Praise for

# THE RED HOTEL

"An unsettling account of how a cadre of foreign correspondents in Moscow during World War II were pressed to acquiesce to the Kremlin's censorship. Philps's thoughtful narrative puts their work into the appropriate historical context. An authoritative history of the terrible ramifications of the silence about Stalin's lies."

—*Kirkus Reviews*

"In a fascinating and surprising narrative, Alan Philps reveals the untold story of the foreign press and its struggle to circumvent the brutal censorship in Stalin's Russia to bring the true story of the brutality of life and war in the Soviet Union to the world. Through fine research and engaging writing, *The Red Hotel* unveils an untold tale of life on the Eastern Front during one of the most titanic conflicts in human history."

—**Laurence Jurdem, author of** *The Rough Rider and the Professor*

"Ostensibly the story of the Allied reporters based during World War II in the Metropol Hotel in Moscow, the real heroes of the book are the female translators who at great personal risk sought to tell the truth about Stalin. A timely reminder of Russia's ambitions and desire to shape the historical narrative."

—**Andrew Lownie, author of** *Stalin's Englishman: The Lives of Guy Burgess*

"*The Red Hotel* is a vivid, intimate, and engaging account of foreign journalists confined to Moscow's Metropol Hotel by Stalin during World War II—and their relations with young women translators sent by the Soviets to spy on and assist them. Philps's fascinating narrative details the brutal suffering of innocent Russians in Stalin's Gulag and evokes dark parallels between Stalin and Putin in their obsession with controlling the flow of information at home."

—**Susan Wels, author of** *An Assassin in Utopia*

"'The truth was the first casualty' in Alan Philps's *The Red Hotel*, a disturbing exposé of Stalin's ruthless control of the media narrative during WWII. At center stage is the harrowing plight of female translators at the Metropol, forced to perpetuate a Soviet disinformation campaign. A timely and sobering reminder of how the absence of a free press can forever change the course of history."

—**Lisa Brahin**, author of *Tears Over Russia: A Search for Family and the Legacy of Ukraine's Pogroms*

"The best histories set in Russia during World War II call to our sensual appreciation of tangible tastes and sensations—lavish wealth with a dark river running through it; passionate courage on the part of the subjugated and impoverished. Alan Philps, veteran Moscow correspondent, skillfully delivers this chilling tale cloaked in a mood steeped in velvet luxury and fitted with a poison lining."

—**Carole Adrienne**, author of *Healing a Divided Nation*

"Alan Philps tells the provocative story about foreign journalists who were sent by Winston Churchill to Russia in 1941 to report on the Eastern Front. *The Red Hotel* exposes the extraordinary lengths to which Stalin went to control the media narrative in World War II. This history may also be critical to our present day appreciation of how Putin, adopting Stalin's playbook, is attempting to control the media narrative, thus swaying public opinion and, ultimately, winning a war. *The Red Hotel* is a must-read for all students of history and public policy."

—**Lis Wiehl**, author of *A Spy in Plain Sight*

"Alan Philps has given readers a true gem. *The Red Hotel* is by turns harrowing and heartbreaking, heroic and squalid, arousing and soul-destroying, epic and claustrophobic. There are a myriad of books of Russia's war time experience, perhaps the most profound episode in the history of the modern West, but *The Red Hotel* stands out among them for its humanity, scholarship, and brilliant, captivating prose."

—**Michael Broers**, author of *Napoleon: The Decline and Fall of an Empire: 1811–1821*

# THE RED HOTEL

# THE RED HOTEL

### MOSCOW 1941, THE METROPOL HOTEL, AND THE UNTOLD STORY OF STALIN'S PROPAGANDA WAR

## ALAN PHILPS

PEGASUS BOOKS
NEW YORK  LONDON

THE RED HOTEL

Pegasus Books, Ltd.
148 West 37th Street, 13th Floor
New York, NY 10018

ISBN: 978-1-63936-427-5

10 9 8 7 6 5 4 3 2

Printed in the United States of America
Distributed by Simon & Schuster
www.pegasusbooks.com

This book is dedicated to the unsung heroes of the international media, be they called secretary-translators or fixers, who enable foreign correspondents to appear well-informed, brave and wise.

'Russia has always had the best stories, ones in which the blood is more sanguineous, the darkness is that much deeper and the heroism that much brighter'
– Mark Galeotti

# Contents

Introduction  *1*

Prologue  *9*

1. June 1941: The accidental war correspondent  *13*

2. July–September 1941: Suitable war work  *19*

3. August 1941: Mother of the British revolution  *33*

4. Meet the Metropol  *47*

5. 1917: The making of a young revolutionary  *63*

6. September 1941: Buttering up the press  *80*

7. October 1941: The trouble with journalists  *106*

8. October 1941: The great Moscow panic  *119*

9. November 1941: The world is much poorer  *138*

10. Winter 1941–42: Feast in time of famine  *152*

11. 1921–23: Carry on spying  *159*

12. 1942: Girls of the Metropol  *176*

13. Summer 1942: Kremlin stooges and fascist beasts  *192*

14. *1931–32: Amerika* 197

15. *Summer 1942: Mr and Mrs Russia at home* 216

16. *October 1942: Prisoner of the Metropol* 237

17. *1942: An army in exile* 255

18. *1943–44: A Polish mass grave* 265

19. *Summer 1943: The visa weapon* 276

20. *Who was the real Ralph Parker?* 288

21. *November 1943: The party at play* 302

22. *February 1944: A taste of abroad* 310

23. *1944–45: 'The Ghosts on the Roof'* 323

24. *The Metropol's invisible wall* 330

25. *May 1945: Winston Smith in Moscow* 338

26. *1947–48: The knock on the door* 345

27. *1951: The Hen and the Eagle* 371

28. *1977: From the Arctic to the Côte d'Azur* 388

29. *Post-War* 395

*Afterword* 419

*Bibliography* 429

*Picture Credits* 435

*Acknowledgements* 437

*Index* 439

# *Introduction*

In early 1943, as the Red Army was preparing to fight the biggest tank battle of the Second World War, which would seal the fate of Hitler's invasion force, the American journalist Edgar Snow tripped and fell as he walked through central Moscow. Gorky Street was the showpiece of Stalin's modernisation of the Soviet capital and in the 1930s the cobbled road had been widened into a six-lane thoroughfare. Trolley buses rolled silently up and down, replacing the scrum of horse-drawn droshkies with their devil-may-care drivers. But even on modernised Gorky Street, the pavements were uneven. Lying on the ground, Snow accepted the helping hand of a Russian man and offered a quick 'spasibo' – thank you – only to see the helper, recognising a foreign accent, turn on his heel and flee. Soviet law required citizens to report to the police instantly any contact with a foreigner, however fleeting. Whether the good Samaritan was running to give himself up to the police or, more wisely, trying to avoid an encounter with a feared organisation, we do not know. Snow tried to file a story to his American readers beginning with the words, 'For the first time in Moscow I met an ordinary Russian. As soon as I opened my mouth, he ran away.' The censor spiked it.

Snow was one of at least fifty of the world's leading war correspondents – and a few intrepid chancers – who made their way to Moscow to cover the biggest story of the war in Europe, the titanic struggle between the then undefeated divisions of Hitler's Wehrmacht and Stalin's largely peasant army whose officer class had been shredded in the purges of the 1930s. Stalin had no desire to welcome British and American reporters to Moscow – he had made life so difficult for foreign reporters that almost all had packed up and left by the time Germany invaded in 1941. But Churchill, who in his youth had been an intrepid war correspondent, believed strongly that gripping eye-witness reports from the Eastern Front would convince the British public that it was worth sending scarce fighter aircraft and tanks to strengthen the hard-pressed Red Army.

With his armies retreating every day and Hitler expected to be in Moscow within weeks, Stalin was in no position to refuse, but he made sure that the eager foreign reporters were kept away from the battle front and had no chance to file the type of stirring reports that Churchill had sent home from colonial conflicts in Sudan and South Africa. He exerted ruthless control through stringent censorship, a visa regime that favoured compliant journalists, a ban on unsupervised travel and prohibition of contact with Soviet citizens except for some 'performing seals'– writers and dancers authorised by the government to speak to foreigners.

When I sat down to write this book I intended to tell the forgotten story of the Allied reporters living and working during the war in Moscow's Metropol Hotel, and how, in their different ways, they dealt with the pressures designed to turn them into mouthpieces of Kremlin propaganda and even assets of Soviet espionage. The more research I did, the clearer it became that the heroes of this story were the female Soviet translators who were the eyes and ears of the visiting journalists. Recruited by the Soviet secret police and believed to be loyal to the regime, some of them contrived, at huge personal risk, to reveal the truth about life under Stalin. This is the first time the story of these women has been told.

The Metropol Hotel, once the most stylish in Moscow, was in 1941 somewhat faded. In the words of Edgar Snow 'it looked and smelled somewhat like a vast but failing whorehouse'. The rooms served as newspaper offices by day, bedrooms at night and drinking dens at just about any time, so it was not surprising that with ready supplies of vodka and the unique luxury of hot water in the en suite bathrooms, the professional and the personal got confused.

This is not a book of academic history but an attempt to recreate the atmosphere of the Metropol Hotel in wartime and to tell the stories of the characters who passed through it. At a time when Russians were existing on a daily ration of 400 grammes of black bread adulterated with various fillers, the Metropol was an island of high living in which the journalists were pampered with caviar, cream cakes and cheap liquor. Kept tantalisingly distant from the greatest battle in history, the journalists had everything they needed except the freedom to write a genuine news story.

It is worth asking why this episode in the Second World War should be of interest now. I would argue that it is more topical than ever. With Russia's brief period of democracy coming to a close, Stalin is once again acclaimed as a great leader. The Red Army's victory in what the Russians call the Great Patriotic War is the origin of the militaristic spirit that Putin has instilled in the Russian people during his two decades in power. Stalin crushed Ukrainian nationalism at the end of the war and restored the boundaries of the Soviet state to those of the Tsarist empire. Eighty years on, Putin is following in Stalin's footsteps and pursuing a war to eradicate the Ukrainian state and prove that Russia is still a great power. Today, it is good to be reminded that there were some courageous Soviet citizens in the 1940s who kept alive the flame of truth.

Today's media environment is totally different from the 1940s, when the printed press was king, and radio and film were the disruptors. Stalin already controlled all the printed media, and in 1941 he issued a decree impounding all the radio sets in the country and the terrified populace handed them in. But even with this total mastery of the media at home, Stalin was determined to muzzle the foreign correspondents so that no banned information could leak back into Russia. This policy served him well: his regime survived and thrived, unlike that of his predecessor, Tsar Nicholas II, who lost his throne in the First World War.

This lesson is not lost on Putin, who consolidated his grip on the Russian media in the early years of this century, so that when he launched his attack on Ukraine it took only a couple of days to silence the last remaining independent TV and radio stations. There was no need to institute formal censorship. Domestic and foreign media were so rigorously policed that a wrong word – such as referring to the invasion of Ukraine as a 'war' – would lead to jail and closure of their outlets for domestic journalists and to expulsion for foreigners. Even with Russian TV stations spewing out non-stop pro-war propaganda, it remains to be seen how long Putin will manage to retain control of the narrative of a war he thought would last only three days.

A few words on how I came to write this story. I first stayed in the Metropol when, as a 15-year-old schoolboy, I came with my Russophile mother on a package tour of the USSR. At Moscow airport, the tour guide had divided up the tourists among different hotels. 'You're lucky – you've got the Metropol. It's the best,' he told us. When we arrived at the Metropol there was furious argument underway in the hotel lobby: a French tour party had been told their promised reservations in the hotel did not exist and an angry Frenchman was shouting '*Ce sale pays!*' while he glared at me and my mother, the new arrivals, as though we were complicit in his humiliation. Tourists could eat with coupons in a cafeteria built on to the outside of the hotel with a long menu of unavailable dishes. One that was on offer was chicken with apples. As a nerdy schoolboy I piped up, 'It must mean chicken and potatoes, not apples, it's the same word on French menus.' But no. When it came, it was a scrawny chicken with little stunted apples in a watery sauce. After that we stuck to the 'stolichny' salad – potato in mayonnaise with chopped up sausage.

My first job as a foreign correspondent was as a Reuters trainee in Moscow in 1979 when the system of press control perfected in 1941 was less invasive but still recognisably the same. After Moscow I opened a North Africa bureau in Tunis where I befriended an extraordinary Russian woman serving as the BBC correspondent. Although she was more than twice my age, the difference in years was immaterial because she was such fun to be with, so full of energy, and had so much to teach me. As a young woman in Moscow, Tanya had secured a wartime job as a translator in the Metropol and had married Ronald Matthews, an eccentric British correspondent. She had followed Ronald to Paris and then to Tunis and when he died, took over his BBC job. In her magnificent house in the blue and white seaside village of Sidi Bou Said, she regaled me with stories of her time in the Metropol, trying to get hold of a wedding dress in wartime Moscow when there was – literally – nothing to buy in the shops. I filed away these memories. After two more stints as a newspaper correspondent in Moscow, I found myself back in the Metropol at a charity ball held in the hotel's vast banqueting hall. Under a magnificent painted glass dome, tables were arranged around a white marble fountain in which carp of heroic size swam in pre-revolutionary times, the whole set-up illuminated by uplighters looking like gilded palm trees and adorned with lamps whose glow was reflected back on the diners by huge mirrors set in the walls. It was a century-old scene of luxury designed to loosen the purses of the Russian new rich.

During the pre-dinner cocktails, a friend I had invited gave me a present, a newly published history of the hotel. Between courses, I slipped out of the dining room, book in hand, and stole away up the back stairs to the third floor. Away from the hubbub of the ball, as I made my way down one of the endless corridors wide enough to drive a tank through, I was overcome by a feeling of unease. It was here, in a makeshift office set up in one of the 'deluxe' rooms, that Lenin had greeted delegations of factory workers. Stalin had walked these corridors as he planned the liquidation of his enemies and I felt that at any moment one of his henchmen would step out in front of me. On reaching my room there were signs that someone had been snooping around – and didn't care if I knew it. I searched the book for Tanya's name in the chapter on the hotel's wartime years and came across the remarkable Nadya Ulanovskaya, whose burning sense of justice in the face of a ruthless dictatorship appears in the following pages.

\*

A word on Russian names, always an obstacle for foreigners. For example, I have called Nadya Ulanovskaya 'Nadya' throughout, even on occasions when it would be more appropriate for her to be addressed in the formal way, with first name and patronymic, as Nadezhda Markovna. As for her husband, he is referred to as Alex, even though he was universally known in Russia by his nom de guerre Alyosha, a diminutive form which to the foreign ear sounds feminine.

Likewise, I have referred to Charlotte Haldane by her first name, when at the time she would have been always 'Mrs Haldane', her married name. Her biographer chooses to refer to her as Charlotte, and this usage is further supported by the fact that the Haldane family never fully accepted her as one of theirs. Among other journalists the naming is frankly subjective. Ralph Parker, who tended to rub people up the wrong way, appears as Parker. And as for Tanya Matthews, one of the prime movers of this story, I recall her saying mischievously, as she passed the harissa to her best friend over a Tunisian lunch of couscous, 'Live dangerously, Mme Benattar.' But I don't recall anyone, even in those more formal times, addressing Tanya as Mme Matthews.

# Prologue
## Odessa, April 1919

On the harbour front in Odessa, a teenage girl was handing out leaflets to French sailors milling around her in an undisciplined mass. They grabbed the leaflets with a smile and a polite 'Merci, mam'selle'. Produced in a clandestine printworks, the leaflets called on the French sailors to join the Bolshevik revolutionaries who less than two years before had executed Tsar Nicholas II and his family. Esther, aged sixteen but able to pass for two years older, was so full of revolutionary zeal that she did not give a thought to the consequences of inciting the sailors to mutiny.

Esther had a ready market for her propaganda. The sailors just wanted to go home. At the end of the Great War they had been sent to southern Russia to support the White armies, the remnants of the doomed imperial regime, against the superior forces of the Red Army. The sailors could see this was a battle they could not win.

The quiet chorus of 'Merci, mam'selle' was suddenly silenced by a shout of 'Bolshevik!' Esther had carelessly thrust a leaflet at a French officer, who grabbed her arm and blew his whistle. She found herself surrounded by French military police. A freckle-faced comrade who was leafleting nearby ran to her aid and was promptly arrested too. They were both dragged off to a police station. When they started to search her, terrified of being stripped naked, Esther demanded to be seen by a woman. She was told: 'When you engage in such activities, you get treated like a soldier.'

Esther and her comrade were taken to the French headquarters in a magnificent estate outside Odessa, where they were separated and subjected to the summary justice of a military field trial.

'Are you a Bolshevik?' she was asked.

'I am a worker.'

'I am asking which party you belong to.'

'But all workers are Bolsheviks.'

Esther was told that incitement to desert was a capital offence. She was taken to a room and left on her own. She imagined her commander, with whom she was secretly in love, dwelling on the memory of her heroic death. Before she had time to think of anything else, she was led out into a courtyard and put up against a wall next to her red-headed comrade. A five-man firing squad was drawn up in front of them. Her comrade's face went so pale that his freckles stood out, even on his lips. She whispered to him: 'We're going to die anyway and so let's show them how we die.' He gave her a pitiful smile through his pale lips.

The soldiers raised their rifles. The officer who had arrested her gave a command in French, but no shots rang out. Instead, the boy was taken away and Esther was left alone with the officer. It seemed she was being released but the officer had other ideas. He grabbed her and tried to drag her into the bushes. She managed to fight him off and ran to the fence. Now she was in sight of a queue of soldiers, some in horse-drawn carts, stopping and starting along the road. The officer who had arrested her caught up with her and started beating her. From the road a French voice shouted, 'What are you up to, beating a woman?'

'This isn't a woman – it's a Bolshevik.'

'Very well then, beat her.'

With people watching, she was able to break free and lose herself in the chaos of the White soldiers and their families fleeing to the port in the hope of being evacuated. Esther never found out what happened to the freckled boy.

Since embracing the Bolshevik Revolution she had turned her back on the enclosed world of Bershad, the shtetl where she was born, and had put out of her mind a legend that had comforted her family for generations. One of her ancestors, a rabbi and a holy man, was called to testify in court against a Jew accused of theft.* Though the Jew was guilty, the rabbi did not want to testify against him, for fear of inflaming Russian incitement against the Jewish community. But neither could he tell a lie. He asked God to let him die before the court case. In return, the family would never be wealthy, but none would die a violent death for seven generations. So it happened that the night before he had to testify, the rabbi passed away in his sleep. Esther was the seventh generation to benefit from the rabbi's deal with the Almighty.†

---

* Many stories are told of Rabbi Raphael of Bershad (1751–1827) whose refusal to tell a lie was so adamant that he preferred death to uttering a falsehood even when other religious scholars would deem it justified. See Shnayer Z. Leiman, 'From the Pages of Tradition: R. Raphael of Bershad's Commitment to Truth', *Tradition: A Journal of Orthodox Jewish Thought* 40, no. 1 (2007): 79–86.
† Nadezhda Ulanovskaya & Maya Ulanovskaya, *Istoria Odnoi Semyi*, 3rd Edition (Inanpress, 2013), p. 20.

With the rabbi's blessing continuing to protect her, Esther never shied away from danger; nor did she lose the burning sense of justice that had driven her as a teenager to risk her life by inciting foreign sailors to mutiny. Over the course of her life she went by many names, but in this book she will be known as Nadya, the woman who twenty years later in wartime Moscow set herself the near-impossible task of breaking the wall of silence around the true nature of Stalin's rule. Hers is one of the untold stories of the brave women who worked in the Metropol Hotel, the heart of Stalin's wartime disinformation campaign.

# 1

## *June 1941: The accidental war correspondent*

It was 9 o'clock in the morning of 22 June 1941, and Alice-Leone Moats, the darling of the Moscow diplomatic scene, was still fast asleep, the faded velvet drapes of her room in the Metropol Hotel doing a good job of keeping out the sun's rays. She had only been in Moscow for a month, but no gathering of the foreign community was complete without her. As a rare unattached woman, and one who spoke five languages fluently, she livened up diplomatic receptions with her glamorous looks and mischievous indiscretions. Being from America, a country still neutral in the war, she drifted effortlessly between the self-segregating camps of the belligerent powers: the Germans and Italians on one side, and the British and their allies on the other.

That Sunday morning, she was rudely awoken by the loud ringing of the telephone beside her bed, and was surprised to hear the voice of John Russell, a British diplomat to whom she had said goodnight only a few hours before at the end of a convivial dinner at the Aragvi restaurant.*

'I don't think it would be a good idea for you to go for that drive in the country today,' Russell said casually. 'The Germans launched their attack at four this morning.

* Alice-Leone Moats, *Blind Date with Mars* (Doubleday, 1943), p. 229.

The war has finally come to Russia.' Fearing a repetition of the London Blitz, and with the hotel being close to the Kremlin, Russell told Alice to leave the Metropol immediately. She would think about it over breakfast, she replied, and rang the bell on the wall next to a drawing of a running waiter. When the elderly waiter shuffled in an hour later, she noticed no change in his behaviour – clearly he did not know that his country was at war.*

At noon, while packing, she heard the loudspeakers positioned all over the city burst into life.† Looking out of her window she saw people standing in groups listening in silence. It was Molotov, Stalin's foreign minister, announcing that Nazi forces had launched an unprovoked attack on the USSR. The enemy was not the German people, he said, the tremble in his voice clearly audible through the loudspeakers, but rather 'a clique of bloodthirsty, fascist German rulers'. Only two years earlier Molotov had signed a friendship and non-aggression pact with Germany, the 'gangster pact' that shocked people of the Left throughout Europe. During those two years not a word of criticism of Germany was allowed in the Soviet press, and Nazi uniforms were seen among the guests at the May Day parades on Red Square and in the Metropol. Now Molotov was saying the German government were Nazi gangsters who had enslaved most of Europe. As for Stalin, he was silent, hiding away in the Kremlin. As soon as the broadcast ended, the people drifted away.

Downstairs, while Alice waited for her bill to be

* Moats, *Blind Date*, p. 229.
† Alice-Leone Moats, Russians Are Like That'. *Collier's* magazine, July 26, 1941.

prepared, a stream of people came up to the hotel receptionist and asked, 'Are we really at war?' Each time, the
receptionist simply replied, 'Yes,' and shrugged her shoulders. When the bill came, Alice found she was 500 roubles
short, so she would have to go to the American embassy
where a diplomat was looking after her money in his safe.
The taxis that waited outside the hotel had vanished and
so she decided to go on foot. The early morning sunshine
had given way to a light drizzle. She expected to see signs
of pandemonium and thousands fleeing the city, as had
happened during the fall of France. But the Moscow streets
looked as they did on any other Sunday afternoon, except
that the policemen were now carrying gas masks. Where
was the anger at Hitler's treachery? The only sound came
from the loudspeakers announcing a blackout and air-raid
precautions followed by blasts of stirring martial music. As
a new arrival in Moscow, she was struck by the expression-
less faces of the passers-by. They showed no traces of
alarm. What John Russell had told her on the phone that
morning came back to her. His maid reacted to the news
that her country was at war with the words, 'If we must
die, then die we must,' and she picked up her rag and went
back to work.*

Alice's reason for coming to Moscow was a secret she
wanted to keep from the Russians. It all began as a whim.
In a New York restaurant in July 1940 she bumped into
Laurence Steinhardt, a friend of the family who was serving as US ambassador to Moscow. She stopped by his
table and laughingly asked, 'When you go back to Moscow, will you take me with you?' 'Of course, Dulcie and

* Moats, *Blind Date*, p. 232.

I would love to have you to stay,' he responded automatically. Later he was to bitterly regret this off-the-cuff invitation.

Even though she had no journalistic experience beyond writing a few celebrity profiles, Alice persuaded *Collier's* magazine to commission a series of articles about her journey through Japan and China to Russia. There was no chance of her getting a press visa for Moscow – they were as rare as hens' teeth – so she asked the State Department to stamp her passport 'Good for the USSR via the Orient, for purposes of study', and the space for 'occupation' was left blank. Steinhardt supported her visa application and even lobbied the Soviet ambassador in Washington, who promised to use 'dynamite' to get it approved.

When Alice applied for a passport and the State Department learned who she was travelling with, there was no stopping the tide of gossip between Washington and New York. Could it be true that old Steinhardt had thrown caution to the winds and was returning to Moscow with a 32-year-old socialite who had worked as a fashion model? Steinhardt tried to get hold of Alice to talk her out of coming to Moscow, but she was with her parents in Mexico. By the time he tracked her down early in the morning of 8 August, the day they were due to sail together from San Francisco to Japan on the first leg of their journey to Russia, he was in a state of great agitation. 'You and I simply can't travel together. It's all your fault – you have been so indiscreet. It will cause a scandal. It already has. I forbid you to come with me.'

Undeterred, two weeks later Alice was on the next boat to Japan. She was fully committed to an adventure that had started as a joke. When she finally arrived in

Moscow in May 1941, Steinhardt was not at the airport to meet her.

When she finally arrived in Moscow in May 1941, Steinhardt was not at the airport to meet her. He sent a clerk. The ambassador was spending the day at his dacha.

As an American journalist, Alice was a member of a species on the way to extinction in Moscow. The 1930s had been a golden age for foreign correspondents, the profession glamourised in Hitchcock's movie, *Foreign Correspondent*, and their lavish expense accounts and Olympian self-regard mocked in Evelyn Waugh's novel, *Scoop*. Kings, presidents and dictators throughout Europe opened their doors to American special correspondents. But not in Russia, where the Kremlin needed to hide the human cost of turning a peasant economy at breakneck speed into an industrial power: a famine that killed millions in Ukraine and southern Russia. The *New York Times* correspondent Walter Duranty who had won the Pulitzer Prize in 1932 for his reports on the success of Stalin's planned economy did his best hide the extent of the famine – 'Russians hungry but not starving' was the paper's headline on March 1, 1933. But visiting correspondents such as H. R. Knickerbocker* of the Philadelphia *Public Ledger* were not as biddable as Duranty. Knickerbocker wrote after a tour of Russia: 'Zeal and terror are the two psychological instruments for accomplishment of the Plan'.

The Soviet press department was soon driving journalists away by restricting travel and tightening censorship. In 1940, with the Nazi-Soviet non-aggression pact in force,

---

* Deborah Cohen, *Last Call at the Hotel Imperial: The Reporters who Took on a World at War* (William Collins, 2022) p. 120

Stalin was a non-belligerent ally of Hitler, supplying the grain to sustain the Wehrmacht in its defeat of France and the fuel to power the bombers that devastated London. Stalin had no need of Anglo-American correspondents in Moscow.

Duranty's successor in the *New York Times* bureau, G. E. R. Gedye, wrote that Moscow correspondents had been 'reduced to the role of precis-writers of TASS and the official press'. In a bitter cable to the *New York Times* after he quit Moscow and closed down the bureau, he wrote: 'As a news centre Moscow has ceased to exist, and every correspondent still there knows that his work is entirely valueless.'*

By the time Alice arrived in Moscow, it was a journalistic desert. But once Hitler invaded the Soviet Union, it was a desert in which war correspondents from all the Allied countries were competing to pitch their tents. Covering the titanic battles on the Eastern Front would be the biggest story of the war in Europe. With his forces retreating across a broad front and desperate for supplies of American and British aircraft and tanks, Stalin could no longer afford to isolate the USSR from foreign media. This was the starting gun for a race among journalists to be the first to get to the Soviet capital and unravel what Churchill called the 'riddle wrapped in a mystery inside an enigma' that was Russia.

---

* Article sent to *New York Times* on the closure of its Moscow bureau, 30 July 1940, Imperial War Museum, GERG23 iii

# 2

## *July–September 1941: Suitable war work*

It was a sunny day in July 1941 and Charlotte Haldane was hurrying down Gray's Inn Road towards Kemsley House, a building she was familiar with in her role as air-raid warden for the London borough of St Pancras. Six months earlier it had taken a direct hit, killing three people and destroying the office of Lord Kemsley, the newspaper magnate. Today she was going there for a very different reason, for a job interview with the editor of the *Daily Sketch*. She had already been turned down by the editors of two Fleet Street newspapers who said they had their own men to send to Moscow. This time she had marshalled arguments that no editor could dismiss.

Having worked in the newspaper business before, she knew that getting on required drinking in the right pubs and, for a woman, to be able to hold her drink like a man. A chance meeting with a sub-editor in a Fleet Street pub provided her with the intelligence that the *Daily Sketch* was still looking for a suitable journalist to cover the war on the Eastern Front. When she telephoned Sidney Carroll, the editor, he asked her to come in and see him the next day.

Arriving at Kemsley House, Charlotte could see the bomb damage had been speedily repaired. As she waited to be summoned to the editor's office, the doorman recounted with pride how the edition of 6 January, the morning after the air raid, came out as usual with only a small delay. In the editor's office, as Carroll rose to shake her hand, she launched straight into a well-rehearsed argument. A woman reporter would be welcomed in Russia – the Red Army did not discriminate against women and would take her to the heart of the action on the front line. And thanks to her Communist Party membership the Russians would rush through her visa application and she would be well placed to get an interview with Stalin and scoop the world's press. She stopped short when she saw the editor nodding in agreement. He told her he himself had no problem in appointing a woman to this important post, nor did it matter to him that she was a Party member, but he might have difficulty in convincing Lord Kemsley, a 'fanatical anti-Bolshie', to employ a well-known communist. 'Leave this to me,' he told her as they said goodbye.*

As she left Carroll's office, Charlotte thought how bizarre it was that she should be angling for a job on a conservative tabloid, and one better known for its dramatic pictures than fine writing. Still, it was her only prospect of a ticket to Moscow.

The weather was fine and Charlotte decided to walk home through the streets she had driven around during night-time air raids, inspecting bomb damage and offering support to those who had lost their homes. Now that the Blitz was over, she had more time on her hands.

She walked up Gray's Inn Road and turned into Sidmouth Street, pausing in front of the bomb-damaged St Peter's Church on the corner of Regent's Square. All that

* Charlotte Haldane, *Truth Will Out* (Weidenfeld, 1949), p. 191.

was left of the showy, two-tiered clock tower which had been a local landmark were the stumps of its slim Ionic columns. She walked up Portland Place and into Park Crescent. Although she had seen it before she was still affected by the devastation of London's most elegant street. Almost half of the crescent had been reduced to rubble.

She crossed the road into Regent's Park and decided to take a look at Bedford College, which had been damaged during one of the last big air raids in May. Strolling among the trees in full leaf and beside the lake alive with water-fowl, for a moment Charlotte stopped thinking of the war. The trees gave way to a bomb site. Ahead of her, sur-rounded by rubble, was the hulk of the Bedford College dining hall. All that remained was the steel framework that had held up the roof, looking like the skeleton of a big beast that had been picked clean by scavengers.

This was the women's university where she, as a bright schoolgirl, had been destined to complete her education. Instead, after her German-Jewish father had lost his for-tune, she was forced to enrol in a shorthand typing course to support herself. During this period – which she recalled as the most miserable months of her life – she would walk home to Swiss Cottage past Bedford College as the stu-dents were leaving, chatting in their posh accents and visibly enjoying the academic life that should have been hers.

Through sheer force of will, and thanks to her lan-guages and writing ability, she had transformed herself from a secretary–receptionist at a concert agency to a journalist at the *Daily Express*. She was hired as a gossip columnist covering the social lives of the idle rich, the editorial role she was least suited to by character and upbringing. Still, she managed to produce the fawning copy the paper required, and worked her way up to become one of the few female news reporters to work at both the *Daily Express* and *Sunday Express*, working seven days a week covering a range of beats including the criminal courts, the House of Lords and Buckingham Palace.

On marrying J. B. S. Haldane, a leading biologist and geneticist, she had given up daily journalism and devoted herself to popularising his scientific breakthroughs, turning him into a household name in the process. As the war clouds gathered over Europe, she devoted herself to the anti-fascist struggle in the Spanish Civil War, helping international volunteers to make their way to Spain and accompanying Paul Robeson, the American singer, on a front-line tour to raise the spirits of the soldiers fighting on the doomed Republican side.* Given her commitment to the cause, she felt she could not stop her 16-year-old son from her first marriage joining the International Brigade. Her varied career so far included writing *Man's World*, a dystopian sci-fi novel in which a male scientific elite has divided women into sterilised 'entertainers' and sainted 'breeders' – widely seen as a precursor of Aldous Huxley's *Brave New World*, published six years later. Despite all this, she still felt she had something to prove.

Coming from an immigrant background and lacking the university education she craved, she was made to feel inferior by the high-achieving Haldane family and their donnish social circle in Cambridge, who mocked her

*Judith Adamson, *Charlotte Haldane: Woman Writer in a Man's World* (Macmillan, 1998), p. 119.

'cockney' accent and looked down on her trade as a journalist. She recoiled from the arrogance of the Cambridge 'highbrows' and this drew her towards Marxism. She had visited the USSR once before in 1928 with JBS – as everyone knew her husband – and had come away with the view that, whatever the faults of the Soviet system, a new and more equal society was taking shape there.

Life with her husband proved not to be the idyll she had imagined. Though they were feted in far-left circles as the model progressive couple, by the late 1930s the marriage was no more than a facade. Both wanted to have children together, but as Charlotte confided to her daughter-in-law many years later, JBS was impotent, perhaps as a result of an injury in the First World War, and wore a truss.*

At Cambridge Charlotte, with her 'looks of Romany princess concealing the heart of a lion'† and questioning intelligence, was a magnet for gifted students, and academic non-conformists would gather in her drawing room to discuss art, science and progressive ideas. On arrival, they would find one of JBS's research students playing jazz on her Bechstein grand piano. JBS had invited Martin Case to live in his house instead of university digs, and before long he became Charlotte's lover.‡ By the time she went to the *Daily Sketch*, Charlotte and JBS were living apart.

Now that the Soviet Union had joined the war and was allied to Britain, she saw an opportunity to relaunch her

---

* Adamson, *Charlotte Haldane*, p. 62.
† Adamson, p. 60.
‡ Adamson, p. 73.

journalistic career. She would tell her readers about the heroic deeds of the Red Army, which was crushing Nazism and with it the most evil manifestation of anti-Semitism. After their visit to Russia in 1928, she had let JBS do all the talking. He had given interviews and lectures. This time it would be her turn.

When she got back to her flat in Swiss Cottage she sat by the phone. Late that afternoon the editor called – she had got the assignment. She would be paid £20 a week, more than three times the average wage at the time, plus expenses – once again she would be self-supporting and independent. She would have to sort out how to get herself to Moscow – only the British Ministry of Information could arrange transport. The editor told her to get on to the ministry straight away as he wanted her in Moscow before the *Express*.

*

In Moscow, another woman was looking for war work. When the Germans launched their surprise attack on the Soviet Union in June 1941, Nadya Ulanovskaya thought she should work in an arms factory – that would keep her in Moscow, and she would be doing something useful for the war effort.

'A munitions factory is no place for you,' said her husband Alex, a civil war hero, now a captain in the Red Army. 'Let me talk to Solomon.' Solomon Lozovsky was a comrade from Alex's revolutionary youth. They had met as political exiles in Paris when Alex was organising strikes in the Renault factory and Lozovsky had a cushier position as director of a cooperative bakery. He was now deputy foreign minister and would act as spokesman for the foreign press, some of whom were already en route to Moscow.

Nadya took a tram to see Lozovsky. On her way to the city centre she saw how the authorities had mobilised architects, painters and set designers to camouflage key buildings in readiness for the inevitable German bombing raids. The red brick walls of the Kremlin were painted yellow and black, with designs to make them look like ordinary apartment blocks. The luminescent ruby-red stars on top of five of the Kremlin towers were switched off and covered up, and the gold domes of the Kremlin churches disguised. The squat pink marble form of Lenin's mausoleum on Red Square – as symbolic to Moscow as St Paul's Cathedral is to London – was hidden under a pitched roof that cast a long shadow in the summer sunshine, a better disguise than a mere paint job. (Lenin's body had been secretly removed to Siberia.) A fake wooden bridge had been built over the Moscow River to confuse German navigators. Some of the camouflage efforts were weirdly overzealous: the Maly Theatre used a backdrop from Ostrovsky's play *The Forest* to give it a rural look, though how this would mislead a bomber on a night-time raid was not clear.

As she got off the tram outside the Bolshoi Theatre, Nadya saw that the classical facade with its giant marble pillars had been draped in a huge net. The square in front of the theatre was painted to look from the air like a village roofscape. Police were shooing away children who tried to play there in case their presence revealed the disguise to a spotter plane.

Nadya was one of the few people in Moscow who knew why so much effort had been put into camouflaging the city. In her job teaching English to army officers, she was given special dispensation to read the foreign press. She was impressed that the British newspapers were able to describe the devastation inflicted on London during the Blitz, while not revealing military secrets to the enemy or denting the morale of Londoners. In the Soviet press, the Blitz was mentioned only in passing, and this was not accidental, because this was the period of the non-aggression pact with Hitler.

The foreign ministry building where Nadya was heading lay close to the Lubyanka, the headquarters of the security police. Nadya's first impression of Lozovsky was that he was not like other Soviet bureaucrats who took pride in their proletarian or peasant origin. With his thick hair worn long, his broad moustache and his square pepper-and-salt beard, he looked like a French statesman of the nineteenth century. In the suavity and polish of his manner, he had lost all traces of the shtetl where he was born. He received Nadya with a paternal beam and, before she could utter a word, he told her he had a plan for her. With her command of English and experience of living in New York, she would be well suited to work with the British and American correspondents who would shortly be arriving in Moscow. With the Soviet Union now allied with Britain, and hopefully soon with America too, these correspondents needed not just translators but someone who understood their ways.

'I'd rather not work with foreigners,' Nadya blurted out before he could go any further. 'I am afraid that when the war is over, me doing this type of work could harm Alexander Petrovich' – she used the formal mode of address to refer to her husband – 'given the kind of work we were doing for so many years abroad.' Nadya did not need to spell out what she meant. Stalin was suspicious of everyone who had worked abroad or with foreigners.

Lozovsky shut her up. 'What are you talking about? Will we even be around when the war is over? Smolensk has fallen, and the Germans are heading to Moscow. The only question is, are we going to survive?'*

He explained that supplies of American aid depended on how the correspondents wrote about the war, and guiding them could not be left in the hands of ordinary Soviet bureaucrats with no knowledge of the outside world. 'Our people, even with the best intentions, sometimes commit gross errors or act stupidly,' the old revolutionary told her. Nadya was given to understand that she was not just being asked to translate for the correspondents, but she had a second, and more important role, which was to present the friendly face of Stalin's regime.

She had one last stab at turning down the offer. 'How am I going to explain to the Americans what I was doing in New York?'

Lozovsky dismissed her concern. 'You'll just say you were accompanying your husband who was working at the Soviet trade mission in New York. So don't hide that you lived in America.' He offered a word of advice: 'The less you lie, the better.'

These words signalled the end of Nadya's job interview. Lozovsky picked up the phone to arrange an appointment for her to meet the head of the foreign ministry Press Department. This was Nikolai Palgunov, a baby-faced former journalist whose brown hair stood up on end like a

* Nadezhda Ulanovskaya and Maya Ulanovskaya, *Istoria Odnoi Semyi*, 3rd edition (Inanpress, 2013), p. 71.

hedgehog and whose bottle-glass spectacles were the thickest Nadya had ever seen. Evidently, he too thought that Nadya was well suited for the job and, as it happened, an American correspondent had just arrived and needed her help immediately. But before she started work, there was just one thing she had to do – have a chat with 'another comrade'.

After questioning her at length, this comrade – who never told her his name – revealed that the American correspondent was staying at the Metropol Hotel. He needed a secretary-translator and here was his room number. 'Of course, we will be in touch with you from time to time. We need to know who these journalists really are, what they think of the Soviet Union and so on. I will be calling you. Don't worry – we won't leave you on your own. We will be giving you instructions on what you need to do for us.' Nadya did not like the sound of any of this but she could see no way out.*

*

On 23 June 1941, the day after Hitler's surprise attack on Russia, a team of police watchers began a surveillance operation on 73 Albert Road, a substantial home opposite a park in the English seaside town of Southport, Lancashire. The focus of their investigation was Ralph Parker, a journalist who had worked for *The Times* in Prague, with his Czech future-wife Milena as his assistant, during the German takeover of Czechoslovakia. As the Nazis tightened their grip on the country and were about to arrest Milena, Parker escaped with her to work in Yugoslavia. Now, several

* Nadezhda Ulanovskaya and Maya Ulanovskaya, *Istoria*, p. 71.

months later, Ralph and Milena had returned to the safety of his family home. As he told a reporter from the local paper, 'I left England for Prague with one suitcase as a single man, and returned with a wife and lots of luggage.'*

The watchers observed that Parker spent a lot of time in the back garden. They saw him posting a thick parcel. On inspection, this turned out to be a manuscript, Chapter 14 of a book about the origins of the war, which Parker was writing with his wife and sending to an agency to be typed up. Otherwise, Parker left the house only twice in the course of the week-long surveillance operation. Nobody came to visit. His wife was said to be very ill in bed. The neighbours understood that he had been working for '*The Times* in New York' and was now on leave from the War Office, which explained why a 34-year-old man was not doing any war work. The Special Branch police officer in charge of the watchers ended his report with a comment bound to raise a red flag with his superiors: the whole family, he wrote, were of 'an extremely nervous temperament, and all seem ill at ease in the presence of strangers'.†

The Metropolitan Police special branch had moblisied the watchers as part of an investigation by MI5, the British spy-catching agency, into an allegation of treachery against Parker. MI5 assessed Parker as a 'timorous fellow' who could easily be broken down by a 'thorough and aggressive' interrogation.

The allegation related to Parker's time in Yugoslavia at the beginning of the war. He had gone to Yugoslavia as a correspondent for *The Times* and the *New York Times* but

* *Southport Visiter*, 5 July 1941.
† TNA KV6 120/7a.

within weeks had been recruited by British intelligence to spy on Albania under diplomatic cover. When he was forced out of Yugoslavia, he had continued his undercover work in Istanbul, producing wartime propaganda. There was nothing surprising in wartime about this career change from reporter to spy.

But according to the British Secret Intelligence Service station in Istanbul, Parker had been contacted by a notorious German agent. While staying in the Pera Palace Hotel, the city's finest, built to accommodate passengers arriving on the Orient Express, the agent had made three calls to Parker's apartment. When Parker was asked to explain on his return to England why he was in contact with an enemy agent, his interviewer observed that his responses were 'shifty', and he clearly had 'a guilty conscience'.

While MI5 searched for more evidence against him, Parker lined up character witnesses, including the president and foreign minister of the Czech government in exile, to attest to his anti-fascist sympathies. Prior to his interrogation, he wrote to MI5 that his wife was extremely anxious about what might happen to her. Having escaped the clutches of the Nazis in Czechoslovakia she feared that the MI5 investigation could lead her to being imprisoned or interned in Britain as an enemy alien.

Despite MI5's assessment of him as timorous and likely to crack under pressure, Parker mounted a crafty defence. He explained that, if his answers had appeared shifty during his initial questioning, this was because he had not wanted to reveal information to the discredit of his colleagues working for British intelligence in the Balkans. If MI5 could show him the dates when he was supposed to have spoken with the German agent – which they had failed to do – he could prove he had not been at home but in his office. His trump card was to suggest that the German agent's calls were accidental: he wanted to get hold of the owner of the flat, with whom he had business interests, and did not know that the owner had let it out to a tenant.

In his note on the interrogation, an MI5 desk officer wrote that the evidence was too skimpy to pursue the case against Parker. What sealed his decision to close the investigation down was MI6's belief that Parker, if allowed to resume his work as a foreign correspondent, 'can produce information of interest to them'.* It was, however, less than a clean bill of health from the spy-catchers: MI5 concluded that Parker was 'quite harmless' and 'by now far too frightened to risk any move which might arouse further suspicions.'

This opened the way for Parker to get his next assignment – as Moscow correspondent for *The Times*.† The newspaper had been impressed with his work in Prague where, with the help of Milena, he had produced readable copy under the eyes of the Gestapo. And now, the Secret Intelligence Service was keen to have him as a source in Moscow. On 11 August, Parker was cleared to get a permit to travel to Russia. MI5 wanted to be informed of the date of his departure and his route.‡ Having completed his apprenticeship in Prague, now a quiet corner of the German Reich, and with some experience of wartime espionage and propaganda, Parker was heading for the country where the fate of the war in Europe would be decided.

* TNA KV6 120/8a.
† TNA KV6 120/13a.
‡ TNA KV6 120/13a.

The files released by the National Archives of this war-time period reveal the close working relationships of the British press and the intelligence services, which often led to foreign correspondents wearing two hats. But the efforts of the intelligence services, monitoring of his phone and mail, the close surveillance of his home and rigorous inter-rogation, failed to uncover elements of Parker's private life that would define his time in Moscow, and indeed the rest of his life.

One can imagine the ferment in Parker's mind as he waited in September 1941 for the telephone call from the Ministry of Information telling him which railway station to report to at the start of his journey to Moscow. Stung by the accusation of treacherous contacts with Nazis and drained by the effort of defending himself, a small part of him must have been relieved to be leaving England, with its class divisions, economic crises and unemployment, for a country that had done away with all these ills.

He was not the only journalist assigned to cover the Eastern Front in 1941 to experience heightened emotions. For Charlotte Haldane, the opportunity to report on the heroic Red Army created in her a state of exultation. For Nadya, working for the journalists was her patriotic duty but it would require all her mental strength to suppress the doubts about Stalin that had nagged at her since the Great Terror of the 1930s. Once installed in the Metropol Hotel, the journalists and their translators would face the most draconian media censorship and would, in their different ways, experience the benefits accruing to those who toed the Soviet line or the terrible punishments meted out to those who stepped over it.

# 3

## *August 1941: Mother of the British revolution*

'Do Russian girls pay for drinks at the bar?' The question, from a young man in the blue-grey uniform of the Royal Air Force, provoked titters all around, as he had intended.* For the past hour, Charlotte had been lecturing a group of airmen aboard a troop ship heading for Russia on what awaited them when they arrived. She painted a glorious picture of life in the Soviet Union where men and women had equal rights, loveless marriages could be dissolved in minutes, and factory workers and scientists were the only aristocrats. Some of the all-male audience – not especially interested in a lecture on her topic, 'Domestic Life in the USSR' – felt it was time to puncture her rhetoric and get some practical advice on how to pick up Russian girls. With her years of anti-Nazi activism, Charlotte was used to dealing with hecklers and she shot back at the questioner: 'Girls buying drinks at the bar? Not just in Russia. I'll stand you a round at 5.30.' The young airmen cheered.

It was August 1941, and Charlotte was aboard the *Llanstephan Castle*, a 30-year-old luxury liner that had been pressed into war service as a troop ship. As she had

* Feliks Topolski, *Fourteen Letters* (Faber, 1988), unpaginated.

promised the editor of the *Daily Sketch*, the Soviet embassy rushed through her visa and the British Ministry of Information found her a berth on the first Arctic convoy heading for the Russian port of Archangel. Most of the passengers were members of a 500-strong Royal Air Force mission to beef up air defences in the Russian north. If the convoy survived attack by German U-boats and torpedo bombers, Charlotte would – as she had promised – be in Moscow ahead of the rest of the British press.

Besides Charlotte only three other members of the press had managed to get berths on board – an American reporter, a BBC broadcaster and a graphic artist. They were to be the nucleus of an Allied press corps in Moscow to cover the Eastern Front where the Soviet armies were retreating in the face of Hitler's divisions, so far unbeaten in continental Europe.

The press pack met up for the first time for lifeboat drill on deck. Charlotte was unpleasantly surprised to see Feliks Topolski, a fashionable Polish-born artist. In Charlotte's eyes, Topolski represented the worst type of bourgeois reactionary who had no place in a post-war socialist Europe after Stalin's victory over Hitler. His credentials as a war artist, however, were impeccable: Stalin allowed no foreign photographers on the Eastern Front, so Churchill had recruited Topolski to provide a pictorial record.

The oldest member of the press pack was Vernon Bartlett, a veteran journalist who had recently been elected to parliament on an anti-appeasement platform. He was to make a series of live broadcasts from Moscow for the BBC. The lifejacket that barely encompassed his John Bull-like frame seemed to have swallowed up his neck so it looked as though the MP's well-fleshed head was being served up on a yellow platter. Thus constrained, he attempted a courteous bow to Charlotte, who was dressed for mud and snow on the front line rather than for promenading on deck. Topolski noted acidly that she was wearing 'the truculent costume of a leftist suffragette gypsy.'*

The solemnity of the evacuation announcements was undermined by the fourth member of the press party, the American Wally Carroll, European diplomatic editor of the United Press agency, who whispered to his colleagues that if the ship was torpedoed there would not be enough room for everyone on the lifeboats. He had heard on good authority that it would be every man for himself. And as for the lifejackets, they were a waste of time – no one would survive more than two minutes in the icy waters of the Arctic.

*

The *Llanstephan Castle* had been built for the Southampton to Cape Town line, one of the sinews of the British empire in Africa, and its salons were equipped with cooling fans for the comfort of first-class passengers as they crossed the equator. Its voyage from Liverpool would take the ship to a far colder clime, to the north of Iceland and through the Barents and White seas. The convoy's circuitous route way above the Arctic Circle was plotted to stay as far as possible beyond the reach of German spotter planes and bombers based in Norway. In preparation, the liner had been painted grey, and had machine guns installed on the boat deck and a three-inch gun at the stern. Inside the cabins, signs in English and Afrikaans testified to the ship's

* Topolski, *Fourteen Letters*, unpaginated.

long service with colonial settlers. Now, in wartime, a polite message had been added: 'Passengers and crew are warned that they must not divulge the route or details of the escort to anyone. Remember – we have to get back.'

On 12 August, the *Llanstephan Castle* set sail from Liverpool for its first stop, Scapa Flow, the naval base in northern Scotland, where the liner took its place beside five freighters laden with tin, rubber and wool (to make the Russian soldiers' felt snow-boots) and, lashed to their decks, giant wooden crates containing the parts of fifteen Hawker Hurricane fighter aircraft. The RAF contingent included a New Zealand-born wing commander and all the crew and service personnel needed to assemble the Hurricanes and to set up an air defence operation to protect the supplies brought to Russia by future Arctic convoys. Such a small consignment of fighter aircraft was not going to compensate for the catastrophic losses of the Soviet air force – just in the first hours of the German invasion it had lost at least 1,200 aircraft, most of them on the ground and poorly camouflaged.* It was a down payment on the once unimaginable alliance between Stalin and Churchill.

Among the passengers was a contingent of Polish officers who were going to Moscow to serve in a nascent army to bring their country back to life. Under the terms of the 1939 'gangster pact', Hitler and Stalin had divided up Poland between them and Stalin had deported tens of thousands of Polish officers and civilians to Siberia to ensure that Poland would never rise again. Now, after Hitler had launched his surprise invasion of Russia and Stalin had become Britain's ally, the Kremlin dictator executed a

* Richard Overy, *Russia's War* (Penguin, 2010), p. 76.

volte-face to please Churchill. He even proclaimed his support for Poland as an independent state.

If the convoy, made up of six cargo ships sailing in a strict formation of two lines and guarded by Royal Navy vessels, managed to get to Archangel and back, it would open a tenuous supply route from Britain to support the hard-pressed Red Army in its fight to the death with the Wehrmacht. As the convoy headed out to sea, it was reported that the *Tirpitz*, the newest and heaviest German battleship, had left the Baltic after sea trials and was heading north to prey on allied shipping in the North Sea.

Despite the dangers ahead, for the first few days there was a holiday atmosphere on board, with the passengers sunbathing on deck, looking out for schools of spouting whales and porpoises, and gorging on a supply of oranges left over from a voyage back from Cape Town.* At odds with this party mood was the festering antagonism between Topolski and Charlotte. Topolski scorned her as the 'mother of the British revolution'. For him, anyone who saw Stalin as the saviour of the Polish nation had to be an enemy. As for Charlotte, she made it clear she had no desire to 'fraternise' with him or any of the other 'reactionaries' on the ship. Perhaps, she admitted later, her fellow passengers may have found her priggish and intransigent.

Vernon Bartlett and Wally Carroll were old friends and, as ever when two journalists are in a confined space with no copy to write, they drank and swapped stories late into the night. Under the influence of the young RAF officers, Bartlett – despite being nearly fifty and an MP – lost all pretence of dignity and cavorted around the ship

* Vernon Bartlett, *And Now, Tomorrow* (Chatto, 1960), p. 70.

making a lot of noise, earning a dressing-down from the commodore of the convoy.

Steps were taken to enforce discipline on board among the passengers. An army medic summoned them on deck every morning for physical exercises to drive away their hangovers. A daily schedule of lectures was hastily put together, which were so popular that the morning one was repeated in the afternoon, and Russian lessons were organised.

The first lecture was given by Hubert Griffith, a playwright with a keen interest in Russia whose play, *Red Sunday*, had been banned from the London stage by the Lord Chamberlain because its portrayal of the ultra-conservative Tsar Nicholas II was likely to upset King George. Undeterred, Griffith published his play with the words 'Banned by the Lord Chamberlain' emblazoned on the cover. Now the rebellious writer had been conscripted to serve as adjutant to the RAF wing commander and navigate the tricky relationship with their Soviet hosts.

Griffith told the RAF men to put out of their heads everything they had heard or read about Soviet Russia: it would be either 'exaggerated adulation from writers who pretend that everything in modern Russia is an earthly paradise, or else exaggerated detraction, pretending in the past years that Russia is largely governed by lunatics, fanatics and incompetents.'

They should keep one fact in their minds: when the Bolsheviks took over in 1917, Russia was not twenty, or thirty or forty years behind Western Europe, but several hundred years behind. For this view he cited Maurice Paléologue, the last French ambassador to the royal court at St Petersburg, who considered himself a friend of the

Tsar. In 1914, at the start of the First World War, 90 per cent of Russian soldiers could not read, could not spell out the simplest placard, and did not know if the Germany that they were fighting was 'a man or a woman or a thing'. In only twenty-five years, Soviet Russia had advanced so far that it was now fielding an army that aimed to fight on equal terms with Hitler's, which, he reminded the flyers and their technicians, had proved to be beyond the capacity of the combined armies of Britain and France to fight.

There was no point in comparing the Soviet Union with Britain. Creating such an army in so short a time inevitably left other things behind such as comfortable living and consumer goods. Some of the grandparents of the people who would be building and flying the Hurricanes would have been born as serfs, 'peasants who belonged to the landowner and were bought and sold with his land just like cattle'. Remember this, he said, when you reach the camp – probably wooden huts in a muddy field in the wildest part of Russia. 'We will have to grin and pretend we like it.'*

Another officer in the RAF team had a more complicated message to deliver. Brought up in Tsarist Russia, Flight Lieutenant Hodson had landed with British forces in Archangel in 1918, an ill-starred venture at the end of the First World War whose aim was to support anti-Bolshevik forces and keep Lenin out of power. Ignominiously, they had to withdraw within a year, their forces totally inadequate to the task. Britain's then secretary of war had described the mission as an attempt 'to strangle at birth the

* Hubert Griffith, *R.A.F. in Russia* (Hammond, Hammond Ltd, London, 1942), p. 23.

Bolshevik state'. That man was Winston Churchill, now prime minister and Stalin's ally. The omens suggested that this latest British intervention force would soon be cutting and running too.

Then it was Vernon Bartlett's turn to talk about the situation in Europe. The airmen were more interested in the MP's views on British domestic politics, and they had lots of questions to ask. Why weren't company profits controlled in wartime? After the war, would there be a return to the discredited old order, just as there had been in 1918? And why did the BBC refuse to play the Internationale, the national anthem of Soviet Russia who was now our ally, at the end of its daily broadcasts? With the British establishment riddled with pro-fascist right-wingers, would the war end with Britain attacking Russia? The mood of the troops was clear: they would fight to rid the world of Hitler, but they would vote to see the British establishment taken down.

Fascinating, flirtatious and dynamic was the RAF officer Eric Carter's view of Charlotte. Not surprisingly, her lecture created a real stir among the young men of the RAF. The enthusiasm was mutual. She was impressed at the questions they put to her and the other speakers. 'These boys had brains and were using them. I was proud to be going to Russia with them.' As the only independent female – the other women were the wives of Polish and Czech diplomats travelling to Moscow – she was the focus of lively speculation among the men, who kept an eye on her cabin to see which if any of the officers she might favour. As Carter recalls in his memoir, revealing the double standards of the time, Charlotte was 'rather taken with Pilot Officer Dicky Wollaston and he had been spending time with her in her cabin. I wouldn't like to suggest what they got up to in there, but I doubt they were discussing the weather.'*

Throughout the voyage Topolski was 'skipping about the ship like a cheerful gnome, never ceasing drawing'.†Everyone from the commodore to the RAF technicians and the cooks below decks wanted the 'gnome' to sketch their portrait, which afforded him a unique opportunity to assess morale on board. As his pencil danced over the pages of his sketchpad, he puzzled over what had brought these people of different nationalities and political persuasions together on the ship, and what they could achieve. As a Polish patriot he was desperate to convince himself that he was taking part in an epic journey, a twentieth-century *Iliad*, which would lead to the glorious restoration of Poland.

Topolski observed that the young RAF men on the lower decks, despite the hurried preparation and uncertain outcome of their mission, were 'panting with life' and keen to fight alongside the Russians to defeat the Nazis. But the first-class section, the mahogany-panelled dining saloon with a sweeping double staircase that led to the lounge where the senior officers and diplomats congregated, was a seething cauldron of political plotting. As he put in his diary, there he was surrounded by 'the insane intrigues of rulers, lackeys, blimps and candidates for people's tribunes'. It is not hard to see Charlotte as the Stalinist 'people's tribune' he had in mind. During the white nights, when passengers gathered on deck to watch the rim of the

* Eric Carter, *Force Benedict* (Hodder, 2014), Kindle loc 1483.
† Griffith, *R.A.F in Russia*, p.22.

sun sink just below the horizon at midnight before beginning to rise half an hour later, Topolski avoided every
chance of a tête-à-tête with her, knowing she would try to
convince him to abandon his bourgeois nationalism.

Charlotte's faith that Stalin would succeed in turning
back the conquering German armies never wavered, and
she was able to arouse the sympathy of the British people
for 'the glorious fighters' of the Red Army.

The radio reports they heard as the liner ploughed
through the cold seas were discouraging. The Red Army
was being overwhelmed. Kiev, the cradle of the Russian
state, was encircled and the Red Army was struggling to
extricate hundreds of thousands of its men from a Nazi
pincer movement. The Russians had been forced to blow
up the Dnieper dam, the proudest achievement of Stalin's
first Five-Year Plan, ahead of the advancing Germans.
And now, the Polish wireless listeners had heard that the
dreaded *Tirpitz* was already hiding in one of the Norwe-
gian fjords and was ready to strike at Allied convoys.

On Sunday, 24 August the passengers began to place
bets on which day enemy aircraft would locate them – with
Wednesday or Thursday the favourites. The crew checked
the lifeboats for water and rations. Descending from the
bridge, the RAF wing commander, wearing his gold-
braided hat for the first time, announced that he was now
second-in-command aboard the *Llanstephan Castle*. 'The
Huns are about,' he declared.

A damp, clinging murk enveloped the convoy as it
reached the danger zone around the North Cape of Norway, shielding the ships from enemy eyes. The convoy
moved silently on a slate-grey sea through a labyrinth of
mist that thickened at times into an impenetrable curtain

of cold and damp. The leading ships trailed floats called fog-buoys 100 yards behind so the vessels following could stay in formation and not get lost. The RAF men donned duffel coats and the machine-gunners were allowed to leave their posts and tramp the deck for a few minutes to keep warm.

All the fears among the RAF boys and the Poles that they were heading into a trap crystallised when the convoy reached the rendezvous point where the Soviet navy was to escort it into Archangel. There was no sign of the promised Soviet escort ship, the *October Revolution*. The convoy stopped, drifting in radio silence with all engines shut down, so that the smoke from their funnels would not give them away. The dense fog had given way to low, thin cloud that obscured both the horizon and the near distance but occasionally thinned sufficiently to allow a glimpse of blue sky. Charlotte and the other passengers heard a German spotter plane circling overhead. Beneath the thin safety blanket of cloud, a cat-and-mouse game was played. The convoy would be safe if the fog outlasted the spotter plane's fuel reserve. If there was a gap in the cloud, German bombers would be on to them in minutes. In the end, the fuel ran low, and the spotter plane returned to base. Rather than waiting like sitting ducks, the commodore ordered the convoy to proceed through the Soviet maritime defences towards Archangel, minesweepers in front and destroyers behind.

The absence of the promised escort and the fact that the Germans knew the location of the convoy prompted an anguished question: had the Russian authorities – or a spy – tipped off the Germans about the convoy's itinerary? There was no evidence to confirm either suspicion, but it added to the pervasive atmosphere of distrust. The commodore preferred to focus on the weather, not conspiracies. 'It was hazardous, but yesterday's fog did its bit,' he said.*

As the convoy approached the Russian coastline, the air cleared, and a lighthouse appeared. Charlotte exclaimed: 'Russia – the lantern of the world.'† She could no longer hold back from delivering her lecture to Topolski, who by this time had downgraded her to the 'Babushka of the British Revolution'. Charlotte took him aside. 'Before you set foot on Russian soil, you must decide whose side you are on. You are either a communist or an enemy.' She jabbed a finger at him. 'In this conflict there is no middle way.'

'You're wrong. There is a middle way,' Topolski insisted. 'Both sides have to be honest and be ready to compromise. It's not just up to us Poles to make all the sacrifices.'

'But Stalin has made huge compromises. The Poles who were detained in Russia are being freed, and are being allowed to form an army corps to liberate their country. With the support of the Soviet leadership Polish progressive forces will restore your country. You have to join them.'

Topolski was about to ask why he should trust Stalin, who had joined Hitler in destroying Poland and was now claiming to be the country's saviour, when Madame Fierlinger, the fur-clad wife of the Czech ambassador to Moscow, stepped in between them, uttering cooing words in French.‡

* Topolski, *Fourteen Letters*, unpaginated.
† Topolski, unpaginated.
‡ Topolski, unpaginated.

With the danger of German bombing having passed, Charlotte gave full rein to her exuberance, predicting that the convoy would be greeted on arrival by cheering crowds in Archangel harbour. As the Soviet maritime pilot climbed aboard and guided the ship past the sandbanks of the Dvina River to its berth, there was silence. On the quayside, no one responded to the waves of the RAF men except a small boy, too young to understand the complexities of allied politics.* A shot rang out as an excited Russian soldier woke up to see blue-clad troops stealing into the port and, taking them for German saboteurs, opened fire and wounded an RAF serviceman in the hand.

Charlotte still did not moderate her enthusiasm. Wally Carroll, who had never been to Russia before, found himself leaning on the ship's rail between Charlotte and a Royal Navy officer. Delighted at the sight of workmen on the quay building a ramp of logs, Charlotte said, 'Have you ever seen workmen work like that before? Look how carefully they sweep up the chips and shavings. You wouldn't find men working like that in a capitalist country.'

The naval officer beside her almost exploded. 'I've never seen such sloppy work.' Looking around the wooden wharves, which seemed too fragile to take the weight of the tanks that would be delivered by future convoys, he exclaimed, 'They've been at it for twenty-five years and this is all they have to show.' Carroll looked around too, but he could not see any difference between the workmen on the quay and those he had seen at American lumber

* Bartlett, *And Now, Tomorrow*, p. 72.

camps. What was the argument about?* It was a lesson for Carroll: Soviet Russia was not just a country. It was a blank screen on which visitors projected the preconceptions they had come with.

Charlotte had one more battle to fight before she could get to work. The British Embassy had booked a plane to fly the important people – the diplomats and the other two journalists, but not her – to Moscow. She and the other 'small fry' would have to go by train, which could take many days. This she saw as a punishment by the British Embassy for her being an unapologetic communist and she protested at the gross insult to her newspaper and its proprietor. She made such a fuss that the Embassy caved in and gave her a seat on the plane to Moscow.†

* Wallace Carroll, *We're in This with Russia* (Houghton Mifflin, 1944), p. 53.
† Haldane, *Truth Will Out*, p. 194.

# 4

## *Meet the Metropol*

The most generous thing you could say about the Metropol Hotel in 1941 was that it had seen better days. When it opened in 1905, it stood as a shining example of the Art Nouveau style, combining the designs of avant-garde British and Russian architects with highly coloured elements of décor drawn from Russian folklore. At that time the capital of the Russian empire had for two centuries been St Petersburg on the Baltic coast, reducing Moscow to 'a village with four hundred churches'. Despite this cruel label, Moscow at the start of the twentieth century was the home of Russia's wealthy merchants, who at the time were leading art collectors, patrons of the country's cultural elite and nurturers of progressive ideas. The Metropol was their showcase and their playground.

The year of its opening was a time of mass protests throughout Russia demanding reform from the autocratic Romanov dynasty. One of the first grand occasions held at the hotel was a dinner to celebrate the unpopular Tsar Nicholas II granting the Russian people the right to elect a parliament. Feodor Chaliapin, the great operatic bass who was the son of a peasant, marked the occasion by climbing up onto a table under the vaulted glass ceiling of the dining room – the space was originally designed as a theatre, hence its huge dimensions – and singing unaccompanied the revolutionary anthem, the 'Song of the Volga Boatmen'. He then passed a hat around the diners to collect donations to support the strikers.

As Russia recovered from the upheaval of 1905, the hotel proved an instant hit for those with money to spend. Sugar barons flaunted their wealth with rivers of French champagne, and cavalry officers invited ballerinas from the nearby Bolshoi Theatre to join them for a post-performance supper. Tsarist gallants invited their guests up to one of the private rooms on the first-floor balcony where they could look down on the diners below or close the curtains for an intimate soirée.

The British diplomat and spy Robert Bruce Lockhart captured the dissolute atmosphere of the hotel when he first visited in January 1912 and, having put off the call girls who pestered him by phone, went down to the restaurant. 'My first impressions were of steaming furs, fat women and big sleek men; of attractive servility in the underlings and of good-natured ostentation on the part of the clients; of great wealth and rude coarseness, and yet a coarseness sufficiently exotic to dispel revulsion. I had entered a kingdom where money was the only God.'*

Unsurprisingly, the hotel acquired a reputation as a place where bourgeois mothers did not want their daughters to be seen – the phrase 'girls of the Metropol' would be used with a knowing wink for decades to come.

Bruce Lockhart describes gaily lit windows on the first floor with doors opening into the *cabinets privés* where,

* Robert Bruce Lockhart, *Memoirs of a British Agent* (Putnam, London, 1932), p. 53.

hidden from prying eyes, 'dissolute youth and debauched old are trafficked for roubles and champagne for songs and love'. The restaurant was a maze of small tables, crowded with officers in badly cut uniforms, Russian merchants with scented beards, and German commercial travellers with sallow complexions. At the end of the dining room was a dais where a red-coated orchestra played, led by a Czech violinist who performed from a little pulpit. Sometimes the orchestra crashed out a waltz loud enough to drown the popping of corks and clatter of plates. At other times, the violinist turned round to face the diners and brought tears to their eyes with his doleful gypsy tunes.*

When the Bolshevik Revolution overthrew the provisional government that had replaced the Romanov dynasty in November 1917, Tsarist officer cadets chose the Metropol to make their last stand in Moscow against the victorious Reds. They were forced to surrender when the revolutionaries brought up field guns to bombard the hotel; the damage was still visible on the walls in the 1940s.

Bruce Lockhart was uniquely well placed to chart the hotel's abrupt transition from playground of the rich to a bastion of the Bolsheviks. When he returned, after the Bolsheviks had seized power, he was the guest of Leon Trotsky, firebrand of the Revolution. Trotsky was haranguing members of the new Bolshevik government from the same dais where the Czech violinist had until recently entertained the cream of Moscow society.

In that year the Bolshevik leader Vladimir Lenin had moved the capital back to Moscow from St Petersburg – an imperial city too closely associated with the Tsars to

* Ibid., p. 54.

suit the workers' state – and he requisitioned the hotel as a dormitory and offices for the new rulers. The hotel was renamed the Second House of Soviets and became the home and workplace of senior Bolsheviks. It was from here that the fateful telegram was sent ordering the Reds to massacre Tsar Nicholas, the Tsarina Alexandra and their five children in Ekaterinburg in 1918. Lenin and Stalin both addressed grand occasions in the hotel's dining room.

The new communist rulers paid no heed to the upkeep of such a bourgeois icon, and standards fell rapidly. The depths to which the hotel had sunk after the Revolution are described in a 1920 account by a Russian official. While blood was being shed in the civil war, the Metropol was filled with people getting drunk on vodka, champagne, and wines from the Caucasus. 'Dirt and cigarette butts were everywhere . . . residents chopped firewood and used primus stoves in their rooms, clogged the sinks and toilets with garbage, lay on the beds with their boots on, carried food and hot water up and down the stairs, hung up their wet clothes in the halls, brought in unauthorised guests, claimed to be someone they were not and often behaved in a rude and downright outrageous manner.'*

Clare Sheridan, a British sculptor who visited Moscow in the early 1920s, wrote in her diary of life in the Metropol: 'The drain smells are such that one climbs the stairs two at a time holding one's breath! There are bits of the Kremlin that are enough to kill the healthiest person, but the Metropole [sic] baffles all description. Inside the offices it is all

* Yuri Slezkine, *The House of Government* (Princeton University Press, 2017), p. 224.

right, but the double windows everywhere are hermetically sealed for the winter, and I wonder that people do not die like flies.'*

Arthur Ransome, who reported from Moscow in the 1920s and later became the author of the children's book *Swallows and Amazons*, described how people lived in the absence of room service. 'And all the time people from all parts of the hotel were coming [to the kitchens] with their pitchers and pans, from fine copper kettles to disreputable empty meat tins, to fetch hot water for tea.'†

By the 1920s the sleek and fur-clad clientele the hotel was built for had either fled abroad and were working as taxi drivers in Paris or Shanghai, or were lying low as 'former people' whose wealth, property and even clothes were requestioned by the Revolution. In their place came commissars in leather jerkins demanding accommodation, peasants from far-flung provinces bringing written notes of the progress of the civil war or the spread of famine, and all manner of desperate people begging for a square meal from the Metropol's dining room, now a cafeteria.

The Revolution had set out to destroy 'bourgeois morality', leading to an outburst of sexual liberation, prompted by the reputed comment of the revolutionary theorist Alexandra Kollontai that 'the satisfaction of sexual desires, of love, will be as simple and unimportant as drinking a glass of water'. The revolutionary 'glass of water theory' of sexual relations after women were liberated from the

---

* Clare Sheridan, *Mayfair to Moscow* (Boni & Liveright, New York, 1921), p.164.
† James Rodgers, *Assignment Moscow: Reporting on Russia from Lenin to Putin*, (I. B. Tauris, 2020) Kindle edition loc 896.

bourgeois norms of marriage was hotly debated in Russia in the 1920s – and denounced by Lenin\*. Alexandra Kollontai did indeed describe sex in terms of a human need like water, but the origin of the sentence which is often attributed to her remains unclear. The hotel manager appointed by the Bolsheviks tried to stop the Metropol becoming a brothel. When he stopped 'non-party women' coming to visit a senior member of the Cheka, the new secret police, the latter told him: 'You are not my father, priest or protector.' In the manager's eyes, Moscow had become a 'bubbling, rumbling, rotting and gurgling swamp'.†

Some semblance of order was restored in the mid-1920s when the government found a new use for the hotel. Having recovered its pre-revolutionary name, it was designated as the place to accommodate influential visitors from the West. The face of Soviet hospitality looked very much like the Tsarist version, minus the fine crockery that had been pilfered in the years of chaos. With the Bolsheviks believing that worker-led revolution was fated to take over the world – and that Soviet power was not safe in Russia until that happened – a new industry arose to market the Soviet Union abroad. In 1925 the All-Union Society for Relations with Foreign Countries, known as VOKS, was set up to ensure that visitors received a positive impression of the emerging Soviet state. Guides and interpreters were put through a 160-hour training course to ensure that

---

\* Clara Zetkin, Lenin on the Women's Question, *My Memorandum Book*, 2004. https://www.marxists.org/archive/zetkin/1920/lenin/zetkin1.htm

† Slezkine, *The House of Government*, pp. 226 & 266.

influential visitors – 'useful idiots' in Lenin's term – went home with an impression of peace, progress and bountiful supplies of everything, even when famine was stalking the land. A VOKS guide, according to Ekaterina Egorova, historian of the Metropol, was not a hired servant, as in the West, but a companion who was 'a comrade with a rigorous political foundation'. Guides should present Soviet achievements 'in the appropriate context and scale'. They were required to inform on the visitors they were showing around: who they met, what interested them and what questions they asked. Stock answers to tricky questions were supplied as part of the training course, such as 'Are infectious diseases widespread in the USSR?' Answer: 'Since the application of our social legislation, infectious diseases have ceased.'

Or this one: 'Do convicted bribe-takers enjoy the right of early release from their sentences?' Answer: 'No, like all members of the intelligentsia who have not emerged from the ranks of the proletariat, they do not enjoy this right.'*

These bone-headed responses might suggest that the charm offensive was cack-handed and ineffectual. While the guides reported that some visitors were inveterate anti-communists and Russophobes, this propaganda barrage worked on a stream of progressive academics, liberal clergymen and others who clung to the Soviet experiment as a way out of the poverty and unemployment that gripped the capitalist world following the Wall Street Crash of 1929.

Most famously, George Bernard Shaw, the Irish playwright, avowed communist and winner of the Nobel Prize

---

* Ekaterina Egorova, *Metropol – Stolitsa Moskvy* (Sever, Moscow, undated), p. 235.

in Literature, visited Moscow in 1931 to celebrate his seventy-fifth birthday. The Russians honoured him with banquets at a time when food was in short supply. In the absence of his wife, who was ill, Shaw was accompanied by Nancy Astor, a Conservative MP and the first woman to take a seat in the House of Commons. Despite their clashing political views, they admired each other and had a lifelong friendship. While in Moscow, Lady Astor provided a muted counterpoint – she liked to denounce communists as thieves – to Shaw's fulsome praise of the Soviet system. No flattery was spared for Shaw: on a visit to the theatre, the whole cast unrolled a huge banner in praise of the writer. Stalin accorded the Shaw/Astor double act a two-hour meeting, unprecedented for a visiting literary figure. The smooth progress of the charm offensive stuttered briefly when the Metropol lift broke down between floors with Shaw and Lady Astor in it and they had to be pulled out.*

On return to Britain, Shaw's impressions dominated the headlines. Ever the provocateur, he said he had never eaten better than in Russia. Within a year, the quickening pace of Stalin's collectivisation of agriculture had unleashed famine on Ukraine. Shaw did not speak of the prison camps that Stalin was filling with real or imagined enemies, though Lady Astor had had the courage to confront Stalin and ask him why he was killing so many Russians. There is some doubt that Stalin's interpreter dared to translate the question correctly.†

In 1935, the British Fabian socialists, Sydney and

* *Chicago Tribune*, 22 July 1931, p. 15.
† Christopher Sykes, *Nancy: the Life of Lady Astor* (Collins, 1972), p. 339.

Beatrice Webb, stayed in the Metropol and then published their two-volume panegyric to Stalin's Russia, *Soviet Communism: A New Civilisation?* For later editions, published in wartime after the USSR joined the Allies, they removed the question mark.

As the 1930s drew to a close, Stalin unleashed a two-year reign of terror known as the Great Purge, which saw residents of the Metropol regularly dragged from their beds. One of the many thousands of Stalin's victims was Evgeny Veger, a rising star of the Communist Party, who lived in two rooms on the second floor of the hotel with his pianist wife Solange and their children. On the night of 25 June 1937, the tramp of boots was heard in the corridor, then a woman wailing and a male voice trying to comfort her. After that, silence. The next morning, one of the rooms occupied by the Vegers was closed with a leaden seal. The sound of weeping drifted down the corridor from the Boyarsky Zal, a function room where Solange had sought refuge to hide her distress from the children. Veger was executed five months after his arrest. Solange did not suffer the usual fate of wives of victims of the Terror – a spell of forced labour in a camp for 'families of traitors to the motherland' – and was placed in a psychiatric hospital instead.*

After Stalin's death in 1953 the political elite were no longer at risk of arrest in the middle of the night, and the Metropol settled into a more comfortable role, as the best of a bad bunch of Moscow hotels with a restaurant serving poor food where no one could get a table. In the 1960s the

* Veger's arrest is described in Eugen Ruge's novel, *Le Metropol* (Chambon, Paris, 2021), pp. 101 & 243.

visiting Labour politician Tom Driberg, openly homosexual at a time when homosexuality was illegal in Britain, discovered behind the Metropol a 24-hour urinal which appeared to be the only gay pick-up place in Moscow. On Driberg's recommendation, Guy Burgess, the Soviet spy who had fled Britain to live in Moscow, went there and found a companion in a young electrician called Tolya.*

After the long era of stagnation under Brezhnev, the death of Communist Party rule was marked by a celebratory dinner at the Metropol in 1991. The exiled cellist Mstislav Rostropovich had returned to Moscow to support demonstrators resisting the hard-line Communist putsch against Mikhail Gorbachev; his concert outside the White House, the bastion of the anti-putschists, was one of the defining moments of the resistance. Afterwards, he and his wife, the soprano Galina Vishnevskaya, celebrated the defeat of the putschists at a dinner in the Metropol – the place where more than thirty years earlier they had first met and fallen in love, before leaving Russia in the 1970s.

In 1993, when Michael Jackson stayed at the hotel, there was a faint echo of Chaliapin's performance almost ninety years before, albeit against a less heroic backdrop. The pop star had climbed onto the stage at one end of the dining room to examine the harp that is played each morning during breakfast. He plucked a string and – such was the hotel's hold on the collective imagination – launched a rumour that he had given an impromptu performance under the glass dome.

* Francis Wheen, *Tom Driberg: His Life and Indiscretions* (Chatto & Windus, 1990) p. 311.

The Metropol has been owned since 2012 by Alexander Klyachin, a Russian businessman and owner of an international hotel chain, who has modernised it, while preserving the unique features of a significant cultural monument.

*

Since its opening in 1905, the Metropol has been witness to the seminal events of Russia's tempestuous twentieth-century history. From its beginnings as a symbol of modernity and progress, to a ramshackle headquarters of the new Bolshevik government, to a slum in the 1920s and then an island of plenty where influential foreigners were schmoozed, the hotel obligingly played its part. In 1941 two characteristic traits of the Metropol's history – its louche reputation and its role as a place to hoodwink influential foreigners – came together in its role as the wartime press centre.

By the end of the 1930s Stalin had made working conditions for foreign journalists so difficult that most of the resident press correspondents had packed up and left. Now, as a precondition of Russia's wartime alliance with Britain, and later the United States, Stalin was obliged to accept inquisitive foreign reporters desperate to unravel what Churchill called the 'riddle wrapped in a mystery inside an enigma' that was Russia. The question for Stalin in 1941 was whether the system of getting foreigners to swallow the Soviet version of reality created in the 1930s would work on tough-minded war correspondents. This time it was not just a question of Russia's image in the West: supplies of American and British tanks, aircraft, lorries and other war materiel to bolster the struggling Red Army against Nazi Germany depended on positive reports coming out of Moscow from a supposedly independent foreign press.

When the reporters arrived at the Metropol they were slotted in among the long-term residents, of whom the main contingent were old Bolsheviks – Stalin's comrades in the Revolution – who had survived the purges of the 1930s. The foreign journalists and the elderly revolutionaries, even when living under the same roof, inhabited separate worlds – it was too dangerous for the Russian residents to fraternise with foreigners – even Allied ones – and very few journalists had enough Russian to make conversation with the people they came across in the corridors whose identities, if they had discovered it and got them talking, would have yielded a world-class scoop. Every foreign journalist who came to Moscow wanted to know the truth about the Great Purge and what had made so many leading Bolsheviks confess to implausible crimes of treachery before they were shot in the back of the head. They could have found the answers from those who had survived the Great Purge and were living just a few doors away.

For much of the war, arriving journalists found the famous dining room closed, its centrepiece fountain no longer bubbling into a now dry and dusty marble pool, in which tradition required someone to be dunked on New Year's Eve. The hotel's assistant manager, a cockney turned Bolshevik named Jack Margolis, explained to one journalist that the dining room was closed to keep the guests safe in the event of a direct hit on the famous glass ceiling. But the closure served another purpose: to isolate the journalists from other guests in the hotel and to exclude outsiders they might want to invite to dine with them.

Instead of eating under the glass dome, the journalists were served their meals on the first floor, enjoying 'ambassador level' rations, which included caviar and a daily cream pastry, one of only a few hundred baked each day for the whole population of Moscow. Service was slow: all the waiters were doddery old men brought out of retirement. The oldest, who had begun his career as a waiter as long ago as 1896, brought to mind the elderly retainer Firs who fussed over the samovar in Chekhov's play, *The Cherry Orchard*. The journalists' assistants – secretary-translators and couriers – were allowed one meal a day in the hotel, a benefit more important than their wages in maintaining their health and strength. The food they saved to take home, plus hunks of bread and sugar lumps given them by the journalists, helped feed their families. For the waiters, a couple of lumps of sugar would do as a tip.

For the journalists living in the Metropol Hotel, the nerve centre was room 346, the office of the American news agency, United Press. This was, in the words of the American reporter Harrison Salisbury, a 'gloomy cave', albeit one fitted with velvet curtains. There were three tables piled high with newspapers, and a cabinet full of tea things. Among the sugar cubes and crusts of black bread were some cans of food, provided by the US embassy after reporters complained their teeth were falling out due to lack of vitamins in their diet. Some slivers of cheese could be seen on a shelf, to be scattered on the floor to keep the mice out of the food cupboard. A two-burner hotplate was sited incongruously below a crystal chandelier. There was a small sleeping nook for the overnight reporter, and a bathroom hidden behind a heavy green curtain. The overall impression was of squatters having taken over a haunt of the rich.*

Looking out of the window of the United Press office in winter, you could see in the courtyard young women in padded cotton jackets chopping up wood for the hotel's furnaces. In December 1941, the first winter of the war in Moscow, it was exceptionally cold, with temperatures dropping well below minus 35 Celsius. The hotel was rarely without some form of heating during the war – unlike ordinary homes in Moscow, where the centrally supplied heating was switched off, there was no running water, and people had to go to the public baths to wash. On the occasions in winter when the hotel's heating failed there was usually hot water and correspondents tapped out their stories wearing boots and a hat and coat, and those with bathrooms filled up the tub so that the steam took the chill off the room.

For the Russian women who worked as interpreters for the foreign press, the view into the hotel's courtyard was a sobering reminder of how privileged they were, and what jobs awaited them if they lost their posts at the Metropol. With all the men at the front, able-bodied women were conscripted to go to the forests in summer to collect wood for fuel. Standing in the river with the water up to their knees, they grasped the logs with long-handled hooks and lashed them together into huge bundles to be winched out of the water by crane. Keeping the Metropol warm was a huge endeavour. From time to time thirty or more female members of the hotel staff – cleaners, bookkeepers, administrators and cooks – were deployed to the forest to collect

* Harrison Salisbury, *Disturber of the Peace* (Unwin, 1989), p. 88.

the timber to keep the furnaces going. The physical strain of the work and the danger of injury was a spur to any woman not used to physical labour to find supposedly vital war work in an office.

With the German army advancing towards Moscow, huge quantities of livestock were driven east through the capital, between the Metropol and the Bolshoi Theatre. Muscovites were astonished to see herds of cattle and pigs on the streets of the city centre, the occasional animal disappearing as it was snatched and taken into a dark alley for butchering. Everywhere jerry-rigged chimney pipes protruded from houses at odd angles to allow residents deprived of modern sources of heat to burn wood in a stove at home.

By day, the hotel appeared to be running as a tightly policed press centre. In the ill-lit lobby, described by one resident as 'like being at the bottom of a pond'*, the NKVD men in their ill-fitting suits lounged around, while the assistant manager Jack Margolis stood behind the reception desk telling new arrivals that he had no record of their booking or, if they were lucky, handing them a key. The glass lift was taken out of service to save energy for the duration of the war, and Jack would apologise for not showing the guests to their rooms – his weak heart was not up to climbing the stairs. In the reporters' rooms, the Russian secretaries mechanically translated the bland, propagandistic reports in the Soviet press while the correspondents scratched their heads, increasingly desperate as the day went on to find a new angle. The reporters' couriers – generally young women of student

* Tanya Matthews, 'Going Back', BBC Radio 4, 27 December 1993.

age – dashed in and out of the hotel. In the morning they might go to the special store on Gorky Street where vodka could be bought with coupons only available to foreigners. Later in the day, they carried the reporters' articles to the 'Nark' (after the Russian abbreviation Narkomindel, the People's Commissariat for Foreign Affairs, whose press department oversaw foreign journalists) and waited while they were censored, and then took the copy, now covered in blue marks, back to the reporter. If there was enough left of the original article to be worth sending, the courier hot-footed it to the Central Telegraph Office for transmission. At the end of the working day, the secretaries and couriers left to go home, taking in their bags scraps of food to share with their families.

To all appearances, the system designed to control the journalists' output was running to plan. The journalists were frustrated at being muzzled, but were powerless in the face of a system designed to control every word cabled from Moscow. At night, however, when the Metropol was a dark presence with all its lights smothered in the blackout, the outward display of order and discipline melted away. The anarchic spirit that had pervaded the hotel at different times in its history seeped back in under cover of darkness.

# 5

## *1917: The making of a young revolutionary*

The American reporter that Nadya had been assigned to was Archibald Steele of the *Chicago Daily News*. He bore a striking resemblance to Abraham Lincoln and Nadya found him as uncommunicative as the president's sculpted face on Mount Rushmore. With nothing to report to the 'comrades' about his political views, she was forced to invent some trivia to fill the vacuum. It was the second correspondent she worked for, an Australian named Eric McLaughlin, who would give her more food for thought, even though their first meeting was a disaster. 'He likes a drink but don't worry, he's harmless' was how he was introduced to her.

Nadya recalled these words when she reported for work at his room in the Metropol Hotel. She found McLaughlin sitting in semi-darkness at 10.30 in the morning. The worn velvet drapes were closed, and the oxblood-coloured walls swallowed up what little daylight penetrated through the tattered fabric. Under the dimly glowing chandelier hanging from the high ceiling was a round table covered with a cloth that had once been dark blue but had turned a greenish black. On this table sat a typewriter, a pile of newspapers and an overflowing ashtray. The bed was still unmade.

McLaughlin motioned to Nadya to sit down. Having

removed a few books, she perched on a chair and had barely started to list her skills when he interrupted her. 'No need for any of that. Let's have a drink.'

She could tell he had already been drinking. She accepted a glass out of politeness. 'Of course, I need a translator, but the most important thing is I just need some human warmth. I can see you are a decent sort.'

After pouring himself another glass of vodka, he waxed lyrical on his sympathy for the Soviet Union and his admiration for the steadfastness of the Soviet people in wartime. He told her not to confuse the Australians with the British, who were a load of snobs. 'We Australians are very democratic, and we side with the underdog,' he said. 'Here in Russia the people want to decide their own fate, and they put up with all the hardships that entails.'

He had heard that the other correspondents were complaining about their working conditions. 'Don't worry – I won't have a problem with the censor. I'll never write anything that could harm the Soviet Union. So you'll have an easy time.'

While McLaughlin grew ever more expansive, Nadya kept silent. She knew that all correspondents were subject to the strictest censorship. It wouldn't be long before McLaughlin found this out for himself.

He poured himself another glass while Nadya was still on her first. His tone changed. 'As for where we will live when I've got out of this hellhole, I'll let you decide. We can rent an apartment if you want. I'm easy to live with.'*

Nadya was shocked. How could this foreigner, apparently

* Nadezhda Ulanovskaya and Maya Ulanovskaya, *Istoria Odnoi Semyi*, 3rd edition, (Inanpress, 2013), p. 73.

cultured and with progressive views, have so misunderstood her duties as his secretary-translator? Even if she was the type to enjoy amorous adventures – which she wasn't – she had neither the time nor the energy to indulge in such things, with a husband out of contact at the front and three children evacuated with their grandmother to the Urals and living on God knows what. She had only taken this job because she was told it was important war work, and here she was wasting her time on a fantasist who understood nothing about the Soviet Union. She would be more use working in an arms factory.

Standing up and raising herself to her full height, she took on the role of outraged innocent – 'Excuse me, you have got the wrong idea about my duties' – and marched out of the door.

The next morning a completely sober McLaughlin approached Nadya and said, 'I hope I didn't say anything to offend you.'

'Don't worry about that, but you can't expect me to work for you.'

In the end, after his colleagues pleaded McLaughlin's case, Nadya relented and agreed to translate for him as well as for Steele, the *Chicago Daily News* correspondent. From then on, he behaved irreproachably. In the morning he stayed sober and worked, only turning to drink in the afternoon.*

*

If McLaughlin had known even the barest details of Nadya's past life, he would have hesitated before treating

* Nadezhda Ulanovskaya and Maya Ulanovskaya, *Istoria*, p. 74.

her as an NKVD-provided mistress. Nadya was born Esther Fridgant in 1903 in the shtetl, or Jewish town, of Bershad, then part of the Russian empire but today in Ukraine. Throughout her life she went under many guises, using first names such as Maria, Elaine and Charlotte, and surnames as varied as Sorokina, Kirschner, Goldman and Zhuratovich. Amid this confusion of identities, one thing was clear: growing up she disliked her birth name of Esther, which tied her forever to the shtetl, and was determined to rid herself of it. Her parents would always call her by the affectionate name of Esterka.

The biggest influence on her early childhood was her grandfather, a free-thinking rabbi with a close-trimmed beard who allowed his precocious granddaughter to listen in when he delivered religious judgments on family disputes and matters of religious law. She was a fast learner and zealously followed the Jewish rituals and even tried to catch out her grandfather in his inconsistencies. She noticed that whenever a chicken was brought for him to judge whether it was kosher to eat or not, he would enquire whether it came from a rich or a poor household. When Esther asked why this mattered, her grandfather answered that if the bird came from a rich household, he forbade them to eat it, but if the family was poor, it was permitted.

'But if the poor family eats treif, they will go to hell,' Esther objected.

'No, the sin will be on me,' her grandfather replied. 'God is not so severe. He understands that a poor family needs to feed its children.'*

From her grandfather she inherited a burning sense of

* Nadezhda Ulanovskaya and Maya Ulanovskaya, p. 11.

justice. At the age of nine she gathered her friends together to re-enact the sensational trial of Mendel Beilis, a secular Jew who was accused of the ritual murder of a Russian boy. The Beilis case was a cause celebre in Russia and was followed with alarm in Europe and America as a sign of the rising tide of anti-Semitism under Tsar Nicholas II. Esther assigned different roles to each of her friends and, of course, appointed herself as chief defence lawyer.

The girls were performing on a balcony, and an elderly neighbour overheard Esther's summing-up of the defence case, which she gave in Russian not Yiddish. 'You should have heard her speech today – like a real lawyer,' the neighbour told her grandfather. 'She'll go far, that girl.' In the Kiev courtroom, Beilis was acquitted after the defence demolished the evidence against him.

Once Esther, sitting quiet as a mouse under her grandfather's desk, was shocked to hear her grandfather confiding in his closest friend that he did not believe in the existence of a god with a grey beard sitting up in heaven on a throne, but only in some kind of higher force.

1917 was a pivotal year for Esther. Her beloved grandfather died, and she quickly lost her faith. In February, when she was fourteen, a merchant arrived to discuss business with her father and remarked, as an aside: 'Have you heard there has been a revolution? The Tsar has abdicated.' Her father turned to Esther for confirmation. 'That cannot be,' she said. 'A revolution means barricades and shooting. We've seen nothing like that here.' A few days later, newspapers arrived and confirmed the rumour.*

Not long after that her father moved the family to the

* Ulanovskaya p. 14.

port city of Odessa in search of work. In Bershad the family had lived from hand to mouth, constantly moving to ever more cramped flats. Her father was not cut out for business, but having married the daughter of a rabbi, it was socially unacceptable for him to work with his hands, and he had pursued a string of unsuccessful commercial ventures. Now in Odessa, it was a relief for him to be employed as a worker in a flour mill.

By the time the family moved to Odessa, Esther was ready to embrace all the freedoms offered by the most cosmopolitan city in Ukraine. She had already begun to feel the constraints of life in the muddy shtetl where the only excitement was the arrival of peasants on market days, and they just wanted to get drunk.

In Odessa it was springtime and the trees lining the city's boulevards were coming into leaf. Her family rented a large flat in the centre of town and they took in lodgers to cover their costs. Even though her mother was working her fingers to the bone, Esther exempted herself from having to cook, clean and look after her three younger siblings. Her parents were so proud of her precocious abilities that they let her come and go as she pleased.

She explored the city streets, reading the wall posters summoning people to meetings of a bewildering number of political parties. She found herself in a meeting of high school students. 'Has anyone got anything to say?' asked the first speaker after he had finished. Esther surprised herself by shooting up her hand. She stood up and out spilled all the ideas that she had been longing to share. International capitalism was the enemy of the working class, she proclaimed. Even in wartime the capitalists kept on trading, while setting the workers against each other so they would fight and die in battle. Unable to control the rising pitch of her voice, she appealed for the workers of the world to unite. She was invited to join the group aged just fifteen.

As 1917 drew to a close a second revolution – with real barricades and shooting this time – swept aside Kerensky's weak transitional government in faraway Petrograd and installed Lenin's Bolsheviks in power, with a promise to pull Russia out of the First World War and replace the empire of the Romanovs with a workers' state. A civil war began. For the politically engaged in Odessa, that meant doing more than giving rousing speeches at meetings, and Esther searched for a more significant role.

The new Soviet authorities' hold over Odessa did not last, and soon it was controlled by the White armies, remnants of the old regime commanded by old Tsarist officers who would be supported by British, French and other foreign armies sent to Russia to strangle the Communist state at birth.

Esther became involved with the Young Revolutionary International, set up by students to support the Soviet authorities in Odessa. Everyone in the group had a code name. They already had two girl members, a Vera (faith) and a Lyubov (charity), so to complete the trinity they needed a 'hope' – Nadezhda in Russian, or Nadya for short. In an instant, Esther became Nadya. As a way of protecting the identities of members of a clandestine organisation, this was sloppy tradecraft, but the name stuck.

One day the police raided a building where the young would-be revolutionaries were meeting some older comrades with experience of underground activities. They were all arrested and held in a police station. Among the detainees a fighter called Alex had a Mauser pistol hidden in his pocket and asked the women if one of them could secrete it in her clothing where the police would not search. Nadya was first to volunteer. Taking in her skinny 15-year-old frame in a green polka-dot summer dress, Alex said: 'Step away, miss. Where in the world would you put it?'

After that first meeting, Nadya and Alex's paths crossed regularly as the young revolutionaries came under the command of the experienced clandestine operators. Despite her youth she progressed from schoolgirl dreamer to activist who could fire a pistol and a rifle, and what's more insisted on carrying her rifle on long marches even when men offered her a place on a cart.

One night she was posting flyers on the wall of a power station when she felt a hand on her shoulder. It was the power station guard. 'You're lucky it's me who has caught you. Do you know what you'd be in for if it was someone else?' She did know. It would not be a trial or a prison sentence.

She was not afraid to go on lone missions to prove to the Communist partisans that she was worthy to be one of their number despite her youth. She set out to confront a group of Ukrainian nationalists who had taken over a nearby railway station. At this time of confusion in the civil war when it was not always clear who was fighting whom, the nationalists were supposed to be joining forces with the Reds. But – as rumour had it – they had just killed some of Nadya's comrades, including her closest friend. She was determined to find out the truth. If her comrades really had been murdered, then she would avenge their deaths. Maybe she could even convince the Ukrainian nationalists of the righteousness of the Communist cause. In a word, she would achieve something significant.*

When she arrived at the railway station, which was occupied by the army of the Ukrainian nationalist warlord Symon Petliura, she found banners supporting Soviet power. This was not what she expected. 'I have come to set you right. Your commanders are deceiving you. Petliura is a counter-revolutionary. He is against Soviet power, and I have proof. He killed Reds who came to negotiate with him. I am a Bolshevik, a partisan. You'll see – any minute they'll come and arrest me and shoot me.'

In the middle of her harangue, an officer appeared. 'Young lady, please come with me.'

She turned to the soldiers as she was led away to the stationmaster's office. 'See? They are taking me away.'

An elderly commander sitting behind a desk raised his eyes: 'Can I ask you what you are here for?' She reprised her tirade. 'You killed them. You say you want Soviet power and then you go and kill the Reds.' The commander shook his head. 'I'm sure Mummy and Daddy will be worried about their little girl. Now what are we to do with you?'

Nadya could not stop. 'Do what you do with all our people – shoot me!'

The exhausted officer had had enough. He ordered a guard to arrest Nadya and hold her in a railway wagon. After a while she fell asleep, to be woken up by a huge commotion and the sound of gunfire. The Whites were attacking and the Petliura soldiers were running away. Her guard hesitated for a moment, then cursed and ran off.

* Ulanovskaya and Ulanovskaya, *Istoria*, p. 18.

It was too dangerous for Nadya to try to re-join her partisan group, so she hid in the railway station until some workers appeared. She joined them as they boarded the train to Odessa. She returned to her parents who had heard nothing from her for several days. They made her promise to stay at home and never leave, a promise she kept for all of one week.

After being arrested for handing out leaflets calling on French sailors in Odessa to desert and support the Revolution and narrowly escaping execution by firing squad, she caught up with Alex, who explained that he had intervened to secure her release. Aware that the French were about to leave Odessa, he had warned the French command that unless Nadya was freed, he would throw the evacuation into chaos by opening fire on the crowds massing on the quayside.

Despite Nadya's history of recklessness, Alex was happy to include her in his next action. With the Whites losing control of Odessa, Alex put together a detachment including his teenage acolyte to seize the city's police headquarters. As they approached, the sentry shouted: 'Stop or I'll shoot.'

Alex grabbed the sentry's rifle. 'Tell your boss that Alex has disarmed you.' And with that he opened the gate and entered the police compound.

With the White guards safely locked up in the cells, Nadya found herself sitting in the police chief's spacious office, upgraded to the role of Alex's assistant. In a cupboard she found a bottle of champagne. She had never tasted alcohol before, and she drank some from a tin mug. Lemonade tasted better, she decided.

After three days Alex and his men handed over the

police station to the Red Army and dispersed. Alex was put in charge of a confiscation committee to seize 'surplus property' from the bourgeoisie. They went round the homes of the wealthy, taking all they could carry, and brought it to Nadya in a warehouse where she recorded it all. She was surrounded by piles of clothes, boots, bed linen and saucepans. The bourgeoisie were allowed to keep two pairs of boots, which Nadya thought too generous – she herself did not have a single pair of matching boots. She was allowed to choose something from the surplus piles, and she chose a dress – a rarity with no holes in it – and wore it home. As for Alex, he would not even take a pair of cloths to wrap round his feet, even though he needed them.

The new Red regime in Odessa lasted only three months. The peasants had stopped bringing food to market and the city was starving. The population was happy to have the Whites back. Alex and Nadya fled to the port of Nikolayev* where they rented a room, and he registered Nadya as his wife, which entitled her to Red Army rations.†

Alex was put in charge of an armoured train to spearhead a counter-attack but as the Whites fought their way into Nikolayev, Alex had no alternative but to blow up the train and escape with his troops. On the day of the retreat, he came to check on Nadya and caught a few hours' sleep before joining his men. That evening Nadya heard the voices of White soldiers on the street outside her room. An officer on horseback shouted at her landlady, 'Are there any Reds in your house?' If the Whites were asking that

---

* Today known as Mykolaiv.
† Ulanovskaya and Ulanovskaya , *Istoria*, p. 22.

question all over town, she was convinced that Alex could not have gone far before being captured or killed. She spent a restless night until, just before dawn, she heard a scratching sound at the window. It was Alex, barefoot and in his underclothes. 'I thought you were dead,' she whispered. He replied, 'I'm not dead unless I tell you myself.'

He had indeed been captured by the Whites. They shot on the spot anyone who looked like a Red officer. Alex was wearing a simple sailor's vest and cheap boots. Then they shot anyone who looked Jewish, but Alex, whose birth name was Izrail Khaykelevich, had always been able to pass for a Russian. He was assigned to a group who were to be transported to the White headquarters. They were made to strip to their underclothes and forced into carts with guards manning machine guns. The Whites did not know the city and the drivers kept stopping to ask the way. Alex dozed. The cart jolted to a halt. He opened his eyes and saw that he was right in front of Nadya's building. Although the gates were locked, he remembered there was a broken window round the side. When the guard's back was turned, he slipped over the side of the cart, ran across the road, through the broken window and into the courtyard.

From inside their room, Nadya and Alex could hear the White soldiers wearily counting and re-counting their prisoners. Then there was the sound of carts moving off and they held their breath until the clatter of the horses' hooves had faded away.

Alex was starving, but all Nadya had to offer him was a few lumps of sugar. As ever, he had an escape plan: hurriedly, Nadya cadged some clothes from their landlady – a peasant blouse and trousers for Alex, and a scarf for her – in exchange for a promise that they would leave immediately. Nadya had an old pair of men's boots rescued from the armoured train for Alex to wear, and she went barefoot. Thus a peasant couple on their way to market, carrying a watermelon to complete the disguise, walked past the White sentries to safety.

After escaping the firing squad she never again forgot the legend about her illustrious ancestor, Rabbi Raphael, who had struck a deal with God that none of his descendants would die a violent death for seven generations. While she could claim the protection of a long-dead rabbi, Alex benefited from some extraordinary coincidences that, thanks to his quick wits, boundless charm and a chameleon-like ability to appear in almost any guise, kept him safe.

The couple separated once they had left Nikolaev and Alex was out of immediate danger. Nadya took the train back to Nikolaev to find shelter in a safe house while he continued to walk to Kherson, the nearest town to the south, for his next civil war assignment in the Crimea.

He was walking alone when an open carriage passed him and then slowed right down and stopped. A soldier was sitting beside the driver and behind them was a nurse in uniform. At the sight of the soldier, Alex assumed that his cover had been blown but could not see a way to escape. To his relief he saw the nurse smiling and beckoning to him. He walked cautiously up to the carriage. He recognised her as the young woman who had been keen on him when he lived in Paris before the wars. She offered him a lift in the carriage all the way to Kherson. It was obvious to her whose side he was on, and to warn him, while not giving away his secret to the soldier listening in, she talked at length about how pleased she was that the dastardly Reds were being hunted down and shot in Kherson.

After he had bought some proper clothes, the nurse introduced him as her friend to the family of a White officer and they offered him a room. They treated him very kindly while he spun them a web of lies to give the impression that he was one of their circle. They never suspected his subterfuge and even helped him on his way to Crimea, where the final battle of the civil war in southern Russia was about to take place.

By October 1920 the White armies in southern Russia were bottled up in the Crimean Peninsula. In November, the Reds marshalled armies of overwhelming force to attack and destroy the Whites in their stronghold.

Nadya tried to follow Alex to the Crimea by sea but her ship was battered by storms and forced to turn back. At this time an epidemic of typhus was raging in Russia – up to 30 million cases were recorded during the civil war. Nadya caught the disease and was sick for a long time. A young anarchist called Victor who had been studying in Moscow had returned to Odessa and joined her group of young revolutionaries. Victor was a regular visitor to her bedside, and he caught typhus himself.

When Nadya recovered, a friend told her, 'Alex is dead. He was shot and there were witnesses.' On hearing this, she was heartbroken and felt that at the age of seventeen her life as a revolutionary was over. Victor was a very attentive suitor, and Nadya became increasingly fond of him as she came to terms with losing Alex.

Victor's birth name was Isidore Kamenetsky and his grandfather had been one of the richest men in Odessa. As 'former people', Victor's parents were reduced to living in one three-roomed flat. Without servants the dirty linen piled up in one room and the dirty crockery in another. From time to time someone would take a vase to sell at the market and come back with a cabbage.*

With the civil war drawing to a close, Victor put aside his anarchist beliefs and accepted a job from the Soviet government as director of a flour mill in the Ukrainian town of Pervomaisk. Nadya accepted his invitation to live with him. While famine raged, there was plenty to eat there.

It was 1921, Nadya and Victor had settled into a comfortable domestic routine and Victor would come home for his lunch every day. One day they heard the front door open and in strode Alex, dressed in the magnificent fur-trimmed greatcoat of a Red Army colonel.

'I thought you'd been killed,' gasped Nadya.

Alex laughed. 'Didn't I tell you not to believe any rumours about me? I'm not dead unless I tell you myself.'

They opened a bottle of wine and Alex and Victor got on well. Alex gave Nadya a small present as a reminder of their first meeting and the adventures they had shared together. It was a small Browning pistol, half of the weight of the Mauser she had gamely offered to secrete about her person three years before.

When Victor went back to work, Alex suggested to Nadya they go for a walk. They were soon on the outskirts of the town, with the featureless steppe stretching into the distance.

'I've come to take you back,' he declared.

'But I'm married, and I love Victor,' Nadya said.

* Ulanovskaya and Ulanovskaya p. 25.

'I don't doubt that. You wouldn't be living with him if you didn't love him,' Alex said. 'But maybe you love me just a little bit more?'

As they walked, Alex revealed the real reason he wanted to get back together. He had been approached to go abroad on an undercover mission. Even though the Reds had won in Russia, the Revolution was not safe until the workers of the world had risen up to free themselves from the capitalists who would always be a threat to the Soviet state. 'I need you and I can't do this without you,' he said. After four hours of hearing what a great team they would make, she agreed to leave with him the next day.

At home, Nadya found Victor waiting for her. With one look at her face he understood. 'You're going with him, aren't you?' 'Yes,' she said. Victor was crushed. 'But you said you loved me.' 'But I have to go.'

They talked all night, with Victor reminding her of the comfortable life she was about to give up and she saying she had to respond to the call of the Revolution. Finally he asked her to give him her Browning as a memento. Reluctantly, to calm him down, she handed over the pistol. Dawn broke and it was time for her to leave. As she sat on the edge of the bed lacing up her high boots, she heard a shot and lifted her head. Blood was pouring from Victor's mouth. She leaped up and seized the pistol from his hand. Hearing Nadya's cries, neighbours appeared. Grievously wounded, Victor moaned, 'Damn, I can't even do this right.' In his distress he had tried to kill himself, but the shot went through the cheek. The first task of the reunited couple was to take the spurned lover to hospital in the back of a cart.

As a hero of the civil war, it would have been natural

for Alex to join the Bolshevik party and make a political career in Moscow. This was the path taken by other anarchists who, like him, had fought for Soviet rule during the civil war.

He surprised Nadya when he revealed he had not joined the party. After their victory in Crimea the Bolsheviks had massacred 30,000 White prisoners of war who were no longer a threat to anyone.* 'There was no reason to kill them other than bloodthirstiness,' he told her. They had not just killed officers. The father of one of Alex's friends had also been shot. A respected doctor and revolutionary who had been sentenced to forced labour in Siberia during Tsarist times, he was killed just because he had treated an injured White.

'I am not ready to share responsibility for their barbaric acts,' he said.

'Of course, it is terrible to shoot 30,000 people, it's terrible to shoot anyone,' Nadya retorted. 'But then again, it was done in the name of the Revolution.'†

---

* Serhii Plokhy, *The Gates of Europe: A History of Ukraine* (Penguin, 2015), p. 226. Historians today put the number of victims of the massacre at 40,000.

† Ulanovskaya and Ulanovskaya p. 27.

# 6

## September 1941: Buttering up the press

After six weeks of refusing to offer the foreign reporters any help in covering the war, Palgunov, the head of the Press Department, telephoned a select few British and American correspondents, opening the conversation with the stern warning: 'Don't share what I am about to tell you with anyone.' They were to go on a six-day trip to the Smolensk front. The city of Smolensk, two-thirds of the way along the invasion route from the German border to Moscow, had already fallen to the Germans, but in the lull as the Nazis prepared for a final assault on Moscow, the Red Army had managed to recapture the small town of Yelnya, a salient in the front line which the Germans had abandoned after a three-week battle. The Germans' loss of Yelnya was likely to be only temporary, but it was the first German-occupied territory in Europe to be wrested from the Wehrmacht by the Allies, and the Russians were determined to bang their drum about it.

Palgunov advised the chosen few to take warm clothes, high waterproof boots, galoshes if possible, and a minimum of luggage. There was no room for the correspondents to bring their translators. Before he rang off, Palgunov repeated his warning: 'Not a word to anyone until we set off – we can't just take everyone who happens to have a press card.'

The trip was not a secret for long. Charlotte Haldane heard about it and was determined to be included even though she never got the call from Palgunov. Having over-promised to her editor, she could not allow herself to be scooped by the other British papers when they printed their first front-line report. Luckily for her, at that time the Nark decided to launch its wartime media operation in grand style, inviting the growing foreign press corps to meet Soviet colleagues at a banquet for 100 presided over by Lozovsky, the vice-commissar of foreign affairs.* Before they sat down, Charlotte bearded Lozovsky to demand a place on the trip. He confirmed that a visit to the front was indeed planned, but all places were filled. He assured her she would have a place in the next front-line tour.

Feeling despondent, Charlotte moved into the dining room and took her seat at the table decorated with banks of flowers and, in pride of place, a pair of rearing horses sculpted in butter, waving their golden manes. Enormous bowls of caviar were served, followed by little quails with frills around their matchstick legs swimming in a luscious sour-cream sauce, and then a dessert of frozen fruit. Wait-ers served champagne from buckets of ice.

When it came time for the endless toasts that are an important part of any Russian banquet, Charlotte seized her opportunity. Vodka glass in hand, she stood up. 'I ardently hope that if, as I hear may be possible, the foreign correspondents are privileged to visit the Red Army in action, the fact that I am a woman will not disqualify me from being allowed to do my duty to my paper as my men

* Alice-Leone Moats, *Blind Date with Mars* (Doubleday, New York, 1943), p. 380.

[sic] colleagues will be doing theirs.' She noted a twinkle in Lozovsky's eye.*

Now the secret was out, the American photographer Margaret Bourke-White, a pioneering female photojournalist, moved to sit beside Lozovsky as the other guests began to file out of the dining room for coffee and apricot brandy in the salon. Waiters were clearing away the banks of flowers and ice buckets, but on the table the butter horses were still charging towards victory. 'I can't go back to America without photographing the front,' she told him. Lozovsky warned her of the dangers.

'If I'd wanted to stay safe, I would have stayed at home.' This provoked no reaction from Lozovsky and so, taking her cue from Charlotte, she raised the stakes. 'What will I say when my fellow countrymen discover that I have not seen with my own eyes the heroism of the glorious Red Army? Perhaps they will doubt that the noble deeds they have heard so much about actually took place.'†

Bourke-White was a hard woman to say no to. She had been invited in the 1930s to photograph the new industrial cities that Stalin's first Five-Year Plan was conjuring out of the rocky soil of the Urals. More recently, she had had the rare privilege for a foreign photographer of taking a portrait of Stalin, one in which the pockmarks on his face would not be airbrushed away. She and her husband Erskine Caldwell, a campaigning writer on poverty, race and social problems in America, were a powerful force in US progressive politics. They had arrived in the Soviet

---

* Charlotte Haldane, *Russian Newsreel* (Penguin, 1943), p. 64.
† Margaret Bourke-White, *Shooting the Russian War* (Simon & Schuster, New York 1943), p. 221.

Union in May – with 280 kilograms of photographic equipment, including five cameras – at the start of a six-month guided tour. The purpose of the trip, as the Soviet authorities understood it, was to tell the epic story of how Stalin was moulding a peasant society into an industrial powerhouse. In fact, it was the fruit of a hunch by a *Life* magazine picture editor who suspected that the Nazi-Soviet non-aggression pact was only a temporary expedient and that war between the forces of Hitler and Stalin was bound to break out. This indeed happened in June, one month after Bourke-White's arrival in the Soviet Union. Bourke-White desperately needed pictures of the Soviet Union at war to add to her photographic record of iron foundries and smiling peasants.

So it was that at dawn on Monday, 15 September 1941, Charlotte walked to the foreign ministry where the reporters had been told to assemble. Standing at the entrance by a bathtub filled with water to douse fires from incendiary bombs was the roly-poly figure of Vernon Bartlett, her companion on the Arctic convoy to Archangel, who was carrying a British army-issue tin helmet. Charlotte wore the same get-up as she had to visit the front line in the Spanish Civil War, practical rather than stylish – a 'siren suit', a sort of romper suit popularised by Winston Churchill, eminently suitable for a woman in a war zone where she would be in the company of men twenty-four hours a day. It was topped off with a Spanish leather coat that reached down to her ankles. She had two unique accessories: the yellow-and-red badge of the volunteers of the International Brigades who had fought in Spain, and a white tin hat bearing the arms of the London borough of St Pancras – a useful identifier for an air-raid warden in the London blackout, but likely to draw a sniper's eye on the battlefront.

By contrast, Margaret Bourke-White looked like she had stepped out of a fashion plate, wearing a bright red overcoat with smart black-and-white checked slacks. Beside her was a mound of camera cases and a large wooden tripod. The Caldwell/Bourke-White duo had come from China and had no clothes suitable for the Russian winter. Fortunately, the red coat had a black lining and could be turned inside out when in sight of the enemy.

Apart from Philip Jordan, the correspondent for the *News Chronicle* who was smartly attired in the khaki battle dress of a British army war correspondent, the men in the party looked ill-clothed for war. Cyrus Sulzberger, the blue-eyed scion of the family that owned the *New York Times* and the paper's roving correspondent, turned up in what Charlotte described as a piece of white silk torn off a parachute 'wedded to the remainder of a Carthusian monk's habit', an outfit he claimed defiantly to be the latest thing in Yugoslav ski jackets.* The St Petersburg-born Alexander Werth, an intellectual steeped in Russian culture who was working as a special correspondent for Reuters and *The Sunday Times*, had searched for a coat at Moscow's 'commission' shops, where the former bourgeoisie sold off their goods and chattels to eke out their starvation rations. He bought a yellowy-white dog-skin jacket – the seller insisted it was Siberian husky – for the huge sum of £7. The doggy smell it gave off was so overpowering that the reporters who shared a car with Werth gave it a personality of its own, calling it Fido. The *Daily Telegraph* correspondent A. T. Cholerton,

* Haldane, *Russian Newsreel*, p. 65.

the donnish sage of the press corps, cut an eccentric figure – an intellectual from Tolstoy's time with a salt-and-pepper beard in which could be seen traces of whatever food he had most recently consumed.

Under the supervision of Palgunov, the journalists were squeezed into six small cars – the Soviet M1 'Emka' based on a 1934 Ford – each with a soldier behind the wheel. They had to arrange their feet around bags in the footwell, which oddly turned out to contain bottles of sparkling wine.\* Their relief at finally getting out of Moscow after weeks of pleading with Palgunov was dimmed by the knowledge that they were travelling cheek by jowl with their competitors so there would be no chance of an exclusive. They were reconciled to the fact that they would not be embedded in the headquarters of one of the Red Army's generals, but they still hoped to get close to the action.

They set off westwards down the Mozhaisk highway, through a featureless landscape. Charlotte was cast into a gloom by the monotonous forests of fir trees as far as the eye could see. After the first day, they left the smooth highway and travelled on unmade back roads and 'corduroy tracks' of felled logs laid on the sodden floor of the forest.

It did not take long for the journalists to understand that their hosts' idea of a good newspaper story was way off the mark. The first stop was the town of Vyazma, the scene of a major Russian victory against Napoleon's retreating army in 1812. The Germans had claimed to have inflicted serious damage on the town in a bombing raid the night before. Eager to prove that the Germans had missed their

---

\* Bourke-White, *Shooting the Russian War*, p. 222.

target, the local Russian commander in Vyazma sent the journalists back down the road, crawling in low gear for twenty-five minutes until they stopped beside an empty field. In the middle was a small bomb crater which the guides pointed to with great excitement, not shared by the journalists, who explained that they could do nothing – either in words or pictures – with a small bomb dropped in the middle of nowhere. They retraced their route back to Vyazma.

As they approached the front line within range of German spotter planes, the soldier drivers tied birch and fir branches as camouflage to the roofs and wings of the cars. A couple of times, when they heard the sound of an approaching aircraft, they all leaped out of the cars and sprinted for cover under the trees. As the weather deteriorated, they travelled through unceasing autumn rains, their cars constantly stuck in knee-deep mud.

With the roads becoming impassable, a Russian commander diverted a squad of sappers to keep the journalists' cars moving along the liquid roads. The soldiers stood at the side of the road, shovels in hand, ready to dig each car out of the mud and lay logs under their wheels. An army truck was on hand to pull them uphill when they became stuck at the bottom of a deep gorge. Cholerton wrote that the front was 'in the slimy but steel-like grip of General Mud', who was much more incapacitating than the fabled nemesis of invading armies in Russia, 'General Winter'. He wrote: 'We were bogged down dozens of times and we made less than 18 miles in over seven hours.'*

* 'Days with the Red Army Facing Smolensk', *Daily Telegraph*, 25 September 1941.

The good humour of the soldiers, who regarded the foreigners in their little cars as a bit of a joke, impressed the reporters as a sign of high morale among the Red Army. While the cars struggled to make headway, the Soviet Union's new weapon, the T-34 medium tanks, slithered through the mud at 30 miles per hour. The tank may have been less sophisticated than the armour fielded by the Germans, but it seemed perfectly adapted to be manned by Russian countryfolk who were introduced to the tractor only a decade before.

If the mud was daunting, the hospitality was overwhelming. At one stop on the journey to Yelnya, a banquet on a long table was laid out among the trees. The table was spread with several varieties of fish – salted, pickled and dried – little hillocks of caviar topped with circlets of onion and slices of hard-boiled eggs, and slices of ham and sausage and cheese. The main course was roast woodcock in sour cream. In the centre of the table were bowls of 'pigeon-toed Misha bear' chocolates, a children's favourite. The waiters wore white jackets over their army uniforms. Occasionally a German spotter plane passed overhead, alarming the journalists, but their Soviet hosts hardly glanced up from the feast before them. At one point the journalists were led out of the rain to shelter in a front-line dugout. A rubber plant stood in a pot at the head of a flight of stairs cut out of the earth. To their surprise, the dugout was furnished with a grand piano and decorated with posters of Soviet and British pilots shaking hands over Berlin. There was even a library of improving books. Amongst the Russian novels and works of Lenin was a copy of the poems of Heinrich Heine, the German-Jewish poet whose works were burnt by the Nazis. At the appearance of the journalists, a group of soldiers burst into song. It was as if Intourist, the Soviet travel agency for foreign tourists, had organised it.

The old lags among the journalists prepared the new-comers for a nightly trial-by-vodka that was an inescapable part of Russian army hospitality. At every stop there was a banquet of delicacies – caviar, salmon, tinned sprats, tomatoes, bread, borshch, meat, vegetables and fruit compote – and a battalion of vodka and brandy bottles that honour required the hosts and their guests to con-quer. The journalists established a vodka rotation list, with one person each day designated to get sloshed, with the rest propping him up. The women were excused this rite of male bravado. For this relief, however, they had to put up with boozy advances from senior officers. 'There is something glamorous about you, something Spanish about you,' one officer said to Charlotte. 'May I call you Carmen?'*

Charlotte took this in good humour as it brought back a happy memory of the war in Spain where the Repub-lican heroine Dolores Ibárruri, known as La Pasionaria for her powerful Communist oratory, had given her the ultimate accolade: 'Carlota – I don't believe you are an Englishwoman – you must be Spanish.'

As the toasts dragged on, Bourke-White became aware of a soldier with a bunch of flowers hovering shyly behind her. During a lull, he addressed her, 'In the name of the entire Red Army and because of our admiration for your great country, we wish to present you with this bunch of red poppies.' With the sparkling wine that had travelled

* Alexander Werth, *Moscow '41* (Hamish Hamilton, London, 1942), p. 202.

beneath their feet from Moscow, toasts were pronounced to the great people of America, Britain and the Soviet Union. The ice broken, a soldier who described himself as a member of an elite group, 'the meat choppers', invited Bourke-White to dance a waltz to the tune of an accordion. After being whirled around under the trees, she was breathless, but the soldiers begged her to teach them the latest American dance steps. In her tweed slacks, muddy from the knees down, and her earth-caked shoes, she demonstrated the rumba to the accompaniment of an accordion. The swing proved beyond her, but the soldiers greeted her efforts with enthusiasm.*

When it was Sulzberger's turn to face the vodka challenge, he found himself pitted against the political commissar, the senior officer accompanying the journalists. Speaking no English and uncommunicative when asked questions, his face wore a permanent scowl. Equal measures of vodka were poured out and had to be downed in one. Bourke-White acted as referee, making sure the glasses were filled to the brim, downed in one gulp and turned upside down to prove they had been emptied 'to the bottom'. When each drinker had emptied two half-litre bottles of vodka, they moved on to a lethal Crimean brandy. Several toasts in, the commissar raised his glass and with a radiant smile proposed a toast to the visitors in clear and fluent English. To the astonishment of the journalists, under the influence of alcohol the commissar had unmasked himself as an English speaker. In his diary entry, Sulzberger makes himself the hero of this unarmed combat: 'My adversary passes out. He is carried to his straw

* Bourke-White, p. 250.

mattress and spends most of the night vomiting over himself.'*

As usual the whole travelling party, men and women, journalists and army officers, were all sleeping together in a big dormitory. The men called out for someone to come and clear up the vomit, and a young woman appeared with a mop, a pail and a candle. She stumbled around the mattresses looking for the culprit. 'Oh, it's the comrade political commissar!' she exclaimed. Driven out of the dormitory by the stink, Charlotte got up and went into the other room where girls were clearing away the remains of the banquet. Vernon Bartlett joined her there. The Red Army hosts for the night apologised profusely for the commissar's behaviour, but Charlotte felt embarrassed on their behalf for their loss of face. She and Bartlett dozed fitfully until the morning when they awoke to see two officers, with the blue collar-flashes of the NKVD troops, go into the dormitory, drag out the commissar and take him away.

'What do you think will happen to him?' she asked Bartlett. 'He'll be tried,' he said. Unable to resist winding up his Communist friend, he added, 'And then he'll be shot.'†

In Alexander Werth's recollections, another drinking bout ends up with one of the journalists drunk and lying under the table. When the journalists all piled into their vehicles, they noticed he was missing, and went back to drag him out and deposit him in the back of a car. He remained in a comatose state throughout the day and far

* Cyrus Sulzberger, *A Long Row of Candles* (Macdonald, 1969), pp. 168–9.
† Charlotte Haldane, *Truth Will Out* (Weidenfeld, 1949), p. 221.

into the night. At breakfast next morning he was shocked to learn he had missed the one part of the trip where the party had come anywhere near the front line.

In Vyazma, they had some reporter's luck. It was 7.30 in the morning of the second day and two German bombs exploded less than 50 yards from the hotel. The raid was clearly aimed at the hotel, which had been home to Soviet officers turned out of their rooms to make way for the press pack. Keen to catch every hour of daylight, Bourke-White and her husband had risen early. He was shaving and she waiting, toothbrush in hand, for the sole basin to be free, when they heard the screech of a falling bomb. The hotel was shaken by the blast and Bourke-White turned round to see three male colleagues staggering bleary-eyed into the corridor, two of them still in their underclothes and wearing tin helmets. Bourke-White and Charlotte rushed outside to inspect the damage – two wooden houses destroyed. From one house, an old man was being stretch-ered out. In the other, a man and three children lay dead, the two girls with their blonde hair caked in dust, sitting macabrely propped up against a wall.

As an experienced photographer, she was used to the camera insulating her from the grim reality she was cap-turing. 'It is as though a protecting screen draws itself across my mind and makes it possible to consider focus and light values and the technique of photography, in as impersonal a way as though I were making an abstract camera com-position,' she recalls.* But when a woman ran up to the bomb site and sank to the ground, howling at the sight of her lifeless daughter, her desperate moans penetrated even

* Bourke-White, p. 231.

the photographer's shield. When she came to develop the negatives, she could not look at them.

While the women went out to witness the scene, it was all the men could do to stagger downstairs for breakfast and sip a hair of the dog. Clearly, the vodka intake was slowing their journalistic reflexes. As for the women, after what they had seen, they had no stomach for break-fast. The sight of Cholerton holding a dried fish by the tail and nibbling its flesh, getting oil and bones mixed into his beard, made them feel queasy.

One of the bombers involved in the air raid, a Junkers-88, was shot down, and the next day the journalists were invited to view the wreckage and interview the crew. In his mind, Sulzberger could already see the headline in his paper. 'Anyone who's bombed me out of my bed gets space in the *New York Times*.'* For Charlotte, with her German-Jewish background, the chance to meet the crew of a German bomber that had been in action over London and had almost killed them was not an occasion for bravado. The pilot, a pork butcher's son, had the most arrogant expression she had ever seen on a human face. 'Observing him I understood to the full the meaning of Hitler's propaganda about the Her-renvolk, or master people; he was just the sort to lap it up.'†

The pilot told the journalists that 'war with England was inevitable and necessary'. Asked about the war with Russia, he admitted that it had come like a bolt from the blue. They had not known they were being diverted to the Eastern Front until they were almost within sight of Russian territory.‡

* Werth, *Moscow '41*, p. 197.
† Haldane, *Russian Newsreel*, p. 76.
‡ Bourke-White, p. 235.

During the whole trip, the journalists never got to the front line and saw no action. Sulzberger noted that the senior military officers deferred to the political commissar, whose role was to ensure that the army officers did not stray from the party line. The generals let him do most of the talking even though in military matters he was too inexperienced to tell the difference between Russian and German planes and asked the convoy to take cover from friendly aircraft. Clearly, Stalin's fear of the army wresting control of the workers' state from the Communist Party had not eased in wartime.

Tension rose within the press party with each passing day as it became clear that they were being offered hospitality instead of the chance to do any real reporting. The men directed their anger at the two women. They were jealous of Charlotte because they feared that she, as a prominent communist, was likely to get an interview with Stalin, the prize they were all competing for. Her passionate pro-Sovietism – she was so trusted by the authorities that she was allowed to broadcast on Radio Moscow and contribute to the defence ministry newspaper *Red Star* – grated on their nerves. The fact that Bourke-White was the only foreign photographer allowed to work on the Eastern Front and had taken Stalin's portrait seemed to be proof that women true-believers were given preferential treatment over hard-bitten war correspondents. Bourke-White was even more frustrated than the reporters – it rained continually, the light was bad, and the men were always in a hurry to move on and resented the time she took to set up her equipment.

Two of the correspondents, sharing a car with Charlotte, launched into a tirade against her, calling her a traitor to her country. They were angry at a piece of cheap trickery by the

Red Army. They had been taken to a dump of captured German war materiel and had noticed the stamp of the Stalin Motor Works on some of the supposedly German wheels. Charlotte was embarrassed by this unnecessary piece of subterfuge; the men were furious at a gratuitous insult to their intelligence.* An unexpected source of tension came from Charlotte's insistence on taking a grisly souvenir from the battlefield. The German dead were left where they lay, in trenches or shell holes, and covered with soil, with the odd hand still poking through and helmets strewn around. The Red Army dead lay in a great burial mound, encircled by a neat wooden fence with a plaque inscribed: 'Brotherly grave of those who died like heroes in the struggle against fascism July 29 to September 5, 1941.' Morning glories were already growing on the mound.† Charlotte picked up one of these German helmets which still had the soldier's blood and traces of his brains inside and was taking it triumphantly into Cholerton's car with her. Cholerton was horrified and refused to allow her in the car with her trophy. 'Such ghoulishness in a woman makes me sick,' he said later.‡

On the fifth day they were scheduled to go to their final destination – the town of Yelnya, which the Germans had abandoned on 8 September after a three-week Russian offensive. The ever-impatient Sulzberger led the pack in arguing for the trip to be cut short and a speedy return to Moscow; he had already got as much as he could out of the

---

* Charlotte Haldane, *The Truth Will Out*, Weidenfeld & Nicolson 1949 p. 217.
† Wallace Carroll, *We're in This with Russia*, (Houghton Mifflin Boston) 1942 p. 125.
‡ Alice-Leone Moats, *Blind Date with Mars*, p. 385.

trip. The reporters were all exhausted by the slow pace of travel and frustrated by being led around like children in a kindergarten crocodile. They blamed Bourke-White for slowing down their already snail-like pace. But she had yet to get a picture that told the story of the war, and sensed that Yelnya would finally deliver what she needed. She was supported by some of the reporters, who felt it would be the height of ingratitude to demand to cut short the trip. Alexander Werth argued that the Russian military had gone out of its way to keep them moving in near impossible conditions. He singled out the drivers who had been behind the wheel for up to sixteen hours a day, on roads that often disappeared under mud, and who had to sleep in their cars, getting up early to repair the worn-out springs while the correspondents dozed and nursed their hangovers. Over breakfast the argument got so acrimonious that the Russian minders absented themselves. Just as the reporters were about to mutiny and vote to go straight back to Moscow, a steaming mound of mashed potato, with a golden pool of butter nestling in a hollow, was put on the table in front of them. Everyone's spirits rose, and the vote was cast to continue through the mud and rain to Yelnya.

The reporters had a pressing concern. It was clear by now that the trip had been organised so that the Anglo-American reporters could set the scene for an important conference that was due to open in Moscow. American and British envoys – the multi-millionaire businessman Averell Harriman and Lord Beaverbrook, the Canadian press magnate placed by Churchill in the Cabinet as Minister of Supply – were due to confirm to Stalin how many aircraft, tanks, lorries and tons of ammunition and food they could spare for the Red Army. If the reporters' copy about the Red Army's success in pushing the Germans out of Yelnya was to have any purpose, they needed to get their words into print well ahead of the Three Power Conference. The Allies were unlikely to be generous with their promises of military aid if – as Western military experts believed – the Red Army was surrendering so fast that the Germans would be in Moscow in a few weeks and at Lake Baikal by the end of the year.

For the journalists, there was nothing notable to report in Yelnya. In the fading light Bourke-White took her heavy wooden tripod, cameras and flash bulbs out of the car to get the picture she wanted – the disused cathedral where the Germans had locked up the residents while they burnt all the wooden houses to the ground. 'Hurry up, Peggy,' shouted one of the journalists as she set up her equipment. 'We're clearing out of here in five minutes, and we'll be halfway back to Moscow tonight.' With no support from her impatient colleagues, she broke down and cried to the empty road: 'I can't work in this crazy way.'* Throughout the week-long trip she calculated that there had been only sixteen minutes of sunshine.

The censor who was accompanying the party stepped in to get the local commander to rearrange the transport to help the photographer. The other journalists would leave immediately for the inevitable banquet and Bourke-White would follow later. By now the light was so poor that it required a five-second exposure, with two flash-bulbs on long leads, to capture the cathedral, two Russian soldiers, and a lonely chimney pointing to the sky that was all that remained of an incinerated family

* Bourke-White, p. 269.

home.* In truth, the picture is too obviously posed – the two soldiers look like they have been ordered, in true military style, to stand still and look lively – and it hardly justifies the 700-mile journey and the aggravation that the photographer suffered to get it. Still, she got her photograph in the end.

*

There was one incident that was witnessed by the two women in the press party that they never shared with their male colleagues. At 6 a.m. on the fifth day, spurred on by Bourke-White's need for a dramatic picture, she and Charlotte, the only two members of the party not befuddled by the previous night's drinking, arranged to go with one of their guides to view the remains of the village of Dorogobuzh, which had been flattened by German bombing – the 'Russian Guernica' in Charlotte's telling. As they waited for the light to improve, they saw an old peasant woman in a dark shawl, bent against the wind and rain. Bourke-White asked their minder to stop her so she could take a photo, but he said it was forbidden to photograph Soviet citizens outside Moscow. As they sat in the car in uneasy silence, a procession of men came into view. They were carrying primitive farming tools, dressed in rags, their unkempt hair falling to their shoulders, their feet in sandals made of plaited birchbark. Each had a small bag round his neck with a hunk of bread in it. They trudged by in silence, without the strength even to look up at the car with two women in it. To Charlotte it was a scene from Dante's *Inferno*. She thought they must be

* Bourke-White p. 298.

97

prisoners, perhaps collaborators with the Germans, but there were no guards. The two women asked their minder who these men were. He shut down the conversation, saying, 'I don't know.'

Charlotte recalled: 'Never on any of my travels had I seen such a forlornly tragic sight, human beings registering such complete and final hopelessness . . . After about ten minutes, another procession, a small one, followed them. It consisted exclusively of women, also carrying agricultural implements, with the sacks of bread hanging down their backs, their heads and faces bent against the wind, also completely silent. The whole picture might have been a nightmare.'*

For Bourke-White, this was a missed photo opportunity, but for Charlotte, used to images of apple-cheeked peasant women clutching abundant sheaves of wheat, it was the moment when the feeling of exultation she felt at being in the workers' paradise was replaced by a nagging sense of unease. 'I kept my impressions to myself. They were too fresh and raw to be shared with any of my colleagues.'†

Still troubled by the tragic procession she had witnessed the day before, she joined her colleagues and her Red Army hosts for a farewell banquet. It was even grander and more bibulous than the previous evenings. There were the usual cold hors d'oeuvres, with caviar, vodka and sweet pink wine, followed by soup and then meat and vegetables. Glass dishes were piled high with apples and wrapped sweets from a Moscow chocolate factory. As the representative of the British embassy rather

* Haldane, *Truth Will Out*, p. 219.
† Ibid., p. 219.

than as a journalist, Vernon Bartlett rose to thank the Red Army for its hospitality.

By this time, Bartlett had worked out the mystery of the sumptuous feasts they were served. The journalists had spent hours speculating about how it was possible to feed them so well when the evidence of their eyes showed that the supply lines to the front were all but impassable. The mystery was unlocked when one day the lead car in the convoy broke down, and they arrived to find their hosts unprepared and had to wait several hours before dinner was served. Now it was clear: the travelling party provided the food they were served each day, and the Russian officers at each headquarters enjoyed a meal the like of which they had not tasted for months. It was not surprising that the Red Army officers greeted their guests so warmly.

This was not the moment for Bartlett to point out that sharing the officers' usual rations would have suited the guests better than the Potemkin banquets that had been set before them. As required, he gave fulsome thanks to the Red Army for their hospitality, and proposed toasts to the flourishing of the Anglo-Soviet alliance.

On the long journey back to Moscow, Charlotte found herself alone in the back of the car with a thoughtful Red Army officer. With the image of the procession of lost souls she had witnessed in Dorogobuzh still on her mind, she dared to ask the officer for an explanation. It was obvious to him who they were: they were peasants who were still resisting collectivisation, putting their energies into the tiny family plots they were allowed to keep and grudgingly giving to the collective only the minimum of labour they could get away with. 'If only they would work hard on the collective farms they could make quite a good living,' the officer said. His was a very different image of Stalin's Russia from the one she had lapped up this past decade from the pages of the *Daily Worker.**

On the way back to Moscow, Alexander Werth's driver picked up a hitchhiker, a schoolteacher who was serving as a Red Army captain. His wife and daughter were living far away in the Ukrainian city of Kharkov, which was under imminent threat of German occupation, and he could do nothing to protect them. With none of the Press Department minders in the car, the captain seized the opportunity to give Werth a whispered warning. He must have known the risk he was running, but what he had to say was too important to keep to himself. He told Werth not to believe official statements about the war, which hid the catastrophic casualties of the Red Army, the loss of the Soviet Union's industrial heartland, and the suffering of the starving and homeless civilians.

'It is no use pretending that all is well. The flag-waving, the hurrah patriotism of our press is all very well for propaganda purposes to keep up morale, but it can be overdone and sometimes is. And we shall need help from abroad, very important help before we are finished.'

He pleaded: 'If you people have got any influence with the British government, for God's sake, don't say all is splendid.'†

But the brave Red Army captain's plea fell on deaf ears. Werth had never included in his reports even the mildest

* Haldane, *Truth Will Out*, p. 222.
† Alexander Werth, *Russia at War 1941-45* (Barrie & Rockliff, London, 1964), p. 193.

suggestion of criticism of his Soviet hosts and even this revelation – which would have been a scoop in any other war zone – was buried for almost twenty years.

The captain had chosen to confide in the wrong journalist. Werth's colleagues believed that he was identifying wholeheartedly with the Soviet war effort, thanks to his Russian heritage. That was true, but there was another factor. As a White Russian émigré he feared he would be jailed by Stalin if he stepped out of line. He had asked for diplomatic protection from the British embassy, but it was refused.*

All the correspondents agreed to file their copy so that it could be passed by the censor and transmitted in time for publication on Tuesday, 23 September. When Bartlett listened to the BBC news on the radio that morning, he was astounded to hear the broadcaster's summary of the correspondents' reports from Yelnya. The BBC was telling the world that a huge Red Army counter-attack was underway, driving the Nazis westwards, and the Red Army was on the point of recapturing Smolensk. Bartlett, knowing this to be untrue, immediately cabled the Foreign Office to say: 'Very inadvisable to suggest Smolensk advance is great victory and still proceeding.'† The British ambassador, Sir Stafford Cripps, backed up his concerns with a cable explaining that the Russian advance on the Smolensk front had petered out three weeks previously. He accused the BBC of recklessly exaggerating the importance of the advance. 'This type of propaganda can do neither Russia's nor our own public any good in the long run.'‡

* TNA FO 371.29587/4150.
† TNA FO 371 29587/5530.
‡ TNA FO 371 29587/5604.

Cripps blamed 'unbalanced American reports' but the fault lay closer to home. Werth's piece for Reuters was front-page news all over Britain and beyond under the strapline 'Eyewitness story from Reds' Victory Front . . . Nazis pursued west of Yelnya'. With breathless bold headings such as 'SOVIET PINCER DRIVE', the operative paragraph read: 'The Germans are now 11 miles west of Yelnya and still retreating. Smolensk is still in German hands, but the Russians are closing in.'*

Bartlett, a veteran of the First World War, had understood precisely the opposite. In his summary of the trip for the Foreign Office, he had written that Lieutenant-General Vasily Sokolovsky, Soviet chief of staff on the South-Western Front, had told the reporters there was no evidence that the Soviet counter-attack had compelled the Germans to rush reinforcements into the battle from other fronts. In other words, the Red Army did not have the men or the weaponry to pursue their counter-attack, and the abandonment of Yelnya was a setback that at best would only delay the German advance.

Sulzberger's front-page piece was more judicious than Werth's, but some awkward phrasing gave the impression that the Germans were withdrawing in the face of an ongoing counter-attack: 'The Germans have rushed in reinforcements, but their lines are still bending backward'.† He wrote that 'the Nazis have lost their original momentum' on the Smolensk front, which was true, but within

---

* 'Nazis Pursued West of Yelnya', from Reuters Special Correspondent, *Daily Record and Mail*, 23 September 1941.
† 'Smolensk Front a Litter of Ruins', *New York Times*, 23 September 1941.

three weeks the Germans had recaptured Vyazma and obliterated four Soviet armies in the process, in one of the Red Army's heaviest defeats of the war. He placed two more articles, the inevitable 'Correspondent undergoes bombing attack' and a notebook that contained a reference to the 'handsome girls in red berets' who waited on the journalists at their forest blow-outs, a hint at the stage-managed nature of the trip.

As for Charlotte, she received a sneering riposte from Lord Haw-Haw, the British Nazi propagandist with the clipped accent who broadcast on Germany's English-language radio. 'At last the British have managed to get a correspondent to the Russian front. This correspondent was a lady, the representative of the *Daily Sketch*. Naturally she was not highly versed in military matters. But she was impressed by the fact that she found in a dugout the poems of the Jewish poet Heinrich Heine. No doubt, had she looked more closely, she would have found the poems of Shalom Aleichem as well.' Charlotte dismissed the broadcast as 'an absurd pinprick'.*

In London, the concerns expressed by Bartlett and the ambassador about Russian propaganda infecting the BBC percolated through Whitehall. The result was that the military had a quiet word with the BBC on exercising more caution on military reports from Moscow that had passed through the Soviet censor, particularly when the corporation did not have its own correspondent in place.

From the Soviet point of view, the trip was an undisputed triumph of media management. Unduly optimistic coverage of the Red Army was splashed all over the

* Haldane, *Russian Newsreel*, p. 74.

Anglo-American media, in time to provide public support for supplying the Red Army with weaponry that Britain could ill afford to give. At the Three Power Conference in Moscow Stalin received promises of far greater than expected quantities of aircraft, ammunition and food. From then on, dried 'amerikansky' egg was a staple in Russian army rations and meals served at the Metropol.

Most important was the lesson that the Metropol method of media control was producing the desired result. Correspondents kept in a gilded cage in the hotel for weeks were, when finally let out, all the hungrier for news they could sell to their editors. It did not matter that by the time the journalists had been allowed to visit, the news was old, the battlefield had been cleaned up, and there was no one of interest to interview for the quotes that would bring the story to life.

Charlotte understood that the Soviet officials believed that every non-communist foreigner, and particularly a journalist, 'was, is, and always will be, a potential spy and wrecker'. What she could not understand was the naïve expectation that journalists could be 'fobbed with lavish hospitality in lieu of the information they were paid to seek.'*

In Britain, the demand for news about Stalin and the Soviet Union was insatiable. Partly this reflected Russia's status as an 'enigma' – or, more accurately, a political battleground in which the truth was the first casualty – but also the fervent hope that the Red Army with its millions of soldiers would deal the death blow to Hitler's forces that Britain alone could not. With the thirst for information

---

* Haldane, *Truth Will Out*, p. 216.

about Russia not being met by the Moscow-based reporters, the Soviet ambassador in London, Ivan Maisky,
stepped in to fill the vacuum. An unusually charming and
effective diplomat, he had added a publishing arm to the
embassy to fan pro-Russian feeling in Britain.

Summing up his propaganda activities in his diary –
with one eye on the embassy NKVD agents he presumed
would be reading it – Maisky noted on 11 October 1941
that a booklet of Stalin's and Molotov's speeches had
instantly sold 75,000 copies. The embassy's propaganda
bulletin, 'Soviet War News', which had begun with a print
run of 2,000 copies, was now up to 10,000 and increasing
daily. An edition of the USSR in maps had sold out in
three days. But the star performer of the embassy's output
was a forty-six-page war diary, *With a Soviet Unit Through
Nazi Lines*, by the soldier-correspondent Alexander Polyakov. One hundred thousand copies were printed initially,
and the second edition would run to double that number.
'Everything "Russian",' Maisky wrote, 'is in vogue today:
Russian songs, Russian music, Russian films, and books
about the USSR.'*

When Polyakov's diary was published in the United
States, the embassy threw caution to the wind, changing
the title to the uncompromising *Russians Don't Surrender*. No
one seemed to notice that the Red Army had been surrendering territory almost every day for three months and
would continue to do so for many more.

---

* Ivan Maisky, The *Complete Maisky Diaries*, vol. 3 (Yale University
Press, 2017), p. 1172.

# 7

## *October 1941: The trouble with journalists*

Vernon Bartlett had gone out to Moscow to make a series of live broadcasts for the BBC, a privilege which had been flagged to the British public in advance. But after he sent his first script to the Nark for approval, it came back with whole passages obliterated by blue pencil. Bartlett argued with Palgunov for three hours, but the Press Department chief still refused to reinstate a single word. It seemed to Bartlett that the edits had come from a higher authority, even from Molotov himself. In a fit of exasperation, Bartlett threw the script into the air and the pages fluttered to the ground, forcing him into the indignity of getting down on his knees in front of Palgunov to pick up each sheet and arrange them in order.*

With the help of John Gibbons, a Scottish communist working for Soviet radio, Bartlett came up with a plan to fulfil his obligations to broadcast without appearing to be a Kremlin mouthpiece. Gibbons arranged for Bartlett to broadcast a talk with a text approved by the censor, but at a time of day when the atmospherics were so bad that no one could make out what he was saying.† Indeed, thanks

* Vernon Bartlett, *And Now, Tomorrow* (Chatto & Windus, 1960), p. 75.
† Bartlett, *And Now, Tomorrow*, p. 76.

to the crafty technician, Bartlett's words were smothered by the whooshing and hissing of radio interference. Increasingly pained and puzzled telegrams from the BBC in London demanding a repeat of the talk went unanswered.

On his return from the trip to the Smolensk front, Bartlett saw no use in staying on in Russia, and he persuaded Lord Beaverbrook to take him back to Britain on a warship that was waiting in Archangel. It was his last evening in Moscow. He had already had dinner, and was focused on the trip home when he received an invitation to attend a banquet in honour of Beaverbrook and Harriman at the Kremlin that very evening. On arrival the guests were led up a wide staircase and through a great hall where the Soviet parliament met once a year, and into an anteroom furnished with red damask sofas. They were told to wait. The guests spied Stalin at the far end of a long corridor. As he drew closer, they could see he was wearing a fawn-coloured uniform and high boots which gave him a vaguely military look. He was smaller in real life than in his photographs and it occurred to Bartlett that without any medals pinned to his chest he looked like a millionaire's chauffeur.

The guests were ushered into St Catherine's Hall with its green malachite pilasters and walls hung with oyster-coloured watered silk. The whole Soviet leadership was arrayed at the top table that stretched the length of the hall. Between each two guests there were three bottles of wine and two of vodka, which were consumed during more than thirty toasts – to victory, to the fighting services, and to each other's political leaders. Every toast required a short speech, and a response, both translated, with all the guests leaping up each time to empty their glasses. Bartlett's mind began to wander. It was not just the vodka and the sweet

Crimean wine but the experience of eating and drinking in these grand surroundings in the company of the leaders of the USSR that put him in a dream-like state. He was jolted from his reverie by Molotov proposing an unexpected toast to the press. An American journalist working for the US embassy responded with a few gracious words, and to his dismay Bartlett realised he, as the British press attaché, was now expected to speak. 'Give them hell,' whispered a man from the Cabinet Office in Bartlett's ear.*

As he rose to speak, Bartlett needed no encouragement to 'give them hell'. In marked contrast to the previous speaker's flimflam, he astonished the assembled dignitaries by proposing that Stalin and the Soviet leadership raise their glasses to a free press. 'A free people requires a free press,' he asserted. On hearing the translation, Stalin turned to Beaverbrook and said: 'That young man talks too much.' At the end of the meal, as the guests got up from their seats, the British ambassador, Sir Stafford Cripps, came up to Bartlett in a state of ill-concealed fury. 'I gave you a temporary post in the embassy. We've worked so hard to create a good relationship with Stalin,' the ambassador said through gritted teeth.

As they entered Stalin's private cinema to watch the evening's entertainment – propaganda films that sent some of the Soviet leaders to sleep – Bartlett felt like an outcast. Sometime after 2 a.m., all the guests lined up to say goodbye to Stalin. As Bartlett's turn approached, he wondered nervously how Stalin would respond to having been forced to drink to a vigorous press. Stalin did not shake Bartlett's hand as he did with the other guests. Instead, he

* Ibid., p. 84.

grasped Bartlett's hand in both of his. 'English journalist,' he said, and a gruff warning noise issued from his throat. After releasing Bartlett's hand, he wagged a finger in front of the MP's face and smiled at him. Bartlett's small display of rebellion had clearly provided Stalin with some diversion from the empty diplomatic phrases of the evening, while at the same time confirming his suspicions that despite all the fulsome toasts to the Anglo-Soviet alliance, Britain and the Soviet Union could never be true friends.*

During the war, several journalists published interviews with Stalin; indeed, they often recalled these interviews as a high point of their career. In fact, they never met Stalin face to face. Suitably bland questions were put in writing and only answered – in writing – if the Kremlin had something it needed to say. So, it turned out that, after thirty vodka toasts, the *bon vivant* Vernon Bartlett was the only journalist throughout the war to say anything remotely challenging to the marshal's face.

*

Back in August when Charlotte Haldane arrived in Moscow, she was invited to lunch at the embassy with Cripps, her former comrade in the anti-fascist struggle who was now serving as British ambassador. She would never have suspected from his warm welcome that only weeks before, Cripps had been lobbying the Foreign Office to remove her from the list of journalists put forward by their media organisations to go to Moscow. 'We have already evacuated all the women and do not want the responsibility of new ones,' he cabled on 27 July, two weeks before Charlotte

* Ibid., p. 84.

set off on the Arctic convoy. 'I trust every effort will be made to persuade the *Daily Sketch* to send a man instead of Mrs Haldane.' No one in London seems to have taken any action on this.*

Over lunch, Charlotte enthusiastically set out her intention to bring alive the heroic exploits of the Red Army and reveal the superiority of the Soviet system through visits to factories and interviews with ordinary people. Cripps listened patiently as he understood that her views were sincerely held. But when she spoke with confidence about her chances of getting an interview with Stalin, Cripps felt he had to bring her down to earth.

'You must understand, Charlotte, that the Soviet authorities are not interested in the converted. They think that a sympathiser such as you would not be trusted by the British public. Look at me. I have been here for more than a year and I've come to the conclusion that they'd rather deal with someone like Churchill, even though he is an imperialist and a Russophobe.'†

It wasn't just women journalists Cripps objected to. Throughout July and August 1941 he had been fighting a rear-guard action to discourage journalists from flocking to Moscow. He told the Foreign Office that British journalists would never be allowed to provide the 'objective' coverage of the Eastern Front that Churchill had asked for. The Soviet authorities had made it clear that journalists would only be allowed to reproduce official war communiqués.

* TNA FO 371 29587/106.
† Charlotte Haldane, *Truth Will Out* (Weidenfeld & Nicolson, 1949), p. 203.

As the list of journalists who wanted to come to Moscow, not just British but American and Australian, grew longer by the day, Cripps's telegrams became more frequent and more forceful: newspaper editors must be told that there was little point in sending a special correspondent to Moscow. The Foreign Office refused to heed his advice. Whitehall feared that editors would blame the Foreign Office for keeping their reporters away from Moscow, and 'the Soviet embassy would certainly hear of it and would very probably make mischief out of it.'*

As telegrams flew back and forth, a typical bureaucratic compromise was reached. The Foreign Office would no longer decide which journalists should go to Moscow. Instead, editors would have to apply directly to the Soviet embassy in London for correspondents' visas. Thus it would be up to Ivan Maisky, the Soviet ambassador in London, to decide who would go. The Foreign Office would ask Maisky to be 'generous' with the supply of visas, while Britain would quietly limit the number of places available to journalists on transports to Moscow. The result of this compromise was that Maisky had complete control over who could get a visa to report from Moscow and, if he deemed them insufficiently on message, he could refuse to renew their visas.†

\*

If the British ambassador had many problems, the American ambassador had one enduring problem. It was the wealthy socialite and would-be war correspondent Alice

* TNA FO 371 29587/100.
† TNA FO 371 29587/97.

Moats. By her own admission, she tended to create chaos and bring out the worst in people, but more important was the fact that she was so well connected in Washington that no ambassador could afford to ignore her; so well connected in fact that when she ran out of silk stockings, all she had to do was to cable the White House and Averell Harriman, Roosevelt's envoy to Russia, delivered them to her in person.

The arrival of a single, American woman at Metropol Hotel in April 1941 naturally roused the suspicions of the secret police and no sooner had she ordered lunch in her room than there was a knock on the door and the hotel's unctuous assistant manager Jack Margolis, a cockney-born Bolshevik, came in to check on her. Hovering over her while she was eating, he asked her insistently what had brought her to Moscow. Ten times she responded that she had not come to work.

'But surely you write or something?'

'No, I'm just a tourist,' she said.

Margolis tried another line of attack. 'You come from Mexico, I believe. Did you ever meet Trotsky?'

Alice gave another negative response, this time a truthful one.*

Though she had no training in journalism, Alice had taken on board two of its basic principles – keep your foot in the door and stay close to your sources. It was the American ambassador Steinhardt who recklessly opened the door to her coming to Moscow and she never allowed him to slam it shut. She had worked out that the most knowledgeable journalist was Cholerton and the diplomat she

---

* Alice-Leone Moats, *Blind Date with Mars* (Doubleday, 1943), p. 173.

needed to befriend was the German ambassador, Count von Schulenberg. She spent her days enduring the squalor of Cholerton's chaotic apartment, straining her ears to catch the accumulated wisdom that poured in an unstoppable torrent from his mouth. In the evenings she set out to get to know the shrewd but affable German count whom Cholerton called a 'fox-hearted lion'. She succeeded so well that one Sunday lunchtime she was the only guest at the count's dacha, sharing with him a salmon flown in for the occasion from Stockholm.

Throughout the month of June 1941 the foreign community in Moscow was buzzing with rumours that Nazi Germany was about to invade. When one of the German diplomats she had cultivated put his boxer dog on a plane to Berlin, she knew she would have to fight her ambassador to stay in Moscow. Steinhardt was evacuating the embassy wives and was determined that Alice would be among them.

On Friday, 20 June, the day before the American evacuation, Alice decided to lie low and not answer the phone. There was not a word in the Soviet press about the war, but one of the papers had a world exclusive, albeit a 550-year-old one. A Russian scientist had dug up the skeleton of the Mongol leader Timur, known in the West as Timur the Lame, from his mausoleum in Samarkand. Timur's right leg was shorter than his left, the newspaper reported, so the great conqueror was indeed lame.

As night fell and she was feeling relieved to have avoided being shipped out, a handwritten note from Steinhardt was pushed under her door ordering her to 'lose no time in making preparations to leave Moscow'. She had no choice but to go and see him the next day. He got straight to the point and asked when she was leaving.

'I'm not going,' she answered.

'Oh yes you are, and soon,' he insisted. 'By tonight there won't be a single foreign woman left in Moscow and I won't allow you to stay on. The Germans may be in this city in three weeks. I can't take responsibility for permitting women needlessly to risk their lives.'

'As a correspondent for *Collier's*,' she said, failing to mention that she did not actually have a press card, 'I do not count as a woman. I am doing a man's job and willing to take a man's chances.'*

The ambassador told her that he could not offer her shelter at the out-of-town dacha that the embassy had been preparing as a refuge for the remaining staff. Sited between an airfield and munitions plant, it was now clear it would be a German target. 'We shall have to take to the woods and sleep under haystacks.'

'I can sleep under a haystack as well as the next person.'

'I am not going to take the little food I have out of the mouths of the members of my staff just to feed a stubborn woman,' he said. 'I order you to leave.'

Alice tried a different tack. 'You have done your duty. I absolve you of all responsibility for my presence in Moscow. I will take refuge in the British embassy and promise you that I will keep out of the way, and you never need see me again.'

At this the ambassador lost his temper.

'I shall have the Russians take away your visitor's permit,' he threatened.

---

* Moats, *Blind Date*, p.227

In the end, it was agreed that he would tell the embassy staff that Alice was leaving for Iran, but for the time being she would go no further than Baku. Alice had outwitted the ambassador: she showed Steinhardt her passport with blank pages where she should have visas from neighbouring countries that would let her in. With no foreign visas, she was not going anywhere soon.*

On the day war broke out, she accepted an offer from John Russell, a junior British diplomat who 'didn't give a damn what anyone thought and always did exactly as he pleased',† to take refuge in an annexe of the British embassy. She found the building deserted – the servants had fled. She went into the kitchen and fried herself a couple of eggs and ate them with bread and butter and drank some flat champagne. She sat alone in a sitting room reading a detective story while the loudspeakers in the street blared out the blackout regulations and air-raid precautions. Her presence had to be kept secret from the more conscientious British diplomats, who would have worried that harbouring her would damage relations with the Americans. For the first five days of the war she darted between the embassy and the annexe, spending every night in a different room. She wandered like a ghost around the two buildings, carrying her overnight things with her in a basket, prepared to bed down anywhere when the coast was clear.

One evening she and Russell decided to see what was happening in the Metropol. 'We found the hotel very much blacked out. The lobby had always been dark, but now it was an absolute dungeon. When we went into the

* Moats, *Bind Date*, pp 229.
† Moats p. 182.

restaurant we felt as though we were underseas, as all the lights were a ghastly blue.' But it was still crowded, and the orchestra played with its usual energy. Russian lads in shirtsleeves kept coming to their table to ask her to dance, but Russell would not let her. 'So I had to content myself with smiling wistfully at the young men and acknowledging their many toasts across the room.'*

By now Alice was hoping that in the hectic relocation of American embassy staff in the first days of the war, she had been forgotten. But on the fifth day of her squatting with the British, she was summoned to the American embassy by one of its diplomats and told to get on the train to Vladivostok that evening.

'The clerks are taking the train for Vladivostok tonight, and I have reserved a berth for you.' He had a look of grim determination on his face. 'I'm not going to Vladivostok,' she said. Feeling that she had overstayed her welcome at the British embassy, Alice took refuge with the Associated Press bureau chief, Henry Cassidy.

'You'd be crazy to leave. And you are perfectly welcome to stay with me as long as you need a place of refuge.' They both laughed at the thought that the sanctuary Cassidy was providing her was not from German bombs but from the American ambassador. She had sent a cable to *Collier's* magazine asking for written confirmation of her assignment as their Moscow correspondent and was hoping to get a speedy reply.

It did not take long before Steinhardt's men discovered her new hiding place. The tone of the phone calls rose until one of them threatened her: 'You're leaving tonight if

* Moats p. 242.

I have to put you on the train bodily.' When she put the phone down, Cassidy's advice was simple. 'Go straight over to the Nark and apply for a press card,' he said. 'You're a dope not to have thought of that before.' He was on his way there and he took her with him.*

To her surprise, the censor on duty told Alice he thought it would be no problem for her to get a press card, but he would have to raise it with Palgunov. On their return to Cassidy's apartment, the phone rang incessantly with an American official demanding to know where Alice was. The net was tightening so fast that Alice was forced to flee to the one place she would feel safe, and that was at Cholerton's. As she stumbled into his chaotic apartment, now in permanent darkness as he could not find a way to raise his blackout blinds, she cried out, 'Sanctuary.' That evening the Moscow phone lines were on fire as Steinhardt's man called every journalist and diplomat in town to find out where Alice was. Alone among the foreign community, Cholerton and Alice spent a quiet evening together because, as fate would have it, his phone was out of order. She returned to Cassidy's at 11 p.m., by which time the Vladivostok train had left.

The next day, Friday, 27 June, all Alice's efforts came to fruition. She received a cable from the editor of *Collier's* naming her as their Moscow correspondent as she had requested. She walked over to Spaso House, the ambassador's residence, to find Steinhardt in the hall, no longer the best-dressed diplomat in Moscow but wearing an old pair of trousers and a leather jacket while he nailed lids on crates for shipment home. He could not bring himself

* Moats p. 247.

to look up at her when she greeted him. Alice saw the message he had received from the editor of *Collier's*. 'We want Alice Moats to be *Colliers's* staff correspondent. Moscow and the State Department says she may stay if you permit, which we beg you to do.' The editor had gone over Steinhardt's head to his bosses in the State Department and forced him to give in, as was clear from his reply. 'Having explained to Alice Moats the desperate risk she is running, I have no objection to her staying but doubt authorities will grant necessary permission.' The ambassador clearly hoped that the Nark would complete the task that he had failed to do and expel Alice. That evening, however, she heard her press card was in the bag.

Over the course of one week, Alice's fight with the American ambassador had become *l'affaire Moats*, avidly followed in the Moscow foreign community and echoing all the way to Washington, even as the Germans advanced towards Moscow. The resources devoted to trying to remove her would have been inexplicable were it not for Alice's political connections in Washington. As Steinhardt told her in an unguarded moment, he imagined himself returning to America with Alice in a box, and her grief-stricken parents – and no doubt Roosevelt himself – pointing their accusing fingers at him and saying: 'It's all your fault.'

# 8

## *October 1941: The great Moscow panic*

The standstill on the Smolensk front that allowed the Press Department to take journalists to the ruins of Yelnya did not last. At the beginning of October 1941, the German army launched Operation Typhoon and within a couple of weeks, German troops had overrun the areas that the reporters had visited and had advanced to the outer suburbs of Moscow. The autumnal rains that had slowed the reporters' progress had given way to the unseasonably early onset of winter, with freezing temperatures. With no word from the authorities on what the population of Moscow should do, the city was gripped by a sense of anxious foreboding. This was not the first time that Moscow had had an enemy at its gates. In 1812 the city had been evacuated, allowing Napoleon to move in unopposed, only to find that the Muscovites had set their city on fire.

On the morning of 15 October Nadya took the tram into the city centre to work. As she walked from the tram stop to the Metropol, a sinister snow, the black flakes of documents being burnt, blew into her face. In the Lubyanka, the NKVD prison and interrogation centre at the end of the street, and the party headquarters nearby they were incinerating records that were too bulky to move. The Germans could be in Moscow within hours.*

In the lobby of the Metropol the clicking of abacuses never ceased as the guests settled their bills each day, to avoid any delay should an evacuation begin. None of the journalists wanted to miss Hitler's victory parade on Red Square, which would be the biggest story since the fall of France, but they suspected that once the Germans took over they would have no way of filing their reports. The Soviet government had drawn up a long list of factories, public buildings and transport infrastructure due to be blown up if the Germans arrived – including the Central Telegraph, the telephone exchanges, the Bolshoi Theatre, and the electricity supply of the Metro. So many people were involved in plans to mine these buildings with explosives that there was no way to keep these plans secret. Groups of Communist Party members were seen on the streets, standing ready to put into action this campaign of destruction. The old lags among the journalists who had covered the fall of Paris enjoyed spooking their inexperienced colleagues: the Metropol itself was bound to be rigged with explosives so that Hitler could not celebrate the fall of Moscow under the glass dome of the hotel dining room where Lenin and Stalin had spoken. What could not be destroyed was being carted off to safety. Thousands of Muscovites employed in key factories turned up to work that morning to find that machine tools were being shipped to the east in a mad rush, and the premises prepared for demolition.

* Rodric Braithwaite, *Moscow 1941: A City and its People at War* (Profile, 2006), p. 245.

When Nadya arrived for work at the *Chicago Daily News*, Arch Steele's first question was, 'So Nadya, what are you planning to do when the Germans get here?' He had asked this question several times before, and she had always given a stock response: 'I hope they don't come.' This time Steele insisted on a proper answer. 'You can carry on hoping. Here's the situation. All the journalists and diplomats are being evacuated and there's a special train tonight to take us all to Kuibyshev. The Russian staff will be following tomorrow in cars, and you can ride in my car.'

Nadya still couldn't decide what to do. With Moscow in jeopardy, she had placed her trust in Stalin to beat the invader back. That still left the issue of evacuation: as Jews, she and her husband would be in line for summary execution if the Nazis came. But leaving Moscow would cut her off from any contact with Alex, who turned up in Moscow from time to time on army business. And no city was as well supplied with food as Moscow. If she was evacuated she would lose a reliable source of food to send to her mother and three children in Chelyabinsk, though she did not know if the food parcels actually got to them.

As she stepped outside the hotel that afternoon, she noticed that the atmosphere on the streets had changed during the few hours she had been inside the Metropol. With the government saying nothing, anarchy was taking hold and Muscovites were leaving the city in droves. The tram home was full of people clutching bundles, and for once they were talking openly about escaping the city, all fear of being overheard by the police and informers driven away by the sense of impending doom. One peasant woman on the tram did not have a bundle, and people asked her, 'Haven't you got anywhere to go?' She replied: 'Why should

I run away from the Germans? Why would they bother with me?'*

With the German army on the outskirts of Moscow, Stalin summoned his leading commissars to decide whether to defend the city, or evacuate the government to the east. On the streets it was clear that people were not waiting for a government announcement. Anyone with access to a car loaded up their families and their possessions and headed east on roads that were packed with buses, horse-drawn carts and lorries, their progress held back by thousands of people fleeing on foot.

After witnessing the beginning of the mass exodus, Nadya accepted Steele's offer of evacuation and that night saw him off on the train to Kuibyshev (now Samara, its pre-revolutionary name). When she reached the American embassy at dawn the following morning, a crowd had already gathered – not just the correspondents' interpreters, but all the local embassy staff. An official was ticking off names on a clipboard. Nadya was relieved to take her place in one of the cars and wait for the convoy to move off. Through the window she saw a distraught woman approach the official, dragging two small children behind her. Something about her was familiar. Now she was shouting at him, all the time pointing to her children. The official was shaking his head. The woman turned round, and Nadya saw it was a Jewish American communist she had known in New York as Mary who had taken the fateful decision to renounce her US citizenship and make her home in Russia. Now Mary was dragging her children

* Nadezhda Ulanovskaya & Maya Ulanovskaya, *Istoria Odnoi Semyi*, 3rd Edition, (Inanpress, 2013), p. 72.

towards the car. 'Nadya, Nadya, I need your help. You must take my children. I'm not asking for me – I'm not an American any more. But they were born in New York, they are little Americans. Please, Nadya, you're my only hope.'*

Nadya was appalled by Mary's plight, but there was nothing she could do. When the car drove off an hour later, she was still thinking of what would happen to a Jewish Communist and her boys when the Germans came.

*

Charlotte Haldane had remained calm throughout the bombing of Barcelona, the London Blitz and some close calls in China and was surprised to find herself in a state of near panic as the Germans approached Moscow. The sangfroid which had allowed her to retain her self-respect in those war zones deserted her. She yearned for a Churchillian statement from the Soviet leadership to acknowledge the severity of the situation and raise spirits. For several days the morning communiqués had contained no useful information, until on 15 October there was an abrupt change in tone: 'The situation around Moscow has sharply deteriorated.' Apart from that, no one in authority had said anything.

The previous day Charlotte had gone to the British embassy to ask what the arrangements were for evacuating British citizens. She was given the brush-off. 'You will have to make your own arrangements. You came here at your own risk. We must look after our own people first.'†

---

* Ibid p. 72.
† Charlotte Haldane, *Truth Will Out* (Weidenfeld & Nicolson, 1949), p. 227.

That evening Charlotte was dining in the National hotel when two bombs exploded nearby – the first air raid she had experienced in her six weeks in Moscow. She went to bed at midnight to the sound of anti-aircraft fire. She found the roar of the guns strangely comforting after working as an air-raid warden in London. Four hours later, she was woken by the howling of the air-raid siren and a maid banging on her door. She was annoyed that the siren went off just as the raid was coming to an end, but she was keen to take a peek at the top people's air-raid shelter that had been prepared for Lord Beaverbrook and Averell Harriman and was now at the disposal of hotel guests. Though it was only across the square, she was ushered into a waiting car to take her to one of the deepest metro stations in Moscow. Behind a guarded door at platform level the shelter was furnished with thick carpets, enormous couches and armchairs and electric fires. Leading off from the main section were small sleeping compartments, all richly carpeted. It was spotlessly clean and very comfortable.

It was not long before the all-clear sounded and she climbed back up to street level. Back at the National she felt alone and unprotected. She was not part of the Metropol press pack and her own embassy had refused to accept responsibility for her safety. There was only one thing to do. She would go directly to the British ambassador. Over coffee, in the ambassador's gloomy office, hung with huge portraits of British royalty, Cripps assured Charlotte there was no cause for 'undue alarm and despondency'. As a good communist, she chimed in that the 'alarmist stories spread by the fifth column' could be discounted. So it came as a shock when on return to her hotel mid-afternoon she found the lobby crowded with American diplomats, suitcases packed, checking out. They had been ordered to assemble immediately at their embassy. Charlotte rang Cripps. 'Come here immediately, with no more than two suitcases. You can come with me to the station,' he said. It turned out that as soon as she had left the embassy that morning, Cripps had been summoned to a meeting in the Kremlin with Molotov, who told him the diplomatic corps and the press were being evacuated that very evening to the Volga city of Kuibyshev, which would act as Russia's temporary capital. Molotov had given him no choice. 'The Soviet government has decided to make Moscow an arsenal and fight to the last. You have to leave.' Charlotte understood that Stalin was going to decamp to Kuibyshev, where a bunker had been prepared for him.

By good fortune, Charlotte had hired a car and a driver for the day. Having packed her two suitcases, and wearing all her three coats, she was driven through a blizzard to the British embassy. It was going to be a 'perfect brute of a night'. In the few hours since her last visit, the embassy, now almost deserted, had taken on a forlorn look. Charlotte found herself in the kitchen with the ambassador, an admiral, an air vice-marshal and the ambassador's Airedale terrier Joe. They were eating cold chicken with their fingers except for Cripps, an abstemious vegetarian, who was drinking a glass of kefir. Joe did not show his usual enthusiasm for his food. He knew something unpleasant was afoot. There was a smell of burning in the air. Throughout the afternoon staff had been furiously incinerating embassy papers. A junior diplomat put his head around the door and asked what to do with the radio.

'Smash it,' answered the ambassador. From the adjacent room came the sound of hammer blows.*

As the ambassador's car drove gingerly towards the Kazan station through the blacked-out city with only the lights of military vehicles piercing the falling snow, their progress was slowed by crowds of people carrying bundles and mothers dragging their children behind them, all hurrying in the same direction. As the station came into view, the British embassy car broke down. They climbed out, and walked the short distance to the station, the men carrying Charlotte's luggage while she clutched her typewriter to her chest. They stepped over exhausted soldiers lying on the station floor to get to the waiting room. The walls were painted with bright holiday scenes of happy folk dancers, and the room had been emptied to accommodate the diplomatic and press corps. The whole world seemed to have come together in that room, with the officers of the military missions in their uniforms as if on parade – the British in khaki and Air Force blue, and the Poles in their comic-opera hats. The American and British diplomats looked vaguely ridiculous in their Russian fox-fur hats and black astrakhan caps, which Charlotte noticed did not suit their long, horsey Anglo-Saxon faces.† 'The scene had the unreal quality of ballet or grand opera; if everyone had started to sing in Italian, it would hardly have been surprising,' noted Wally Carroll, the ace reporter of United Press, angry that the war correspondents were being forced to flee when they should have been heading

* Charlotte Haldane, *Russian Newsreel* (Penguin 1943), p. 156.
† Haldane, *Russian Newsreel*, p. 158.

towards the sound of gunfire.* Another reporter noted that the diplomats 'stuck out like a bunch of clowns at a kingly levee'.†

Joe the Airedale and the diplomatic corps' other dogs strained at their leashes and growled at each other. Tea, beer and soft drinks were served, and the diplomats strolled around greeting their friends, as if at an embassy reception. Perspiring porters brought in mountains of luggage – heavy coats, rugs, furs, bags and boxes – which were sorted by embassy third secretaries into barricades to mark out the floor space occupied by each mission.

Around midnight word spread among the passengers that their train was ready, and there began an unorganised, politely restrained but determined shoving towards the waiting-room exit. Outside, two lines of armed soldiers secured a passage for the foreign dignitaries through the milling crowd of pushing and straining evacuees. In the pitch dark of the blackout, with the snow still falling, and in fear of getting swallowed up in the crowd, Charlotte held on tightly to the coat sleeve of a senior officer. The first train they tried to board turned out to be the wrong one, but in the end they found the one allocated for the foreigners. Charlotte secured herself a two-berth compartment in one of the two international sleeping cars reserved for ambassadors and senior officers. There were no sheets or blankets but she at least had a mattress. Her three coats made a comfortable nest, in the absence of heating.

* Wallace Carroll, *We're in This with Russia* (Houghton Mifflin, 1944), p. 165.
† Philip Jordan, *Russian Glory* (Cresset Press, London 1942), p. 98.

The 600-mile rail journey to Kuibyshev would normally have taken a day and a half. As the train stopped in sidings for hours at a time it became clear that the foreign VIPs were the least important passengers on the line. As they looked out of their windows, they saw coming from the east trains full of equipment – gun carriers, armoured cars, light tanks and lorries, sometimes with the driver in the cab, looking frozen. Thousands of fresh soldiers from Siberia were pouring into the battle to defend Moscow, replacing the hundreds of thousands who had been killed, wounded or captured during the first two weeks of October. There was equally urgent traffic heading east – flatbed wagons loaded with American-supplied lathes, electrical transformers and switches from the Moscow defence factories that had been dismantled for relocation beyond the reach of German bombers. The American advisers who had provided the know-how for Stalin's breakneck industrialisation were pained to see this precious machinery uncovered, open to the elements, without any tarpaulin, and caked in snow. Would even half of it be serviceable once it got beyond the Urals?*

There was no restaurant car on the train, and a great gulf developed between the hungry and the well fed. The American embassy had brought along three cooks and the contents of its commissary, which included a plentiful supply of canned goods, ensuring regular meals for the Americans on board. There was even canned grapefruit juice to make vodka cocktails, which were cooled with handfuls of freshly fallen snow. By contrast, the British, who had a large stock of iron rations at the embassy for just

* Wallace Carroll, p. 176.

such an emergency, had left everything behind. As the Americans gorged on roast turkey, they joked about the abstemious Cripps gnawing on a carrot. Charlotte took secret delight in the British diplomats' loss of privilege. 'They were, with very few exceptions, the sort of men who, even in wartime, had been used to sitting down three times daily to good regular meals which had been purchased and prepared on their behalf by some other body. They were now for the first time in their lives, many of them, confronted with the symptoms of an empty tummy and nothing to fill it with.'* Cripps could be seen sitting in his compartment, in an overcoat with collar turned up, tapping away on a typewriter balanced on his knees.

Cripps pleaded with a Soviet foreign ministry official to lay on cooked meals at the stations they passed through. This resulted in three meals of cabbage soup and pancakes for everyone over the course of five days. For the rest of the time, whenever the train stopped at a station, the diplomatic corps lapsed into feral mode, leaping onto the platform and laying siege to the buffet. Those with the sharpest elbows would hurl themselves on the food, grab it, sling some money on the counter and carry it off in triumph, under the noses of their anguished competitors. During one long stop at a provincial station the diplomats persuaded the NKVD guards to bring them a cartload of food from the local market. Everyone was too hungry to ask whether the secret policemen had actually paid for the food they brought back. While the Americans feasted, the British diplomats were reduced to asking the train conductors to boil eggs in the samovars that were located in every

* Haldane, *Russian Newsreel*, p. 163.

carriage to provide tea. A pair of British trade unionists caught up in the evacuation tried to capture a piglet for their supper, but it escaped.

For the diplomats and journalists, who were rarely allowed outside Moscow, it was an opportunity to see provincial Russia. Every carriage was guarded by NKVD soldiers with fixed bayonets in smart new uniforms, a long grey overcoat with brass buttons down the front, blue peaked caps with a red band and five-pointed Soviet star in the centre. At the stations where the train stopped, in one case for eight hours, the guards chased away the children begging for coins from the foreigners. The peasants waiting at the station watched the spectacle of the travelling foreigners and their smartly turned-out guards without daring to approach any of them. In their ragged clothes, they seemed to have stepped out of a Tolstoyan past. Trainloads of Russian evacuees – travelling like cattle in freight wagons – coped with the loss of their homes and livelihoods seemingly with little fuss. The men would staunch their hunger by chewing sunflower seeds and spitting out the husks. Women could be seen hopping down from their wagons, sending children to collect firewood from the forest, lighting fires on bricks in the snow beside the railway tracks and boiling potatoes to feed their families. Once the meal was over, they would take the bricks back into the wagon to keep their feet warm.

Charlotte had the good fortune to have a British army officer of Pickwickian plumpness in the next compartment who understood better than the diplomats that an army marches on its stomach. She called him 'Colonel Kettle' because he had brought a tea kettle, and a supply of tea and sugar, tinned bacon and beans, army biscuits, and a spirit stove and cooking pot. With these ingredients supplemented by what could be cadged from the Americans or bought at the stations, the colonel and his three fellow officers cooked meals for eight twice a day. On the last day, they got hold of a chicken which they cooked in the pot, providing an unforgettable meal. With every mouthful, Charlotte recalled the words of the British embassy employee, 'We must look after our own people first'.

'Colonel Kettle' was no ordinary officer. He was George Hill, an intelligence agent with a colourful history of spying adventures in Russia who in his youth had felled an assailant in Moscow with a swordstick. He had been brought out of retirement to liaise with the Soviet NKVD on joint sabotage operations in occupied Europe. The colonel, described by his biographer as 'libidinous', could not fail to be impressed by the other woman journalist on the train. Even without washing facilities Alice Moats cut a glamorous figure, emerging in a fur coat from her compartment 'looking as if she had just stepped out of her boudoir'.* A former fashion model, Alice was in fact mortified by her appearance under the fur coat. The blue skirt and sweater she wore grew more rumpled and grey by the hour. While she could keep her face clean with cosmetics, there was nothing she could do about her neck and hands. As the usually taciturn Arch Steele passed by Alice's compartment each morning, he mocked her: 'You dreadful looking slut.'†

Alice Moats spent the first night in lonely splendour in a four-berth 'soft class' compartment (the USSR had

* Peter Day, *Trotsky's Favourite Spy* (Biteback, 2017), p.161.
† Alice-Leone Moats, *Blind Date with Mars* (Doubleday 1943), p. 411.

renamed first and second class to suit the ideology of the workers' state), but in the morning she was joined by three refugees from the 'hard class' coach: Sulzberger of the *New York Times*, Henry Cassidy of the Associated Press and Quentin Reynolds, a burly Irish-American whose rich voice had enthralled American radio listeners with his dramatic reports from the London Blitz. They knew they had come to the right place when hot coffee was served in a silver pot decorated with the American embassy crest.

Her compartment became the headquarters of a poker game which started after breakfast and continued without respite until 3 a.m. Even her old adversary, Ambassador Steinhardt, joined in. As each day wore on, the compartment's floor disappeared under cigarette packs and butts, whisky bottles, eggshells and watermelon rinds. In the absence of a broom, they ripped up one of Sulzberger's books to sweep the rubbish into the corridor. With the window sealed tight, a fug of cigarette smoke hid the fact that no one had washed or changed clothes for five days.

On the fourth day, they reached the Volga, but the twenty-nine-carriage train stopped until darkness fell so that the Japanese diplomats on board – still neutral but regarded in Moscow as an inevitable enemy – could not assess the vulnerabilities of the bridge.

The five days it took the train to arrive in Kuibyshev gave the city some time to prepare to accommodate the foreign dignitaries. The NKVD took over the best hotel, the Intourist, while the Grand Hotel was cleared of guests to make way for diplomats and journalists.

The Grand reminded Charlotte of hideously furnished hotels she had experienced in provincial Spain. There were no bathrooms, only a mixed washroom with four basins with cold taps on each floor. As she walked into the hotel she was hit by the blended odours of unwashed bodies – soap was nowhere to be had – rancid cooking fat, the sickly perfume from the barber shop at the entrance, and traces of fumigation gas. At least there would be no bedbugs. For the first week the whole diplomatic corps and all the journalists ate in the hotel. The restaurant solved this catering problem by feeding several hundred people beef stroganoff in relays throughout the day, from ten in the morning to ten at night. On Charlotte's first night, as she was eating, her eyes strayed to the ground and she saw a huge grey rat feasting on the crumbs beneath the tables.

It was a disconsolate press corps that Nadya found in Kuibyshev after her four-day journey from Moscow by car. A sort of Metropol-on-the-Volga was taking shape, with journalists, censors, a cable office and the travelling circus of writers and ballet dancers that they were allowed to meet. But when Stalin failed to leave the Kremlin, it became clear that the idea of Kuibyshev as a 'temporary capital' was a lie designed to get the diplomats and journalists out of Moscow so they could not witness the breakdown of law and order in the capital. Six hundred miles from the front line, they were not even allowed to tell the world they had moved to the Volga until after the news had been announced on Tass, by which time it was no longer news.

Cholerton, the *Daily Telegraph* correspondent, had no outlet for his nervous energy and paced miserably around the hotel foyer. Quentin Reynolds growled that he would be more use anywhere in the world but Kuibyshev.

Philip Jordan, a young British socialist who had invested

in a white Astrakhan cap for the Russian winter, had arrived in Russia in two minds. With unusual self-awareness, he knew that his far-left principles were unlikely to survive a collision with the reality of life in the Soviet Union. The dominant fear in his heart, he wrote, was 'that I should discover the Soviet Union to be other than I had always tried to imagine it: that it would be peopled by indelicate savages ruled by gangsters; and that all I had written and preached for five years would dissolve suddenly in my hand like salt thrown into boiling water.'*

Once in Kuibyshev, he decided to leave before his political beliefs were shattered and, on arrival in Tehran, he cabled to his newspaper what he had been trying to write for months but was told by the censors was premature: 'Freed from the intolerable burden of Soviet censorship I can now predict that the Red Army will eventually win the war.' With the army in headlong retreat and the machinery to re-equip it either on a train crawling eastwards or lying in the Siberian snow waiting for a factory to spring up around it, it was a brave prediction.

For Charlotte, it was already too late. All her illusions about Stalin's Russia being a communist paradise were dissolving. Within a few days the city of Kuibyshev was overwhelmed with refugees. They came down the Volga on every form of water transport, in ferries or open barges, hurrying to reach the city before the river froze over, or arrived at the railway station on every train. They were cold, half-starved, wet and tired. Young mothers with babies and old women lay down their bundles in the mud on the quayside or by the railway station. Charlotte had

* Jordan, *Russian Glory*, p. 1.

seen similar flows of refugees in China, but in Russia the scenes were more heart-rending with the cruel winter setting in.

On the day the foreigners arrived in the city, the shops were stacked with loaves of bread and other provisions, giving the illusion of a perfectly supplied Soviet city. But food disappeared from the shops overnight, and queues began to form, and grew longer and longer. Supplies were not replaced. As the city grew hungrier, the authorities opened a special shop for foreigners. The windows were piled high with bread, cheese, butter, cold meats, sausage, caviar, vodka and Soviet champagne. The manager had a book with the names of all those entitled to buy there. The door was guarded by a soldier with a rifle and fixed bayonet. As Charlotte approached to buy a bar of chocolate, she saw an old Jewish man peering in at the window and attempting to enter the shop. The soldier moved him on – 'Not for you, foreigners only.' Charlotte felt ashamed of being one.

She was already shaken by a distressing scene she had witnessed just minutes before. A crowd of women were gathered around an open carriage. In the carriage were two weeping women, one elderly and one young. The young woman was holding a small cardboard box decorated with white and red paper flowers. In it lay the corpse of a two-year-old child dressed in its best suit of pale-blue wool. The child had died of starvation, and they were on their way to the graveyard.

Charlotte knew that children died all over world, and particularly in wartime, and that the callous indifference of the 'haves' towards the plight of the 'have-nots' existed at all times and in all places. So she was surprised at her reaction to this tragic scene. One thing she knew: whatever the faults of British society, while she was working for the London Borough of St Pancras she had ensured that no bombed-out family had to suffer the indignity of a pauper's funeral. It was as if she had woken up from a deep drugged sleep. In the four years since she had joined the Communist Party, ideology had suppressed her sense of morality and clouded her mind.

'Standing by the side of that dead baby,' she writes in her autobiography, *Truth Will Out*, 'I swore a silent oath that never again would I get on any platform, anywhere, at any time, to use my oratorical or persuasive gifts to convince an audience of working-class men, women and children that the Soviet Union was the hope of the toilers of the world.'*

That night, as she lay on the filthy sheet and thin and lumpy straw mattress in the Grand Hotel, she repeated to herself, 'I'm free, I'm free.' She felt a strong sense of guilt for betraying her old comrades, especially those who had gone to fight and die in Spain with her support. But there was no going back. Her faith in the Communist Party had gone for ever.†

It was time for Charlotte to leave Russia. She could not cover the war so far from the front, and the interview with Stalin that she had promised her editors was an impossibility. She now accepted that Stalin would never favour a fellow traveller with an interview, knowing that a mainstream publication would carry much more weight. After a final complaint to Konstantin Oumansky, a senior

* Haldane, *Truth Will Out*, p. 233.
† Ibid., p. 239.

official in the Soviet foreign ministry, that even her simplest request to visit a Moscow factory had been ignored, she boarded a flight to Archangel with a delegation of British trade unionists who were heading by sea back to Scotland.

When she had arrived in Archangel two months before, she had been full of praise for the dock-workers. As she embarked on the *Ville d'Anvers*, the ship that was to take her home, she accepted without demur the captain's word that the dock-workers were prison labourers who were guarded by NKVD soldiers. The checkers who recorded the details of the incoming cargo were all young women. They worked long shifts, were blue with cold, and ate and rested in a wooden hut on the quayside. A British captain offered one of these checkers a hot meal, but she refused, though with tears in her eyes could not resist the offer of a hot cup of coffee. She drank it, and was never seen again. Beyond the confines of the Metropol Hotel, the rules of non-fraternisation were enforced with unrelenting watchfulness.

Once installed in her cabin, Charlotte got out her typewriter and sat down to write a short book about her experience as a war correspondent in Russia. She was a fast worker but *Russian Newsreel* would be the hardest book she had ever had to write; she would have to find a way to skate around the contradiction between her Communist Party membership and the revolution in her personal beliefs after her epiphany in Kuibyshev.

# 9

## November 1941: The world is much poorer

When Ralph Parker arrived in Kuibyshev in November 1941 to begin his posting as correspondent for *The Times*, he was reunited with his friend Cyrus Sulzberger, who was astonished to find the journalist in such a low mood at the start of his new adventure. Sulzberger had known Parker since 1939, when the Englishman was a keen young reporter in Prague at the time of Hitler's takeover of Czechoslovakia and had appointed him as a stringer, or part-time reporter, for the *New York Times*. Parker did not feel comfortable working in the *New York Times* bureau – an ethnic German member of staff was suspected of being pro-Hitler – so whenever possible he worked outside the office with a more congenial assistant, Milena Markova, a young divorcee who was a reporter for the newspaper *Lidove Noviny*. It was no secret to the Nazis that Milena was a Czech patriot and an anti-fascist. In June, Parker was invited to 'spend a couple of hours with the Gestapo' so that he would be in no doubt they were watching him.

Over the summer of 1939, as Czechoslovakia was brought under Hitler's control as a 'protectorate' of the Reich, Prague was gripped by fear and suspicion. In this tense atmosphere, Parker and his assistant Milena fell in love and their fates became entwined, he protected by his status as a British journalist but she vulnerable to Nazi persecution. In August, Milena received a tip-off that she was on a Nazi arrest list.

The couple fled Prague by car in the middle of the night and headed for the Hungarian border. Despite having the Nazis on their tail, they could not leave Czechoslovakia without making an important detour and stopped in the south Bohemian village of Bechyne, where Milena's two daughters were spending the summer with their grand-mother. Milena hated to wake the little girls, but she needed to hold them close and tell them she loved them as she had no idea when she would see them again. Early the next morning the couple crossed the border into Hungary.

Later they would learn that their midnight flit had saved Milena's life. Her colleague and friend, Slávka Částková, was arrested shortly after their departure and held in prison until 1942 when, as an example to other anti-fascist Czechs, the Nazis beheaded her. Milena's mother Clara was arrested on a charge of spying against the Germans, but following the intervention of a relative, an Austrian army officer, she was released after six months. Milena's ex-husband was held in a Berlin prison under sentence of death, but thanks to the efforts of German lawyers of his acquaintance who secured stays of execution, he survived the war. Despite being trau-matised by five years in a Gestapo prison, he went on to introduce basketball to Czechoslovakia, which became a source of great national pride even if the Czechs were always under orders to lose to the Soviet team.*

While in Hungary, Parker received a cable from Sulz-berger proposing that he continue to work for the paper from

* Family history kindly provided by Zsuzsanna Szunyogh, May 2022.

Belgrade. Parker readily agreed. The capital of Yugoslavia was a hotbed of intrigue where foreign correspondents had gathered to cover the next stage of the war in the Balkans, many of them moonlighting for rival intelligence services. It was not long before Parker was sought out for full-time intelligence work.

One morning he received a phone call from Julian Amery, whose position as the press attaché at the British embassy was cover for working in the clandestine sabotage outfit Section D ('D' standing for destruction), a precursor of the more famous Special Operations Executive or SOE. Amery had been asked for a memo on what was happening in Italian-occupied Albania. Utterly ignorant of that country, Amery asked Parker if he knew any Albanians. Parker said he knew a couple, and he invited Amery to meet them for a drink at his flat. Based on what the Albanians told him, Amery wrote up a quick report and handed it to his boss, the chief of Section D in the Balkans, with the words, 'This might throw some light on the general picture.' In the great British tradition of amateurism, this hastily concocted document went up the chain of command to shape British policy towards Albania – and Parker was recruited to Section D as a regional expert. Abandoning journalism, in June 1940 he was appointed British vice-consul in the small town of Skopje with the mission to spy on the Italian army in Albania. His transition to working full time in the undercover world was complete.*

Two weeks before their arrival in Skopje, Parker and

* Malcolm Atkin, *Section D for Destruction: Forerunner of SOE* (Pen & Sword, 2017), Appendix 2, online.

Milena had married in Belgrade, with Julian Amery as best man. Their first marital home was a flat in Skopje from where, under cover of picnicking and fishing on a lake in the Shar Planina mountains, they reconnoitred the Albanian border.

One day Sulzberger came to Skopje to see what his protégé could offer him by way of a story. After a tour of the Yugoslav-Albanian border area, Parker showed him a map the Italians had produced which revealed the parts of Yugoslavia they planned to incorporate into a greater Albania after the war. These lands included the major Serbian towns of Niš, Bitola and Skopje. Sulzberger's story, 'Italy Said to Plan a Greater Albania'*, was a propaganda coup for Britain that caused a rift between Germany and its Italian ally: just as Germany was about to incorporate Yugoslavia into the Reich, Italy was promising to give Albania territory of historic importance to the Slavs. With its dateline of Skopje, Sulzberger's article pointed unmistakeably to Parker as his source.

Parker's propaganda coup was too successful: the Germans were furious and demanded that the Yugoslav government expel him, and for the second time in a year he and Milena had to pack up and leave at short notice. They decamped to Istanbul, where Parker resumed his undercover work, producing wartime propaganda for the British Ministry of Information. His cover this time was as assistant editor of a French newspaper. But he was already suspect in the eyes of his new employers. A fellow agent had described his behaviour in Skopje as 'reprehensible' – his job was to maintain a low profile and spy on the

* *New York Times*, 29 July 1940.

Italians, not to get expelled.* His colleagues also blamed him for a leak which led to the identity of a British agent in the Balkans being revealed. A few weeks after his arrival in Istanbul, he was dismissed. In September, 'for various reasons, not all of them valid in my opinion', Parker was ordered back to Britain, 'just as the magnolias were at their best but before the famous Judas trees.' Parker wrote to a Czech friend, 'We packed up our icons, our embroideries and our clothes, and carted them all the way across Syria and Palestine to Cairo.'† From Suez they took three ships around the coast of Africa, stopping in Cape Town for a ten-day break.

While on board, the newlyweds enjoyed each other's company, reflected on their shared adventure and, with a child on the way, planned the next stage of their lives. They set about writing a book together about the origins of the war, which was almost complete by the time they reached Britain. The book was never published, but it is a fair guess that its themes were the failure of the British policy of appeasement, Chamberlain's betrayal of the Czechs that gave Hitler a green light to incorporate Czechoslovakia into the Reich, and the reluctance of Britain and France to work harder to create a united anti-Hitler front with Stalin. For the last three weeks of the voyage to Britain, the ship's doctor prescribed bedrest for Milena.

As Sulzberger would find out, the cause of Parker's despair lay in crucial information that the British Special Branch

* TNA HS 5/965.
† Parker to Mrs Palkovská, 6 July 1941, courtesy of Zsuzsanna Szunyogh.

police officers had failed to uncover during their watch on Parker's family home in Southport over the summer.

Special Branch had been deployed to monitor Parker's movements as part of an MI5 investigation into some mysterious phone calls to his home in Istanbul from a known Nazi agent. The police watchers reported that Parker rarely left the house and that the residents of number 73 Albert Road appeared 'nervous and ill at ease in the presence of strangers'. Had the watchers stayed one more day they would have witnessed a commotion outside the house. They would have seen the front door open and a heavily pregnant woman obviously in pain being steered down the front steps. With Parker's protective arm around her she made her way into the waiting car, an elderly couple and a maid anxiously looking on. Despite questioning the neighbours and opening the family's post, the watchers had failed to find out that Milena was going through a very difficult pregnancy. Three days after she was rushed to hospital, a healthy boy was born by caesarean section: Jan Ralph Heyrovsky Parker, the last of his given names in honour of a Czech scientist from Milena's family.

Ralph wrote to a close friend, Ludmila Palkovská, the wife of a Czech diplomat in London, to tell her the good news: Milena's stomach was painful and swollen but she was able to feed the baby, and he was thriving.* The local press in Southport reported the birth as a happy wartime story. 'Southport man home from Turkey: Famous Czech name for baby son' reported the *Southport Visiter* on 5 July.

* Ralph Parker to Mrs Palkovská, 6 July 1941.

Four days later a headline on the front page read: 'Southport war romance has tragic end'.*

A grief-stricken Parker wrote again to Palkovská: 'Milena died this morning. I left her a little while ago. Her hair was streaming over the pillow. Her expression was calm and resolute. Her poor body, which has suffered so much, today was quite still . . . Although she had suffered, none of us thought she would die. Yesterday morning she was happy and well – and then collapsed. When I saw her she was very weak, but in the evening she rallied and said: "You will save me. Won't you? I'm so happy." She did not seem, then, to know that her child had been born and asked to see him. She was very happy when they brought him in. Poor mite, he will never remember his mother.'

He was able to pour his heart out to his Czech friend in a way he never could with English people: 'You know how happy we were, and how we completed each other. I think of her as the most wonderful woman I ever met. And by her loss the world is very much poorer – even now when so much is being thrown away. What am I to do without her? I only began to live when we met. And now I feel that all the brightness has gone out of my life. So futile, so wasteful, so cruel that she of all people should have died . . . Everything I have reminds me of Milena and I can't turn without seeing her. Jenicek is such a darling child. He will be all right.'†

When Parker took the train to London on the evening of Sunday, 29 June, for a 'thorough and aggressive

* *Southport Guardian*, 9 July.
† Ralph Parker letter to Mrs Palkovská, courtesy of Zsuzsanna Szunyogh.

interrogation'* by the MI5 spy-catchers over his alleged contacts with the German agent, he was holding on his lap a box containing his wife's ashes. Milena's death had made him realise that Britain was an 'alien country' to her and not a fit place for her ashes to be scattered, so he would entrust them to his Czech friends to take back to her homeland. In the archival record of the MI5 interrogation there is no mention that the suspect had only a week before suffered a catastrophic bereavement. Despite his loss, Parker put up a good defence. But he had to wait another month for a decision: since his time in Yugoslavia a fierce turf war had raged in London between the army, the intelligence service and the new Special Operations Executive (which had swallowed up the discredited Section D) over who would be responsible for sabotage and black propaganda throughout German-occupied Europe.

Parker was caught up in this Whitehall battle. 'I am like a worm being tugged at by two or three birds,' he wrote to his artist friend Julian Trevelyan. 'Which ministry will get me I don't know, but it seems more probable they will pull me to pieces in the process.' Bereaved and unsure about the future, he could not decide whether to take up Trevelyan's offer of a flat in Durham Wharf, the warehouse on the Thames where the artist had his studio which was the focus of a fashionable bohemian set. 'I did think it would have been pleasant for us – when it was a question of "us",' he wrote.† Parker preferred to sleep on the sofas of Czech friends in London, unable to face

---

* TNA KV6 120/6a.

† Parker to Julian Trevelyan, 28 July 1941, Julian Trevelyan archive TREJ 44.10, Trinity College, Cambridge.

returning to the family home where Milena had spent her last weeks. A handwritten note at the bottom of the typed letter says: 'Jan is a good child and in safe keeping.' He had placed Jan in the care of his grandparents, who had hired a nanny.

In mid-August, MI5 ruled that there was no evidence to pursue the allegation that Parker had colluded with a Nazi agent. This opened the way for *The Times* to offer him the job of Special Correspondent in Soviet Russia, at a salary of £750 a year, with a living allowance of £500.

On September 23 he accepted the job, and advised the paper that his only dependant was his baby son.*

On October 11, a Southport paper reported the final chapter of the Anglo-Czech wartime romance, a tale so tragic that it was tucked away on page six, with the title: 'Another Blow for Bereaved Father'.† Jan Ralph, aged three months, had been put down to sleep in his cot by his nanny, a local girl, at 6 p.m. on the evening of October 6. When the girl checked on him at 11 p.m., the boy was lifeless. His grandfather tried to resuscitate him, and a doctor was sent for. All to no avail. The cause of death was recorded as asphyxiation due to regurgitation of food.

On the day of Jan's funeral, October 10, Parker wrote to *The Times* foreign editor, Ralph Deakin: 'My son died through as remarkable and unfortunate a mishap as did his mother. Technically, death was caused by the blocking of the windpipe by a regurgitation of food. He died in his sleep and, naturally, without a sound. The extraordinary thing is that he had never been sick in his short life and

* Times Media Ltd Archive, 23 September 1941.
† *Southport Guardian*, 11 October 1941, p.6.

was in perfect health. We buried him today at St Cuthbert's North Meols to the sound of children playing in a neighbouring schoolyard. Only on Monday, the night he died, I had been told by the Czechs here that in the event of my failing to return from Russia, Jan would have been given a Czechoslovak state scholarship as a tribute to his mother's work for her country. It falls on me now to pick up the threads, the one so firm and strong, the other so short, and to work out the pattern. Then, perhaps, I shall understand the shape of these events.' The next day Parker set off for Soviet Russia.*

In Liverpool he boarded the freighter Temple Arch, part of convoy PQ2 carrying tanks and other war materiel to Archangel. The journey would take seventeen days. While the American journalists on board – Eddy Gilmore of the Associated Press, Walter Kerr of the New York Herald Tribune, and Larry LeSueur of CBS – passed the time playing gin rummy, their English colleague hid his grief behind a Russian grammar book. During the voyage Parker's mind was 'virtually unhinged' and he twice tried to commit suicide.†

On arrival in Archangel the journalists found themselves confined to the ship for six days while they argued with Soviet officials for permission to disembark. When they were finally allowed off the ship, they could not travel to Moscow but had to go straight to Kuibyshev, the 'temporary capital' on the Volga to which all diplomats and

---

* Parker to Ralph Deakin, 6 October 1941, Times Media Ltd Archive.
† Julian Amery, *Approach March: A Venture in Autobiography* (Hutchinson, London 1973), p. 190.

journalists had been evacuated. When they were finally allocated seats on a train, with food for six days provided by the ship's captain, they found themselves inching across Russia for more than three weeks in a great horseshoe pattern, first eastwards to the Urals and then back to the Volga. Cold, hungry and dirty, the journalists were barely on speaking terms when they arrived in Kuibyshev after three weeks on the train. When the American journalist Eddy Gilmore read out the sign *PECTAPAH*, Parker broke his silence to tell him sententiously, 'Russian is pronounced just as it's spelled and what you call *pectapah* spells restaurant.'* When checking into the Grand Hotel, Parker's colleagues ensured that he had a single room – most journalists were living two or four to a room.

While the Anglo-American journalists were in enforced exile on the Volga, the hastily reinforced Red Army turned the tide of the battle on the outskirts of Moscow. Hampered by lack of winter clothing – Hitler had banked on taking Moscow by autumn – and with supply lines stretched to breaking point, the Wehrmacht was forced to retreat. It was a ferociously cold winter, with temperatures down to minus 35 Celsius, and the Soviet soldiers with their sheepskin coats and felt snow-boots had the advantage over the Germans. This was the epic drama – the fall or defence of Moscow – that the journalists had come to Russia to cover, but all they could do was rewrite official communiques. The recollections of a Soviet cameraman give an inkling of the story the foreigners missed. In October 1941 the cameraman's daily journey from Moscow to the front line

* Eddy Gilmore, *Me and My Russian Wife* (Greenwood Press, New York 1968), p. 26.

got shorter and shorter until the Germans were only fifteen kilometres away and the sound of artillery could be heard throughout the city. But the intense cold, and a fierce Red Army counterattack, pushed the invaders back, leaving behind the corpses of German soldiers in their summer uniforms sitting by the roadside: as soon as the exhausted troops stopped to rest, they froze to death.*

Confident that there was no chance of the journalists witnessing scenes of anarchy such as broke out in mid-October – there had been examples of mobs robbing Jewish evacuees– the Press Department began to allow selected correspondents to return to the Metropol in December.

With the fall of Moscow no longer imminent, Sulzberger had a problem he needed to solve urgently: he was to be married in January and needed to find someone to cover for him in Moscow while he was gone. As the nephew of the publisher, Arthur Hays Sulzberger, the young prince had a lot of latitude. So much latitude that he defied his uncle's ruling of 'no more Brits'† writing from Moscow and, and having convinced himself that the grieving Parker was up to the job, offered the role of Moscow stringer to him. Parker accepted.

Parker was now responsible for the two most influential newspapers in the Allied camp, and the *New York Times* was even more important now that the United States had entered the war after the Japanese attack on Pearl Harbor. He was now a prime focus of interest for the NKVD;

---

* Tanya Matthews, 'Going Back', BBC Radio 4 documentary, 27 December 1993, speaking about her first husband.
† Arthur Hays Sulzberger to GER Gedye, Imperial War Museum, GERG27 10.49.

doubly bereaved, he was easy prey and the secret police assigned to him one of their best operatives, Valentina Scott.

Valentina had been a sniper in the Red Army. She had undergone parachute training and taken part in operations against rebellious Siberian tribesmen in the 1930s. She was also, at twenty-eight, beautiful and quick-witted. As her surname indicated, she had an excellent command of English: she had been married to Henry Scott, a black American who came to Russia to improve his educational opportunities. They had met when both were studying law at Moscow State University, but his studies suffered when he unexpectedly found fame as a tap dancer. Having separated from Valentina, he returned to America with a new Russian wife.*

When Parker arrived in Kuibyshev, Valentina was working for Intourist behind a desk in the lobby of the Grand Hotel and had made a reputation for herself among the journalists for getting quick results from an intractable bureaucracy. By the time Parker was allowed to leave Kuibyshev and live in the Metropol in Moscow, he and Valentina were a couple, and he was rarely seen without her by his side. No longer in her Intourist uniform, she lived openly with him in the hotel. Nadya observed that Valentina mixed freely with all the foreign correspondents, coming in and out of their rooms as she pleased.

* For the family history of Henry and Valentina Scott, see 'US and Soviet Sisters Meet at Last', *New York Times*, 5 November 1989, and 'Storybook Meeting in S.D.: Black artists: A Soviet choreographer is introduced to her American half sisters', *Los Angeles Times*, 8 November 1989. Valentina is identified by another surname, Bobsen.

Unlike the other translators, she was not afraid of meeting Russians in the presence of foreigners – apparently she had no fear of being denounced. Nadya concluded that mingling with foreigners was Valentina's real work. As for Parker, he was so smitten with her that he was oblivious to his colleagues' suspicions that Valentina was much more than a translator – and most likely a colonel in the NKVD.

# 10

## *Winter 1941–42: Feast in time of famine*

In the early days of 1942 Moscow still had an abandoned feel, and Nadya could walk from the Metropol to the Central Telegraph through the city centre without seeing more than a couple of souls. But the sense of imminent danger having passed prompted the Metropol journalists to reconsider what they were doing in Russia. After Pearl Harbor, some Americans left to cover the war against Japan, in which they would get closer to the battle front. As for Parker, the successful defence of Moscow reinforced his conviction that the USSR would win the war and take its rightful place as a major power in Europe. And for Nadya, an otherwise routine press trip to a village liberated from the Nazis led to a wartime epiphany.

As Nadya had predicted, it did not take long for McLaughlin, the boozy Australian who had assured her that he would have no problems with the censors, to clash with the Press Department. 'They are crossing out all the best bits of my copy,' he told her. 'They don't understand what's good for them. Not even the most virulent anti-communist has done as much harm to the Soviet cause as the press department has.'

McLaughlin had got off on the wrong foot with Nadya at their first meeting, but as time passed he revealed a heart and a conscience hidden behind his rough exterior. When the Press Department head Nikolai Palgunov – known to the journalists as 'the goon' – announced he would be taking a group of journalists to view the devastation left by the retreating Germans around Moscow, McLaughlin said they should not go empty-handed. He made sure that all his colleagues took some of their rations to share with the villagers, even if only bread and sugar cubes from their lunch tables or tins of condensed milk from the foreigners' store. In a convoy of little cars, they drove to the town of Istra, where the New Jerusalem monastery had been a favourite picnic spot for Muscovites. The Nazis had used the monastery as an ammunition store, which they blew up on retreat, leaving the site in ruins. On the way, in sub-zero temperatures, the correspondents were driven through villages that had been flattened, with only the brick stoves and their chimneys – the hearts of these little houses – remaining. They came to a halt in a village where in pride of place stood the gallows used by the Germans to hang captured partisans, whose bodies were strung up for weeks.

Palgunov rounded up some survivors for the journalists to interview, with Nadya translating. There was a little girl with frost-bitten hands, and old people with gaunt faces and dressed in rags, and others with terrible disfigurements and injuries. The Germans had given the villagers ten minutes to pack their bags and leave. The soldiers robbed the population of everything – crockery, furniture, even clothes and footwear. There was a severe frost, and many villagers froze to death on the road. This was the first time the foreign reporters had witnessed first-hand the extent of Russian suffering.

An elderly peasant blurted out something that was not in the official script: 'In the beginning we were ready to welcome the Germans,' he said. 'But now, I would be the first to fight them.' With Palgunov out of earshot, Nadya decided it was safe to render this treasonous statement into English.*

Palgunov shepherded the correspondents out of the cold into the only house that had survived the Germans' scorched-earth policy. The door opened and the journalists were taken aback to see a table covered in a white cloth on which was laid out a feast of delicacies by a gleaming brass samovar. How could they tuck into a feast while outside there were starving people who had lost everything? Palgunov had no such qualms. He rubbed his hands together and said, 'Let's eat!' before helping himself.

One of the journalists asked the hostess standing by the samovar how she had survived under German occupation.

'Those Germans – they took every last thing from us.'

'But they left you the samovar?'

The unfortunate woman was silent. It was clear that the feast, the samovar and the tableware had all been brought in specially for the correspondents. Nadya felt ashamed. This ridiculous banquet made a mockery of the suffering of the homeless villagers. McLaughlin was too embarrassed to give their hostess the leftovers they had brought, but Nadya managed to slip a bag of food to one of the villagers before they set off back to Moscow.†

---

* Nadezhda Ulanovskaya & Maya Ulanovskaya, *Istoria, Odnoi Semyi*, 3rd Edition, (Inanpress, 2013) p. 74.
† Ulanovskaya, *Istoria* p. 75.

In the car the correspondents shared their disgust at the banquet served amid such misery.

'What did they think they were doing, setting that woman up with that feast for us?'

McLaughlin vented. 'Do they think we're stupid enough to believe that the food and the samovar were all hers? Don't they understand what kind of impression that gives?'

Henry Cassidy, an old Russia hand, offered an explanation. 'You must understand, for so many years foreigners have been writing that there's famine in Russia. The Russians have always denied this and got into this habit of plying foreigners with heaps of food to show that there is more than enough for everyone to eat. If they had thought about it, they would have realised that it is the Germans who are to blame for all the misery we have seen today. Russia has nothing to be ashamed of here.'

Nadya sat silent in the back of the car. The correspondents were now moving on to more general complaints about living in a gilded cage while never getting near the front line or hearing a shot fired. She realised she was failing in her duty to get the correspondents to write positive articles about the Soviet Union and its war aims, but after what she had witnessed, she didn't have the energy. It struck her that today, for the first time, her reactions to clumsy Soviet propaganda techniques had been no different to the foreigners'.

Nadya now had plenty of material to share at her regular meetings with the 'comrades' from the secret police. She told them how the journalists were frustrated at seeing nothing of the war, while living in luxury at the Metropol. She threw in some of her own experience from reading the

British and American papers which normally no Soviet citizen would have access to. During the London Blitz, the British papers did not hide the devastation caused by German bombing, but this in no way reduced British determination to fight. And the *New York Times* correspondents in London could write what they saw, which increased sympathy for Londoners, at a time when American opinion was still firmly against getting involved in the war. All this she reported back to the 'comrades', in the hope that it might filter up the hierarchy.

Nadya's message did get through, but her frankness had an unexpected result. Shortly after the Istra trip, Palgunov called McLaughlin in to tell him there were too many reporters in Moscow and he needed to return to Kuibyshev. It was clear that he had concluded that McLaughlin was a troublemaker and should be replaced by a more reliable Australian. McLaughlin refused to go back to enforced idleness on the banks of the Volga, and the comrades duly escorted him to Murmansk to catch the next ship to Britain. Over the months she had worked with him, Nadya had found in the gruff Australian a kindred spirit, but she was not sorry to see him go as it was wearisome to work for a lost soul who fancied he was in love with her. His departure opened the way for another Australian to come to Moscow, one whose clear-eyed approach to navigating the press restrictions in Moscow would change for ever the lives of several people, including Nadya.

\*

In December 1941, Charlotte Haldane, once again in a hotel room, found herself back in London, writing *Russian Newsreel*, a short account of her experience as a war correspondent on the Eastern Front. Tapping out 200 pages in a couple of months was easy for her, with her experience of filling newspaper columns. The problem was how to portray her admiration of the Russian people's fight against fascism while skirting around the truth of her disenchantment with Stalin's Russia.

With no one else to confide in, Charlotte screwed up her courage to admit her crisis of faith to her husband. Theirs was no ordinary marriage but a high-profile political union. Both Charlotte and J. B. S. Haldane had suffered public shaming in the press when they had left their respective spouses to marry in 1926, while in leftist circles they were hailed as a model progressive couple. Even though they had begun to drift apart at the end of the 1930s and were now living separately, the British Communist Party valued their union so highly that the leadership asked them to maintain the fiction of a model couple united behind progressive causes. Now, with Britain allied with Stalin against Hitler, Communist Party membership was rising and the last thing the party wanted was a split in the Haldane family – the working classes could be quite conservative when it came to divorce – to disrupt its golden moment.

When JBS came to the hotel to see her, she recalled their visit to Russia together in 1928. She reminded him how impressed they had been that scientists were prospering under communist rule and that factory workers were 'the aristocrats of the new society which was aiming to become a classless one'. She explained to JBS that by the time she left Russia in November, her views had reversed. Society in Stalin's Russia was becoming as rigidly stratified as the British class system. Jobs in the military and secret police were passed from father to son. Higher education was no longer free, meaning that the children of workers were deprived of access to Stalin's self-perpetuating bureaucratic class. While rationing in Britain was far from perfect – the rich could pay for fine food in restaurants – in Russia the overt disparity in rations between the privileged and the ordinary folk was blinding. She chafed at Stalin's abandoning anti-religious propaganda and re-opening churches, which she saw as a cheap ploy to please the Christian lobby in the US Congress.

Her husband listened to her arguments but did not want to engage with them. A brilliant scientist responsible for a string of breakthroughs in fields ranging from genetics to statistics, he was happy to let Communist Party discipline define his political views. He warned her that going public with her change of heart would make her a pariah. Former comrades would shun her, and she would lose all her friends. He showed no hint of understanding her change of heart.*

Unsurprisingly, JBS lost no time in raising the alarm with the Communist Party. When Charlotte went to party headquarters in King Street, Covent Garden, to see William Rust, the Editor of *The Daily Worker*, he had already made up his mind that she had been 'got at' by Trotskyites. But still, he told her, for the sake of the party it was her duty to allow her comrades to 'collaborate' on the manuscript of her book. Charlotte refused to allow the party to censor her work. Having rejected Rust's demands, she was now 'an outlaw, a political leper'.†

* Charlotte Haldane, *Truth Will Out* (Weidenfeld & Nicolson, 1949), p. 256.
† Haldane, *Truth Will Out*, p. 263.

# 11

## *1921–23: Carry on spying*

In late 1921, when Nadya was only eighteen, she and Alex
set off on a clandestine mission to Germany. Their brief
was simple – to bring about worldwide revolution. They
were part of a group of eight divided up into four couples
who were told to make their way separately to Germany
and meet up in Berlin. They had no passports, no visas, no
tickets, and no clear plan of action. Each couple was given
a stash of diamonds and a wad of dollars and pounds, and
Alex kept his in a money belt. The couples agreed among
themselves that once they had reached Berlin, they would
establish contact through the small ads column of a
Russian-language émigré newspaper.

Adventurous by nature, Alex was expecting to repeat
his experience of passport-free travelling around Europe
before the First World War. As a young anarchist he had
been sentenced under the Tsars to exile in Siberia, where
he fell under the influence of senior Bolshevik revolutionaries. Among his fellow political exiles was Yakov Sverdlov,
who would later order the execution of the Tsar and his
family, and a morose Georgian with a pockmarked face
and a luxuriant moustache who was too wrapped up in his
own thoughts to say hello to anyone. None of the exiles
thought Josef Stalin would amount to anything.

Despite the stimulating company and good food – he tasted cocoa for the first time in Siberian exile – Alex was too restless to wait out his sentence. Having stolen a teach-yourself-English book from Stalin's bookshelf, he walked and cadged lifts on river boats for 1,100 kilometres through the midge-infested Yenisei valley until he reached a railway station and managed to stow away on a Moscow-bound train. Caught hiding beneath a seat, he was dragged off the train to the stationmaster's office. He adopted the persona of a wheedling peasant and begged to be let go. When this tactic did not work, he changed tone and revealed himself as a political prisoner, which scared the stationmaster so much that he gave Alex money for a train ticket to make himself scarce. He was the only political exile to escape from the settlement of Turukhansk, so remote there was no need for barbed wire. Such was his charm and guile that on his long journey to freedom no one denounced him, and indeed many helped him.*

Having outwitted the Tsarist authorities, he travelled around Europe working as a stoker on steamships. By this means he supported himself and visited London, Paris and Barcelona and never had any difficulty in trickling across borders.

The first border that Alex and Nadya had to cross, from Russia to the newly independent state of Estonia, was easy. They found a guide who pointed out a way across the fields. The two emissaries of the workers' revolution were under instructions to fit into capitalist society as members of the bourgeoisie and stay in good hotels, which were less likely to

* Nadezhda Ulanovskaya & Maya Ulanovskaya, *Istoria, Odnoi Semyi*, 3rd Edition, (Inanpress, 2013) p. 6.

be raided by the police. But when Alex and Nadya arrived at the best hotel in Tallinn, with no luggage beyond their bundles in a wicker basket, and with Alex's blue Moscow suit being rather too short in the leg, the doorman took one look at them and turned them away. They bought a suitcase, which got them into a lesser hotel, but their huge appetites – Nadya had never seen so much food in her life – showed them up as visitors from a hungry land. In Petrograd, when they had stayed in the Astoria hotel, the city's best, at the start of their journey, they were lucky to get a ration of black bread and fish oil. In Tallinn, they scoffed big plates of meatballs in gravy three times a day while they racked their brains over an unforeseen problem – how to get a visa to Germany without having a passport.*

Alex decided he would find a ship going to Germany and work his passage as a stoker. With no passport, Nadya would return home the way they had come. Distraught that Alex would be fomenting revolution without her, she boarded a train back to Russia. On the train she fell into conversation with an Estonian student who gave her the name of a lawyer in Tallinn who, if paid enough, would pro-vide Estonian passports. She got off the train at the next station and went straight back to Tallinn. Two impressive Estonian passports duly arrived but the lawyer could not get them over the next hurdle – obtaining a German visa. They set about creating a story that would guarantee Nadya a visa for medical treatment in Germany when she had no visible signs of illness. Alex – who claimed Nadya was his sister – told the doctor she had trouble sleeping, had head-aches, was listless and had no appetite, and she used to be

* Ibid., pp. 28–31.

such a lively girl. All this was the result of her witnessing terrible atrocities committed by the Bolsheviks. Her husband had died in the fighting, and she had narrowly escaped being raped. After this performance Alex was sure the medical visa was in the bag, but the doctor winked and said, 'I'm a hypnotist. Maybe I could cure her.' He sat her in a chair, made gestures in the air and mumbled in German. Nothing worked, the doctor claimed, because she did not understand German, and he wrote a letter saying she needed to recuperate in a German sanatorium. They got their visas and took a train to Berlin.

For weeks they searched the small ads in the newspaper for the secret message that would bring the team together to start their mission. Alex got tired of doing nothing and felt bad about wasting the wadge of dollars in his money belt. He went to the Ruhr and found work in a coalmine, sending Nadya his wages while she learned German and every day bought the paper and continued to scrutinise the small ads. When she finally spotted the signal among appeals for help from penniless Russian émigrés, she set off to meet the leader of their group. He was living in one of the best hotels in Berlin, and his wife appeared in the sable cloak she had been given as part of her travelling funds. Appraising Nadya's wardrobe, she told her: 'You have to make yourself into a bourgeois lady.' They were shocked to hear that Alex had gone to work as a miner. 'But they gave you lots of money,' said the boss. As Nadya left, he told her, 'Don't come here dressed like that again.'

Despite all the obstacles they had overcome to get to Berlin, Alex and Nadya were the first of their group to reach their destination, and by several months. The other six members of the group had been arrested in Estonia and had to be sprung from jail, making a big hole in their stash. With the boss now in place and keen to embark on their revolutionary mission, Alex and Nadya eagerly awaited their orders. They were taken aback to learn that their mission was to befriend an elderly White general living in Berlin. They went through the motions of recruiting him, but the plan – establishing an anti-Communist 'Peasants' Alliance' under his leadership which would reveal the identities of the Soviet Union's enemies in Germany – was too thin for even a penniless White general to take seriously.

Alex had had enough. Instead of fomenting revolution in Germany they were being required to recruit informants in Russian émigré circles. They were not working for the Communist International, as they had been led to believe, but for the secret police, the Cheka, the forerunner of the Soviet KGB. Alex wanted nothing to do with the secret police, at home or abroad, and decided to bail out and return to Russia. At least, this is Nadya's recollection of the fiasco. A Russian historian who has reviewed some Soviet intelligence archives has another version. Alex was so confused about what he was supposed to be doing in Berlin that, breaking all the rules of spycraft, he called in at the Soviet embassy and asked the diplomats to seek more precise guidance from the Cheka in Moscow.* The word came back from the Cheka that there was no one on their books by the name of Alex Ulanovsky, and he must be a provocateur who should be kicked out of the embassy. Whatever the truth, at the end of 1922 Alex and Nadya boarded a ship – as passengers this time – and sailed back to Russia.

* Owen Matthews, *Richard Sorge: An Impeccable Spy* (Bloomsbury, 2019), p. 52.

Back home, Nadya was no longer required to acquire bourgeois polish and threw herself into relief work, serving in a soup kitchen feeding starving children. Russia was gripped by famine and in the lower Volga region it was so severe that incidents of cannibalism were reported. When the famine abated and she returned to Odessa, she found no trace of her family. Her father, and her younger brother and sister, had all died of typhus, or more likely from hunger. Her mother had exchanged the flat for two kilos of wheat and had set off back to the shtetl with Nadya's last remaining sibling. He had died en route.*

\*

In 1923 Alex found a new way to satisfy his ambition for clandestine work abroad without having to take orders from the Cheka. The Bolsheviks had founded a revolutionary trade union organisation known as the Profintern, or the Red International Labour Unions. The Profintern hired Alex to set up seamen's clubs in Russian ports to indoctrinate foreign sailors in revolutionary politics. These clubs proved to be popular with visiting seamen, and Alex was sent to Germany to set up a network of clubs in Europe's major ports.

Nadya followed him, with their newborn son Lyosha, travelling by ship to Hamburg under the name of Maria Sorokina. In October of that year radical members of the German Communist Party in Hamburg organised an uprising designed to spark revolution throughout Germany as Lenin's Bolsheviks had done in 1917. They stormed more than twenty police stations and stole weapons. The

* Ulanovskaya and Ulanovskaya, *Istoria*, p. 32.

authorities called in the army to open fire on the rebels and within three days the barricades had been destroyed and more than 100 communists killed. Shortly after the crushing of the uprising, Nadya answered a knock on the door. It was a policeman asking where her husband was. She said her husband – who used the name Peter Sorokin – was away. 'And who is Alex?' he asked. Shocked that Alex had been careless enough to let his colleagues use his real name, she thought quickly. 'This is Alex,' she said, pointing to her baby son. The policeman left, but the authorities had made a connection between the seaman's club – a venue for radical speeches – and the uprising. Alex's cover was blown, and they had to make a quick exit.

Alex's failure to keep his true identity secret did not damage his spying career. Astonishingly, he was given a far bigger job. Soviet military intelligence, then as now a rival to the Cheka and its successors, approached him to be their *rezident*, or illegal station chief, in Shanghai.*

With the revolutionary wave in Europe receding, Moscow's attention turned to the gathering war clouds in East Asia. It was no secret that the old enemy, Japan, had designs on the port of Vladivostok and other Russian lands on the Pacific coast, a short hop from Tokyo but more than 9,000 kilometres from Moscow. With China in turmoil and the Nationalist government facing a communist rebellion, both Japan and Russia were eyeing up opportunities to expand their influence.

Soviet military intelligence – at that time called the army's Fourth Directorate but better known by its later name as the GRU – recruited Alex in October 1929.

* Ulanovskaya and Ulanovskaya, *Istoria*, pp. 34–44.

Within days, he was heading to Berlin to build himself a cover identity. He was accompanied by Richard Sorge, who was born in Russia to ethnic German parents and spoke both languages like a native. He would rise to become one of the Soviet Union's most successful spies. Sorge would travel to China under his own name, and only required a letter of introduction from a Berlin newspaper to be accredited as its China correspondent.

Alex's task was much harder. He needed to build a legend which would hide his past as a communist agent. Claiming to be a German-speaking Czech metals dealer by the name of Kirschner who was heading to Shanghai, he placed adverts in the Berlin press offering to represent companies in China. A firm of arms dealers responded immediately, and appointed him on lucrative terms to smooth the way for the export of weapons to China. There was one problem: Germany was banned from exporting arms to China by the Versailles peace agreement and the League of Nations, but the company was confident that Herr Kirschner would sort out this small detail.

Alex and Sorge boarded a ship in Marseille at the end of November and arrived in Shanghai in January 1930. It was no place for amateurs – the intelligence services of the old colonial powers pitted their wits against spies from Japan and Russia, while British and French police in the international sectors of the city kept a close eye on subversive elements – and recruited a good few of them as informers. Shanghai would test the abilities of the two very different men. Sorge would turn out to be one of the most formidable spies of the Second World War. Alex had to prove that the qualities he had displayed as an underground fighter in the Russian civil war could be repurposed for intelligence gathering in Shanghai, where no one could be trusted, and everyone was for sale.

Nadya was to join Alex in Shanghai to play the role of Charlotte Kirschner, a German-speaking hausfrau from Prague, while secretly working for him as a radio operator and cypher clerk. In preparation, she spent weeks in the Russian countryside cooped up in a cottage with a huge antenna on the roof. A creepy German communist called Willi was teaching her how to encode and decode messages sent by radio. It was difficult work, requiring her to be ready at all hours to receive encrypted messages, and then, under Willi's guidance, to decode them. At the same time, Willi drilled her in spoken German so she could convincingly inhabit her cover identity of Charlotte Kirschner. In the close confines of their cottage, as they sat on a sofa waiting to receive transmissions and sharing the only blanket to keep warm, Willi touched her arm. 'What smooth soft skin – not like Jewish women have,' Willi said. 'On trams, if you brush up against one, it's disgusting. They have such prickly hairy arms.' Acutely aware that she was reliant on Willi to certify her competency to operate on her own, she could only respond coolly: 'I didn't know that communists could be anti-Semites.'

Her first test would be the hardest. Any young woman travelling alone for eight days on the Trans-Siberian railway would attract the attentions of all the bored male travellers, but in her case there was a greater danger, of having her false identity exposed. As she waited to board the train, she told the friend who was seeing her off there were two things she feared most – being in a sleeping compartment with a German and having a Japanese in the same carriage. The Japanese were vigilant spies, and if she aroused their suspicions, she would arrive in Shanghai with a Japanese tail.

To her relief she found herself in a compartment with a Russian. But she had to think on her feet when a Swiss man expressed concern about her sharing with a Russian man and suggested he swap places. She avoided the ordeal of having to make small talk in German for eight days by saying playfully, 'If I have to share with a man, it's better if he's completely foreign.'

She could not avoid small talk with two young German men in the carriage who were clearly Nazis. She thought books would be a safe topic of conversation and mentioned the new bestseller, *All Quiet on the Western Front.* 'You didn't read that disgusting book, did you?' one of them exclaimed. Too late, she realised that a good German housewife would never read an anti-war book. Indeed, it was to be top of Hitler's book-burning list.*

Her permanent state of anxiety was heightened by having to keep in her head a secret code she had been forbidden to write down. She had no respite, day or night. One night she had a dream that the two Japanese men who had been pestering her to come into their compartment were bending over her and one of them was grabbing her by the throat. To her enormous relief, even in sleep she did not betray herself as a Russian, shouting out '*Hilfe!*'

For eight days she had to keep the persistent Japanese and the Germans at bay while not letting slip her identity, and it was a relief when the train at last reached its destination of Port Arthur, today called Lushunkou. From there she boarded a steamship for the three-day voyage to

* Ulanovskaya and Ulanovskaya pp 35.

Shanghai. It was a Japanese ship and as she embarked, she was dismayed to see following her on board the same passengers she had been trying to avoid. Feeling completely wiped out, she found sanctuary in her cabin for a couple of hours until she was disturbed by a loud knocking on the door. It was the two young Germans calling her to dinner and dancing. She hated having to dress for dinner and, despite Willi's best efforts, she was a terrible dancer and felt uncomfortable being pawed by strange men. As the sole European woman on the ship, she found herself the centre of unwanted attention and was invited to sit next to the captain at dinner. While the men were drinking toasts to the 'beautiful lady', all she could think was: 'I've got another two whole days of this.'

As the ship docked in Shanghai, she spotted Alex waiting on the quay. Beside him stood the imposing figure of the man she assumed to be Richard Sorge, tall with chestnut hair, elegantly dressed and looking older than his thirty-five years. As soon as she got into the car she broke down and let go of the tension that had built up inside her. 'Thirteen days amongst Japanese and Germans pretending to be someone I'm not, and nowhere to hide, not even for a minute,' she kept repeating. Sorge looked disapproving, and Alex was embarrassed.

When they got to their apartment, Sorge ran her a bath, telling her a long soak would revive her. He laid out a gorgeous kimono and backless slippers with pompoms, the like of which she had never seen. Before she could relax, she had to pass on the secret code. Over the next few days Sorge took her round the shops to buy a new wardrobe so she would fit seamlessly into colonial life. She would normally have chosen clothes in muted colours, but Sorge insisted she buy silk dresses in bright blues and greens and a full set of delicately embroidered underwear. Returning from a trip to Canton, Sorge completed her wardrobe with a beautifully worked Cantonese shawl, a must-have accessory for going to a Shanghai nightclub.*

At that time Shanghai was one of the most vibrant cities in the world, but all Nadya felt was disgust and alienation. She was appalled at the beggars and cripples with their terrible diseases and infected eyes, sleeping on the streets like animals while she lived in a spacious apartment in the European settlement. She felt uncomfortable taking a rickshaw with the half-naked driver gasping for breath as he ran like a horse, mopping the sweat off his body with a dirty rag. The sight of the Europeans lording it over the Chinese – and the passivity and subservience this engendered in the local population – revolted her.

When Alex arrived in Shanghai, he was under orders to ditch all the agents recruited by his predecessor – they were all said to be compromised – and build a new network from scratch. This came as a nasty surprise to the existing *rezident*, who had no idea until Alex and Sorge arrived that he had been called home or that the network he had built up was to be dissolved. The old chief was not going to go without a fight, and the first weeks of Alex's stay were consumed by a power struggle with the *rezident*, who refused to budge.

There was worse to come. Sorge had persuaded Alex and Nadya that if they really wanted to fit in with the Shanghai expats, they had to start going to nightclubs, and so one evening he took them to the Arcadia in the city's French Concession. No sooner had they walked in than

* Ulanovskaya and Ulanovskaya p. 37.

they were hailed by a loud German voice. 'Alex, wonderful to see you again. Why didn't you tell me you were coming back to China?'

It was a German who remembered Alex from his visit to China two years before when he was making speeches as a fiery Soviet trade union agitator under his real name. The two men had shared a compartment on the Trans-Siberian Express on the way to China, so there was no possibility of Alex claiming mistaken identity.

This was a disaster: the whole point of Alex's cover as Herr Kirschner was to be able to move among Germans who were working as military advisers to the tottering Chinese government. After this chance meeting at the Arcadia, Alex had no choice but to hide from German society, and he had to pad out his meagre reports to Moscow with information gathered from newspapers. Sorge meanwhile was delivering intelligence gold from his German contacts, whom he charmed ruthlessly. Posing as a raffish journalist who rode around Shanghai on a high-powered motorbike with stylish European women clinging to his waist on the tight turns, he had the perfect cover.

While Sorge thrived, the good luck that had saved Alex so many times during the civil war deserted him. On the street he bumped into an old comrade from his partisan days in Crimea during the civil war. Rafail Kurgan had written a memoir of those days, in which Alex featured as a ruthless warrior – a description Alex rejected, preferring to be remembered instead for his guile, such as the time he dressed up as a White officer to rescue two Bolshevik prisoners from a firing squad without firing a shot.*

* Ulanovskaya and Ulanovskaya pp. 9–10.

Alex almost failed to recognise the old partisan in his dishevelled state. After the civil war, Kurgan had joined the Soviet Communist Party, but he lost his faith in the revolution as early as 1924 and began to steal state funds to support a gambling habit. When his fraud was discovered, he fled Russia and moved to Shanghai with his mistress, a fellow Communist Party member who had been working as a Soviet state prosecutor. There was no work for Kurgan in Shanghai, and the couple lived off her meagre earnings as a dance partner for hire. When Alex told Nadya that he had met up with his old friend, she was appalled. 'How can you spend your time with that worthless criminal?' Alex said Kurgan was an old mate, and it was interesting to hear his thoughts. Nadya could only think that he was putting their mission in jeopardy, and indeed their safety.

Nadya was right to be worried. In his desperate state, Kurgan would never leave Alex alone, so Alex paid him to recruit some dubious informants who provided a stream of largely worthless intelligence. Kurgan got greedy – demanding 5,000 dollars for what he claimed was top-secret information about the armed forces of the Chinese government. With approval from Moscow Centre, Alex handed over the money, but three days passed and Kurgan failed to appear with the intelligence. Days later, his mistress came to explain what had happened. On the way to meet his contact for the handover, Kurgan could not stop himself entering a casino and he gambled all the money away. Now he was demanding more money to complete the deal, and threatened to expose Alex unless he provided it. Alex refused.

To reinforce the blackmail threat, Kurgan sent a Russian émigré double agent, a notorious fraudster and conman who worked closely with the Chinese police, to Alex's home. Captain Pick, as he called himself, addressed Alex in Russian, but Alex pretended not to understand and said in English: 'Clear off, or I'll call the police.' Pick left, threatening, 'You'll regret it,' but the damage was done. So many Shanghai shysters now knew Alex's real name, his true mission, and his home address, that he had to leave immediately.

With the police watching their apartment, Alex took refuge in a safe house. He had to get permission from Moscow to leave Shanghai, and there was a bigger problem: Nadya only had one passport in the name of Kirschner, so she could not board a ship without the risk of arrest. They needed a way to smuggle her out of the country. While he worked on an exit plan, Nadya lived alone in their six-bedroomed flat, dressing for dinner every evening, even though she was too nervous to eat, so that the servants had no unusual activity to report to the police. Every other day she would meet Zeppel, the residency's German wireless operator through whom she and Alex communicated, for an exchange of messages. Sometimes they would meet at a swimming pool where Zeppel liked to show off his diving skills from the high board. Nadya, also a good swimmer, would exchange a couple of words with him as he ploughed up and down the pool. On other occasions they would rendezvous in a darkened cinema in the afternoon.

Kurgan had spent enough time with Alex to know he would not run away and leave his wife behind to rot in a sweltering Chinese prison cell. Every few days Nadya would go to meet him, her presence assuring him that Alex was still in Shanghai. As they tramped the streets – Nadya did not want him near their apartment – she was forced to listen to Kurgan moaning for hours about his misfortunes, while at the same time threatening to betray her to the police. All he needed to start a new life was a few thousand dollars for tickets for him and his mistress to leave Shanghai, and he would take Nadya with them. But if Alex would not hand over the money, he would have no option but to betray her to the police. If Nadya ended up in jail, it would be Alex's fault. 'What's a few thousand dollars to the Bolsheviks? They're throwing money away all over the world to promote their cause.'

Kurgan thought of himself as a wily fox who was dealing with a naïve and guileless Komsomol girl, but he underestimated her. She was stringing out their conversations until she and Alex had an escape plan.

One night, as she tried to sleep, there was a loud knock at the door. She got dressed – better not to go to prison in her night clothes – and answered the door. It was Zeppel, the wireless operator. 'Why didn't you come today?' he hissed. They had agreed to skip a day, but Zeppel had forgotten the change of schedule. When Nadya had failed to appear, he raised the alarm with Alex, who told him to go and check on the flat. If Nadya had been arrested, Alex would take a revolver and shoot Kurgan. Realising he had made a mistake, Zeppel hurried away – he had to stop Alex before he set out to take his revenge, which would make it impossible for them to sneak out of Shanghai.

Zeppel meanwhile had been using his contacts with German communist seamen to get Nadya and Alex on board a slow boat to Europe. When he had a firm date, Nadya adopted her Komsomol-girl persona and told Kurgan that Alex had agreed to provide the money for the tickets and they would all leave together. Nadya said she would meet him in five days' time to give him the details.

When the ship was about to sail, they were able to sneak on board and slip out of Shanghai, unnoticed by the police or by Kurgan. Their Chinese adventure had lasted all of six months.

In Moscow, Alex's handlers assumed their *rezident* was 'a real terrorist' who would not have shrunk from liquidating a low-life blackmailer like Kurgan. But in truth too many people knew Alex's real identity for a single shot to have resolved the problem.

As for Kurgan, when Nadya failed to meet him on the appointed day, he went looking for her. On finding their apartment empty, he shot himself. He had pinned on Alex any hope he had of paying off his gambling debts. The death of Kurgan was big news in the Shanghai papers. Captain Pick profited from the scandal, selling to reporters juicy details of the lives of the two spies who went by the name Kirschner.

Alex and Nadya's first port of call was Hong Kong, where Sorge was now working. Having left the Shanghai network in good time, he miraculously avoided any shadow of suspicion falling on him as a result of the Kurgan affair.

Alex shared with Sorge lessons learned from his experience. In future, he told his colleague, who moved effortlessly in bourgeois circles, Soviet agents should be taught dancing, golf, tennis and bridge to provide 'a good foundation for small talk'. Colourful silk dresses and a Cantonese shawl were not enough.*

* Owen Matthews, *Richard Sorge: An Impeccable Spy*, p. 74.

# 12

## *1942: Girls of the Metropol*

For many decades the phrase 'girls of the Metropol' had been a polite way of referring to prostitutes. This reputation was refreshed during wartime by a play, *Kremlin Chimes*, which premiered at the Moscow Art Theatre.

> Father (Zabelin): 'I shouldn't be surprised if our daughter turns out to be a street walker.'
> Mother (Zabelina): 'How can you say that – it's our daughter you're talking about.'
> Father (Zabelin): 'You should know that just one hour ago our daughter entered the Metropol Hotel with a man.'*

With unattached men from Britain and the United States flooding into Moscow to staff the military missions, the British embassy thought an analysis of the Metropol Hotel's sex-trade subculture was in order, particularly given the security aspects of liaisons with Soviet citizens and the near impossibility of taking a Russian bride back home. In a drab and hungry city where, with men absent

* English translation in *Three Soviet Plays* (Foreign Languages Publishing House, Moscow, no date).

at the front, women's work was likely to be twelve-hour shifts of manual labour, the Metropol offered a tempting vision of comfort and luxury.

'On first arrival at the Metropole [sic] Hotel to take up residence there, foreign bachelors soon find that they receive telephone calls practically every other night from Russian girls, complete strangers, who know not only the room number but the name of the occupant. There seems to be a most efficient bush telegraph operating among these girls, who would come under the heading of floozies.'* So runs the opening paragraph to a guide to the 'Good-Time Girls' of the Metropol compiled for the British embassy by an anonymous resident of the hotel.

The 'floozies' generally spoke only a few words of English and were well known to the hotel administration. They had to give the hall porter the number of the room they were going to, and around midnight the occupant of the room would receive a phone call to tell his guest to go home. The existence of these young women was precarious. One day a 23-year-old known as Big Vera, who had been a fixture at the hotel for several months, disappeared. Her friend Lyudmila explained that she had been picked up by 'the bluebells', a reference to the colour of the NKVD uniform. Vera's 'hobby' is dismissively described in the document as 'eating' – not surprising given that most Russians were half-starved. A more forgiving label of the young women's trade would be 'hunger prostitution', a term used by the *Telegraph*'s Cholerton who knew better than any other foreigner the privations of Russians who lived outside the magic island of the Metropol.

* TNA FO 371 43305/214.

About thirty students from the foreign language institute frequented the Metropol, and three lived openly with Americans. They believed, rightly or wrongly, that they had special latitude to improve their English. The institute's teachers preferred British English to the US variety and, even though Americans had more expensive gifts to offer, there was a saying in the institute: 'Find an Englishman with a hundred pairs of stockings and stick with him.'

As Nadya noticed ever more young women hanging around the lobby, she guessed that some of them had been sent by the comrades to entrap a foreigner. But she knew that every woman who fell in with foreigners, whether sent to spy or looking for excitement and silk stockings, was doomed. The NKVD would exploit them as informers and then, when the war was over, they would be declared ruined by contact with foreigners, and sent to the Gulag. As a loyal communist Nadya should not have interfered with the comrades' use of young women as bait, but when she came across a student from the Institute of Foreign Languages in the room of an American correspondent she decided on impulse to save her from her fate. Although two Russians meeting in the presence of a foreigner always treated each other with suspicion, she took a risk and gave the student her room number.

When she appeared, Nadya sounded her out. 'Aren't you afraid to be with this foreigner?'

'Yes, I'm very afraid, but is it wrong that I've come to see him? Tell me about him.'

Nadya told her that the American correspondent, Walter Kerr, was a decent fellow but seeing him was very dangerous. The student became very upset; she did not want to stop seeing him. 'It's so interesting to learn about life in another country and besides, isn't he an ally?'

The student left, and Nadya regretted that she had not been more forthright. She should have told her that after two or three visits she would be called in by the NKVD and they would say: 'So you've been going to the Metropol. Carry on. Get to know as many people as possible. We will give you a code name and you will bring us useful information. If you do good work, we will reward you.' She would work for them as long as they needed her, and then they would put her in prison. In the eyes of the NKVD, any girl who had associated with foreigners had ceased to be a Soviet citizen.

Nadya bumped into the student a second time, and this time she did not hold back. She told her exactly what lay in store for her, and that she was risking not only her own freedom but the well-being of her whole family. She was never seen in the Metropol again. Looking back on her time working with foreigners, Nadya saw this as a mitzvah, a good deed in a naughty world.*

\*

When the American journalist Edgar Snow arrived in Moscow he was appalled to see how shamelessly reliant the correspondents were on their translators. Snow had made his name by tracking down Mao Tse-tung, then a communist revolutionary hiding in the depths of the Chinese interior, and introduced him to American readers with his 1937 bestseller *Red Star Over China*. In his diary of October 27, 1942, he wrote:

* Nadezhda Ulanovskaya & Maya Ulanovskaya, *Istoria, Odnoi Semyi*, 3rd Edition, (Inanpress, 2013) p. 76.

'Many correspondents do not leave the hotel for weeks in winter but rely on secretaries and newspapers. Secretary orders breakfast in the morning, arranges pillow under your head while you eat it, shops for cigarettes and vodka, translates, interprets, teaches you Russian and sometimes goes to bed with you. In exchange the correspondent brings back titbits from the dining room – bread, cake, cheese and meat. It's a daily event to see correspondents trooping up to their rooms with a plateful of bread and cheese.'

As time passed, he understood that a secretary-translator was not a nursemaid, but a crucial figure whose interaction with the journalist would define the correspondent's access to information and their view of the Soviet system. He noticed that Nadya, who he knew was no supporter of Stalin, quietly reinforced the sceptical views of Soviet communism harboured by the correspondents she worked for. 'Secretaries undoubtedly influence the POV [point of view] of correspondents. Or is it simply that instinctively the correspondent drifts toward the one who will support his POV?'*

After six months in Moscow, during which time his editors at the *Saturday Evening Post* described his output as 'boring', Snow tallied up the number of sources of information he could count on among the Russians. These were:

'Three Russians from whom I can get expressions of disillusionment with the regime; two Communist Party

* Papers of Edgar Snow, Book 40, 29 March 1943.

members for frank discussions on public questions; one from whom I get the "see no evil" position; and one conditioned to rationalise all decisions as perfect.'

Looking at his staff, his two translators and his courier, he had to admit that each of them contributed something to his point of view. In contrast to his own rather thin contact list, Parker was doing much better – with the help of Valentina, whom Snow recognised as 'the most efficient of the lot', Parker had acquired eight Russians who could be counted as reliable sources in the journalistic sense.*

The sense of impotence that Snow felt in Moscow was no doubt shared by many of his male colleagues. A very different view comes from Charlotte Haldane, who felt 'deaf, dumb and blind' on arrival in Moscow and saw her translator, Lily, as a true colleague, endowed with the competitive spirit that drives a good reporter.

'She was intelligent and took a real interest in her work so that it was possible to get her genuinely excited about a story. She was also, as every normal woman should be, capable of healthy cattiness and malice. She liked scoring over her rivals, the other secretaries, and ipso facto over the other correspondents who were being "run" by them, as I was being "run" by her.'†

Not all the secretary-translators working in the Metropol were who they appeared to be. One of the most popular was Tatyana Sofiano, who had worked before the war for the American chamber of commerce

* Papers of Edgar Snow, Book 40, 16 November 1942.
† Charlotte Haldane, *Russian Newsreel* (Penguin 1943), p. 57.

in Moscow. In 1937 she had been sentenced to an eight-year term for espionage – she was lucky not to have a death sentence – and sent to a forced labour camp in Kazakhstan. When working in the Metropol she spoke openly to the journalists about milking cows in the Gulag and recalled her long conversations with imprisoned intellectuals in the evenings. She was a warm, outspoken woman with a bubbly personality who seemed to have no fear of being reported to the NKVD. Only Alice Moats voiced any suspicions about her, noting that she was 'as brave as a lion, especially considering she had served three and a half years of an eight-year sentence in prison camp'.* She had told the correspondents she had secured early release from prison by protesting her innocence in a letter-writing campaign. But this was only part of the truth.

Her prison record provided by Memorial, the organisation that for thirty years documented the victims of Stalin's repressions until it was closed down by Putin, tells a different story about her early release. In 1940 she was moved from Kazakhstan to the Lubyanka in Moscow, where her task was 'to work on detainees in their cells'. In other words, the price she had to pay for early release was to work as a stool pigeon, providing a friendly ear for detainees to reveal secrets they would not disclose to their interrogators. She was released in April 1941, just in time to find work at the Metropol. Several members of her family had suffered in Stalin's repressions, one reason why her nephew, the nuclear physicist Andrei Sakharov,

---

* Alice-Leone Moats, *Blind Date with Mars* (Doubleday, New York, 1943), p. 424.

became the Soviet Union's most famous dissident in the late 1970s.*

*

Getting a job as a secretary-translator with a foreign correspondent at the Metropol was a dream for many, but success was restricted to those approved by the NKVD. Without their approval, it required luck, persistence and not a little detective work, as shown by the experience of Tanya Svetlova, a provincial outsider who, despite her bourgeois origins, achieved the impossible.

It all started with the search for a good meal. Before departing for the front, Tanya's estranged husband Nick, a Soviet documentary film-maker, gave her something far more valuable than cash – a book of vouchers. Each voucher provided a bowl of hot soup, a plate of fish or macaroni, and a saucer of red jelly. Also on offer was a 100-gram ration of vodka, which Tanya turned down. This was served in the closed dining room of the Moscow House of Actors. If she had not had her five-year-old daughter with her, Tanya could have spent the afternoons in the warm dining room surrounded by elderly thespians. At home Tanya, her mother and daughter lived off mashed potato peelings and 400 grams a day of black bread and, when they got their rations, horse meatballs and millet gruel.

One day the director of the House of Actors interrupted her lunch. 'Comrade Svetlova – I hear you speak English. Can you help us?'

He told her he was organising a concert of English and

* See websites https://ru.openlist.wiki/Софиано_Татьяна_Алексеевна_(1903) and http://www.pmem.ru/index.php?id=400

American music for Russia's allies, and had invited all the
Anglo-American diplomats, senior military officers and
press, and he needed someone to introduce the programme.
Tanya said she would be delighted to be the compere. Her
next thought was, what could she wear? She had nothing
suitable for such a grand occasion.

She borrowed a black dress from a friend and put on
her only pair of silk stockings and tried not to think
about the ladder in them. She walked to the House of
Actors in her party shoes. The concert began with the
orchestra, accustomed to playing Glinka and Rimsky-
Korsakov, struggling through two short pieces by the
only English composer whose music they could find,
Cyril Scott. Then Tanya, unfamiliar with musical terms
in English and not sure if she was pronouncing them
correctly, hesitantly introduced the next piece, 'Con-
certo and Minuet', also by Cyril Scott. There followed a
respite from Scott with extracts from *Rose-Marie* by the
Canadian composer Rudolf Friml – the closest the con-
ductor could find to American music – before Tanya,
growing more confident in her English, pronounced
loudly, 'Now for the finale, "Gavotte" by Scott,' to loud
laughter from the audience.

At the drinks party afterwards, Tanya found herself
surrounded by British and American officers who had
turned away from the weak Russian beer on offer and who
asked her questions, while she stood smiling and silent.
Their language was so different from the English of Soviet
textbooks. She could not follow it. A middle-aged man
with mischievous eyes behind silver-rimmed glasses pushed
his way up to her and shook her hand. It was the American

Ambassador, William Standley. ' "Gavotte" by Scott! Ha ha ha. And who are you?'

'I'm just an English teacher.'

'And may I introduce you to Admiral Miles and Commander Palmer?' Turning to the two naval officers, he said, 'Meet Miss Gavotte Scott.'

Commander Palmer – so that was his name, the handsome young officer she looked out for every morning. At 9 a.m. he would emerge from the building across the street, immaculate in his dark blue uniform, his head tilted slightly to one side, as he accompanied the admiral with his weather-beaten face and gold braided cap to a car flying a Union Jack pennant. She even had a secret name for the admiral – the old British sea wolf.

Tanya blurted out, 'I know you – I live in the new red-brick block opposite you. From my window I see you drive away every morning.'

The sea wolf said, 'I didn't know that a pair of beautiful eyes was watching me. I must be more careful in future.' Then he added, 'Can I give you a lift in my car?'

For a moment Tanya was confused. She knew that an English lift was an American elevator. Why was she being offered an elevator? But then she understood he was offering to take her home in his car and gratefully accepted.

Walking down the stairs beside the dashing Commander Palmer, she was in seventh heaven. As they drove away in the car with the Union Jack pennant, she looked over her shoulder and saw they were being followed by a black vehicle with three men of military age in it. The admiral patted her hand. 'Don't be alarmed – those boys are my bodyguards,' he joked. Nevertheless, Tanya asked to be dropped off at the end of the street. 'Goodnight,' she said, 'and thank you for the elevator.'*

Despite the attentions of the diplomats and naval officers, Tanya, at the age of twenty-seven, was feeling old and stale. The thought of standing in front of students for the rest of her life making them repeat the unpronounceable 'th' sound depressed her. What she really needed was to talk to native speakers and train her ears. Her success at the concert gave her the push to give up her teaching job and look for work in organisations where they needed English speakers. She had high hopes of VOKS, the All-Union Society for Cultural Relations with Foreign Countries, where her friend Valya worked. But Tanya was not prepared for the question that every prospective employee had to answer: Where were you when Moscow was evacuated in October? Replying truthfully, she said she had stayed behind in the city. In the eyes of the officials who had left Moscow and were now returning, she was admitting she was a Nazi lover who had been standing by to welcome the Germans. There was no job for her.

To cheer herself up on her twenty-eighth birthday she went to the hairdressers and found herself sitting next to a foreigner called Joe or Doe who spoke English and told her there were jobs going with journalists at the Metropol Hotel. Desperate to ask him how she could meet such a journalist, she was afraid of being overheard by the hairdressers, and held her tongue. As soon as her hair was dry, she dashed outside but Joe or Doe had vanished. As she stood on the pavement, she thought what a wonderful job

* Tanya Matthews, *Russian Child and Russian Wife: An Autobiography* (Gollancz, London 1949) p.275.

it would be. They would speak real English – good training for her ears – and they would pay decent wages, and
there was bound to be tinned fruit. She cursed herself for
letting this opportunity slip through her fingers.

She pulled herself together. The correspondents lived
at the Metropol Hotel. That's what Valya had told her too.
And one of them, an English one, had recently given a talk
at VOKS. She had said his name was Parker. Maybe he
needed an assistant. She would try her luck – it was her
birthday after all.

In her flat there was a locked room with a telephone
for the use of the fire brigade during air raids – and perhaps also for spies who wanted to keep an eye on the
British officers living over the road. Tanya had managed
to persuade the fire watchers to let her have the key to the
locked room in exchange for a promise to dust it every
day. On her return from the hairdressers, she unlocked
the door, sat down by the telephone and dialled the number of the Metropol. 'Mr Parker, please,' she said in her
best English.

It was Parker who responded. 'You don't know me – I
compered at the concert the other day. You went? I mean,
did you attend?'

'No, but I heard all about you from Admiral Miles. He
says you have pretty legs.'

Words then spilled out of Tanya's mouth in no particular order. 'I went to the hairdresser today. It's my birthday.
I met a man who said that journalists in the Metropol need
secretaries. Mr Parker, do you need a secretary?'

'I have a secretary already. But come along at five to
room 75 and we can have a chat.'

Room 75 was divided in half with a heavy velvet

curtain in front of which stood a big empire-style desk. Tanya's attention was irresistibly drawn to a plate of sand-wiches piled high with black caviar next to a typewriter and a pile of papers. Parker introduced Tanya to his secre-tary Valentina, who was looking the visitor up and down. He had remembered it was her birthday, and opened a bottle of Georgian white wine and handed Valentina and Tanya a glass. Valentina said, 'We must do something for Tanya. Let's call Fatty.' Parker agreed.

Fatty, or Mr Matthews as he was introduced to Tanya, turned out to be a tall, corpulent man with kind eyes and a stern face wearing the British military correspondent's khaki uniform. What a great bear of a man, thought Tanya. Parker poured Matthews a glass of wine and Mat-thews, after a perfunctory birthday toast to Tanya, launched into an assessment of the wines of Australia, from where he had just come on an empty oil tanker surrounded by lurking Japanese submarines. While Tanya tucked into the caviar sandwiches, Parker offered Matthews a new-comer's briefing on British diplomats in Moscow who were worth speaking to, with Matthews exclaiming every so often, 'Oh, we were at Oxford together.'

When this topic was exhausted, Matthews turned to Tanya. 'Can you type?'

'No.'

'Do you know shorthand?'

'No.'

'Have you worked as a secretary before?'

'No.'

Matthews told her he had just arrived and needed an experienced secretary, but he would call her tomorrow. Tanya left the Metropol feeling very low.

Matthews did not call the next day, nor the day after. Her high opinion of foreigners was shattered, but she decided not to give up until she had a firm refusal. She called Parker's secretary and told her she had heard nothing from the big man. 'With foreigners you have to press them up against the wall and squeeze out of them what you want,' Valentina told her. She was clearly a woman who knew how to get her way. 'Come here at 5 o'clock and we'll see what we can do.'

That afternoon Matthews was pressed up against the wall, and he put up very little resistance. 'The thing is, I need someone with more experience, but I'll give you a two-week trial, and if you don't prove to be what I require, there'll be no ill feeling.'*

The next day Tanya appeared promptly at 9 a.m. clutching a pile of Soviet newspapers. Matthews was dressed, shaved and smelling of soap and waiting for her with a notebook and silver pencil in his hand.

'So what's the news today?' he barked. Tanya translated column after column from the front page of *Pravda*, with Matthews taking notes, and then moved on to other papers. Matthews stopped writing. 'You're reading the same article all over again. Can't you find something different?'

'They all carry the same articles,' Tanya responded, to a distrustful look from Matthews.

'I need some colour – some interesting details to bring my copy to life.'

Tanya found a front-line article in *Red Star*, the army newspaper, about a Soviet unit that ran out of machine-gun

* Matthews, *Russian Child*, p. 281.

ammunition, but with the Germans about to overrun them, strapped grenades to their chests and threw themselves in the way of the advancing enemy tanks, detonating the explosives underneath them. She seemed to have found what Matthews wanted. 'That will be enough,' he said, and started to hammer away at his typewriter.

Tanya watched in fascination as the foreigner got to work. 'To help him concentrate he always had a handkerchief in his teeth when he was working,' she recalled in later life. 'From time to time he would stop typing and pull a small tube of Colgate out of his breast pocket, take a nip of toothpaste and then replace the tube. The gesture was totally automatic. Then the handkerchief would go back between his teeth and the typewriter would start to rattle again in a very fast and efficient way.'*

When minutes later she was still standing in the middle of the room, he seemed surprised. 'Don't you know your duties?' She did not, and he had to tell her.

'By noon this despatch must be taken to the Press Department to be censored. Wait till the censor has done his worst. If there are cuts or alterations, bring the copy back to me. If there are no cuts, take it to the telegraph office. Be back here at four o'clock with the evening papers.' He paused for breath. 'There should be some rations for me at the foreigners' store which you might collect. Here is my card. Deliver these empty bottles and get two litres of vodka. You can get some fruit if there is any at the store. You are entitled to one meal here at the hotel. Get yourself a book of vouchers downstairs. Be back here at a quarter to twelve.'

* Tanya Matthews, 'Going Back', BBC Radio 4 documentary.

For five days Tanya rushed around like a 'salted hare' to provide Matthews, aged thirty-nine and unmarried, with a daily supply of journalistic colour and bottles of vodka, while also securing him a bigger room at the hotel, procuring a radio (possession of which was illegal for Soviet citizens in wartime) so he could listen to the BBC, and darning his socks. She got the job.

# 13

## Summer 1942: Kremlin stooges and fascist beasts

By the middle of 1942, one year after the outbreak of war on the Eastern Front, it was clear to the British and American journalists that the conditions they were working in were immutable. This realisation crystallised a split in the press corps between the 'Kremlin stooges' and the 'fascist beasts'. The 'stooges' came in two forms. Some were happy to polish up Kremlin propaganda for Western consumption, because they believed that Stalin's victory would usher in an era of peace and progress throughout Europe in place of the dictatorial politics of the 1930s. Others, more cynical, did whatever was necessary to keep their press passes that allowed them to live tax-free in Moscow while supplementing their salaries by writing books about Russia which were assured of huge sales.

The material benefits of being a 'stooge' are satirised by Iris Morley, wife of the *Daily Express* correspondent Alaric Jacob, in her 1946 novel, *Nothing But Propaganda*. The heroine Catharine Sarcy works in a communist bookshop in Bloomsbury and is visited by Noel Reed, a correspondent back from Moscow who has just written a book about Russia. From Reed's reports in print and on the BBC she believes he is 'emotionally pro-Soviet', so she is shocked when he tells her over lunch at the Savoy that the Russian people are 'controlled by a dangerous and unscrupulous government with boundless ambition'. All he can talk about is 'censorship, spies, secret liquidations and general inefficiency in all spheres'. Back at the bookshop, Catharine asks her colleague to explain the contradiction between the private and the public Noel Reed. 'My dear, he is on to a good thing. If you can make £2,000 a year by being pro-Soviet, who is Mr Noel Reed to refuse? Every word he says here in public has got to have plenty of visa-appeal, and he knows it.'* 'Visa-appeal' was a reference to journalists' practice of not saying or writing anything in London that might jeopardise their return visa to Moscow.

As for the 'fascist beasts' – a Soviet term of abuse for any foreigner who made the slightest criticism of Stalin's rule – they struggled to reconcile their duty to support an ally with their journalistic instinct to reveal the truth about Stalin's blood-soaked climb to power and his plans to subsume eastern Europe into a buffer zone of satellite states after the defeat of Hitler. They spent their energies fighting the censor, and losing.

Parker and Valentina were the power couple at the head of the Kremlin stooges. So recently inconsolable in grief, Parker had recovered his equilibrium and was thriving under the tutelage of Valentina, who had set him on a journey to becoming a Kremlin propaganda asset.

Exactly the opposite could be said of Tanya. By any measure of loyalty to the Kremlin, she was an unfit

* Iris Morley, *Nothing But Propaganda* (Peter Davies, London, 1946), p. 128.

person to work in the Metropol. Because of her origins in the 'rotten bourgeoisie',* – her grandfather had been a priest – she was banned from higher education, and wherever she earned a crust, whether as jazz singer or teacher, she was harassed by the NKVD to inform on her friends and colleagues. With her bad background, she could not say no, but only run away and try to keep one step ahead of them. While in the Metropol she was a walking encyclopaedia of the horrors of life under Stalin – her hungry childhood chewing grass, the abortions without anaesthetic she had had to endure, and the housing shortage which forced her family to sleep eight to a room just to be able to live in Moscow.

As for Matthews, he was too much of a freethinker to meet the stereotype of a correspondent of the *Daily Herald*, the leftist paper he was working for. As he wrote later, 'Even those of us who came to Russia with some indulgence for the Tyranny – because it was at that time our ally against an almost worse regime, that of the German Hitler – came in the end to feel it had no excuse.'†

Matthews' devotion to the Catholic church seemed stronger than any political allegiance, and his habit of keeping a tube of toothpaste in his breast pocket and sucking on it, occasionally at parties offering fellow guests a suck as if it were a hipflask of whisky, cemented his reputation as a true English eccentric. Nadya called him

---

* Tanya Matthews, 'Going Back', BBC Radio 4 documentary.
† Ronald Matthews, *Red Sky at Night* (Hollis & Carter, London, 1951).

'spineless' and 'a loser'.* While Parker hewed ever more firmly to the Kremlin line, even arguing that Stalin's dictatorship was in fact a democracy, Matthews and Tanya became the standard bearers of the Fascist Beasts, fighting a quixotic and sometimes farcical rear-guard action against official propaganda, a struggle which at moments of crisis led to fists flying in the press room.

If Nadya had been doing her job properly – that is, guiding the press corps towards the NKVD-approved path – Tanya would have been on the first train to Siberia. But somehow Tanya was able to charm her. Nadya seems to have recognised in her a kindred spirit, a child of the Russian provinces who like her was desperate to rise above her origins and get out into the world.

The British Foreign Office had abandoned any hope that the output of the press corps in Moscow could be in any sense 'objective', but they were concerned at how quickly Ralph Parker had been converted from a trustworthy informant of the Secret Intelligence Service – which had endorsed his appointment to Moscow – to an asset of Kremlin propaganda. This emerges from the record of a private chat that a British official had over drinks in New York with Larry LeSueur, the CBS radio correspondent recently returned from Russia. The official steered the conversation round to the lack of balance in Parker's reports. LeSueur hesitated to criticise a former colleague with whom he had suffered so many privations on the hungry journey from Archangel to Kuibyshev, but said Parker had been 'over-propagandised by

* Nadezhda Ulanovskaya and Maya Ulanovskaya, *Istoria, Odnoi Semyi*, 3rd edition, (Inanpress, 2013) p. 77.

the Russians'. To avoid Parker's fate, LeSueur added, no journalist ought to stay in Moscow more than a year. The
conversation ended on a topic of prurient interest to male
reporters and diplomats around the world – the girlfriends
made available to their colleagues in Moscow by the NKVD.
'Any such companions,' LeSueur replied sniffily, 'are constantly questioned and occasionally sent away.'*

* TNA FO 370 2294/42.

# 14

## *1931–32: Amerika*

In 1931 Alex and Nadya sailed from Cherbourg to New York as a Canadian couple called Goldman, travelling in style aboard the luxury liner *Bremen* in a suite bigger than any Moscow apartment they could ever have lived in. Nadya had bought two new dresses in Paris to complete her disguise as a bourgeois lady, but this extravagance was not enough: in first class it was de rigueur to appear in a different outfit each evening, so when her wardrobe ran out, Nadya pleaded a headache and skipped dinner.

After the intelligence fiasco in China, it should have been clear to Alex's controllers that he was too ill-disciplined for undercover spy work. Yet Yan Berzin, the military intelligence chief, who admired Alex for his civil war heroics, appointed him as *rezident*, or station chief, in New York. His assignment to America was something of a demotion: the United States was seen by Moscow at the time as a land of plutocrats and starving workers without a serious communist party that could be a contender for power.

America had something else to offer – technology that the capitalists were ready to sell. Stalin was spending millions of dollars buying US technology to transform a peasant society into an industrial powerhouse. Now that factories based on Henry Ford's mass production techniques were up and running in Russia, Stalin wanted American designs for tanks, submarines and other military kit the Russians could build for themselves. Alex and Nadya were in New York to steal these plans.

Alex's New York spy network was made up of recruits provided by the American Communist Party who would be working in the party's 'underground apparatus'. Members of this secret arm of the party sought out sympathetic workers in naval yards and arms industries who could provide blueprints of military technology for copying and sending to Moscow.

Alex's first recruit was Whittaker Chambers, a gifted writer who was working as an editor of a Marxist journal, *New Masses*. Chambers would be a courier, receiving technical plans from communist sympathisers and delivering them to the Russian spies. The recruitment of Chambers was a typically reckless step by Alex. In time, Chambers would expose to a shocked American public the extent of Soviet penetration of the Roosevelt administration, setting off a 'Reds under the Bed' spy scare that poisoned US politics in the 1950s.

Chambers was already well known as a party member and by habit not one to blend into the background. While other recruits hid their revolutionary zeal behind a facade of ordinariness as dentists or carpenters, Chambers stood out as a shambolic figure with a mouthful of rotten teeth who either dressed in a rumpled, ill-fitting suit or went hatless and tieless in khaki shirt and slacks.* He despised the consumer culture and suburban lifestyle that the American

---

* Whittaker Chambers, *Witness* (Andre Deutsch 1953), p. 203.

middle classes aspired to, choosing instead to live at the end of a dirt track in a barn about sixty miles from New York City, near Glen Gardner, a town in western New Jersey. The barn had no electricity and only a kerosene stove to heat it, but Chambers said it met his need as a country boy to be in touch with the land, even if it required him to walk six miles over the hills to the train station when his ancient car broke down. When Nadya was invited to visit, she found Chambers' wife Esther to be equally eccentric. She wore dresses of unbleached linen, but bought her gloves from expensive New York stores. It was incomprehensible to Nadya that sophisticated Americans would choose to live in what seemed to her to be the Siberia of the East Coast.*

Tradecraft required the use of code names. Chambers was 'Bob', Alex was 'Ulrich' and Nadya was 'Maria', or sometimes 'Elaine'. Nadya was not supposed to know Bob's true identity or anything about him, but that did not last. They travelled together to meet communist contacts, a couple being less suspicious than a man on his own.

At his first meeting with Alex, Chambers found 'Ulrich' pacing the floor to dissipate his nervous energy. 'He had taken off his jacket. I thought his expensively tailored, but many-pleated gray trousers, his sweat-soaked silk shirt, slight stoop and gait made him look a good deal like a gangster.'† He quickly understood that Alex was too much of an anarchist to abide by the rules of clandestine work and so he assumed Nadya was a communist enforcer, 'the

---

* Ulanovskaya and Ulanovskaya, *Istoria Odnoi Semyi*, 3rd edition (Inanpress 2003), pp. 47–48.
† Chambers, *Witness*, p. 211.

party's eye' on her husband.* Having cast her in that role Chambers was surprised to see that Nadya was pregnant, true communists in his eyes living only for the cause. A daughter, Maya, was born in October 1932. Alex and Nadya had left their son Lyosha in Russia with his grandmother as a guarantee that they would return home.

The relationship between Chambers and Alex changed when a senior American communist slipped Chambers a piece of paper with the name and address of a Trotskyite doctor who, he assured him, 'Ulrich' would want to 'deal with'. Given that Stalin's priority was the elimination of Trotsky's supporters at home and abroad, there was no doubt what 'deal with' meant. Unwilling to be responsible for threats against or even the death of a fellow communist, Chambers hesitated before handing the paper to Alex. When Alex read it, he looked Chambers in the eye and said: 'I don't think Uncle Joe is interested in this – he has more important things to deal with.' He crumpled up the paper and tossed it away. This act of indiscipline placed Alex at Chambers' mercy, and from that moment on Alex was 'the only Russian who was ever to become my close friend'.†

To begin with, Nadya's role was to work in a laboratory hidden at the home of a sympathiser where documents and technical drawings were photographed. She hid the microfilm in the frames of pocket mirrors for shipment to Moscow. Nadya bought the mirrors at five-and-dime stores, where the profusion of cheap goods was a source of wonder for visitors from communist Russia who back home might spend a lifetime searching for a bath plug.

* Chambers p. 213.
† Ulanovskaya and Ulanovskaya p. 49.

Unlike in China, where the couple had been unable to let their guard down day or night, life was easier for them in New York. Once on American soil they adopted the false identities of deceased Russian immigrants – producing these documents was a lucrative source of funding for the American Communist Party – and claimed to be working for the Soviet trade mission. It was no problem getting to know American communist sympathisers, whose ranks had been swelled by the Wall Street Crash of 1929.

During her two years in America Nadya appreciated the freedom that Americans enjoyed and that, unlike in Europe and China, people did not feel they had to abase themselves before the rich. Nadya was taken aback to see that the unemployed lining up outside the Depression-era soup kitchens were better dressed than her friends back in Moscow. She looked for the workers' hovels that featured so widely in Soviet propaganda, but she did not find any housing that she considered a slum. On a visit to an unemployed family, Nadya expected the wife to tell her they were too poor to buy food. But no, the woman complained she had no money to buy linoleum for the kitchen floor. The woman assumed Nadya would find it shocking that she had to wear the same coat for three years. In Russia, coats were still prized items after a decade of use.*

As she began to feel more relaxed, Nadya hatched a plan that entailed a gross breach of spycraft. America did not have a counter-espionage agency at the time and Nadya liked to say that if you wore a sign saying 'I am a spy' on Fifth Avenue, you still might not get arrested.†

* Ulanovskaya and Ulanovskaya p. 45.
† Allen Weinstein, 'Nadya: A Spy Story', *Encounter,* June 1977.

Alex was learning to drive and she suggested a practice trip to West Chester, Pennsylvania. She had failed to tell him that this town was the home of her uncle Yaakov, who had left the shtetl of Bershad in 1913 to start a new life in America. She had never told her controllers in Moscow that she had close relatives in America. This was already a serious offence, and now she was compounding it by breaking the rule that they could only meet Americans for the purpose of intelligence gathering.

As they approached West Chester, she revealed the reason she had directed him there. Alex was shocked, but eventually gave in and dropped Nadya off in the centre of town and drove back to New York alone. Searching Market Street for the address her grandmother had given her, she saw sitting on a bench two figures recognisable even after eighteen years. 'Esterka, *mein shvesterkind*! Where have you sprung from?' her uncle greeted her.

Yaakov had worked as a truck driver until he lost an eye in an accident and had then started a window-cleaning business. Nadya was happy to see that, despite the ravages of the Depression, her uncle and aunt were living in a five-room apartment with their own bathroom. They had become real Americans: they even had orange juice for breakfast. Over a chicken supper her uncle expressed his disappointment with life in America. The sons and daughters of his friends back in Russia had become doctors and engineers, while one of his sons had given up his dentistry training to work for a communist newspaper and the other was a worker heavily involved in the trade union movement. Both reproached him for taking them away from the Soviet Union.

'Should I have stayed? What do you think?' he asked his niece. She could not lie to him. 'Although you are a window cleaner you live better than our engineers. Nobody back home has orange juice for breakfast or chicken for dinner.' Her uncle's eyes widened. 'And nobody has a flat like yours. Me and Alex, we live in just one room, have no bath and share one toilet with twenty other households.' Yaakov was stunned. 'How could that be?'

That evening his two sons dropped by. They did not ask about living conditions in Moscow – in her smart clothes Nadya seemed to be living proof of a thriving Russia – and she told them what they wanted to hear. 'Our workers in Russia feel like they are masters of the country. With our blood and sweat we are constructing a beautiful edifice. We shall finish building it and then we shall have everything.' The two sons were delighted to hear this, but Nadya later regretted that she had parroted the party line. It was a missed opportunity to rescue David, the elder son, who had not yet joined the party.*

The American newspapers were reporting that Russian peasants were resisting Stalin's collectivisation of agriculture and they were slaughtering their stock rather than join the new collective farms. Nadya had dismissed these reports as anti-communist bias until she had a chance to speak to a visiting Soviet official she was showing round an American factory – at that time Russia was legally buying US-made goods in addition to the technology the spies were stealing. He told her that, far from being the success trumpeted by the party, state-enforced collectivisation was a catastrophe and untold numbers were dying of hunger in southern Russian and Ukraine, the country's breadbasket.

* Ulanovskaya and Ulanovskaya pp 52–53.

In early 1933, towards the end of their stay in New York, the loyalty of American communists was tested by Stalin's role in facilitating Hitler's rise to power in Germany. Stalin had decreed that the German communists should not work with the social democrats in fighting fascism, a policy motivated by his distrust of any leftists who were outside his control. Once in power, Hitler set about liquidating the German Communist Party, once the biggest in western Europe.

Chambers recounts that Nadya organised a party to get him drunk and force him to reveal any anti-party sentiments.* Nadya, who generally agrees with Chambers' account of their time in America, takes issue with him here, denying that she and Alex would have organised any trial by alcohol – that would have been the practice of the rougher spy chiefs who came after them. Still, there was a party, drink was taken – bootleg alcohol, as this was still prohibition time – and Chambers, who was not used to spirits, launched into a drunken rant and started a brawl. When Nadya tried to break it up, he pushed her over.† In his telling, when he woke up in the morning, he found a dishevelled Nadya sitting on a couch, refusing to speak to him. Alex, who had spent the night on the floor, spoke coldly: 'Do you know what you did last night? You denounced the party and when Maria defended it, you knocked her down. You also knocked me down.'‡ He told Chambers that when he was drunk he had accused the Soviet government of betraying the German communists,

* Chambers p. 226.
† Ulanovskaya and Ulanovskaya, p. 50.
‡ Chambers p. 227.

making Russia complicit in the murder of German comrades in Hitler's prisons.

Chambers feared Alex would liquidate him for this gross disloyalty to the party, or have him summoned to Russia to rot in jail. To his surprise, Alex came over to him and put his hand on Chambers' shoulder. 'You're all right, Bob. You're the real thing,' he said. Alex cared only that Chambers was a true revolutionary, not an apparatchik; the twists and turns of party policy meant nothing to him.

Nadya was not so forgiving. 'I believe in the saying, *in vino veritas*. If you really liked me, you wouldn't have knocked me down,' she told him. Later, Chambers recalls, Nadya told him stories, in a casual way, about communists who secretly hated the party and had betrayed their hatred in little ways that nobody noticed at the time, but eventually they had broken with the party. It seemed to Chambers that she was giving him a warning, but she could equally have been revealing something about herself.*

*

When the Ulanovskys returned to Moscow after two years in America, Nadya decided she would not accompany Alex on his next assignment. She needed to reconnect with the reality of Soviet life. She remained a convinced communist but in America, she recalled, 'My horizons expanded and my rigid principles softened.' She came across a Soviet school textbook which described the exploitation of Ford car workers. But she knew that in America cars were widely accessible and that Ford workers

* Chambers, p. 227.

received a minimum of $5 a day and one could live decently on that. Capitalism wasn't all bad.

Having joined the revolution in her teens, Nadya had never completed high school, but now back in Moscow she was determined to get an education. With the Fourth Directorate pulling strings, she enrolled in the Foreign Languages Institute.*

Alex was sent to Denmark to take charge of intelligence gathering on Germany, now that Hitler was in power and it was too dangerous to operate a Soviet spy network in Berlin. It was a delicate mission, and one that proved beyond doubt that Alex's charming dilettantism was out of sync with a world heading for war. Alex ignored advice to avoid recruiting Danish communists, who were likely to be infiltrated by the police. The Danish police bided their time until February 1935 when Alex had called together the top-level agents in his network. The police raided the meeting and arrested Alex and ten of his informants, including four of the top Soviet illegals in Europe, and a leading American lawyer.

Nadya suspected something had gone wrong when Alex failed to turn up in Moscow for a promised visit home. After weeks of hearing nothing, and with the Fourth Directorate suggesting that a letter may have gone astray, she took matters into her own hands. In the foreign languages library, the only place in Moscow where it was possible to read the foreign press, she found a Canadian paper with a brief mention of the arrest of some spies in Copenhagen. This had to be Alex's network. Armed with this information, she demanded to see the deputy director

* Ulanovskaya and Ulanovskaya p. 56.

of the Fourth Directorate. When he tried to brush her off, she rebuked him: 'How can you treat me like this?' She reminded him she was not just the wife of a *rezident* but that she herself had worked for the service for the past decade. The deputy director then adopted a fatherly tone, confirming that they were both part of the same big family. In a convoluted compliment, he reminded her that Napoleon's fortunes plummeted after he parted company with Josephine. Alex's Danish catastrophe was not quite as ruinous as Napoleon's invasion of Russia – two years after he divorced Josephine – but in intelligence terms it came pretty close.*

Alex served an eighteen-month sentence in a Danish jail, and never worked again for military intelligence abroad. He rescued the last shreds of his reputation by refusing to admit in court that he was a Soviet spy, insisting that he was an American citizen, providing as proof the passport he had fraudulently procured in New York.

\*

As Alex stepped off the train at Moscow's Leningrad station, Nadya enthused, 'You know, Stalin is a great man after all.'† Her doubts about the Soviet leader had been softened by a sense of relief that the harsh times of civil war, famine and forced collectivisation were now in the past. Alex was non-committal. 'I'm glad you think so. It will make your life easier.'

At that time Stalin was fostering a mood of optimism, famously launching a slogan in 1935: 'Life has become

---

* Ulanovskaya and Ulanovskaya p. 56.
† Ibid., p. 58.

better, comrades, life has become gayer.' He won over the intelligentsia the following year by promulgating a new constitution which promised rights and freedoms unknown anywhere in the world. But Alex remained wary of Stalin. And he was right. Life was about to get a lot darker.

In December 1936 the first of Stalin's show trials opened, with two of his leading Communist Party comrades, Grigory Zinoviev and Lev Kamenev, accused of being part of a network of spies and wreckers. They and fourteen other defendants were all sentenced to death. Despite the lurid and scarcely credible charges, Nadya convinced herself they were all guilty of treason and deserved to be executed. Even when old friends from her partisan years during the civil war gave her eyewitness reports of the disastrous consequences of collectivisation, she refused to believe them. By this time, it was widely known that many thousands of prosperous farmers – the so-called kulaks who resisted expropriation of their land – had been arrested, deported and killed, and millions of peasants had died in the ensuing famine. She told herself that these former comrades had become anti-Soviet people who exaggerated the negative.

As the year 1937 dawned, the pace of arrests speeded up and the frenzied search for 'wreckers' and 'spies' moved from the top layer of the party through mid-level bureaucrats and down to ordinary people, even the schoolmistress in the remote village where Nadya's children were spending the summer with their grandmother. Nadya was shocked to hear of the teacher's fate, but it was not until Naum Naumov-Glatman, a close friend of Alex's and a colleague from Soviet military intelligence, was expelled from the party for no apparent reason that she allowed herself to think the unthinkable. Naumov-Glatman said to Nadya: 'I want you to promise me something. If they arrest me, don't waste your time thinking of a reason. I've done nothing wrong. You must understand that they arrest people for no reason at all.' That was the last time they spoke. He was arrested in October 1937.

As she found out later, the NKVD broke his spine to get him to confess to imaginary crimes, and then shot him in March 1938. The family was told that he had been sentenced to ten years in prison 'without right of correspondence', a lie commonly used by the authorities to conceal an execution from the family. His widow Sara was sentenced to eight years in a labour camp as a wife of a traitor to the motherland.*

Now forced to confront the truth about Stalin after the arrest of their dear friend, Nadya begged her husband: 'Alex, explain to me how it has come to this?'

Alex responded calmly. 'Why is it only now that you're upset? When I told you they had shot all those White officers in the Crimea, did that bother you? When they liquidated the bourgeoisie and the kulaks, didn't you justify it? And why is it only now when it gets to us and our friends that you ask why? It's been like this from the start.'

Nadya argued back. 'I understand killing people is terrible but in the past we knew that it was necessary for the

---

* Information from Russian websites which have now become unavailable. – For more on the history of Naum Naumov-Glatman and his family: https://urokiistorii.ru/school_competition/works/aleksej-naumov-istorija-moej-semi.

revolution. But there's no explanation for what is going on now.'

Alex led her back through all the killings and deportations that she had justified on the grounds that the Soviet Union was the cradle of world revolution and the hope of mankind, and these deeds were a historical necessity. They could not avoid the question: when did it all start to go wrong? Was it when the peasants had their farms taken from them? Was it Stalin seizing power and liquidating all his rivals? Was it the untimely death of Lenin in 1924 before he had stabilised the country? Could it have been the ruthless tactics of the Red Army in the civil war? Or did they have to go still further back? Nadya was horrified by this thought, but she could see that it had long been maturing in Alex's mind, and she had finally caught up. The Bolshevik Revolution of 1917 was the root cause of the horrors that followed.

In her memoir, Nadya recalls the distress she felt at their fateful conclusion. 'My friends had died for the revolution. It was only by merest chance that I survived. My friends had killed for the revolution. It was pure accident that I had not committed murder for the cause. God saved me.'* Maya, the Ulanovskys' daughter born in the United States, recalled that her parents 'turned away in horror from the Soviet regime' in 1937. At home, she was taught to believe that the pre-Revolutionary regime had been unjust, but that 'everything that had happened in Russia (after 1917) was a gigantic error'.† This dissident

---

* Ulanovskaya and Ulanovskaya, *Istoria*, p. 60.
† Irina Kirk, *Profiles in Russian Resistance* (Quadrangle, New York, 1975), p. 259.

upbringing was to have terrible consequences for Maya in her teenage years.

*

Alex's judgment that his wife's disillusion with the Communist Party stemmed only from her friends falling victim to Stalin's purges was too harsh. There was another factor: she had unusual access to first-hand information from inside the NKVD from Naum Lerner, a childhood friend from Odessa. Impressed by her transformation from shtetl girl to well-travelled Moscow lady – and also not a little in love with her – he could not resist the temptation to boast of his own rise through the ranks to become a senior NKVD interrogator, and from time to time would reveal a juicy detail about this secret world. To keep him talking, she had to keep her emotions in check, but her interest in what he had to say, while her friends were being picked off one by one, was all-consuming. He bragged that he had interrogated Genrikh Yagoda, the former head of the secret police who was arrested in 1936 and shot. He boasted about playing chess in the Lubyanka with Nikolai Bukharin, the darling of the Communist Party moderates whom Stalin had executed in 1938.*

Relaxed and happy after spending a pleasant evening chatting to Nadya, Lerner would put on his coat and walk the short distance to the Lubyanka. There he would

---

* Lerner survived Stalin's purges and had the rare good fortune to be dismissed from the NKVD in 1940 and to rebuild his reputation as an army officer during the war. Biography here: https://nkvd.memo.ru/index.php/Лернер,_Наум_Моисеевич and https://cyclowiki.org/wiki/Наум_Моисеевич_Лернер

conduct an all-night interrogation of one of Stalin's victims
who had been forced to stand up all day and been deprived
of sleep. When one of the show trials was in progress, he
would dash off, remarking with studied casualness that he
had to coach one of the detainees to make sure he did not
deviate from his confession.

Nadya never intended to reveal to Lerner her true feelings about Stalin's rule, but one evening she could not
contain her exasperation. 'I don't believe that you lot are
exposing wreckers and spies,' she said. 'I think it's the
opposite. Enemies of the people with criminal intent are
arresting honest Soviet citizens.' Her sudden outburst
shocked him. 'How dare you say such things knowing that
I won't denounce you?'

Nadya summed up Lerner as 'a bit of a coward, petty-
minded and self-interested, but not an evil man'.* Under a
different system, she concluded, this man would have lived
an 'ordinary respectable life'. She had good reason to be
forgiving of this boastful careerist: he was her family's
guardian angel who used his position in the secret police
to protect Nadya and Alex at times of greatest danger.

Once, a colleague of Alex's in military intelligence
falsely denounced him as an Austrian spy. Lerner burst in
on the investigation and bullied the accuser into withdrawing her testimony. In 1937 Alex was hired to lecture trainee
spies of the Fourth Directorate. Never having learned to
watch his words, he told the class that the unemployed in
Denmark were better looked after than Soviet workers, his
point being that workers in the West could not be bought
just for money. One of the trainees denounced him, but

* Ulanovskaya and Ulanovskaya p. 65.

Lerner used his contacts to transfer Alex from military intelligence to a military academy to teach English. This saved Alex's life. Tucked away in an army establishment under the protection of the NKVD, he escaped Stalin's root and branch clear-out of military intelligence. Five of the department's bosses, including Alex's patron Yan Berzin, were shot between 1937 and 1939.

Nadya could not slam her door in the face of her protector, so he continued to come and drink tea with her and stroke her cat. The most shocking of Lerner's revelations came after he and some of his Moscow colleagues had been sent to Leningrad to replace an NKVD team that had been arrested and then thrown into the same meat grinder they had been stuffing so loyally. 'I couldn't do what they asked me to do,' he told Nadya on his return from Leningrad. 'How was I to make four thousand arrests? They had already shot all the political prisoners from the Tsarist era and arrested all the Latvians [who had played a big role in the Revolution but were now suspect in Stalin's eyes].' Nadya hung on to his every word. Until then she had not understood why people were taken. Now it was clear. Just as in any other Soviet institution, there was a target to meet.* The Kremlin would impose a quota of arrests on the regional authorities throughout the USSR and indicate which social or ethnic groups were scheduled for punishment. It was up to the local officials to decide how to meet these quotas and place the appropriate label – kulaks, spies, saboteurs, anti-social elements – on those executed or sent to forced labour camps.

As Nadya was losing her faith in communism, in

---

* Ibid., p. 64.

America Whittaker Chambers was plotting how to escape from the party he had devoted thirteen years of his life to. By 1938 Chambers had risen from courier for an industrial espionage outfit to become the lynchpin of a Washington spy network that was extracting high-grade intelligence from the heart of the US government.

But Chambers had had enough. He was shocked at Stalin's murderous Great Purge and the dictator's paranoid pursuit of Trotskyites around the world. When three of his comrades disappeared in suspicious circumstances and Chambers heard that he too was suspected of Trotskyism, he fled Washington with his wife and two children.* In April 1938 he delivered his last consignment of microfilmed documents and fled with his family to Florida. He cut off all contact with the Communist Party and its underground network, making sure his controller knew that, if they killed him, there was enough evidence in a bank safe deposit to blow the whole spy network into the open.

A year later, in August 1939, he was stunned by the news that Stalin and Hitler had agreed on a non-aggression pact – and then proceeded to divide Poland between them. Now that Hitler and Stalin were allies in this 'gangster pact', the intelligence Chambers had been collecting could end up being read by Hitler himself. Chambers asked for a meeting with Adolf Berle, US assistant secretary of state and Roosevelt's intelligence liaison. Within days he was sitting on the lawn in Berle's garden, a cool wind freshening the Washington night air, reeling off the names of communist agents in the US government and media. As

---

* Sam Tanenhaus, *Whittaker Chambers: An Un-American Life* (Old Street Publishing, 2007), p. 136.

soon as Chambers left, Berle went to his study and typed up a four-page memo with the names of highly placed communist agents. Berle was unsure what to do with the list. His immediate concern was that revealing the extent of communist penetration of the administration would destroy public trust in Roosevelt even as the president might have to call on the American people to fight an unpopular war.*

Chambers was careful not to divulge to Berle that he himself had spied for the Russians. Such an admission could result in a twenty-year jail sentence for espionage. While certain he was doing the right thing, it still pained him that after so many years as a loyal communist he had now become an informer. To his old comrades, this was the lowest level to which a party member could sink.

For Chambers, it was a difficult decision, but the course of action he had to take was clear. For Nadya in Moscow, having reached her own fateful conclusion, it was not clear what steps she could take and remain alive.

* Chambers p. 318.

# 15

## Summer 1942: Mr and
## Mrs Russia at home

In the summer of 1942 Nadya was granted two weeks off from her work at the Metropol to travel to the Urals to visit her husband in hospital and her children in the remote village of Uzhovka, where they had been evacuated with their grandmother. For months since the start of the war, Nadya had heard nothing from Alex. Desperate for news of him, she went to the flat in a military settlement where they had lived before the war but found no letters from Alex there. The commandant showed her to a room with the floor piled high with undelivered mail. She got down on her knees and sifted through the heap of letters until she found a postcard from Alex several months old saying that he had been wounded in November and was in a military hospital in Sverdlovsk in the Urals.

Before setting out on her journey she stocked up with food as well as bottles of spirits and packets of cigarettes from the foreigners' store. She found Alex seriously wounded in the thigh but still in good spirits and cheering up everyone around him. Alex was enthusiastically exercising his leg and vowing to get the better of the doctors, who predicted he would never return to active service.

After three days with Alex, Nadya continued her journey to Uzhovka. The train took her only as far as the city of Chelyabinsk, where she arrived in the middle of the night. The village was twenty kilometres away, so she lit up a cigarette and waited for someone to respond. Soon enough a peasant with a horse and cart appeared, and he agreed to take her to Uzhovka in exchange for a bottle of vodka. As dawn broke she opened her eyes to see that the cart was passing through ruins which reminded her of the villages blown up by the retreating Germans.

'What happened here? Why has this village been destroyed?'

The cart driver answered with one word. 'Collectivisation.'

She was horrified to find her children so dirty that they were in danger of catching typhus, the louse-born disease that had almost killed her during the civil war. She gave her mother the precious supply of soap she had brought from Moscow.*

In the recollections recorded by her daughter Maya, Nadya does not say how she felt about seeing her children again, or indeed which of her three were there, or how they greeted her. It must have been Maya and the youngest, Irina, with the boy Lyosha already mobilised for war. Lyosha was killed in battle in 1943, while Irina died after the war due to a medical mishap. Neither of these tragic events appears in Nadya's recollections: she saw her life story not in personal terms but through the lens of the politics of the twentieth century.†

On her return to Moscow Nadya started working for

* Nadezhda Ulanovskaya and Maya Ulanovskaya, *Istoria Odnoi Semyi*, 3rd edition, (Inanpress, 2013) p. 84.
† Conversation with Alexander Yakubovsky, July 2022.

the newly arrived Australian Godfrey Blunden, an ambitious roving reporter of the Sydney *Daily Telegraph* – no connection with the similarly named British paper – whose despatches were syndicated in the *London Evening Standard*. In the words of Fay Anderson, an academic expert on Australian war reporting, he was part of a group of ambitious Australian journalists – most notably Alan Moorehead, who later became a successful author of popular histories – who established their reputations in Europe during the war. He was 'particularly intrigued' by Russia and fully aware of the journalistic and literary value of the fourteen months he spent in Moscow.*

Blunden had applied to come to Moscow immediately after Hitler's invasion. He had ambitions beyond filling newspaper columns – in 1935 he had published a novel, *No More Reality*, about an Australian country town, and he arrived in Moscow ready to immerse himself in a story as grand and expansive as the country itself.

In Moscow, Blunden needed to fill his notebook and required an enabler who trusted him enough to share the secrets that the Kremlin had hidden since Stalin's rise to power. Luckily for him, Nadya was available for work. By 1942 her disillusion with Stalin's implementation of the communist ideal was complete. The dreary perusal of the Soviet newspapers every morning soon led to frank conversations between Nadya and Blunden. At last, Nadya had found a correspondent who was on her wavelength.

A spirit of rebellion was brewing among the journalists

* Email from Fay Anderson, co-author of *Witnesses to War: The History of Australian Conflict Reporting* (Melbourne University Publishing, 2011).

in the Metropol. Except for the minority of convinced Stalinists, they could see that their dream posting had been a mirage – all they were allowed to write was 'toothpicked' from the propaganda-heavy Soviet newspapers. They blamed Palgunov, the eternally unhelpful head of the Press Department, for preventing them from witnessing any front-line action and imposing a censorship regime so strict that it banned any news, however trivial, that was not 'official'.

The journalists' anger boiled over when they were invited to meet a poet, Vera Inber, who had been flown out of Leningrad and would tell them the truth about the conditions in the Nazi-besieged city. Of all the stories the journalists were not allowed to report, by far the biggest was the blockade of the old imperial capital. The journalists knew that the Nazis were starving the population to death, bodies were piling up in the streets and there were rumours of cannibalism. Excited that they would at last be able to tell the full story of the Leningraders' struggle to survive, the journalists packed the press room to hear Inber speak. She read from a prepared text with Nadya translating: in a cheerful voice she assured the press that life in the besieged city was continuing normally, the theatres were open and mothers cooked dinner – modest ones – for their children.

When Inber had finished, one journalist asked what the bread ration was. Flustered, she mumbled, 'I don't remember exactly. But it's enough.'*

There were mutters of disbelief. Paul Winterton, the correspondent of the *News Chronicle* and the BBC, rose to

* Ulanovskaya and Ulanovskaya, *Istoria*, p. 85.

ask why they had been summoned to hear Inber's lies. 'Madam Inber says she does not remember the size of the bread ration. If I had to endure such a siege, I would remember that until my dying day.' The journalists bombarded her with new questions, and she left the briefing room in tears.

Nadya recalls this briefing as the most shameful incident during her time at the Metropol. The journalists wanted to know why Inber had been chosen for the task. It was a typical story of Stalin's Russia. She was a second cousin of Leon Trotsky, all of whose relatives were confined to the Gulag on the Stalinist principle of family guilt by association. Only Inber had avoided that fate, thanks to her output of patriotic verse in praise of Stalin. Even in her diary – which she knew could be read by the NKVD – she adopted a tone of undying loyalty. 'There is something irresistible about Stalin's voice,' she wrote after hearing him speak on the radio. 'You can feel from the sound of it that its owner knows everything, that he will never be a hypocrite.'*

In the hope of undermining Palgunov, the journalists arranged a briefing with his boss, Alexander Shcherbakov, the head of the Sovinformburo, who never usually spoke to foreign journalists. When Shcherbakov, an imposing figure in high boots and a capacious army field shirt hiding his huge belly, arrived for the press briefing, the journalists launched into their complaints – they could not travel anywhere, they never got close to the front and the censors' blue pencil struck out any information of interest to their readers. The Kremlin was throwing away a chance

---

* Vera Inber, *Leningrad Diary* (St Martin's Press, London, 1971), p. 117.

to show the human side of the Russian people in their struggle against Nazism.

Shcherbakov waved a hand to cut them short – 'And when will you open a second front?' This silenced the journalists. Stalin had been using this line to embarrass his allies since Roosevelt had recklessly promised to launch an amphibious assault on German-occupied France in 1942, an operation that Churchill knew was beyond the Allies' capacity for at least two more years. As long as the Russians were fighting the Wehrmacht alone in Europe, and dying in their hundreds of thousands, while the British army was defending its empire in a sideshow in North Africa, raising the question of when the 'second front' would be launched in Europe was a sure-fire way of asserting Soviet moral superiority. The journalists' bravado seeped away and they began asking for small favours, all of which Shcherbakov dismissed crudely. As Nadya recalls, the journalists left the room with their tails between their legs and Palgunov's position enhanced.*

Palgunov knew what he was doing. In 1944 he was rewarded with one of the top jobs in Soviet journalism, director-general of the TASS news agency, which he kept for sixteen years. Once elevated from bag carrier to boss, he set out his ideas on the organising principle of Soviet journalism, the first of which was to know what to leave out. 'News must be organised, or else it is news of mere events and happenstance,' he said in a 1955 lecture. 'News is agitation through facts. In selecting the news topic, the writer of the news story must proceed above all from the realisation that not all facts, and not just any event,

* Ulanovskaya and Ulanovskaya p. 84.

should be reported in the press.'* The facts and events that Palgunov believed should be ignored covered just about everything that the foreign journalists considered newsworthy.

The disappointed journalists grumbled among themselves about Palgunov's intransigence and spent their time rehearsing the insults they would deliver to him on leaving Russia. As he did not speak English the insults had to be delivered through the quavering voice of a translator. Edgar Snow called him a 'liar, hypocrite, defeatist, obstructionist and outstanding saboteur of Soviet-American friendship' who was doing more harm to Russia than Goebbels.† Sulzberger addressed Palgunov in French – the Soviet official had been a TASS correspondent in Paris – and called him *'espèce de morpion mécanique'* – a mechanical crab or pubic louse. History does not record whether Palgunov's experience of Parisian lowlife had acquainted him with this insect.‡

Blunden decided not to waste his energies on fighting the Press Department but to work within its restrictions. What was most important was to get to the front line, or as close as he was allowed. Even if the news from the front was late and the copy lacked vivid characters, a competent journalist could still turn the thin gruel of a guided tour into a feast.

---

* Leo Gruliow, 'The Soviet Press: "Propagandist, Agitator, Organizer"', *Journal of International Affairs*, Vol. 10, No. 2, *The Press in World Affairs* (1956), pp. 153–69.

† Edgar Snow, *Journey to the Beginning* (Random House, 1958), Chapter 12.

‡ Cyrus Sulzberger, *A Long Row of Candles: Memoirs and Diaries, 1934–1954*, London 1969, p. 213.

In an article published on 8 May 1942, Blunden warned his readers, in a roundabout way that would pass the censor, that they could not expect front-line coverage from him – or from any other journalist in Moscow. Nadya arranged an interview with David Ortenberg, editor of *Red Star*, the army newspaper, who jealously guarded his right to publish original news from the front, some of which had the flavour of battle. Under the headline 'Soviet Reporters Die for News', Blunden painted a portrait of a newspaper unlike any other in wartime. Its reports were largely written by serving military officers and men, not by professional journalists, and any correspondents embedded with the Red Army had to fight, and sometimes die, with the soldiers they were reporting on. Ortenberg had lost fourteen of his correspondents in battle, including two of his best writers, and one had committed suicide to avoid capture. 'We know that the enemy will have no mercy on those who shape ideology,' Ortenberg explained.

Borrowing a technique from *Pravda*, where the key information was often to be found in the last two paragraphs, Blunden addressed his readers at the end of the article: 'That's *Red Star* for you, surely a newspaper unique in the world of newspapers, whose reporters you have been reading for 10 months, whether you knew it or not, for *Red Star* covers almost exclusively the greatest war front in history.' If his readers cared to read between the lines, he was revealing to them that all war reporting from Moscow was second- or third-hand even if it appeared to be eyewitness copy.*

* *Daily Telegraph* (Sydney), 8 May 1942. Blunden's articles can be found at the National Library of Australia website: https://trove. nla.gov.au/newspaper/

Having surreptitiously apprised his readers of the censorship regime he was working under, Blunden felt able to mine rare nuggets from the Soviet press and embellish them in the lively style his newspaper required. Sometimes he slipped in a detail that the censors were keen to hide, such as a clue to the size of the bread ration in besieged Leningrad. In September 1942 he reported that Leningraders were living off 'one slice of inferior bread a day'.* (In the winter of 1941–42 the ration went down to 125 grams of rye bread, of which half was fillers with little or no nutritional value.)

At other times, his desire to play Palgunov's game led to headlines that were plainly misleading. One of his first articles, 'Plenty to buy in Moscow – clothing, foodstuffs efficiently rationed', beggars belief. It was impossible for a newly arrived correspondent to gauge the availability of goods in Moscow – reporters were forbidden to visit TSUM, the department store a five-minute walk from the Metropol, without permission from the Press Department.

The rationing system was indeed efficient – but only in the sense of feeding those whose labour was deemed vital to the war effort, such as workers in arms factories and privileged sectors such as Communist Party officials and, indeed, foreign journalists. If you were not capable of doing hard labour or fortunate enough to be a member of the elite, you were eternally hungry, with a ration of 400 grams of bread a day, but unable to afford the high prices in the market where the peasants sold milk and butter

* Leningrad Faces New Winter of Siege, *Daily Telegraph* (Sydney), 17 September 1942

from their private plots. Some peasants amassed piles of cash, but there were no goods to spend it on – nothing was being produced except what the army needed. Hungry city dwellers could barter an upright piano with a peasant for a sack of grain, but grand pianos were of no value – too big to fit in a peasant home.

On 10 July, Blunden reassured his readers that Muscovites were not dismayed at the 1,000-kilometre retreat of the Red Army from Russia's borders to the banks of the Volga. The Russians, he said, were 'playing the old game of letting the enemy stick out his neck'.* In reality there was a dangerous crisis of morale in the Red Army. Vasily Grossman, one of *Red Star*'s correspondents, wrote in his novel *Stalingrad* that the army was in the grip of a 'psychology of retreat'. Soldiers were euphoric when allowed to climb out of their foxholes and escape the onslaught of German tanks and aircraft.

'The retreat had developed its customs and routines; it had become a way of life. Army tailors, bakeries, food shops and canteens had all now adapted to it. Men thought they could keep retreating, yet carry on with all their usual activities. They could work, eat, chase after women, listen to the gramophone, get promoted, go on leave, or send packages of sugar and tinned food back to their families in the rear. But soon they would be on the edge of the abyss.'†

With the Nazis bearing down on Stalingrad, the loss of which would seal the fate of Stalin's regime, Grossman describes one of his journalistic colleagues cadging a tyre

---

* No Pessimism in Russian Retreats, *Daily Telegraph* (Sydney), 10 July 1942
† Vasily Grossman, *Stalingrad* (Vintage Classic, London, 2020), p. 336.

inner tube to help him to float to safety across the Volga when the battle was lost.

Stalin was all too aware of the defeatist mood, and on 28 July 1942 issued Order No. 227 demanding 'panic mongers and cowards' be liquidated on the spot. 'Not one step back without orders from higher headquarters! Commanders . . . who abandon a position without an order from higher headquarters are traitors to the Motherland.' From then on, 'not one step back' would become the defining slogan of Stalin's war.

Nadya obtained permission for her husband to continue his recuperation in Moscow and he joined her in her room at the Metropol. Alex and Blunden got on well. On New Year's Eve Blunden turned down an invitation to an embassy party, choosing instead to see in 1943 in the company of Nadya and Alex. First they went to the theatre together and then returned separately to the Metropol where Blunden joined them later in their room. They sat talking well into the night, Alex regaling Blunden with tales of his exploits in the civil war when he had repeatedly outwitted the White officers. Blunden, keen to find out the truth about Stalin's elimination of his Communist Party rivals in the Great Purge of the 1930s, had brought with him a weighty tome, *Soviet Communism: A New Civilisation* by Sidney and Beatrice Webb. This was the fellow travellers' bible, published in 1935 before Stalin had cemented his hold on power, and recently re-issued in Britain. 'Let's see how many senior Bolsheviks in this book perished in the purges.'*

Blunden ran his pencil down the index of the Webbs'

---

* Ulanovskaya and Ulanovskaya p. 75

book, reading out each name, with Alex and Nadya interrupting him whenever they recognised a purge victim. He put a tick by the names of sixteen of the top leadership who had been executed, four who had committed suicide while under threat of arrest, and two including Trotsky who had been assassinated by Soviet hit squads. Nadya revealed that not just the party elite but millions of ordinary Soviet citizens, even down to village schoolteachers, had been executed or sent to labour camps. There was no mention of this in the Webbs' account of Stalin's Russia. Bizarrely, the Webbs described 'Iron Felix' Dzerzhinsky, the ruthless founder of the Soviet secret police and architect of the post-Revolution Red Terror, as a humanitarian who devoted himself to caring for homeless children.

When Blunden returned to his room in the Metropol it was past 3 a.m. He did not go straight to bed. He took out of his pocket a notebook, and wrote every detail of Alex's civil war memories and Nadya's revelations.

*

The end of 1942 marked a turning point in the war. Nadya's grim description of provincial Russia – a deindustrialised society reliant on horse and cart with a currency the peasants had no use for – told only half the story. In the year since the Soviet Union's most advanced factories had been dismantled and dumped in the snows of Siberia and the Urals, a miracle had taken place. The factories had been rebuilt, staffed by starving women, first producing arms of questionable quality but soon churning out tanks in quantities that would overwhelm the German army. By the end of 1942 only fifty-five out of 1,500 major factories moved to the east were still idle. In the second half of 1942 the Soviet economy produced over 13,000 tanks and 15,000 aircraft, at the price of scrapping almost all civilian production.*

Stalin's order of 'not one step back' was enforced rigorously – and at huge cost in Soviet lives – to defend the Red Army's toehold in Stalingrad on the west bank of the Volga. During the winter of 1942 all available soldiers, even the cooks mentioned by Grossman, were moved across the frozen river under German fire to reinforce the hard-pressed defenders. Most of these raw recruits were killed before they reached the front line. The Red Army kept its toehold.

The Sixth Army of General Friedrich von Paulus was now struggling too: progress in gaining control of the bombed-out city where the defenders were hiding in every basement and refusing to surrender was painfully slow. Most significantly for the outcome of the battle, Stalin's acute sense of self-interest at times of great danger forced him to abandon his pretence of being a strategic genius and to delegate war planning to the professionals. On 19 November, Soviet General Georgy Zhukov launched Operation Uranus, a brilliantly conceived, masterfully concealed and fully resourced pincer movement to encircle Paulus's troops. The five-month battle of Stalingrad was entering its decisive phase.

After so many months of retreats, spirits rose in Moscow and the journalists at the Metropol were excited at the prospect of visiting a battlefield where the tide of war had turned. As a second-ranking journalist Blunden was not on the list. Nadya understood this was a catastrophe for him, and she pulled every string until the Press Department got him

* Richard Overy, *Russia's War* (Penguin, 2010), p. 171.

on the trip. As she recalls, half in jest, what she did for Blunden in January 1943 justified what happened to her later.

In the second week of January Blunden was taken on a 2,000-mile trip to the outskirts of Stalingrad to interview General Malinovsky, who had inflicted the first large-scale defeat on a German tank army. In February, after the German surrender, Blunden met the defeated General von Paulus, a nervous wreck who had defied Hitler's invitation to commit suicide rather than surrender, and interviewed the victorious Soviet generals Chuikov and Rodimtsev. The articles he wrote from Stalingrad made his reputation as a war correspondent. There was more to come. In March he followed the Red Army to the city of Kharkov, the former capital of Ukraine and the first major European city to be liberated from the Nazis.

In a powerful 2,000-word despatch from Kharkov, titled 'Nazis Used Ukraine as a Slave State', Blunden focused on the Nazi massacre of the Jews, a topic not previously documented by foreign journalists in Russia. 'The first thing the Germans did on entering Kharkov was to announce a "Crusade" against Jews and communists,' he wrote. They began by shooting or hanging prominent people whose Soviet identity cards showed them to be Jewish. Then they rounded up all the Jewish women and children and drove them to a camp outside the city: 'Two days after being sent to the camp, they were made to dig ditches. Then a company of SS men with sub-machineguns shot them all, making them stand in the trenches they had dug so that they fell into their own graves. The Soviet authorities at Kharkov today estimate that 15,000 were killed in this way.'*

* *Daily Telegraph* (Sydney), 4 March 1943.

The Nazi genocide of the Jews was no secret to the Red Army soldiers as they pushed westwards, and Vasily Grossman, then a front-line war correspondent for *Red Star*, wrote a searing essay in 1943 entitled 'Ukraine Without Jews'. It was blocked by the military censor (though a version appeared in Yiddish) because Stalin had decreed that all Soviet nationalities were equally victims of Nazism, and the Jews should not be singled out for special mention. Stalin's own anti-Semitism manifested itself in his postwar campaign against 'rootless cosmopolitans'.

In their reports from Kharkov, neither *The Times* of London nor the *New York Times* focused on the annihilation of the city's Jewish population, the latter paper printing a short piece by the United Press agency playing down the anti-Semitic element of the Nazi occupation and mentioning only that some 'eminent professors' had been shot or hanged because of their Jewish origin or their refusal to collaborate. Cholerton, the *Telegraph* correspondent with many years of experience in second-guessing the censors, also reported on the massacre of the Jews of Kharkov, but his story relegated this Nazi genocide of the Jews to the end of a long piece, and the language used was less forthright than Blunden's.*

This is not to say that the reporters in Kharkov were free to report everything they saw and heard. None was able to mention a startling sign of the ferocity with which Stalin had begun crushing the Ukrainian nationalists, who were bitterly opposed to the reimposition of Soviet rule. In his diary, Edgar Snow records that the Press Department censors briefed the journalists on the Nazis' reign of terror

* 'Kharkov's 15 months of Nazi Persecution', *Daily Telegraph* (London), 1 March 1943.

in Kharkov and then led them to the Gestapo prison to view its 'horror chambers' where thousands of Ukrainians were tortured and killed. To the journalists' surprise, they heard disturbing noises coming from inside the prison, and there were weeping women outside. The censors had made a big mistake. The building had indeed been the Gestapo headquarters but it had been taken over by the Ukrainian branch of the NKVD, who were using their cellars to torture and shoot suspected Ukrainian nationalists. The correspondents were moved speedily on.*

A sanitised reference to this incident is included in Alexander Werth's 1964 book, *Russia at War*, where he mentions archly that the return of the Russians was not 'an occasion for unanimous rejoicing in Kharkov.'† He saw large letter boxes on the street for posting anonymous denunciations – which he noted provided plenty of scope for ugly vendettas – and witnessed civilian prisoners being escorted by the NKVD into the torture chambers only recently vacated by the Gestapo. Not surprisingly, nothing so sensational could ever pass the Soviet censor in wartime.

Blunden received accolades from far and wide for his hard-hitting reports from Stalingrad and Kharkov. Michael Foot, editor of the *London Evening Standard*, later to become leader of the British Labour Party, used Blunden's interview with a 'swaggering' German prisoner of war to warn the British public against complacency that Hitler was about to surrender.‡

* Papers of Edgar Snow, Book 40, p. 244a.
† Alexander Werth, *Russia at War 1941–45* (Barrie and Rockliff, London, 1964), p. 616.
‡ Reproduced in the *Daily Telegraph* (Sydney), 27 January 1943, https://trove.nla.gov.au/

The months Blunden had spent sitting beside Nadya while she translated the newspapers bore fruit when his Australian paper turned over its news pages to Blunden's answers to readers' questions about every aspect of Soviet life, from Stalin's plans for Poland to the food served at the Metropol and how it compared with ordinary people's rations. Relaxing the rule against publishing praise from readers, the paper printed a letter from Margaret Senior in Coffs Harbour, New South Wales. She asked why no word from readers ever appeared in praise of Godfrey Blunden's journalism which, she wrote, ranked easily with the despatches from the most famous Allied 'ace correspondents'. The 'purple patches' of these aces were never more vivid than Blunden's 'bald yet sensitive descriptions of men and things seen, facts pertinently marshalled, and opinions soberly deduced'. In a line that would surely have made the would-be novelist's day, she concluded that in wartime 'it is the war correspondents who fill the gap in contemporary literature, even through the filter of world censorship'.*

Blunden had one last request to make of Nadya before he left Moscow to cover the liberation of western Europe by the US army. 'Nadya, you've done so much for me already, but I have another favour to ask you. I've never visited a Russian home. Can you help me with this?'

This was a huge favour to ask of her. This was the kind of feature that a British or Australian trainee reporter would be asked to do, but correspondents could spend years in the Metropol without ever visiting an ordinary Russian home. Nadya had once organised such a trip

* *Daily Telegraph* (Sydney), 26 May 1943.

through the press department for the *Daily Express* correspondent Paul Holt, the grandson of a weaver who wanted to see how the family of a Moscow weaver lived. It took almost a year for the Press Department to find a suitable family for him to visit, and Nadya accompanied him as his interpreter. They were greeted at the door by a smiling woman who, as she showed them around, declared that it was only under Soviet rule that she could live in such a flat, which, to Nadya's astonishment, had three generously proportioned rooms. The illusion of luxury collapsed when, on further questioning, the weaver woman revealed that it was not just her and her family living there. She shared with eight people who just happened to be absent that day. The secret of how ordinary Russians really lived remained intact.*

Nadya warned Blunden that Soviet citizens who welcomed a foreigner into their home risked losing their freedom. She thought long and hard about who to approach. In the end she asked her friend Rakhil Afanasyevna, a widow who often came to Nadya's room at the Metropol to have a hot bath. Rakhil agreed on condition that the foreigner should come in secret and no one else would know. Despite their cramped living quarters and sharing a hallway, a kitchen and a toilet, people in Moscow's communal apartments had learned to preserve a measure of privacy away from the prying eyes of the other residents.

Rakhil and her childhood friend Lidia Romanovna shared one room in a communal apartment near Smolenskaya Square in central Moscow, overlooking the route on

* Ulanovskaya and Ulanovskaya p. 81.

which Stalin's motorcade was regularly seen speeding between the Kremlin and the marshal's dacha. The day before, Nadya went to the foreigners' store to buy food and drink and delivered it to Rakhil so she would have something to offer her guest.

On the appointed evening Nadya, dressed in her beaver coat, stood just inside the entrance of the Revolution Square metro station, scrutinising the faces of the people coming into the light from the blackout. She was pleased when a figure appeared, dressed in the shabby overcoat she had bought him in the commission shop and with a fur hat pulled down over his ears. The disguise was let down by his shoes, which looked too smart, even with a covering of snow. Greeting Nadya with a silent smile, Blunden followed her down the escalator and onto a crowded train. It was only two stops to their destination. Unused to the ways of the Moscow metro, Blunden failed to push his way to the door in time and found himself struggling to get out against the tide of passengers forcing their way into the carriage. By using his elbows, he managed to thrust himself out onto the platform before the doors slammed together with a great crash. Once outside in the blackout, they walked together without speaking. People brushed past them, but their footsteps made no sound on the fresh snow. They turned into a side street, and she led him into a doorway. She put a finger to her lips. She was waiting to see if they were being followed. She lit a cigarette and when she had finished they crossed the street and pulled open a heavy door. They went from the gloom of the blacked-out street into total darkness and were hit by the pungent smell of Russian tobacco and damp. They felt their way up one flight of stairs and Nadya banged on a door while Blunden lurked against the wall. She called out and an old woman's voice answered. The door opened and a beam of light sliced the darkness. After ensuring the old woman had gone back to her room, Nadya beckoned Blunden inside and led him along a long corridor and into a small room.

The room was tiny, just twelve square metres. There was a single bed with an embroidered coverlet, which the women shared, and a small table, two chairs and a little wood-burning stove against the wall. A fold-up bed in one corner had been used by Rakhil's son when he was living with them. Nadya was impressed by how graciously the two women received their guests and how beautifully the food was presented, on a white tablecloth with each guest handed a folded napkin. Blunden understood that they had once lived a very different life. With Nadya interpreting, Rakhil and Lidia took turns to relate the story of their lives. Rakhil's husband had been a wealthy Siberian fur trader. In the early 1930s he was arrested as one of the 'former people' and disappeared into the gulag. Rakhil moved to this tiny room where she brought up her son and supported them both by making hats. Her son had graduated from the Institute of Foreign Languages and was working as a teacher when he was arrested in 1941, and she had not heard of him since. All she wanted now was to be left in peace. Lidia's husband, a prominent lawyer, had also been arrested in the 1930s for his bourgeois origins. She was of noble ancestry and supported herself by knitting sweaters and making buttons to sell at the market. Conversation flowed until Blunden and Nadya had to leave before the midnight curfew.*

* Ulanovskaya and Ulanovskaya p. 78.

Now Blunden had everything he needed to write a book on Russia and, weakened by chronic dysentery, he was ready to leave. As Nadya said goodbye, she reminded him, 'Don't forget that this book you are writing could have bad consequences for us Russians.'

'There's no need to be afraid, Nadya. It's going to be a novel.'

# 16

## *October 1942: Prisoner of the Metropol*

Ronald Matthews had arrived in Moscow with a bag full of soap which, a fellow Englishman in Tehran had assured him, could secure the favours of any Russian woman. At the end of Tanya's second day of work, Matthews offered her a bar of soap and asked if she would like to have a bath. For months there had been no hot water in her flat, and washing meant standing at a basin and splashing cold water on her face and neck. It was bliss to step into the hot bath and wash herself with scented foreign soap. When she finally emerged from the bathroom, he asked her if she wanted to take the soap home with her and she gratefully accepted. The next day another bar of soap was produced, she had another luxurious bath and took the second bar home with her. This was repeated for six days. On the seventh day, as they were drinking tea and going through the afternoon papers, Matthews got up, walked over to her chair and dropped on one knee.

'Tanya, I have never met a girl like you . . . I've got a set of false teeth . . . and I want to have a son as soon as possible . . . Will you share the life of a modest writer and moderately successful journalist? Will you be my wife?'

'It's a little sudden . . . Ronald,' Tanya said, using his Christian name for the first time.

Matthews kissed her hand, returned to his chair and Tanya resumed translating the article about Ukrainian partisans.*

Two months later, Ronald Matthews stood waiting in the lobby wearing his freshly pressed British war correspondent's uniform. His gaze was fixed on the staircase which wound round the gilded mesh of the lift shaft. His habitually stern features broke into a smile at the sound of footsteps tripping down the threadbare carpet on the marble stairs. He had travelled the world and he had never met anyone like Tanya, and today she was to become his wife. When Tanya reached the bottom of the stairs, she stood up on tiptoe and reached up to give her English bear a big kiss.

Tanya had arrived at the Metropol early that morning and gone straight up to Marjorie Shaw's room. Shaw, the *Daily Mirror* correspondent, who was one of the few female reporters in Moscow at the time, had promised to lend her a blue-green silk dress for the day, and when she saw Tanya had nothing to keep her warm, she pressed on her a smart coat and, as a wedding gift, a box of fine French powder. The effect of this borrowed ensemble was marred only by Tanya's shapeless old Soviet shoes.

Paul Holt, the *Express* correspondent, and Tanya's friend Irina, the Russian-American wife of a US naval commander, were the first of the wedding party to join Matthews and Tanya in the lobby. The American Edgar Snow arrived carrying a couple of onions by their stalks which he had just cadged off a waiter. 'These two will keep me going for a couple of days,' he said by way of explanation. Snow was

* Tanya Matthews, *Russian Child and Russian Wife* (Gollancz, 1949) p. 284.

convinced he had scurvy from the lack of vegetables in the Metropol diet and feared losing his teeth. Marjorie appeared wearing a black coat with astrakhan trim. Tanya thought how wealthy she must be to have two coats.

As the party walked to the trolley-bus stop, Tanya noticed how the propaganda posters had changed over the past year. No longer were people being asked to 'strangle the Nazi viper'. Now the posters featured military heroes from Russia's imperial past – Kutuzov, Suvorov and Prince Alexander Nevsky – calling on the people to defend Mother Russia as they had done in centuries past. As the party pushed their way onto the bus, there were murmurs of '*inostrantsy*' – foreigners. Matthews, clumsy and not used to travelling on buses, knocked a woman's hat off. People could be heard exclaiming '*nekulturny*' – uncultured; and then muttering '*Gde vtoroi front?*' – Where is the second front? Tanya was about to assure the passengers that the second front would be launched within months, but something held her back. She realised that her borrowed finery had put a barrier between her and her people, the ones on the bus in their drab clothes, carrying crusts of bread in cloth bundles. Earlier that morning, on the tram to the Metropol dressed in her shabby coat, she had been Tanya from provincial Grozny. Now, on the trolley bus to the register office, in the eyes of her compatriots she had become a foreigner, even before she had signed the marriage register.

The ceremony was due to take place in a new red-brick building. They passed through a dark corridor into a small room where a little bespectacled woman in a heavy overcoat sat under a bas-relief depicting Stalin smiling down at a little girl handing him a bunch of flowers. Released from the artificial world of the Metropol, Snow and Holt appeared to have forgotten they were witnesses at a wedding. Holt gazed round the room, trying to decipher the signs in Russian on the walls, and Snow was busily writing in his notebook. Only the two women behaved with appropriate solemnity for the occasion. Tanya handed over three documents: her and Ronald Matthews' passports and a pink slip he had received at the Russian border. The registrar had Matthews down as 'Matsy Ronal' and asked Tanya if she wanted to change her name to Mrs Ronal, and Tanya saw to her dismay that the pink slip had her future husband's names in the wrong order.* This could be the excuse the bureaucrat was looking for to call the marriage off. Tanya pointed to the surname in the British passport and to her relief, the registrar addressed her: 'Citizen Matthews – sign your name here.' With the paperwork completed, the unsmiling bureaucrat became more human. She picked up the documents and handed them back to Tanya with a faint smile. 'Congratulations, maybe your son will grow up in time to open the second front.' Snow's ears pricked up. 'What did she say about the *vtoroi front?*' he asked the bride. Tanya interpreted, and Snow scribbled in his notebook. Finally, it was time for the witnesses to kiss the bride and shake the groom's hand. Outside the register office, Matthews said, 'I think the occasion calls for a little celebration. Besides I feel quite thirsty.'†

They walked to the only bar open in wartime Moscow, the Cocktail Hall on Gorky Street. There was a long queue outside and every so often one or two people would emerge

* Papers of Edgar Snow, Book 40, 1942-43, p. 39.
† Tanya Matthews, *Russian Wife Goes West* (Gollancz, London 1955), pp. 8–12.

and the doorman would allow the same number inside. Foreigners were entitled to jump the queue, and soon enough the doorman ushered them in. The Cocktail Hall, with its décor of dark wood and chromium and long bar fitted with high stools, had been built in the late 1930s when Stalin was turning Moscow into a showcase of Communist Party rule. Silence reigned, with the clientele – a mixture of shabbily dressed civilians and officers in uniform – downing their cocktails and ordering another until the doorman decided they had had enough and turned them out into the cold street. The wedding party ordered six of the cocktail du jour – the Taran, or tail-rammer, in honour of a Soviet fighter ace who, having run out of ammunition, sliced off the tails of German planes by ramming them. He was reputed to have survived this desperate manoeuvre twice and parachuted to safety. The cocktail was pink and tasted of vodka.

Irina raised her glass and shouted '*Gorko*' and Tanya leaped up and kissed her new husband. He looked bewildered but all the drinkers in the bar were soon raising their glasses and shouting '*Gorko*', which obliged her to keep kissing him. *Gorko* means 'bitter', and it is a Russian tradition to force newly-weds to kiss to make life sweeter. By the time they left, all the dour drinkers were smiling at them, and even the all-powerful doorman joined in, congratulating Edgar Snow on his marriage to Irina.

The wedding reception was held that evening in the office of the Associated Press, a two-room suite in the Metropol. Sandwiches and bottles of Caucasian wine were laid out on tables among the typewriters and piles of newspapers and on the lid of the grand piano in the corner, one of the many pianos randomly located around the hotel. First to arrive at six o'clock was Admiral Miles, the head of the British military mission, and the dashing Commander Palmer, followed by the newlyweds' journalist friends: Parker, Blunden, Werth, Holt and Henry Cassidy of the Associated Press, and Tanya's friend Katya who, alone of her Moscow circle, thought it safe to attend the wedding party because she worked with foreigners at VOKS, the All-Union Society for Cultural Relations with Foreign Countries. The guests stood together in small groups, drinks in hand, the journalists discussing their favourite topic: how the censor had mauled their copy. This was not the wedding party that Tanya had envisaged – no long table piled high with food for everyone to sit at, no extravagant toasts, no one shouting '*Gorko!*', no singing, no dancing, no excitement. She tried to get her husband's attention in the hope that he might help her get the party started, but he was too involved in his conversation to respond. In desperation she put a record on the gramophone, climbed onto a table and started to dance. No one joined in, and she jumped down.

By 3 a.m. most of the guests had drifted away, leaving behind a few hard drinkers. The sombre mood was reinforced by Henry Cassidy playing soulful American songs from the 1930s on the grand piano, skilfully avoiding the keys with out-of-tune notes. Tanya was sitting on a faded plush sofa chatting to Paul Holt when there was a commotion at the far end of the room. Matthews had drunk himself into a stupor and two RAF officers had decided it was time to put him to bed.

Tanya turned to Holt. 'The joke is that I spent my wedding night with you.'

'It's our secret, something to laugh about when we are

old and grey.' Holt patted her hand reassuringly. 'You're starting a new life. When you get your British passport you will be free to travel the world.' By this time Tanya knew she would always occupy fourth place in her husband heart – after journalism, reading and alcohol – but no matter, he was her 'exit'.*

'I'd like to go to America,' she said sleepily.

'Of course you can go to America, you can go anywhere. You're going to be very happy,' he said in his soft voice.

At this point, the doors to the bedroom were flung open and her husband reappeared, scantily clad and singing the Carmagnole, an anthem from the French Revolution, demanding another drink. The two RAF men turned him around and manoeuvred him back inside the bedroom as skilfully as the doorman at the Cocktail Hall. The wedding reception was over.

*

Once married to Matthews and living at the Metropol, Tanya was shocked to discover that her path to freedom was full of pitfalls. The Metropol administration had no rulebook for dealing with someone like her. They lurched between treating her as a foreign wife and a Soviet citizen. As a secretary-translator Tanya was entitled to a book of meal tickets each month that she gave to her mother and daughter while she shared her husband's rations. After her marriage, Matthews had to make a fuss in the manager's office at the end of every month to get her next book of tickets.

She might have been eating black caviar and half a

* Tanya Matthews, 'Going Back', BBC Radio 4.

cream cake every day while most Russians survived on potato peelings, but she lived under the same constraints as the journalists. Her friends were fearful of visiting her in the Metropol. Katya, who had thought it was safe to attend the wedding party, lost her job at VOKS a week after the marriage, with no explanation. Tanya's oldest friend Ida was given permission by the NKVD to visit Tanya occasionally, on condition that she did not attend any parties or other big gatherings. As young women in Rostov, they would go together to the railway station to watch the Moscow trains come and go, dreaming of the time when they would live in the capital. Unlike Chekhov's three sisters, they both achieved their goal. Ida would come for a bath and something to eat, and bring news from the outside world, but as time went on they had less and less to talk about.* Social life for Tanya meant drinks with the war correspondents, every evening going to a different room under the same roof. As a non-drinker, this was purgatory.

Nadya recalls sharing a table with Tanya's mother in the secretaries' dining room. It was upsetting to see her tired face. In her hearing the other women were gossiping maliciously about her daughter. 'Can you believe it? She's got herself an English husband and soon she'll be off, leaving her daughter behind.' Nadya thought about engaging the mother in conversation, but this was not a place to speak freely. Normally so judgmental about the young women who came to the Metropol to find a foreign husband, Nadya did not condemn this exhausted woman for being her daughter's accomplice. She understood that there was no future in the Soviet Union for Tanya, indeed

* Matthews, *Russian Wife Goes West*, p. 16.

*(above)* A downed German bomber is displayed in front of the Metropol Hotel in Moscow. British and American correspondents lived and worked in the hotel throughout the war. They called it a 'gilded cage'.

*(left)* The author and journalist Charlotte Haldane came to Moscow in 1941 as an ardent communist, but the experience destroyed all her illusions about Stalinism.

*(below)* Correspondents were allowed to visit the war zone only rarely, and then on escorted trips. They experienced the full force of Red Army hospitality including a nightly 'trial by vodka'.

*(above)* The remains of the town of Yelnya after its liberation by the Red Army in September 1941. It was soon back in German hands.

*(left)* In the autumn rains, the roads became liquid. Red Army sappers were deployed to dig correspondents' cars out of the mud near the Smolensk front.

*(above)* Alex Ulanovsky, 1932. A civil war hero, he was sent abroad with his wife Nadya to spy for the Russians in Germany, China and the United States.

*(above)* Nadya Ulanovskaya, 1932. A teenage convert to revolutionary socialism, she worked as a translator for the foreign reporters in the Metropol Hotel throughout the war.

*(left)* The Ulanovsky family in 1960 after release from the Gulag. Alex and Nadya in the rear, in front from left: Maya and her son Sasha (in later life Alexander Yakobson), Irina's son Shurik (in later life Alexander Timofeevsky), and Nadya's mother Rivka.

*(above)* Valentina Scott was the most successful of the Soviet assistants in persuading foreign reporters to follow the Kremlin line.

*(above)* Tanya Svetlova in Russia in the 1930s. She secured a job in the Metropol to find a way to escape Stalin's Russia.

*(left)* Godfrey Blunden, (second from right) with other Australian war correspondents in France. Blunden put the secrets he had learned in Russia into a novel.

*(above, left)* Ralph Parker with his Czech bride, Milena Hofbauerová, in 1940. 'I only began to live when we met,' he said.

*(above, right)* Milena in more carefree times in the 1930s.

*(left) The Times* correspondent Ralph Parker (right) was a young Tory at Cambridge but moved to the left under the influence of the pro-communist artist Julian Trevelyan (left) with his wife Ursula Darwin and his mother.

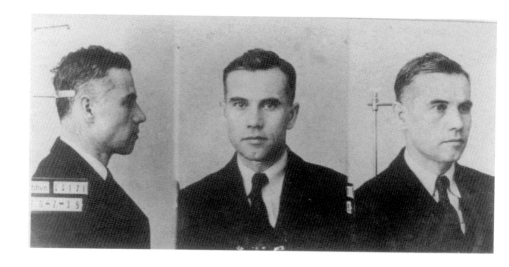

*(above)* Mugshot of Alex Ulanovsky under arrest in Copenhagen in 1935 after his spy network was by penetrated by Danish police.

*(left)* More than one million Poles were deported to Russia when Hitler and Stalin divided up Poland in 1939, some trekking over the mountains of Turkestan to freedom in Iran in 1942.

*(above, left)* Edgar Snow, the American reporter whose views were sought out by Roosevelt, at the entrance of the Metropol, 1943. Snow said: 'The correspondent's aim was to get a fresh, original and honest story and the [Soviet] press department's purpose was to frustrate him.'

*(above, right)* A would-be journalist with an acerbic tongue and talent for creating chaos around her, Alice-Leone Moats achieved her goal of becoming a foreign correspondent in the unlikely setting of wartime Moscow.

*(left)* The *Daily Telegraph's* A T Cholerton was the longest serving correspondent in Moscow. He was denied a re-entry visa in 1943 and his assistant was sentenced to a decade in the Gulag.

*(above)* Vasiliy Ulrich (centre) signed thousands of death warrants and was known as Stalin's 'executioner No. 1'. He lived in the Metropol hotel but none of the journalists knew of his blood-soaked career.

*(above)* Tanya Matthews (nee Svetlova) at home in Sidi Bou Said, Tunisia, aged seventy-two in 1985. She became a fearless reporter of events in North Africa for the BBC.

*(above)* Nadya Ulanovskaya in a camp in Mordovia, 1956, after eight years in the Gulag. Prisoners were allowed to wear their own clothes after Stalin's death in 1953.

no future for her mother either, but her daughter at least had a chance to escape.

Maybe Nadya recognised something of herself in Tanya. Both had grown up in distant provinces and from an early age were given the freedom to roam. As teenagers they sought to escape their origins. Tanya befriended American technicians working in the oil industry in her home town of Grozny, learned English from them and almost persuaded one of them to take her back with him to Oklahoma. When Nadya's father was forced to leave the shtetl in search of work in Odessa, she seized the opportunity to become part of the revolution. In the 1940s, they were both freethinkers in a society where independence of mind had been crushed by Stalin's dictatorship. Nadya had always refused to join the Communist Party, even though this was the easiest way to make a career.

There was one significant difference. Nadya's family were officially classed as proletarians, which meant she could only move upwards in the workers' state. Tanya, by contrast,* would never escape the consequences of her 'spoilt biography'. Her grandfather had been a priest of the sort who might feature in a Bolshevik anti-religion poster. He lived in a twenty-room house with a stable of horses which he rode to church every morning, had a cellar of good wine and a succession of mistresses. After the Revolution, the Bolsheviks requisitioned the house, and moved the priest and his wife into two stuffy rooms in a peasant's house on the outskirts of town.† Tanya's grandmother, who had never worked in her life, supported the couple

* Matthews, 'Going Back'.
† Matthews, *Russian Child and Russian Wife*, p. 33.

selling kvas, a cloudy drink of fermented bread, in the market.

In 1919, while the teenage Nadya and her Bolshevik comrades were raiding the homes of the Odessa bourgeoisie and confiscating their clothes, boots and valuables, five-year-old Tanya was standing by the dining-room window in the family home in a Cossack village outside Grozny when she was excited to see a cart decorated with bright red ribbons draw up outside the gate. Four people carrying guns – three men, one with two holes in his face instead of a nose, and a woman – jumped down from the cart and burst into the house. The man with no nose pushed a gun into her grandmother's belly. 'This is the doctor's house – we have nothing of value,' her grandmother protested.

The noseless man ignored her and shoved all the family's silver spoons and forks into a sack. Tanya watched as the woman rifled through her mother's clothes and, standing in front of the mirror, pulled her mother's best lace dress over her head. Finding it too small, she ripped the top off and squeezed herself into the long skirt. Tanya heard her mother screaming from the hallway, 'Not this one, please, it's the only warm one he has.' One of the looters was carrying off her father's fur-lined coat, dragging her mother along as she clung on to it.

By the time winter came, Tanya's father had no need of a warm coat. He died that year of typhus. The family had a document attesting that he had succumbed to the epidemic while in sole charge of a hospital for Red Army soldiers, all the other medical staff having run away. Despite this, Tanya's family lived under a cloud of suspicion. Somewhere in some archive it was recorded that, as a bourgeois, he had been shot by the Reds. After being forced out of their spacious house, Tanya's mother got a job in a clinic for workers at the Grozny oil refinery, which came with one room in a communal flat. There were other benefits – constant hot water and the staff received weekly food parcels, including Canadian white flour, which was kept for special occasions. With their mother at work, six-year-old Tanya and her little brother ran free. Until the age of twelve, Tanya did not own a pair of shoes. She went out in winter with her feet wrapped in newspaper and rags.* When Tanya's mother bought two nanny goats, Tanya became a goatherd, driving the animals every morning to find fresh pasture in the valleys outside town. When she and her little brother got hungry they would creep under the goats and suck the rich milk from their teats. Their mother complained of the disappointingly low milk yield, but delighted in her children's plump cheeks.

As a teenager Tanya dreamed of going on the stage and when she left school at seventeen she wanted to apply to drama schools. Her mother would have none of it, insisting she train for a serious career. Not wishing to spend her life in a stuffy office, she opted for the forestry institute but her application was rejected on the grounds of 'improper social origin'. The clerk at the office said, 'You must be of proletarian social origin to study here.' Tanya remonstrated, telling him she had a right to higher education because her father, a doctor, had died working in a Red Army hospital. 'He gave his life during the Revolution like a soldier.' This argument did not impress the clerk, and she met with the same response from every institute she applied to. Even at the drama school, to which she applied secretly,

* Matthews, 'Going Back'.

there were the same rules, except for the children of artists and actors.

Tanya's mother persuaded the dean of the oil refinery institute to accept Tanya for evening classes to study organic chemistry and higher mathematics plus the mandatory course on 'dimet', dialectical materialism. In the daytime she got a clerical job at the refinery. It was there that Tanya befriended the American oilmen who were installing a new catalytic cracker. With their ready smiles and relaxed attitude, they seemed like visitors from Mars. Tanya's visits to the House of Specialists where the Americans lived opened up a new world, one of colour magazines, refrigerators, hot water on tap and delicious meals of roast beef and canned fruit for dessert. In the room of one of the Americans – his name was Harold Armstrong* but she called him Horse Face due to his row of big strong teeth – stood two unopened trunks. Surprised to learn that one man's possessions filled two trunks, she offered to unpack them and found inside enough clothes to stock the local department store. They also contained toilet paper, the purpose of which Armstrong had to explain with the help of a dictionary. What do Americans do with newspapers? she wondered.

To celebrate her eighteenth birthday, she organised a tea party with fellow students and the young Russian wife of a French oil technician, who brought along two Spanish men. Armstrong arrived with a gramophone and some jazz records. They ate canned fruit from the oil refinery's stores and apple pie. For three hours Tanya forgot the grim reality of life outside, where people were starving and in the market lean and shady men whispered, 'Got any bread?' She learned

* Matthews, 'Going Back'.

that she could exchange her bread ration for three pieces of sugar or a lump of butter, which would transform the taste of her breakfast of cornflour porridge.

The day she had been dreading finally came when the plant was handed over to the Russians and the American oilmen began to decamp. Tanya was heartbroken – in Russia she would never find a man like Armstrong, who had recognised her abilities and given her a responsible job, while displaying rare thoughtfulness in the gifts of food he provided.

One day when Tanya, still a student, was conducting an experiment in the chemistry lab, a man appeared in the doorway. 'Comrade Svetlova, can I have a word with you?' He handed her a piece of paper with an address on it. 'You must go there immediately.' She recognised the address as the local headquarters of the secret police. The building was very grand, and a clerk led her along narrow corridors with closed doors on both sides. He knocked on one of them and waited for a reply before motioning her to enter and shutting the door after her. A corpulent man with an 'unpleasant blank face' sat behind a big desk.*

'Citizen Svetlova, sit down,' he ordered. 'Now tell me how you came into contact with foreigners.' He knew everything about her. He knew that she had been paid in dollars and suggested that the Americans had tried to recruit her to be their agent. He knew that she was friends with the Russian wife of a French technician and implied that the Frenchman was more than just a technician.

She was horrified at his recasting of her innocent friendships as unpatriotic and potentially criminal and

* Matthews, 'Going Back'.

found herself searching for words to convince him otherwise. He gave her no time to think. 'With your knowledge of English, you could be useful to your country. Now tell me, do you want to work for your country?'

'Do I have to decide now?' she stammered. He told her he would give her two weeks to think it over and then she must return to continue their conversation. Before she left, he made her sign a paper promising, on pain of prosecution by a military tribunal, not to mention this conversation to anyone.

Tanya knew she was trapped. If she accepted the offer she would have to inform on all her friends and family. Unable to confide even in her best friend, the next few days were agony for her.

One evening, just before the two-week deadline, an opportunity to escape the secret police presented itself. Her best friend dragged her along to Grozny's central hotel to a party given by a documentary film crew whose bohemian ways were tolerated so long as they produced the stirring propaganda the state required. When a cameraman offered her a shot of vodka she asked instead for a glass of water with a big piece of sugar in it. His name was Nick, and under his kindly gaze, Tanya released all her pent-up anguish. She told him about the hell she was living in after her summons to the secret police and how she wished she were dead. 'You must leave this town immediately,' Nick told her. 'Marry me and I'll take you away.' Two days later, they became a couple and the next day left Grozny. By hitching herself to the peripatetic film crew, she was banking on staying one step ahead of the secret police. For three years she did indeed stay beyond their grasp but her life was empty: a loveless marriage, no fixed abode and abortions without anaesthetic. After a near-death experience following the traumatic premature birth of a baby who died, she decided to take control of her life and applied for evening classes in English at Rostov University, a provincial college that was happy to have her. She became the star pupil and was soon given her own students to teach. With her knowledge of English she was talent-spotted to sing American love songs with a jazz band that had a Sunday radio show. Her rendition of 'Life is Just a Bowl of Cherries' was a hit among young people in Rostov.*

Now that she was out in the world again, it was no surprise that early one morning there came a knock on the door and she opened it to a man who could only be a secret policeman. 'Tell your mother you are going to the passport office, and come with me,' he said. The building she was taken to was much bigger than the one in Grozny and had the same long corridors with closed doors on both sides. The man across the table was bulkier than her previous tormentor, had a shaven head and the same blank stare. This time Tanya was determined to stand up for herself. 'We have received information from Grozny. Shall we pick up where we left off?' was his opening shot.

'What is there to pick up?' Tanya was amazed at her own defiance.

'All we want from you is to keep your eyes and ears open. Tell me about that professor you are teaching.'

Tanya said the professor needed her help translating articles in English on chemistry.

'What's his apartment like?'

She said the professor had an oak chest of drawers and a leather armchair in his study, and she was surprised to see that even these trivial details were being written down.

* Matthews, 'Going Back'.

'I suppose you know he is from the former people, that his mother's a countess, I mean an ex-countess.' Tanya pictured the frail and timid old lady who opened the door to her. 'I'm afraid you will have to do without me. I'm in poor health. I nearly died from an operation a year ago. I still haven't recovered. I'm a semi-invalid. I can't take on this responsible work.'

After being made to stand in the corridor for two hours, she was called back in. Another man, taller and thinner, asked her to explain why she was refusing to do her patriotic duty when she was fit enough to sing on the radio. 'All my life I've wanted to be a singer,' she said with tears streaming down her face. 'I'm no good for the work you want me to do.'

The tall man said, 'Give her the form to sign,' and left the room. For the second time Tanya signed the non-disclosure form. As she was escorted out of the building, she was exultant that she had got the secret police off her back, but as time passed, she had to ask herself, for how long?

Tanya's third encounter with the secret police took place in December 1941 and this time it was in the Lubyanka itself, the headquarters of the NKVD in Moscow, nicknamed the 'Big House' by those too fearful to mention its real name. By this time Tanya's life was transformed. She had divorced Nick and was living with her mother and daughter in a communal flat in Moscow, and had just landed a job teaching English at a teacher-training college.

The NKVD officer sitting opposite her was a young man who reminded her of one of her students. He had no thick file in front of him and Tanya assumed her biography had been destroyed in the panic-burning of documents in October when the Germans appeared to be on the point of storming into Moscow. The officer worked through a prepared list of questions that Tanya easily batted away. Clearly he was learning on the job. He finally got to the point of her summons: Why had she stayed in Moscow and defied the order to evacuate? Was she eager to welcome the fascists?

Tanya explained that her daughter was ill at the time, and her husband had a car – she omitted that they were divorced – so they could have escaped at any time. 'We did not think for a moment that Moscow would fall,' and then she said, knowing it would do the trick, 'And of course my husband was decorated for his film, *The Defence of Moscow*. I'm sure you've seen it.' The young man stood up, shook her hand and even apologised for taking up her time.*

Tanya's victory in the Lubyanka in no way lessened her ambition to live in a world of freedom, a concept she barely understood but which to her meant the end of fear and lies, the end of reciting chapters of Stalin's works in a tone of conviction that convinced no one, the end of condemning 'enemies of the people' at workplace meetings, and the end of pretending that nothing had happened when a neighbour or family member was taken away in the middle of the night. Marriage to Matthews was a step towards freedom, but the immediate effect was the opposite – to make her a prisoner of the Metropol. Friends and family were forced to shun her, and it was dangerous to go outside the hotel unaccompanied. She could be picked up by the NKVD and ordered to move to Siberia.

There was one place she could go in safety. Every Saturday evening Admiral Standley, the American ambassador

* Matthews, *Russian Child and Russian Wife*, pp 260–261.

who at the concert a year before had cheerily greeted her with the words 'Gavotte by Scott', invited the Anglo-American colony to his residence for a film show. Every week he asked Tanya if there was any progress on the exit visa she had applied for and she always replied, 'No news.'* One evening, in the summer of 1943, he told her that he had found a way to force the Soviet authorities to let five Russian wives of Americans, including one with a baby, leave the country. For months their departure had been blocked. He had come up with the idea of linking their case to the Soviet Trade Mission's request for visas for its officials and their families to go to New York. Within two weeks, the five exit permits for the Russian wives miraculously appeared. What, Tanya asked herself, was the British embassy prepared to do to secure her freedom?

* Tanya Matthews, *Russian Wife Goes West*, (Gollancz 1955) p.19

# 17

## *1942: An army in exile*

While most of the journalists evacuated from Moscow to Kuibyshev spent their days in enforced idleness, Alice Moats set out to discover what had happened to the hundreds of thousands of Poles who had been rounded up by the Red Army when Stalin and Hitler were carving up Poland between them. The two dictators had wiped Poland off the map in 1939 but, now that they were at war with each other, Alice was fascinated by the prospect that the martyred nation of Poland could rise again. Her interest had been piqued a few months previously during a dinner at the Aragvi restaurant with a Colonel Exham, one of the newly arrived British officers who were competing for the attention of the only unattached foreign woman in Moscow. Seeking to impress, the colonel told her that two Polish generals were dining upstairs. Would she like to join them? He could arrange it. She jumped at the chance, and soon they were forcing their way past a dozen Soviet security men to a private dining room. The two generals were sitting at a table littered with the remains of a great feast in the company of senior NKVD officers. One of the Polish generals was a handsome fellow in the pink of health with thick blond hair who had fought in the disastrous Norway campaign and had just arrived from England. But it was 49-year-old General Anders whom Alice was drawn to. He stood up to greet her, and Alice saw he was tall, erect and stick thin. His head was shaven, and his face was drawn and haggard. This only accentuated his luminous hazel eyes, which radiated the warmth and power of a natural leader.

With Colonel Exham looking jealously on, Alice and Anders fell into conversation in French. He told her he had just emerged from a two-year stretch in the Lubyanka and had been put in charge of recruiting a liberation army from Polish deportees in Russia. In a few days he would be travelling to his army headquarters in Buzuluk on the Volga.*

'I wish you'd take me with you,' Alice blurted out.

'Not this time, but maybe next time,' Anders said. Switching to Russian, he turned to the NKVD major next to him. 'There wouldn't be any objection to Miss Moats visiting Buzuluk would there?'

'Of course not, she can travel with us in our plane,' the major replied. Inevitably, Alice never got permission to visit.†

Over the next few months Alice and Anders met frequently for dinners in Moscow and then in Kuibyshev, which was a staging post for Polish deportees on their way to join the 'Anders' Army' in the training camp on the edge of the bleak Kazakh steppe. On these occasions, out of earshot of the NKVD, Anders revealed to Alice how he

* Władysław Anders, *An Army in Exile* (Macmillan, London, 1949), p. 54.
† Alice-Leone Moats, *Blind Date with Mars* (Doubleday, New York, 1943), p. 334.

had ended up in the hands of the Russians. When the Germans launched their blitzkrieg on Poland, Anders was in command of a Polish cavalry brigade which was no match for the combined might of the German tanks and air force. Ordered to retreat, Anders withdrew so far that his men backed into the Red Army, which, by agreement between Hitler and Stalin, was invading from the east. As Anders tried to disperse his forces so they could travel to safety over the Hungarian border, he received a serious wound in the back and was captured by the Russians while being treated in hospital.* After he refused to accept a Soviet invitation to join the Red Army – he had served in the Imperial Russian army in the First World War – he was kept for two years in the Lubyanka, the first seven months in solitary confinement. He had lived off 600 grams of black bread a day and little else, and been deprived of medical attention.

One day in August 1941 he was astonished to find his ration of black bread supplemented by 250 grams of white bread and a glass of kefir. From his prison cell he had heard the boom of high explosives and the night-time roar of anti-aircraft fire, and he understood that Russia was at war. It could only be Germany bombing Moscow.†

A few days later, in the course of a few hours, he was transformed from enemy of the state to VIP. The commandant of the Lubyanka himself carried the general's suitcase to a waiting limousine and broke the extraordinary news to him that he had been appointed commander of the a new army made up of Polish deportees in the

* Anders, *An Army in Exile*, pp. 11–12.
† Anders, p. 41.

Soviet Union.* He was driven to a new four-room apartment, with a cook and a maid. Supper was waiting for him, caviar, other delicacies, huge pats of butter and champagne and a choice of wines.† Even though he had tried to restrain himself, he was ill the next day. A new uniform was sewn for him by the finest Moscow tailors using khaki cloth looted from Poland, and embroidered with eight silver stars, one for each of the wounds he had incurred in battle. His three most prized medals lost in prison miraculously reappeared. He happened to mention to his NKVD liaison officer that he liked dogs, and a few days later two of the finest police dogs appeared to keep him company. Having left the Lubyanka on crutches, he was immediately placed under the care of the finest specialists in Moscow and before long he was able to walk with a stick. The rubble outside his apartment building was removed and a smooth concrete pavement was laid down so that the general with his bad leg would not trip up. Such was his newly pampered status when Alice first met him in the private room at the Aragvi restaurant.

Anders made such an impression on her that she decided to write a profile of him for *Collier's* magazine and sought out Polish deportees to interview. After her evacuation to Kuibyshev, she hung around the railway station waiting for trains to arrive filled with Poles released from prisons and slave labour camps scattered across the vastness of the Soviet Union from Arctic Murmansk to the deserts of Central Asia. Alice had to keep a low profile – the Soviet authorities were determined that no one should

* Alice Moats, 'Heart of Poland', *Collier's* magazine, 4 April 1942.
† Anders, *An Army in Exile*, p. 48.

see the wretched condition of these people – and she had to catch them before they were enrolled in General Anders' army. His orders to new recruits were to put their horrific sufferings at the hands of the Soviets behind them. 'Our task now is to beat the Germans. We have no time to waste on personal rancour or self-pity.'*

One day a train arrived with 2,000 Polish deportees in cattle trucks, 'gaunt, hollow-eyed, half-starved and dressed in rags', among them the corpses of sixteen men and women who had died of malnutrition during the journey.† In their past life many had been lawyers, professors, engineers or members of the Polish nobility, and they were incarcerated with murderers and other criminals. Hunger forced the women to trade sex for bread, venereal diseases were rife among them, and many were pregnant. The men and women had to work twelve hours a day, at heavy manual labour such as loading ships and trains or cutting timber in the forest in deep snow. Sometimes they had to walk five or six miles to work. They did this on a daily ration of 600 grams of black bread, a mug of tea for breakfast, a mug of soup in the middle of the day and a small portion of millet porridge in the evening. In the forests, they were required to cut six and a half cubic metres of wood a day, and if they failed to meet their norms their rations were cut, which made them even less able to work.

By coincidence Alice came across someone she had known in Vienna ten years before, when he had been a well-fleshed man about town. It was not until he told her

---

* Moats, *Blind Date*, p. 432.
† Moats, 'Heart of Poland', *Collier's* magazine.

his name that she recognised him. Although over six feet tall, he weighed only eight and a half stone. His face was gaunt and grey, most of his teeth were gone and the stubble on his head left by the prison barber was white. Three days before Stalin had ordered the release of all Polish prisoners he had been condemned to death, and he was still dazed by his miraculous escape. Alice interviewed a former university professor, wearing a prison-regulation quilted cotton jacket with nothing underneath, a towel round his neck like a scarf, and a pair of shoes with soles full of holes. In Poland he had been arrested by the Russians for teaching 'bourgeois theories'. He bowed low over Alice's hand and kissed it, as if they were in a drawing room. He apologised for weeping as he told her what he had endured. 'The sight of a woman looking like the women I once knew and addressing me kindly was too much for me.'*

General Anders' task was to create a Polish army corps on Russian soil to fight the Germans and he soon found out that the NKVD, which was responsible for the million-strong population of deported Poles, would work with no one but him. He had to get his fellow countrymen out of prisons and work camps, arrange trains to transport them, secure finance to feed and house them, select from among them the men who were fit enough to be soldiers and the women strong enough to join the auxiliary services and then send them to training camps. The general described to Alice how he had arranged a mass for the first 16,000 recruits at the camp and reviewed his men as they marched past to the field where the service was to be held. 'One in

* Moats, pp 434–5.

four had a shirt, one in ten shoes, one in twenty a coat, and yet they marched past like guardsmen.'*

In due course, the British government provided 100,000 battle-dress uniforms for the Poles. As Cholerton put it, 'They are going to fight the Germans on Russian soil, wearing British uniforms and carrying American arms. There in a sentence you have the history of the Poles.'

*

While the Russians made him feel like a valued ally, it was clear to Anders that this was a charade to please Churchill, who had gone to war against Hitler to restore an independent Poland. In a moment of weakness and isolation after Hitler's surprise attack, Stalin had indeed authorised the raising of a Polish army on Russian soil and allowed Anders to assemble it. But in the longer term, this army could never be under the command of a Polish patriot such as Anders – in Stalin's eyes a bourgeois officer who was aligned with the 'reactionaries' in the Polish government-in-exile in London. After Soviet forces had beaten back the Germans on the outskirts of Moscow, Stalin was not minded to indulge Churchill's sentimental attachment to Polish independence and decided he no longer needed the extra troops from the Polish diaspora to swell the ranks of his armies.

Anders saw what was happening. The rations provided by the Soviet government left his recruits too malnourished for intensive training, and weapons were in short supply. Most worrying, however, was the disappearance of 14,000 Polish officers who had been detained in Russia

* Moats, p. 435.

since 1939. He needed the officers to staff his new army, but most of all to allay Polish suspicions that the officers had been liquidated in secret. The longer the fate of the officers remained unresolved, the more reluctant Anders was to send his ill-equipped and poorly trained recruits to die in battle, with no prospect of achieving a revived Polish state. Some of his officers – the ones that the war artist Topolski had labelled reactionary 'blimps' on the first Arctic convoy to Russia – held more hard-line opinions. For these men, the resurrection of Poland lay not in fighting Hitler alongside the Russians, but in staying out of the war, allowing Germany and Russia to fight to the death, after which the Western Allies could redraw the map of Europe to Poland's advantage. Such ideas inevitably reached the ears of the NKVD spies and through them to Stalin.

Faced with an impossible situation, Anders worked in secret on a plan to evacuate his army and as many Polish civilians as possible to Iran, and from there to link up with the British forces in the Middle East. In what seemed at the time like a miracle, under his direction more than 112,000 Poles – one-third of them women and children – trekked through the deserts of Turkestan or were evacuated by ship across the Caspian sea to safety in Iran. From there the Polish soldiers fought with great bravery in the Italian campaign in 1944.

The evacuation served as a coda to the friendship between Anders and Alice Moats. While in Kuibyshev she had been living on borrowed time, subject to deportation at any moment. The American ambassador Steinhardt, still pursuing his feud with her dating from the time she resisted being evacuated with the 'embassy wives', refused to support her application for a residence permit, which left her in limbo. One evening, during a ballet performance, one of Alice's friends overheard a conversation between Anders and the head of the British military mission, General Mason-MacFarlane, in their box. They were discussing the British and American correspondents. The British general asked Anders if he saw much of Miss Moats.

'Yes, a great deal. Why do you ask?'

'I feel I must warn you that she is very indiscreet. I can't go into details now. I'll tell you when we meet in my office.'

Anders laughed. 'I'm afraid, General, I cannot congratulate you on your timeliness. I have known Miss Moats for two months.'

This conversation was proof that Steinhardt's slurs against her were now treated as gospel at the highest levels of the anti-Hitler alliance. The stress of his job as ambassador, responsible for the safety of his embassy staff in wartime, became too much to bear. This prompted something like a manic episode, of which a major part was his obsession with cutting Alice down to size. In the end, the huge effort he had put into destroying her reputation ended up tarnishing his own. He naturally blamed Alice, telling her that her behaviour had made him the subject of diplomatic gossip from Tokyo to London and Washington DC. Even the Russians had made it clear they would welcome a replacement for Steinhardt, viewing his early and over-zealous plans to flee Moscow ahead of the German advance as a sign of 'defeatism'.

Within days of Mason-MacFarlane's warning to Anders, Alice was on a plane to Tehran, having despaired of ever renewing her residence permit. The irony of '*L'affaire Moats*' was that after the months Steinhardt had spent trying to bully her into leaving Russia, he and Alice departed on the same plane, she to continue her travels in the Middle East and Africa and he to take up the more congenial post of Ambassador to Turkey.*

Anders did not heed the British general's warning. The next time he and Alice met was late at night in her hotel room in Tehran. A British officer had asked her to arrange a discreet meeting with the Polish general to discuss the still-secret plans to transfer Anders' Army to the Middle East. Alice could not retire discreetly as they needed her to interpret. There were no chairs in the room, and all three sat on her bed. 'This is a strange place for a military meeting,' laughed the Englishman. Anders replied, 'I don't imagine this is the first time a matter of military importance has been decided on a woman's bed.' Alice made a point of forgetting everything they said.†

* Moats, *Blind Date* p. 452.
† Moats, *Blind Date*, p. 461.

# 18

## *1943–44: A Polish mass grave*

One year after the evacuation of Anders' Army to Iran, on 13 April 1943, German radio made an explosive announcement that would present the journalists in the Metropol hotel with their toughest challenge of the war. German troops had discovered a mass grave in the Katyn woods near the city of Smolensk in western Russia. In a huge pit lay the bodies of 3,000 Polish officers, neatly stacked in twelve layers and wearing their greatcoats and boots, with insignia of rank still visible on their uniforms. They had all been killed with a pistol shot in the back of the head. They had documentation in their pockets establishing their identity, as well as letters and newspaper clippings which showed they had probably been killed between April and May 1940. The Germans set up a committee of inquiry which in their view established that the Polish officers had been shot while in the custody of the NKVD.

It took the Kremlin three days to respond to the 'slanderous fabrications' of Goebbels' 'gang of liars'. The Soviet statement was confusing: it acknowledged that the Polish officers were all dead – hitherto Stalin and Molotov had suggested they were alive – but seemed to dismiss the mass grave as a forgery. Ten days later, *Pravda* weighed in with an editorial attacking the Polish government-in-exile in London under the headline, 'Hitler's Polish collaborators'.* The basis for this accusation was that the London Poles' call for a Red Cross investigation into the massacre had, by unfortunate coincidence, come on the same day that Berlin requested the same investigation. This was the nugget that allowed *Pravda* to pursue a devastating line of attack: the London Poles had swallowed Hitler's bait and were collaborating with the Führer in a vile anti-Soviet campaign.

With hindsight, the inconsistences of the first Soviet statement make perfect sense. Stalin had been looking for an excuse to break with the London Poles, who were wearying him with their questions about the fate of the detained officers. General Sikorsky, the president of the Polish government-in-exile, had come close to calling Stalin a liar to his face – not something he took lightly – when the dictator had assured him that all the Poles in Russia had been 'amnestied' and so the missing officers would soon show up. By the logic of dictators, Stalin could not admit to a mistake or be caught out in lie. Now Goebbels had provided him with the opportunity to explain the death of the Polish officers – the Germans did it! – and to break his commitments to the London Poles and cast them adrift. The announcement was, in the opinion of one historian of the Katyn massacre, 'a godsend' that allowed Stalin to complete the process of marginalising the London Poles.† Stalin was confident that the British and the Americans would place more value on their alliance with

* *New York Times*, 20 April 1943.
† George Sanford, *Katyn and the Soviet Massacre of 1940: Truth, Justice and Memory* (Routledge, 2005) , p. 127.

him, now that he looked invincible after the Red Army victory at Stalingrad, than on their obligations to the Polish leaders in London.

In the Metropol Hotel, the diplomatic struggle over Poland was mirrored in journalistic farce. On 26 April the British and American reporters were alerted that Vyshinsky, the deputy foreign minister, would be making an important announcement on the Polish crisis at 4 p.m. Vyshinsky was a star performer in the propaganda war: as the state prosecutor in the Moscow show trials of the 1930s he had dominated the proceedings by extracting implausible confessions of treachery from the victims of Stalin's Great Purge. The scheduled press conference would clash with a British embassy cocktail party, but as the day wore on Vyshinsky's show was postponed until 8 p.m., allowing the reporters to enjoy embassy hospitality for at least an hour. While they were swilling back the embassy whisky they heard that the press conference was further delayed until 9 p.m., and finally to 10 p.m. By the time the reporters assembled in the deputy foreign minister's anteroom they were, in the words of the American journalist Eddy Gilmore, in dangerously high spirits. The reporters were already angry with the Press Department for excluding their Free French journalist friend Jean Champenois on the grounds that the press conference was restricted to members of the Anglo-American Correspondents Association. So when Ralph Parker appeared with Valentina by his side, with the clear intention of taking her into the press conference, the Reuters bureau chief Harold King was spoiling for a fight. Pacing up and down as he waited for the press conference to start, he bellowed: 'This is an outrage. A professional journalist, one of our colleagues, was barred from the conference and here we find other influences.'

Parker, almost six feet tall and powerfully built, advanced on King. 'Are you referring to me, King?'

'Yes, you and your . . .' History does not record exactly what he said, but he implied that Valentina was a spy.

Parker clenched his fist and punched King on his nose. Eddy Gilmore grabbed Parker from behind by the arms to restrain him. As he did so, Matthews reached around Gilmore to land a blow on Parker's face, sending his glasses crashing to the floor in splinters. Blood gushed from his nose. Valentina leaped to her lover's defence but, misjudging which of the men was Parker's assailant, she jumped on Gilmore's back, cursing and clawing at his arms to force him to release Parker. Gilmore, using more force than necessary, shook her off, and she landed against a glass door panel which shattered, showering her with broken glass.*

Into this scene of mayhem walked a flunky to summon the reporters to the press conference. Valentina combed the glass out of her hair, made a semi-apology to Gilmore for assaulting the wrong man, and took her seat, Parker being in no fit state for work. Vyshinsky announced that the USSR was suspending relations with the Polish government-in-exile. The journalists reported the news in full, and the result of the evening's fracas was that the person they wanted to exclude from the press conference ended up carrying out her first reporting assignment.

It was not long before Parker got his revenge on his

---

* Eddy Gilmore, *Me and My Russian Wife* (Greenwood Press, New York, 1968), p. 184.

colleagues. The prize that all journalists were fighting for was an interview with Stalin, and they regularly sent lists of questions to Uncle Joe. Stalin had made himself so inaccessible that any words to a reporter were treated like ingots of gold. On 5 May, the press chief Palgunov phoned Parker to tell him there was an important letter from the Kremlin – Stalin had responded, only the second time in the war that he had favoured a journalist with a response. Parker had proved the benefits of toeing the Kremlin line. In the memoirs of some of the reporters from that era, indeed even in their obituaries, Stalin's written answers are recorded as interviews, but in the course of the whole war Stalin never answered questions from the Metropol reporters in person.

It is worth quoting Parker's Q&A with Stalin in full:*

Q: Does the Government of the USSR desire to see a strong independent Poland after the defeat of Hitler's Germany?

A: Unquestionably.

Q: On what foundations is it your opinion that the relations between Poland and the USSR should be based after the war?

A: Upon the basis of sound good-neighbourly relations and mutual respect, or, should the Polish people so desire it, on the basis of an alliance providing for mutual aid against the Germans, as the principal enemies of both the Soviet Union and Poland.

* 'Marshal Stalin's Statement to "The Times" [sic]', *The Times*, 6 May 1943.

The questions were bland, the answers non-committal and they clarified none of the outstanding issues – the future borders of Poland and whether the Poles would be allowed freely to choose their own government. But it was a scoop, and Stalin's answers did offer a fig leaf to those British officials whose consciences were uneasy about abandoning their ally to the mercy of the Kremlin: Stalin had made a commitment to preserving Poland as 'a strong independent state', whatever he might mean by those words.

By the autumn of 1943, the Red Army was rolling back the Wehrmacht after the failure of its last offensive on Soviet soil, at the Battle of Kursk. By September the Russians had recaptured Smolensk and the Katyn woods where a large group of Polish officers had been buried and discovered by the Germans. The Russians gave themselves three months to prepare a propaganda bomb as big as the one Goebbels had set off the previous year. NKVD forgers worked in secret to change the dates of documents and letters found in the dead officers' pockets to prove that the Poles had been alive until 1941 when the Germans invaded. A Potemkin-style inquiry was set up, its title revealing in advance the conclusion its members were required to give: 'The Special Commission for Determination and Investigation of the Shooting of Polish Prisoners of War by German-Fascist Invaders in Katyn Forest'.*

In January 1944 the British and American correspondents were taken by train to Katyn to see the evidence. And some trip it was – the train was so extravagantly equipped

* https://soviethistory.msu.edu/1943-2/katyn-forest-massacre/katyn-forest-massacre-texts/report-of-soviet-special-commission/

and staffed that it must have seemed to have belonged to the Tsar, with snow-white linen and waiters in white jackets. A British embassy official cabled to London: 'No Press excursion to any part of Russia has been arranged with greater luxury than the Katyn party.'* Kathy Harriman, the 25-year-old daughter of the American ambassador who was acting as his diplomatic hostess in Moscow, added a touch of glamour to the party. She had worked for *Newsweek* in London and had been given the poisoned chalice of summing up the Soviet evidence in a report for the US State Department.

The journey to Katyn made an indelible impression on the American journalist Harrison Salisbury, who had arrived in Moscow only a week before. He recalls dining in luxury at tables laid with crystal glasses and silver plates of caviar, while through the lace curtains he saw wounded soldiers with heads in bloody bandages travelling in the opposite direction on freezing freight trains.†

In the forest the reporters found a forensic laboratory set up in tents amid the snowdrifts, with surgeons sawing open skulls, and the overpowering stench of rotting flesh. The witnesses who testified that the Germans had committed the massacre looked shifty – one of them had been the Nazi-installed deputy mayor of Smolensk, who clearly had been let out of prison on condition he delivered his lines correctly. The reporters were not allowed to put any questions to the people presented as witnesses to the German 'crime'. 'Unexpected questions flung at

* TNA FO 371 39387/1097.
† Harrison Salisbury, *Disturber of the Peace: Memoirs of a Foreign Correspondent*, (Unwin, 1989) p. 80.

# THE RED HOTEL

the Commission by some of the American correspondents were received with noticeable irritation,' the Foreign
Office cable reported. As usual there was an odd array
of 'performing seals' to add lustre to the occasion, in this
case Alexei Tolstoy, a pro-Soviet writer known as 'Comrade Count' who was a remote relative of the author of
*War and Peace,* and a bishop of the Russian Orthodox
Church. The visitors watched as the 66-year-old Red
Army surgeon Nikolai Burdenko conducted a post-
mortem before their eyes. Out of one of the corpses he
dug a greenish piece of stinking liver and waved it at the
journalists. 'How lovely and fresh it looks.'*

The huge mise en scene in the forest was designed to
give an aura of scientific respectability to the conclusion
that the officers were killed by the Germans in 1941, but
no convincing medical evidence was offered and the cir-
cumstantial evidence was confusing. For some of the
journalists it was the boots that clinched it. Alexander
Werth, always keen to present the Russian case in the best
light, argued that Russian executioners would never have
buried their victims without stealing their precious boots.
The journalists were told that shooting in the back of the
head was a Nazi method of execution – it was still a secret
to the journalists that a shot in the back of the head had
been used by the NKVD on hundreds of thousands
throughout the 1930s. In his book *Russia at War,* published
twenty years after the end of the war, Werth reveals his
mindset at the time. Prisoners of the NKVD may have
died from overwork, bad food and exposure to cold, he

* Alexander Werth, *Russia at War 1941–45* (Barrie & Rockliff,
1964), p. 662.

argued, but the secret police never engaged in mass murder. His astonishing naïvety is testament to the success of the Soviet policy of keeping the journalists ignorant of the basic facts of Stalin's rule – and to the willingness of the press corps to accept the conditions they worked under.

The journalists saw that the evidence of German guilt was poor, the presentation sloppy and the lack of independent expertise troubling. But they could only report the evidence they saw. 'The censors killed all sceptical remarks and deleted references to the caviar,' Harrison Salisbury noted in his diary.*

The report written by Kathy Harriman and forwarded to the State Department was not hedged with much doubt – the Germans were guilty, which was the finding that the Roosevelt administration wanted. She had been impressed that the Russians had pulled incriminating documents from the clothes of the murdered Poles. 'While I was watching, they found a letter dated 1941, which is damned good evidence,' she wrote to a friend.† In 1952, after the American romance with Stalin had curdled and the hunt was on for Red traitors, she changed her view under questioning by a House of Representatives committee and accepted that the guilt belonged to the Soviets. Henry Cassidy, the Associated Press reporter, admitted that he had not been convinced by the Soviet version of events at Katyn, but had reported it nevertheless.

The truth about Katyn was kept secret until after the

---

* Salisbury, *Disturber of the Peace*, p. 83.

† Letter to Pamela Churchill quoted in Averell Harriman and Elie Abel, *Special Envoy to Churchill and Stalin, 1941–1946* (Random House Inc., 1975), p. 302.

Soviet Union's collapse in 1990, when the Russian president, Boris Yeltsin, opened the safe in his office where the most secret papers were kept. They told a simple tale. On 5 March 1940, Lavrenty Beria, the Soviet Commissar for Internal Affairs, had proposed to Stalin the execution of 14,700 Polish officers and gendarmes on the grounds that they were 'hardened, irremediable enemies of Soviet power'. They were to be killed without being informed of the charges against them or of their death sentence. The document is signed by Stalin, and five other senior Bolshevik leaders, with some amendments in Stalin's own hand.* The decision to liquidate them was not a rush job prepared in secret by rogue elements of the NKVD, or an action forced on the Soviet leadership by the prospect of war. It was just one bureaucratic procedure among thousands in the extinction of the old Poland to make way for one cast in the Soviet mould. On his deathbed the Red Army surgeon Burdenko is said to have confessed to a man who later defected to the West that the NKVD was indeed responsible for the massacre, and that the soil of Russia was full of Katyns.

*

In 1944 Stalin's plan to build a new Poland on Soviet lines was moving into overdrive. The departure of General Anders and his evacuation of 116,000 of his supporters from Russia still left a huge population of Poles in the Soviet Union. With Anders gone, the Kremlin sought out one of his senior officers, Zygmunt Berling, to form a new

* Anna M. Cienciala et al., *Katyn: A Crime Without Punishment* (Yale University Press, 2007), p. 118.

Polish army corps. The Polish Communist Party, which had been dissolved in 1938 when Stalin liquidated its leaders, was allowed to reconstitute itself under Boleslaw Bierut, a former Soviet intelligence agent who was one of the few of the party cadres to survive the purge, as the nucleus of the new regime in Poland. The task of rallying the Polish diaspora in Russia was given to a group of Soviet-aligned Polish politicians who called themselves the Union of Polish Patriots, or UPP. These 'Polish Patriots' had been dismissed by diplomats as a front organisation with no popular support. The task of telling the world that the UPP was now the embryo of the future Polish state was given to Ralph Parker.

In a long article under the title, 'The Poles in Russia: Soviet Encouragement of a New Patriotic Movement',* Parker told *Times* readers how he had been invited to visit a Polish orphanage in the Russian town of Zagorsk where 100 boys and girls were learning to smile again. Overall, 16,000 Polish children were being taught in nearly 200 Polish schools using newly printed Soviet textbooks. Now that the UPP had taken over the running of Polish schools in Russia from the London-based Polish government-in-exile, a new generation of Polish children was being educated along Soviet lines. The 'patriots' now enjoyed 80 per cent support among the Polish diaspora in Russia, he wrote, without stating how this figure was arrived at. Not only was education in safe hands, but a new Polish army was being created on Russian soil. This was a great achievement, Parker suggested, given the 'unhelpful attitude' of exiled Poles over the Katyn massacre.

* *The Times*, 17 April 1944.

# 19

## *Summer 1943: The visa weapon*

In July 1943 disturbing news reached the journalists in the Metropol. Cholerton, the grand old man of the foreign press corps, had been refused a visa to return to Moscow after taking a short break in Britain. Even worse, his secretary-translator, Natalia Vodovozova, who had worked alongside him for sixteen years, had been arrested with her husband.

Cholerton was not just the most experienced journalist in Moscow. He was the institutional memory of the press corps, generous with his time in answering the questions of newcomers about Stalin's rise to power in the Great Terror of the 1930s. He could have been an academic historian – he had been awarded a fellowship at Cambridge – but he never took up the post, preferring to go to Moscow as a newspaper reporter in 1927 to pursue his obsession with Russia. The Kremlin followed his reports closely, as did the British embassy. While other correspondents came and went, he was an immovable part of the Moscow landscape.

Before he left Moscow in June the Soviet Press Department had assured him he would get a new visa when he wished to return, and with a light heart he set off for

Liverpool on an Arctic convoy. 'I never came away from Russia feeling so easy in my mind,' he wrote.*

Just as he was preparing to take his young daughter fishing in Wales, he got a cable from Moscow alerting him to the arrest of his translator. He had already been notified that his visa was ready to collect, so he rushed to the Soviet consulate to pick it up and head back to Moscow to try to rescue her. On arrival at the consulate, he was told there had been a 'mistake' and the visa was not ready. He knew this was no mistake. The NKVD had seized the opportunity of his holiday in Britain to remove him from Moscow without having to formally expel him.

On 6 July, Cholerton poured his heart out to his friend, the British ambassador Sir Archibald Clark Kerr, begging him to persuade the Soviet government to reverse the visa ban. In a seven-page letter written from London, Cholerton had no choice but to reveal the truth about his complicated love life, a secret he had kept hidden from all but a few of his closest friends. Natalia was far more than a translator: they had been lovers for twelve years and she was the reason he had stayed so long in Moscow. 'I had an abominably unhappy life until I met her. She nursed me from death, found me doctors to cure me, made me work. But those are minor points. She is, with my child, my whole life.'†

In 1927 Cholerton had married a Russian woman, Katerina Batiushkova, but soon after the birth of their daughter Katya, they grew apart. During Stalin's Great

* TNA FO 800/301, pp. 104–110.
† TNA FO 800/301, pp104–110.

Terror, divorce was out of the question – Cholerton feared that as a divorced woman Katerina would have no right to escape to safety in England and could end up in Siberia, depriving Katya of a mother. When Stalin dialled back his terror campaign in 1938, Katerina left Moscow with their daughter to live with Cholerton's sister in England. Despite her relationship with Cholerton, Natalia remained at home with her husband, a senior engineer at the Stalin Motor Works in Moscow, who was content to share his wife with the eccentric Englishman. This *ménage à trois* was no secret to the NKVD, but the couple deemed it wise to keep up appearances. When war broke out, and Britain was allied to the Soviet Union, they relaxed a little. Natalia's husband would come to Cholerton's flat to have a bath when the pipes were frozen at his home and Cholerton would get some fresh air on Saturdays when he visited Natalia's dacha. Cholerton ended his letter to the ambassador with a blunt message: 'Get me a visa,' he wrote. 'My life to some extent is now in your hands. I apologise for that, and for writing at such length. I am too hurried to condense.'

Clark Kerr went into action. He approached Molotov for an explanation for the refusal of Cholerton's visa, but the foreign minister said he had no knowledge of the Cholerton affair and promised to investigate. On 2 August the ambassador appealed personally to Molotov to take an interest in Natalia's case and so 'restore happiness and peace of mind to Mr. Cholerton, who is a man of high value and a devoted friend of this country'. Natalia was a Soviet citizen, so Clark Kerr was in no position to ask any such thing, but it was a clear sign of the embassy's respect for Cholerton that he dared to make such a request.* There was silence from the Kremlin until the end of August, when Molotov forwarded a terse message. 'A S Rupnevsky [Natalia's husband], former section chief in one of the Moscow factories, has been detected in espionage. His wife has also been detected in espionage. All these circumstances make Cholerton's return undesirable.'†

The term 'detected in espionage' meant no more than being in contact with a foreigner. There was no need for the NKVD to provide evidence. During a twelve-hour search of Natalia's home the NKVD officers showed particular interest in items which could be used to build up a case. These included tinned food which Cholerton had cadged from the RAF to sustain her during his absence. Cholerton had warned the ambassador that Molotov might use the RAF rations as proof that she was engaged in military espionage. He explained that Natalia was in poor health, suffering from scurvy and septicaemia – not working at the Metropol, she had no access to diplomatic-level rations. The NKVD men also took away a photograph of Natalia's father in the uniform of a tsarist general.

Cholerton cabled a cringing appeal to Stalin to let him return.‡ Anthony Eden, the British foreign secretary and future prime minister, was persuaded to step in with a personal endorsement of Cholerton as 'a good friend of the USSR which had become his second home'. Cholerton, he wrote, 'is a man of unquestioned honour and integrity

---

* TNA FO 800.301, p. 150.
† TNA FO 371.37007, p. 85.
‡ TNA FO 800/301, pp. 200–201.

and we are all persuaded that he has at no time associated himself with any kind of espionage.'*

The British Foreign Office originally thought that the cause of the visa ban could be that Natalia had worked too efficiently – alerting Cholerton to items in the Soviet press which had been passed by the censor but which the NKVD did not want broadcast abroad. Cholerton was more clear-sighted. It was nothing to do with Natalia's work. After losing control during the panicked evacuation of Moscow in 1941, the secret police were now back in charge of all the levers of state and hungry for new victims.

'The old NKVD knew me through and through and no longer suspected me, except on principle,' he wrote. 'I always worried them because they couldn't classify me. They felt somehow I was too big for my reporter's boots . . . I remember one of them saying: "We know everything about him, except his soul".'

He feared the new NKVD men more than their pre-decessors of the 1930s, whom he called 'their wicked-er liquidated uncles'. He wrote: 'I also have the feeling that they are rebuilding their files, thrown into deliberate disorder during the Purge, perhaps burnt during the evacuation.'

Cholerton understood that his position, living in his own home and relatively free to meet Russians beyond those approved by the secret police, was no longer accept-able to the NKVD. The diplomatic corps was 'pretty well blockaded', and the other reporters were 'penned in the Metropole with their police hacks'. The aim of the author-ities, he wrote, is to place 'everybody into pens'.

* TNA FO 371.37007, p. 96.

By the end of the year, the Foreign Office decided there was nothing more they could do in the face of the 'disgraceful' behaviour of the Soviet authorities. Clark Kerr asked the Foreign Office to tell his friend, 'I am really sorry that I have failed here.'*

\*

Though he had been in Moscow for sixteen years and considered it his second home, Cholerton never drew on his vast experience in Russia to write a book. By contrast, almost every other foreign reporter wrote one book or two claiming to decode the enigma of the country they had spent just a few months in, mostly within the walls of the Metropol. With very few experts to speak to, these journalist-authors pocketed Cholerton's apercus and enlivened their accounts with descriptions of the eccentric English sage. Reviewing four books by American journalists about wartime Moscow, the American magazine *The New Republic* noted a curious fact: the books all told the same story, with similar organised trips to cleaned-up battle fronts, except that their authors could not agree on Cholerton's whiskers, variously described as a 'long brown beard', a 'stubbly black beard', a 'goatee' or, more cautiously, as 'a full beard'. The article was entitled 'Mr. Cholerton's Beard'.† In a small diary item, the *Daily Telegraph* asked its correspondent for clarification on this point, and he insisted that, despite the passing years, his beard was totally black.

Cholerton's apartment, on the fifth floor of a crumbling building at 3 Maly Levshinsky Pereulok, was a haven

---

* TNA FO 371.37007/85.
† Malcolm Cowley, *The New Republic*, 2 August 1943.

where journalists could escape the confines of the Metropol without joining in the grim round of diplomatic parties or going to the Bolshoi to watch *Swan Lake* for the umpteenth time. Cholerton could be relied on to challenge the diplomatic consensus – at the start of the war when the British and American embassies were predicting that Moscow would fall within weeks, he insisted that the Red Army soldier would fight, even without the weapons to match those of the Germans. When the would-be correspondent Alice Moats first visited his flat she found the sitting room uncarpeted and furnished with a day bed, a broken-down chaise longue, and a desk with two typewriters surrounded by a clutter of bottles, glasses, shoes, the spectacles that Cholerton habitually misplaced and a telephone whose wires he got caught up in whenever the unreliable instrument rang and he picked up the receiver. The double doors of a closet hung open to reveal several years of copies of the *Daily Telegraph* tied up with string. His wife's bedroom – she was living in England – served as a storeroom, every inch of floor taken up with empty bottles. The dining room was dominated by an ancient fridge whose rumbling was loud enough to drown out the sounds of German air raids.*

As a keen student, Moats arrived with a list of questions to put to the sage, but in five hours she never got beyond the first one, his mind too cluttered with names, dates and events to give a simple answer. Henry Cassidy, the AP correspondent, advised getting Cholerton to speak in French, which slowed his delivery. When Moats asked for a carbon copy of his latest article, he delved into the

---

* Alice-Leone Moats, *Blind Date with Mars* (Doubleday, 1943) p. 207.

closet and rummaged in drawers, emerging triumphantly with what turned out to be copy from a show trial from the 1930s. It was so engrossing she forgot what she had asked for. Some of his bon mots stuck and became the accepted wisdom of Moscow's foreign community. When questioned on what really happened to make Stalin's rivals in the Bolshevik party confess to taking part in patently ludicrous conspiracies, he answered: 'Everything is true except the facts.'* He had come to Russia as a wide-eyed socialist and, not surprisingly for a freethinker, had quickly lost his illusions about Soviet communism. As the years passed he called himself a 'conservative rebel' though he insisted he never lost his 'indignant love' for the Russian people.†

When Quentin Reynolds, an American journalist famed for his radio broadcasts from the London Blitz, came to Moscow he drew an alarming picture of Cholerton in winter. There was no heating in the building and water was leaking through the ceiling from a burst pipe. Cholerton plugged in as many electric heaters as he could lay his hands on and rigged up two big umbrellas he got from the British embassy over his bed. He spent the cold months under the covers of his bed, tapping on a type-writer perched on a wooden stand.

Distracted as he often appeared, Cholerton could display a fierce temper when aroused. At the first press conference called by the Soviet spokesman Lozovsky, Cholerton launched into a speech in French demanding that the correspondents should have access to wider

* Malcolm Muggeridge, *Daily Telegraph*, 28 October 1982, p. 18.
† Moats, *(Blind Date)*, p. 207.

sources of news. 'We are filing little that is of interest to the outside world, and nobody can get a colour story.'

Lozovsky attempted to humiliate the Englishman into silence, telling him that his French was unintelligible – even though Cholerton's first wife had been French and he had lived and studied in France for several years. Confident that he could beat the journalist into submission, he told him: 'The war is not a game, nor is it being fought for the pleasure of correspondents.'

This bullying approach failed to shut Cholerton up. Tugging his beard with greater violence than usual, Cholerton told Lozovsky that the BBC was desperate for news of the Red Army, but found nothing worth broadcasting from the daily papers, so its news bulletins were filled with trivial domestic items. The British and American publics expected to hear stirring first-hand reports about their gallant allies, and were instead getting old news picked up from the Soviet press. Unused to being challenged by a reporter whose volubility brooked no silencing, Lozovsky retreated, and agreed to the reporters' demand that there would be two military communiqués a day instead of one. It was the first, and pretty much the only, battle won by the journalists against the censors.*

*

In his letter to the British ambassador, Cholerton wrote that he could not be sure of the immediate cause of Natalia's arrest, which might be 'a chance denunciation, or a provocation or a brutish muddle'. The only certainty was that the NKVD would never let go. 'These beavers will go

* Moats p. 260.

on building it up, as a matter of routine, into a big affair unless they are stopped early.' On this point, Cholerton's instincts were spot on. The wheels of the NKVD ground slowly on until, after the war, it was the turn of Natalia's daughter Maika, a fifth-year piano student at the Moscow conservatoire, to be fed into the maw. For nine years the NKVD kept working on their 'big affair', concocting an anti-Soviet conspiracy involving the army's chief medical officer Sergei Yudin, a loose-tongued Red Army general named Nikolai Voronov, the British ambassador Clark Kerr, and Cholerton, who appears in the interrogation reports as the link between Dr Yudin and the ambassador. The conspiracy was so ludicrous that neither the general nor Dr Yudin was ever convicted, but in 1952 Maika, at the age of twenty-eight, received a ten-year forced labour sentence for passing 'suspicious packages' from Dr Yudin to the British ambassador.* One of these was a Christmas card for Winston Churchill.

Only once after her arrest did Cholerton hear from Natalia, the love of his life. She had been sentenced to ten years in the Gulag. Cholerton's daughter Katya, who in adult life uses the name Katerina, recalls the scene when she, as a young woman, was staying in the south of France in the 1950s with her father and his new wife, Charlotte Trautschold, the widow of a pre-revolutionary Russian diplomat. 'When I was staying with my father on the Mediterranean he got a letter from Natalia. This was the

---

* For details of the persecution of Natalia Vodovozova and her family: Alexander Sannikov, 'Academician Sergey Sergeyevich Yudin – The Reasons for the Arrest' (in Russian), https://proza. ru/2021/02/14/1790

only time he heard from her.' Cholerton and his wife discussed at length what to do, and whether Natalia would suffer even more if he sent a letter to her in Moscow. 'In the end, they decided it was safer for her if he didn't respond.'*

*

Not surprisingly, after the Cholerton case, Clark Kerr described the visa as 'the most powerful weapon of all' wielded by the Soviet authorities to control journalists. 'A very careful discrimination is exercised in admitting or re-admitting them, and correspondents whose work, inside or outside the Union, has at any time met with Soviet displeasure are unlikely, unless they have particularly influential connections, to obtain a re-entry visa,' the ambassador wrote.†

Cholerton's absence from Moscow was a huge loss to the Metropol journalists, who had no one to guide them, and was keenly felt by British diplomats, who were even more restricted in their movements than the journalists. Ralph Parker was keen to fill Cholerton's shoes as the embassy's confidential contact, but this was never going to be easy. He had angered the embassy with 'mischievous' articles criticising the weakness of British wartime publicity in Russia and his parroting of Kremlin talking points about British tardiness in opening the 'second front' in continental Europe was intensely annoying to the diplomats. Parker was also in bad odour with his journalistic colleagues, for usurping the position of doyen of the press

* Interview with Katerina Porter, 25 August 2022.
† TNA FO 271 47718.7449.

corps. At a lunch with Shcherbakov, the head of the Sovin-formburo, to air the reporters' complaints about not being able to do their work, Parker took the floor and spoke for half an hour, reading out a wartime PR strategy that he thought Shcherbakov should adopt. It was laboriously translated into Russian by Alexander Werth. When Parker had finished, Shcherbakov stood up and, without having touched his food or said a word, walked out.

When Parker wrote a rare article which the embassy agreed with there was a suggestion that he might be thanked – an idea dismissed by the embassy's counsellor. 'This article is quite sensible but is not, I think, any more interesting than a great many articles sent by Mr Cholerton at various times.'*

* C. F. A. Warner, TNA FO317 329.323.86.

# 20

## *Who was the real Ralph Parker?*

In the words of one of his colleagues at *The Times*, Parker was 'a talented man who seldom appeared to be at ease with others or, possibly, with himself.'* To understand why he made a poor impression on members of the British establishment it is worth going back to Parker's childhood in Southport, a Lancashire seaside resort where the class differences in English society were on display with unusual clarity. In summertime, the wealthy holidaymakers would take a taxi from the station to a fine hotel on Lord Street, a canopied boulevard that recalls the broad thoroughfares of Hausmann's Paris. The day-trippers from the poorer parts of Liverpool would be directed by a policeman from the railway station straight to the beach, away from the posh parts of town.

The Parker family business, a wholesaler of small goods to the corner shops of Manchester – anything from stockings to tins of brass polish – provided a comfortable life for his father and uncles. There was enough money to send young Ralph to a boarding school, which enabled him to get a scholarship to Cambridge and softened his Lancashire

---

* Iverach McDonald, *The History of The Times [sic] 1929–1984* (Times Books, 1984), p. 85.

accent. He never mentioned the family business – the wholesale trade was nothing to be proud of. The note-paper of the family home, a three-storey villa in the smart part of town, grandly proclaimed the address as 'Seventy Three, Albert Road, Southport', but the family occupied only the first-floor flat. In later life Parker would admit to being depressed by his family 'living such blind, futile lives, sending their children to public schools but not being able to afford to buy books . . .'

While living in Moscow he invented a childhood in which he was a socialist rebelling against the 'close-clipped lawns and outward respectability' of his bourgeois parents. He claimed to have befriended a working-class boy called Frank with rough hands and a torn shirt on his back whom he met on the beach. To the annoyance of his parents, he went to stay with Frank in a worker's cottage in Oldham, a Lancashire mill town, where he learned 'the dignity of the worker, certain of his rights'. In a Soviet-published polemic, *Conspiracy Against Peace*, Parker suggests he was a budding socialist at Cambridge. He writes: 'I adopted the aspirations and dreams of those older than me who had been at Cambridge, as well as their curiosity about everything concerning the Soviet Union, although in those years I sorely felt the lack of reliable information about the country.'* This is a lie. He was an ardent young Conservative, seemingly preparing himself for a career in that party. Proof of this comes from a 1929 pamphlet edited by Parker, 'A Declaration of

* Ralph Parker, 'Gorod Otkrytykh Serdets', in *Angliiskiye Pisatelye o Strane Sovetov* (Lenizdat, 1984), p. 208.

Tory Principles'.* In the lead essay, 'Reason and Instinct in the Conservative Philosophy', Parker wrote that social-ism 'is by its very nature inimical to the institutions of this country'. Among the contributors to the pamphlet is the aristocrat and future Tory Lord Chancellor, Quintin Hogg, and other students who on graduating from Cam-bridge effortlessly slipped into careers in politics and the professions. But Parker lacked the polish and sense of entitlement of the British elite. He was never one of the gilded youth at Cambridge and he spent his final year anxious about getting a job. He left university with no career lined up.

Parker graduated in 1929 and two years later he was still, according to a friend, a 'sturdy reactionary'.† A cou-ple of years after that, Parker was a changed man. He was helping to produce an opera in an 'unemployed settlement – a good, honest to God radical club in the Manchester tradition'. In 1934 he was 'having great fun putting on plays in the slums. Last night we acted in a children's theatre – 200 lads under ten – and all the actors save me unemployed. I in [sic] only because none of the others could sing.'‡ The explanation for his political rebirth lies in the influence of his old Cambridge friend, the bohemian artist Julian Trevelyan, with whom he bonded over a common love of art and travel through the Balkans. At six feet three

---

* A. R. Parker, R. Gresham Cooke, Felix Green (eds), *A Declaration of Tory Principles. Essays by Undergraduates of Oxford and Cambridge* (Heffer & Sons, Cambridge, 1929), British Library.

† Julian Trevelyan, *Indigo Days*, (Macgibbon & Kee, London, 1957), p. 35.

‡ Letter to Julian Trevelyan, Trinity College archive, TREJ 45.20.

inches tall with a mop of chestnut hair and the self-confidence that comes from belonging to a well-connected family of poets, artists and intellectuals, the charismatic Trevelyan embodied everything that Parker, an insecure provincial, wanted to be. Parker's carefully drafted letters to him betray a yearning to be part of the stylish set that met up in Trevelyan's Thameside studio at Durham Wharf in Hammersmith.

By 1937 Trevelyan was sending money to the British Communist Party and raising funds for an ambulance to tend volunteer fighters in the Spanish Civil War, and Parker had taken to dropping into his correspondence a reference to the triumph of the Third International, better known as the Comintern, whose goal was the worldwide spread of communism.

For MI5, the British counter-espionage service, Trevelyan was not an artist but a suspected communist agent. The spy-catchers spent two decades trying to establish whether Trevelyan was the elusive communist agent working under the alias 'Joe Pascoe' who had travelled to Moscow in 1934. In 1956 MI5 wound up the investigation by concluding that Trevelyan probably had once used the name 'Joe Pascoe', but the purpose of the Pascoe mission to Moscow was never discovered.*

MI5's investigation into Trevelyan as a communist agent was hampered by the absence of some information that emerged many years later. Anthony Blunt, the 'fourth man' of the Cambridge spy ring, had been a contemporary of Trevelyan at Trinity College, and with their shared passion for art they became close friends. Blunt went on to

* TNA KV2 3931/69a.

have an illustrious career as an art expert, as surveyor of the King's – and then Queen's – pictures, a position he held from 1945 to 1972. Blunt did not confess to spying for the Kremlin until 1964, when he was granted immunity from prosecution and his past was hushed up to spare the Queen embarrassment. It was only in 1979 that Blunt's name was made public by Margaret Thatcher, who had been appalled at the establishment cover-up of this traitor in their midst.

Apart from wartime, when Blunt had access to useful intelligence, his role was as a scout for the Soviets. Blunt would no doubt have considered recommending Trevelyan to the Russians, and Trevelyan may indeed have slipped off to Moscow in 1934, but it seems unlikely he would have been considered fit for espionage. Trevelyan's second wife, the painter Mary Fedden, confirmed that her husband had indeed been a close friend of Blunt. Julian had told her: 'He would have recruited me as a spy, but I was such a gossip he couldn't trust me.'* Trevelyan did not fit the typical profile of a spy who could infiltrate the decision-making centres of the British state as Kim Philby had done; MI5 described his usual attire as 'odd trousers'. But Parker's transition from young Tory to communist sympathiser would not have taken place without the influence of Trevelyan, who was one step away from the Cambridge spy ring as a close friend of both Blunt and Guy Burgess, whom he visited in Moscow in 1960.†

When Trevelyan published his autobiography, *Indigo*

---

* British Library, National Life Stories Collection, Artists: Mary Fedden.
† Letter from Burgess to his mother, TNA KV2.3932/75a and KV2.3932.74.

*Days*, Parker was hurt to see how lowly a place he occupied in the life of someone he considered his best friend. He appears as a 'communist journalist'* with whom the artist had once fallen out – though not permanently – due to Parker's inability to pay his way on one of their foreign adventures. (Parker never joined any communist party, either British or Soviet. He was, however, often in debt as a young man, even with a subsidy from his father.)

When Parker was appointed Moscow correspondent for *The Times* he went with the blessing of MI6, who trusted him to 'produce information of interest to them'.† He had already developed a taste for intelligence work, first in Czechoslovakia and then, having been recruited by Julian Amery, working as a British spy in Yugoslavia under diplomatic cover. After his expulsion from Yugoslavia, an Italian-language newspaper in New York memorably described Parker as 'a fake newspaperman but a genuine spy'.‡ Keen to play a role of greater significance in Moscow than that of mere reporter, Parker was ready to offer his services to the Allied cause, both to the British – to whom he was an 'old friend' – and to the Russians. There can be little doubt that he was a confidential contact of the NKVD; the only uncertainty is the level of his involvement.§

Pavel Sudoplatov, a former Soviet intelligence agent

* Trevelyan, *Indigo Days*, p. 35.
† TNA KV6 120/8a.
‡ *Il Progresso*, New York, 22 October 1940, in TNA FO 371.25031/298.
§ Stewart Purvis and Jeff Hulbert, *Guy Burgess: The Spy Who Knew Everyone*' (Biteback, London, 2016), pp. 336–337.

who played a role in the assassination of Trotsky and after fifteen years in the Gulag wrote several books about Soviet spies, casts Parker as a valued agent of the NKVD. He claims that Parker was first contacted by Soviet intelligence when he was working undercover for the British in Yugoslavia. When he came to Moscow in 1941, he was 'turned' and became a double agent. In Sudoplatov's view, Parker was no less valuable to the Soviet Union in the war years than Kim Philby.* This startling assessment would make Parker's contribution to Soviet intelligence as important as that of any of the members of the Cambridge Five spy ring. In the absence of other evidence, it is clear that Parker could have been a useful contact for Sudoplatov at the start of the war: Sudoplatov was put in charge of a sabotage group working behind German lines, the same activity as the British 'Section D', for which Parker had worked.† Equally important would have been Parker's access to the veteran MI6 agent George Hill, a key member of Section D in charge of training and sabotage who had been assigned to Moscow as the British intelligence liaison officer working with the NKVD. A fluent Russian speaker – he was the resourceful 'Colonel Kettle' who had saved Charlotte Haldane from starvation on the evacuation train from Moscow to Kuibyshev – Hill had written a colourful memoir, *Go Spy the Land*, detailing his attempts to undermine the Communist Party rule in the early years after the 1917 revolution. With that background, Hill was

---

* Pavel Sudoplatov, *Raznye dni tainoi voiny i diplomatii* (Olma Press, Moscow, 2001), p. 62.
† Vadim J. Birstein, *SMERSH: Stalin's Secret Weapon* (Biteback, London, 2011), p. 218.

a subject of great interest for the NKVD, which was never going to trust him. Notably forthright with journalists, Hill did not hide his view that after the war the alliance between Britain and the USSR would collapse into confrontation in Europe.* Parker's usefulness to the NKVD would have declined after the war, when he had no new intelligence to impart and all he could offer was embassy tittle-tattle.

An alternative assessment of Parker's relationship with the NKVD dates his recruitment as a Soviet agent from before his arrival in Moscow, possibly before he was sent to Prague. This comes from Ivan Obyedkov, not an espionage specialist but a researcher who is a relative of Parker's wife Valentina. In a 2014 article, 'Ralph Parker: Journalist or Scout?' he notes that, at the time of Parker's arrival in Russia, the British ambassador Sir Stafford Cripps was complaining that MI6 'are always trying to send spies of some sort out here . . . Of course the Russians find out and it makes them quite properly and naturally suspicious of everyone else.'† Obyedkov suggests a link between Parker's arrival and Cripps's complaint.

Obyedkov argues that Parker's motives for working as journalist cum double agent were high-minded. Parker, he concludes, was 'a member of a small community of foreign correspondents who worked as unofficial channels to share confidential information between political leaders of countries that were allies and even enemies.' Of course,

---

* Papers of Edgar Snow, Book 40, 1942–43, p. 94.

† Stafford Cripps and Gabriel Gorodetsky, *Stafford Cripps in Moscow 1940–1942: Diaries and Papers* (Valentine Mitchell, 2007), diary of 9 October 1941.

double agents from Philby downwards have always presented treachery as committed in the interests of peace and mutual understanding, but such arguments rarely stand up in court. Obyedkov declined to discuss his article with the author.*

While the extent of Parker's role in the cloak and dagger world will remain a mystery until the Soviet archives are opened, his transformation from respected journalist to a willing conduit for Soviet talking points is a matter of record. In wartime, this was not a problem for *The Times*, then a paper noted for accommodating Stalin's ambitions to exert great-power influence in Europe post-war. According to Iverach McDonald, the newspaper's diplomatic editor, *The Times* was 'earnestly seeking a basis of East-West cooperation if the Russians made such cooperation possible'. When Parker was sent out to Moscow, he was strongly encouraged to present the Soviet attitude 'fully and fairly'.† This is an understatement: the paper's editorial line came close to full-throated support for Stalin's ambitions to control eastern Europe as a buffer zone against future invasions.

In his first year, Parker was praised for his news coverage of the war, but by 1942 the foreign editor Ralph Deakin was complaining that Parker's 'effusions' read too much like his personal views rather than news copy.‡ A year later he cabled Parker with a warning: 'Must remind

---

* I. V. Obyedkov, 'Ral'f [sic] Parker: Zhurnalist ili razvedchik?', *Gumanitarnye Osnovaniya Social'nogo Progressa: Rossiya I Sovremennost,* April 2016, p. 146.
† McDonald, *The History of The Times [sic]*, p. 89.
‡ McDonald p. 86.

you that effective presentation of current Russian views requires they be reported with detachment. Spoiled by too much personal advocacy.'* Two months later, however, when Stalin had favoured Parker over all the other correspondents by answering his questions about the future status of Poland in liberated Europe, his position at *The Times* became unassailable. While the foreign editor gritted his teeth, Parker began sending briefing notes – private and not for publication – to the editor, Robert Barrington-Ward, who enjoyed reading them, even if less and less of Parker's output fitted the more detached tone required for the news pages.

Parker's ally on the paper was the assistant editor in charge of its editorial line, Professor E. H. Carr, a former diplomat and historian of Russia who was an ardent supporter of Stalin's post-war aim to be the leading power in eastern Europe. Carr used *The Times*' leader pages to influence British government policy, sometimes having his words toned down by the editor for fear of angering Churchill. When challenged over his Russophilia, Carr offered a sop to his critics in the form of an Anglo-Soviet condominium, with Moscow dominant in eastern Europe and Britain controlling the West. While superficially attractive, this idea ignored the fact that London and Moscow had very different ideas on what a friendly country should look like. In Stalin's understanding, a country close to Soviet borders needed to be made dependent on Moscow, if necessary by the killing or deportation to Siberia of thousands of its citizens.

Parker maintained his influence on the paper by

* McDonald p. 86.

providing Kremlin arguments for Carr to use in his leader page articles. Writing to Carr in April 1944 about Soviet plans for Europe, Parker insisted that Stalin had no intention of imposing communist rule on Poland. Parker advised Carr on how he could disarm his critics in London: by suggesting that Soviet foreign policy was now showing more flexibility – he used the word 'manoeuvrability'.* Parker's missives to Carr were sent to London through the diplomatic bag, a privilege that the embassy had offered to all British correspondents, but which Parker exploited to increase the influence of his writing: his briefings were seen not only by *The Times'* senior editors but also by the British embassy in Moscow, potentially influencing government policy from the inside.

Over this period Parker's relations with the British ambassador, Sir Archibald Clark Kerr, were souring. In 1944 the ambassador had bumped into Parker at the US embassy and told him, 'I am surprised you dare show yourself here.'† A year later a Foreign Office official noted that the ambassador was 'scarcely on speaking terms' with Parker. 'Clark Kerr is terrified that anything he says to Parker will leak to the Russians.'‡ Despite his seniority in the Moscow press corps, Parker could still provoke a kind of allergic reaction. The embassy's number two, Sir Frank Roberts, told an interviewer that his wife had taken an instant dislike to

---

* TNA FO 371.39400, item 111.
† Ralph Parker, *Conspiracy Against Peace: Notes of an English Journalist* (Literaturnaya Gazeta Publishers, Moscow, 1949), p. 200.
‡ Handwritten note by G. M. Wilson, TNA FO 371 39408, p. 82.

Parker. 'We should not have too much to do with Parker,' she advised him.*

Parker still had his defenders in the Foreign Office. A handwritten comment on a telegram from Moscow to London arguing for Parker's removal from Moscow blames his sulphurous reputation on idle gossip. 'Mr P. is undoubtedly the most intelligent and best-informed journalist in Moscow; the trouble is that he knows it and his colleagues know it too. He is also pompous, and the result is that all his colleagues are jealous of him and miss few opportunities of belittling him and of discussing him with members of the Embassy staff.' Instead of asking *The Times* to withdraw him, the embassy should make more use of the information provided by Parker and Valentina.†

Even Guy Burgess, the Soviet spy who fled to Russia in 1951 and welcomed Parker as a whisky-drinking partner to enliven his dull exile in Moscow, did not know what to make of him. He tolerated Parker's company so long as he brought along the whisky he imported with his foreign earnings, but he never trusted him. It was suspicious, Burgess told the Labour politician Tim Driberg, that Parker had his car – a Chevrolet – serviced by a corporal at the American Embassy. 'We all think he's an agent,' Burgess added, 'but we can't make out whose side he's on.'‡

But even while the ambassador regarded Parker as a security risk who was feeding everything he heard to the NKVD, and British diplomats were floating the idea that *The Times* should withdraw Parker, pragmatism trumped

* *The World Today*, Vol. 46, No. 12 (December 1990), pp. 225–30.
† FO 371 43337./2.
‡ Tom Driberg, *Ruling Passions* (Cape, London, ruling 1977), p. 232.

principle. As one British official noted: 'Mr Parker's contacts with Poles and out-of-the-way Russians have at times
proved quite valuable to the embassy'.* The phrase 'at
times' was an understatement. During the final months of
the war, Frank Roberts, defying the advice of his wife, and
the deputy head of mission at the US embassy, George
Kennan, invited Parker to lunch once a month to pump
him for Kremlin gossip and political intelligence.

Roberts later explained the kind of information Parker
provided. In April 1945, a month before Victory Day,
Parker told his lunch hosts: 'Something unpleasant is happening. The party's agitators are going round the factories
and enterprises and their theme is the following: "We the
Russian people must stop regarding the Americans and
British as our friends and allies. It is pure chance that we
fought this war with them on our side against the Germans –
it could equally have been the other way round. They are
our enemies."' Such information was gold dust: it enabled
diplomats who had no confidential contacts in Moscow to
show they had their finger on the Kremlin pulse.†

On the American side, Kennan's game plan was more
ambitious. He saw Parker as a 'bridge to the Soviets',
someone he could talk to unofficially and who would pass
him on to a Russian authorised to open an off-the-record
dialogue to ease the rising East-West tensions. This never
happened: it was naïve to expect Stalin to allow any back
channels of communication with Washington.‡

Nowhere are the contradictions in Parker's behaviour

* TNA FO 371 47918, p. 47.
† *The World Today*, Vol. 46, No. 12 (December 1990), pp. 225–30.
‡ Harrison Salisbury, *Disturber of the Peace* (Unwin, 1989), p. 132.

more glaring than in his relations with the British and American embassies. In private he was trusted as a reliable, even critical, analyst of the otherwise impenetrable world of Soviet policymaking, yet what he wrote was becoming ever more stridently anti-American. In truth, he was buffeted by the changing winds of geopolitics as the wartime alliance soured into open hostility. He wrote what was needed to avoid the fate of Cholerton, who had had his Moscow residency removed, while being useful to the British embassy so that he was never classed as a threat to national security.

With the onset of the Cold War, and *The Times* no longer in the market for apologias for Stalin, Carr's full-time work at the paper ended in 1946 and a year later Parker was dropped. His only option was to write for the *Daily Worker*, the British Communist Party paper, while supplementing his income with articles for Egyptian and Indian publications that required an anti-American take on events. He had left the *New York Times* in 1944 after falling out with the paper's staff correspondent, William H. Lawrence, who took a more robust approach towards Stalin.*

* Papers of Edgar Snow, Book 45, p. 2.

# 21

*November 1943: The party at play*

Holding on to her husband by the sleeve of his war correspondent's uniform, Tanya Matthews joined a queue of
unusually smartly dressed guests lining up to enter the
Morozov mansion, an over-the-top, neo-gothic fantasy
with pointed arches and turrets that had been the home of
a pre-revolutionary textile magnate. It was the evening of
7 November 1943, and the mansion was the venue for a
grand reception the like of which Moscow had not seen for
a generation. For two years, Revolution Day celebrations
in Russia had been muted: in 1941, Stalin had made a
speech before a small audience deep underground in the
Mayakovskaya metro station, in case of a German air raid.
The following year, he had invited a few dozen guests to
the Kremlin. This time there would be 500 guests in one
of Moscow's grandest locations. With the Red Army having beaten back the Germans at Stalingrad and Kursk,
the event was a coming-out party for a Soviet elite that was
emerging from the trauma of imminent defeat to find its
place at the head of a great power in Europe.

For Tanya, whether she would be on the guest list was
a test of her uncertain status. Would the foreign ministry
shun her as an undistinguished Soviet citizen, or invite
her to put on her best frock as the wife of an allied

correspondent? The ministry was in a generous mood –
she got a personal invitation. She felt she had earned
it – five months earlier, on the night of the last German
air raid on Moscow, she had given birth to the son Matthews had wanted so badly. How her life had changed
since they had first met only fourteen months before.*

She had her invitation checked three times as the queue
shuffled towards the entrance of the mansion. Inside, she
found herself walking between two ranks of Foreign Ministry officials clad in the Soviet diplomatic staff's new
uniform: pearl grey for ordinary wear, and for special
occasions such as tonight, black with gold trim and shoulder straps, with a ceremonial dagger hanging from the belt
to symbolise diplomacy as war by other means.† The foreign ministry staff did their best to stand tall, with serious
expressions on their faces, to reinforce the message of the
evening that Russia was once again a force to be reckoned
with. At the end of the two ranks stood foreign minister
Molotov, Stalin's faithful bag carrier, playing the role of
genial host, smiling as he shook hands with each guest. For
years Molotov had been a key member of the Bolshevik
leadership, but his bosses had always kept him in a subser-
vient position. Lenin had described him as 'Russia's finest
filing clerk'. This evening, however, was his to enjoy.

Pressed forward by the crowd, Tanya raised her eyes
and marvelled at the brilliance of the chandeliers. Room
after room was visible with tables covered in white cloths

---

* Tanya Matthews, *Russian Wife Goes West* (Gollancz, London
1955) p. 20.
† Victor Israelyan, *On the Battlefields of the Cold War: A Soviet Ambassador's Confession* (Pennsylvania State University Press, 2003), p. 21.

laden with gleaming silver and glass, and mountains of food. Tanya surveyed the guests and recognised stars from the ballet, opera and theatre worlds. She plucked up the courage to approach Lepeshinskaya, prima ballerina of the Bolshoi Ballet, and told her how much she admired her dancing. Lepeshinskaya was friendly and enjoyed chatting to Tanya until she learned that she was married to a foreigner, at which point the dancer turned away.*

Reeling from this snub, Tanya, who didn't drink alcohol, went off in search of a soft drink. She found herself in a quiet corridor. 'What do you want?' barked one of three men who could only be secret police. She thought quickly and said in English, 'I want water,' making a gesture with her cupped hand. One went off to get her a glass, and the other two stood either side of her while she smiled like a dumb foreigner. In front of them was a large trolley, such as you would find in an operating theatre with the surgeon's instruments on it. It was covered in a white cloth. Under the cloth, she realised, was the food specially prepared and checked for poisons to be served to Molotov and his party. Tanya was in such a hurry to leave she almost choked on her water.

She saw a crowd of admirers around Dmitry Shostakovich, whose Leningrad symphony composed in the city under siege had turned him into a cultural hero of the war. Having taken to heart the evening's formal dress code he was wearing white tie and tails and looked, as Alexander Werth noted cattily, like a college boy who had put on evening dress for the first time. The American correspondent Eddy Gilmore had a revealing conversation with him.

* Matthews, *Russian Wife*, p. 21.

The great composer told him that completing a new symphony or having one acclaimed by the Russian people was as nothing compared to the first swallow of beer after his football team, Zenit Leningrad, won a match.* The composer was not being glib. Music was a cultural minefield and several of his compositions had been denounced for 'modernism', so it was no surprise he took refuge in football; he even trained as a referee.

In his account of the evening, Werth noted the opulent nature of the event: 'The party had something of that wild and irresponsible extravagance which one usually associates with pre-revolution Moscow. There never was to be a party quite like it in subsequent years.'†

Tanya heard raucous laughter and moved to find out what was happening. She came across Marjorie Shaw of the *Daily Mirror* in a state of deep distress. 'I can't bear to look,' she said, one hand shielding her eyes and the other indicating the far corner of the room. 'Our ambassador can't take it any more, oh the poor man.'

Molotov was sitting with his guests of honour, the American and British ambassadors. The trial by vodka was reaching its climax. The US ambassador Averell Harriman, with years of experience of Russian banquets, had barricaded himself into a corner, with the oak panelling on one side and his daughter Kathy on the other. Harriman's tactics ensured that the night's victim was the British ambassador, Sir Archibald Clark Kerr, who unlike the

* Eddy Gilmore, *Me and My Russian Wife*, (Greenwood Press, 1968) p. 191.
† Alexander Werth, *Russia at War 1941–45* (Barrie and Rockliff, London, 1964), p. 753.

teetotal, vegetarian Cripps who had preceded him, was determined to stay close to Stalin and his associates, even as far as – in Churchill's words – 'kissing Stalin's bum'.

It was not going well for the British ambassador. At Molotov's table were two other Politburo members – Mikoyan and Kaganovich – and the three of them took turns in standing up to propose toasts, with the two ambassadors having to respond to each toast by rising from their chairs and draining their glasses in one. Kathy made sure that her father's glass was filled with soda water, but the British ambassador had no daughter to protect him. Each shot he drank was pure vodka. Tanya and Marjorie watched as Sir Archibald rose unsteadily to his feet in response to a Mikoyan toast and, after a few words, downed the liquid and collapsed back into his chair. Another glass was put before him; he stood up, braced himself with both palms on the table and opened his mouth to respond to the toast only to fall face forward onto the table, with a great clatter of glass and cutlery. Molotov and his staff lifted the ambassador back into an upright position. Bleeding from a flesh wound to the head, he pulled himself together and finished his toast.*

Having seen off Clark Kerr, Molotov stood up and left the table and began to circulate among the guests, followed by three waiters bearing trays of glasses and bottles of different sorts of firewater. Every few minutes he would recognise a senior diplomat, stop and in a spirit of great bonhomie propose a toast. Spying a newly arrived American naval commander in full dress uniform who radiated power and polish, Molotov bellowed

* Werth p. 753.

to the officer, 'You – fill your glass. I want to drink a toast to the everlasting friendship between the truly great American people and the Russian people.' The startled officer downed his glass. Amid the cheering and clapping, Tanya saw her husband hovering and noticed a mischievous look on his face. Standing in Molotov's way, Matthews asked politely, 'Mr Minister, I want you to drink my toast.' Molotov agreed.

'I want you to drink to the health of his Holiness the Pope.' Molotov pretended not to understand and indicated to his bodyguard to move on.* The next person barring his way was the Swedish minister, who had been trying to get Molotov's attention for some time and hoped to profit from his good mood. The Swede proposed a toast to 'the everlasting friendship between the great Russian people and the great Swedish people'. On the alert for diplomatic traps after Matthews' provocative toast, Molotov cut him off with the words, 'the great Swedish people are just a little too neutral', and marched away.

The assembled diplomats had never seen anything as rude as Molotov's rebuff to the Swede, and they huddled together discussing what it might mean. Vyshinsky, the deputy foreign minister, who had been tailing his boss throughout the party, now stuck more closely to him, sensing that the evening's vodka-fuelled animal spirits might lead to a diplomatic incident. After much whispering in the foreign minister's ear, a flunky appeared with Molotov's fur-trimmed coat, and he allowed himself to be steered down the stairs towards his waiting car. Before Vyshinsky could fold him safely into the vehicle, Molotov

* Matthews p. 24.

looked up and saw, standing at the top of the stairs, the American naval officer he had so recently summoned for a toast. Despite Vyshinsky's efforts to restrain him, Molotov climbed back up the stairs and threw his arms around the perplexed officer, kissing him full on the lips. 'My great friend,' Molotov beamed to the man he had never met before. Only then could Vyshinsky coax him back to his car.*

Molotov at least was still walking at the end of the evening. Many senior diplomats whose role required them to embody the grandeur of the states they represented were carried bodily out to their cars. As for Tanya, she cadged a lift with the Swedes back to the Metropol and hauled her comatose husband up the staircase to their room.

The next day there was much for the diplomats and journalists to chew over. In Russia there was no lasting shame in a man being drunk under the table, but alcohol tolerance had a way of establishing who was top dog. At his great Kremlin feasts Stalin never appeared drunk – indeed some suspected that the bottles from which his shots of vodka were poured were diluted with water – and he derived amusement from the sight of his subordinates, such as the loyal but underperforming Marshal Voroshilov, sliding under the table. The unequal contest imposed on Clark Kerr, taking place after Molotov had rejected every British plea to rescind the ban on Cholerton returning to Moscow, had established a new hierarchy in Europe in which Russia saw itself as the rising imperial power, fit to supplant the British empire.

For the last two years of his posting to Moscow, Clark

* Eddy Gilmore, *Me and My Russian Wife*, p. 199.

Kerr made clear to London his fears that after the war Stalin would not stop until he had expanded his areas of influence to include half of Europe. As for the Swedish minister, he was asked to leave Moscow within days. If the Swedes considered neutrality to be an honourable stance, the Kremlin did not, and with victory over Nazi Germany within its grasp, it was not afraid to say so.

# 22

## *February 1944: A taste of abroad*

The provocative toast pronounced by Matthews added a new crime to the Russians' charge sheet against him. Earlier in the year, on a long train journey from Moscow to Stalingrad, the press party had stopped in Saratov on the Volga and been treated to the usual banquet, at which Matthews had drunk his fill. At the end of the evening the other journalists held him upright and dragged him through the snow back to the station. Reviving with the cold, Matthews shook his colleagues off and began to harangue the crowd waiting on the platform. 'Comrades, you think you live in a promised land. It's true. You do. For much is promised, but . . .' Before he could complete his sentence, Kozhemyakov, a censor from the Press Department, rushed up to him and pleaded with him to stop. Matthews would not be silenced. 'Get away from me, you despicable lackey. You word killer. You are a murderer of the noblest things in the world – words.'*

The next morning, the British journalists treated their hung-over colleague's behaviour of the previous night as a big joke. Only the thunderous look of the face of

---

* Eddy Gilmore, *Me and My Russian Wife* (Greenwood Press, 1968), p. 156.

Valentina, Parker's translator, showed her contempt for the British reporters indulging their colleague. This cemented Valentina's reputation in the foreign community as a hardened Anglophobe. When word of the incident filtered back to Moscow, Valentina was cast as the guilty party. The head of the embassy's consular service wrote, 'She is a highly intelligent communist, skilled in the apologetics of the Party and, at heart, scornful of the English.'*

The Soviet Press Department staff had respected Cholerton for his rare understanding of Russia but were keen to see the back of Matthews. Having Tanya beside him had reinforced his anti-Soviet views and, for him and the other journalists, she was a ready source of juicy details about the daily struggle of ordinary Soviet citizens, so different from the lives of the pampered ballerinas and authors they were allowed to consort with. Matthews was now desperate to leave but he refused to go without Tanya and their baby Christopher. Stalin had banned Soviet women from emigrating with their foreign husbands – they were decried as selfish 'shirkers'† using the pretext of marriage to avoid the hard graft of rebuilding Russia.

An opportunity to break the deadlock arose in January when Matthews received a cable from his mother. His father had died, and she begged him to come home and bring her new daughter-in-law and grandson with him. Matthews asked the British embassy to request permission for Tanya to go to England on compassionate leave. The embassy's number two, Jock Balfour, secured a meeting with the deputy foreign minister, Vladimir Dekanozov, a

* Thomas Brimelow, TNA FO 317.49718/94.
† 'Shirkers' is the word used by Vyshinsky, FO 369 3025/88390.

hard man even by the standards of the Bolshevik leadership: he had overseen the execution of thousands of Red
Army officers just before the war and then had enforced
the 'Sovietisation' of independent Lithuania by the simple
expedient of deporting its political leaders and middle
class to Siberia. To the surprise of everyone at the Metropol,
this ruthless operative gave permission for Tanya to go
abroad on her Soviet passport. It was explained that this
was an exceptional case, and did not set a precedent for
the dozen Soviet women married to British subjects who
were being prevented from joining their husbands abroad.*

Tanya was in a hurry to pack up and leave before the
Soviet authorities changed their minds. There was one
problem to resolve: she had to get permission from her ex-
husband Nick to take their daughter Anna with her. Nick
had always promised to let Anna go abroad with Tanya if
she was ever to be allowed out, but when Tanya went to see
him at their old flat, his attitude had changed. A few days
before, he had been summoned to the Soviet visa department and told that it would be unpatriotic of him to allow
his daughter to live in the hostile world.

'So you're saving your own skin,' Tanya rebuked him.

Nick shot back: 'And you sold yourself for cheap comfort and chewing gum.'

Tanya spat in his face, Nick slapped her and she hit out
at him blindly with clenched fists.

In all their years together they had never fought. Now
all their unspoken recriminations were coming out.

Tanya said: 'You're taking revenge on me, but it's Anna
who will suffer.'

* Tanya Matthews, *Russian Wife Goes West*, Gollancz, 1955 p. 30.

She knew there was no chance of Nick changing his mind – he had been warned by the visa department there would be consequences for him if he let Anna go. The thought of leaving Anna behind filled her with unbearable pain, but what choice did she have? She knew what happened to Russian women who stayed behind after their foreign husbands had left. Unless they were willing to work for the secret police they could never find employment, and even if they did become informers they still risked ending up in a labour camp in Siberia or Kazakhstan. If that happened she would be separated from both her children, for fifteen to twenty years.

On the day of their departure they arrived at the airport at 4 a.m. with only Tanya's mother to see them off. All Tanya could say, again and again, was: 'Mama, somewhere, somehow, we'll all be together again. Believe me, one day we'll be together.' She could see that her mother did not believe her. Indeed, it would require a miracle.*

After a day's flying they landed at Baku airport, from where they were taken by bus to the Intourist hotel to spend the night. Early the next day, they drove back to the airport and stayed on the bus waiting for permission to board the plane which stood a few hundred yards away. Minutes stretched into an hour and then two hours, and Matthews and some of the passengers strolled about in the thin February sunshine but Tanya and her baby remained on the bus. After three hours, a border official appeared and called out Tanya's name. 'The boss wants to see you.' Leaving her baby in the arms of a passenger, she summoned

* Tanya Matthews, *Russian Wife*, p. 31.

Matthews and together they walked to the border guards' office. 'Citizen Matthews – you cannot continue your journey,' said the chief. Tanya's heart stopped. She had always known the cruelty of the regime she was escaping from, but she never expected such a heartless trick. Was she about to be arrested, 1,000 miles from any help from the British embassy?

Outwardly she remained calm, and asked what the problem was. The chief said, 'There is an irregularity in your passport. I have received a telegram from Moscow ordering me to stop you boarding the aircraft.'

She asked how long they were going be delayed. The official said he was awaiting a decision from Moscow, but added, 'Of course, your husband can leave on this plane. He can go now.'

She translated and Matthews turned red in the face and started shouting insults at the official. He yelled: 'Tell this bastard I will not dream of leaving you behind. And I will kick up the mother and father of all rows with our ambassador about our abominable treatment.'*

All they could do was watch the other passengers board the plane. Returning to the hotel in the empty bus, for the first time in her life Tanya doubted that she would leave Russia. She saw how small and defenceless she was in the face of the cruel machine. She could not eat, finding it hard to swallow. At the end of the second day there was still no news from Moscow. With a baby, they could not stay imprisoned in the hotel indefinitely and reluctantly she faced the prospect of returning to Moscow. It

* Ibid., p. 33.

was time to persuade her husband to get them back to the Metropol.

The Foreign Office archives contain many pages about the struggle of Soviet wives of British citizens to leave the country, but they shed no light on what happened next. It could have been a case of bureaucratic muddle – a senior official in Moscow could not understand why, in defiance of all the rules, Tanya was being allowed to leave the country and took it upon himself to prevent her leaving. Perhaps he had not been told that giving Tanya permission to leave was the only way to get rid of the troublesome Matthews. More likely, the exit permit granted to Tanya was a trick right from the start. The plan was always to halt Tanya's journey at the scheduled stop in Baku, in the hope that Matthews would leave without her, and then she could be quietly exiled to Siberia. Many British husbands, particularly members of the military mission, had been forced to abandon their Russian brides. But Matthews' stubborn nature and devotion to his wife and son were an unforeseen obstacle to the plan.

Tanya woke early on their third day in the hotel and there was still no news from Moscow. Later, there was a knock on the door. It was a man from the Intourist bureau. 'You are free to leave. We are holding the plane for you at the airfield. How long do you need to pack?'

'Five minutes,' Tanya whooped with joy. They rushed down to a waiting car. As she entered the plane, Tanya was handed back her Soviet passport. As they flew over the high Elburz mountains into Iran, she looked for any sign of 'irregularities'. Not a word had been changed.*

* Ibid., p. 35.

Tanya's first impression of 'abroad' was the abundance of fruit, the stalls piled high with oranges and lemons in quantities she had never seen before, and you could go into a shop and buy whatever you desired, and there were no queues. The people on the streets of Tehran were not quite what she expected – some of the men wore long garments – and to cross the roads you had to step over a stream of running water, as if pipes had never been invented. As she grew accustomed to Tehran, she realised that the bit of 'abroad' she had landed in was not so far from her childhood home, the oil town of Grozny in the Caucasus. In the mornings she would slip out of the hotel and buy salty, sharp-flavoured goat's cheese such as she had eaten as a girl. This made Matthews cross: he told her it was 'not done' – whatever that meant – to eat goat's cheese for breakfast, a meal that had to feature bacon and eggs.

One evening they were invited to a dinner party at the British embassy. As she recalls, 'There was candlelight, flowers and subdued conversation as if someone were dead. The food was served by smoothly moving native servants.'* As she took her place at table she was horrified to see three forks and three knives on either side of her plate, and a spoon at the top. She had never used more than one knife and one fork which Matthews had taught her to hold in her left hand. She had no idea what to do with three of each. To her relief soup was served and she grabbed the spoon, only to see everyone around her sipping the soup straight from cups. From then on she watched her neighbour's choice of cutlery so assiduously that she could not make polite conversation. Worse was to come. When the

* Ibid., p. 38.

hostess rose from her seat, Tanya assumed her ordeal was over and went to join to her husband.

He gave her a stern look. 'The party's not over yet. Run along and join the ladies.' She found herself sitting for a whole hour with five women who ignored her, while discussing babies, servants and 'someone called Julia who had run away with someone else's husband'. At last the men came in, talking louder and looking redder about the face. On the way back to the hotel, Tanya confided to Matthews that she liked the Metropol parties much better.

After ten days in Tehran they flew to Cairo, which turned out to be more like the city of Tanya's dreams, with its bright sunshine, busy streets, white houses and shop windows full of exciting things she had not even known existed. It was here she received her British passport, dark blue with gold lettering. To celebrate her becoming a subject of the King, Matthews took her on her first shopping trip. He suggested they take with them a female colleague to help her select appropriate outfits. But Tanya put her foot down. This was the first time in her life she would be able to choose her own clothes, and she would do it herself. That evening, Tanya put on the white evening dress she had bought in the afternoon as they were going out to dine with some journalists and a British general. The terrace of Shepheard's Hotel, with its palm trees, soft lighting and Egyptian waiters gliding about in their white robes with broad red belts, was the place to be seen in wartime Cairo. While the journalists were amusing each other with their 'when I was in . . .' stories, Tanya wondered what a British general would look like – probably short and bulging out of his uniform, with a weather-beaten face and grey hairs growing out of his ears. It was a shock when General Joe

Baillon turned out to be tall and slender with dark wavy hair and a small moustache, wearing a well-cut uniform. What's more, he turned out to be an accomplished dancer – the only Englishman she had met who could follow the rhythm of the orchestra. 'Do you play tennis?' asked the general as he steered Tanya around the dance floor.

'Very badly,' replied Tanya. 'In Russia it is considered a bourgeois game.'

'Well, I'd like to teach you a bourgeois game,' he responded. 'I'll invite you to play at the Gezira Club.'

As they parted, Matthews told the general that he would shortly be leaving Cairo to cover the war in Europe and asked him to keep an eye on Tanya while he was away. 'One day she might need your advice.'

At the end of March, Matthews left for Britain to cover the D-Day landings on the Normandy coast, the 'second front' that the Russians had been demanding since the start of the war. Tanya threw herself into learning to play tennis. At the Gezira Club five days a week she practised with a professional, and on Wednesdays she played with the general. Joe, as she now called him, took her out to dinner and dancing every Saturday night.

One day she was asked by a prim Englishwoman to give a talk for broadcast on the BBC Middle East service. The subject would be Russia in wartime. Tanya outlined what she wanted to say – the potato-peel diet, the freezing temperatures of the unheated apartments, Russians' hatred of Stalin's regime such that in the early months of the war whole armies surrendered to the Germans hoping for liberation. The BBC woman was horrified. 'We are allies, the Russians saved England from Hitler's invasion. You should not say such wicked things about this great people.' It was clear to Tanya that she was not going to be broadcasting her views on Russia, so she suggested she might sing some Russian folk songs instead. Visibly relieved, the woman accepted her offer.*

More alarmingly, one day after a game of tennis Tanya found a telephone message inviting her to call in at the British Embassy at her earliest convenience. What could this mean – had something happened to her husband Ronnie in France? When she arrived at the embassy her name seemed to be familiar to the receptionist. As she waited in an anteroom, embassy employees walking past appeared to be sizing her up while trying not to be too obvious. She was ushered into the office of a young first secretary. 'Mrs Matthews, we can facilitate your passage to England.' Air passages to London were in short supply, he continued, but he thought he could fit her on the first available plane.

Astonished at the suggestion, Tanya told him that she had no plans to leave.

'I'm afraid you have to leave. Your husband undertook an obligation to take you to England with him.'

Tanya reminded him that her husband was in France; she knew nothing of any obligation, and besides she had nowhere to live in England – Ronnie's flat had been destroyed by a buzz bomb – and she needed to stay in Egypt until she had a home to go to.

The diplomat was not pleased by her response. As she left the room, his parting words were, 'I will let you know about further developments in your case.' Tanya was confused. If there was a case, that suggested she had done

* Ibid., p. 47.

something wrong. It took a journalist colleague to explain that the whole of Cairo was abuzz with gossip about the affair between a pretty Russian blonde and a British general who were flaunting their relationship on the tennis court and the dance floor.

'But I only see him twice a week,' Tanya protested.

'You're so naïve. People love gossip and they say you're inseparable. You only left Moscow a few weeks ago. I shouldn't be surprised if the military police are searching your rooms for signs of espionage while you play tennis at the Gezira Club.'

Tanya was indignant at these revelations and told him she was not going to be forced onto a plane to London. In any case, she was planning to escape the heat of Cairo by moving to the coast for the summer. Her friend reassured her that once she had left Cairo she would be forgotten, and the foreign community would find someone else to gossip about.

The question of Tanya being a Soviet spy was not just empty gossip. The British embassy in Cairo asked the Foreign Office to run a security check on the young Russian woman who was cavorting with the chief of staff of the British Army in the Middle East. A response came in an unsigned cable from Moscow: 'Nothing is known against her on security (repeat security) grounds, but I doubt her trustworthiness.'*

The comment about her trustworthiness signalled the beginning of acrimonious exchanges over the nature of the deal with the Russians that had allowed Tanya to escape. In the months to come, British diplomats would

---

* TNA FO 369/3025, cable of 16 June 1944.

paint Mr and Mrs Matthews as evil masterminds of esca-
pology whose underhand tactics had embarrassed the
British government and ruined the chances of other hos-
tage wives joining their husbands abroad. The truth was
more complicated.

The exit permit, issued under 'exceptional circumstances' in January, was supposedly to enable Tanya to
visit her widowed mother-in-law in Britain. Jock Balfour
had arranged this permit as a favour for Matthews who,
according to Foreign Office archives, had been 'reduced
to a highly nervous condition' by the delay in getting his
wife out.* Now, with Tanya creating problems for the
embassies in both Moscow and Cairo, Balfour railed
against her in a cable to London. She had settled herself
down 'to enjoy the fleshpots of Cairo'. Her behaviour, if
known to the Soviet authorities, 'will certainly not predis-
pose them to make any similar concessions in the future.'†

There was worse to come. To add weight to his argument that Tanya should be allowed out on compassionate
grounds, Balfour had indicated to Molotov that Tanya
would be returning to the USSR after her visit to
England.

The idea that Tanya, a married woman, would return
to Moscow after her visit to London was patently absurd,
as would have been clear to both sides. She had, after all,
devoted her life to escaping the Bolshevik state, and the
NKVD would have known this. Nevertheless, the Russians pocketed this promise and used her failure to return

* TNA 369 3025/1577.
† Ibid

as a pretext for refusing to help the dozen other wives of British citizens to leave.

With Tanya refusing to move from Egypt, the Foreign Office decided to put pressure on Matthews to order his wife to relocate to Britain. As Matthews was following the Allied armies through Europe, urgent missives from the Foreign Office failed to reach him. When he finally responded in October 1944, he insisted that neither he nor Tanya had made any promise to the Soviet authorities. And if they had done, 'I consider that undertaking would have been automatically voided when, at the frontier airport of Baku, those authorities tried to hold my wife and child captive, on the pretence of a non-existent visa irregularity and to persuade me to leave the country alone.' He ridiculed the idea that a promise to return would have been taken seriously by the Russians. The Soviet authorities, he wrote, 'may be boors but they are not buffoons . . . and must have known that she would never come back.'*

In London, a despairing official concluded after reading this letter that there was no point in pressing any further 'an unprincipled man of this type'. We do not know how much the diplomatic stink left by Tanya's departure harmed the chances of freedom for other Soviet wives of British citizens. The indisputable fact is that Tanya had found her saviour and escaped Russia, and she could never be forced to return.

* TNA FO 369/3025, item 11754.

# 23

## *1944–45: 'The Ghosts on the Roof'*

In the spring of 1944, Ella Winter, a leading light of the American left, arrived in Moscow at the start of her dream posting: she was to spend six months writing features for the *New York Post* about daily life in Russia. As the widow of Lincoln Steffens, who had famously declared of the Soviet Union, 'I have seen the future, and it works', she might have expected one of the better rooms at the Metropol. But when she arrived in the hotel lobby, the assistant manager Jack Margolis could find no trace of her booking. She was shown to a 'windowless den on an airshaft that was dark all day' and she had to use a shared bathroom with a rusty tub standing in an inch of smelly water.*

Some guidance from Nadya would have helped her settle in, but Nadya avoided her: they had known each other in America – and not just as friends. In the early 1930s in New York, the communist agent Whittaker Chambers had approached Winter twice to work for the Ulanovsky spy ring, but she turned him down. Alex made a third attempt to recruit her, this time in person, but she was not interested in clandestine work. Nadya was worried that Winter

---

* Ella Winter, *I Saw the Russian People* (Little, Brown and Co, Boston, 1946), p. 11.

could reveal her past as a Soviet intelligent agent, and put off the inevitable reunion.

Noticing a newcomer who seemed a bit lost, one of the young women hanging around the Metropol lobby 'took pity' on her and offered to help her collect her sugar ration. When Winter said she did not take sugar, the young woman asked if she could have her ration, and Winter readily agreed, not knowing that sugar was a precious commodity in the Soviet barter economy and more valuable than cash; a pound of sugar was worth $100 under the rigged exchange rate that foreigners had to use. Winter fell for the same trick again, this time from a correspondent who wanted to buy gifts for his Russian girlfriend and asked her if she needed the coupons she had been allocated for the foreigners' store where clothes and household goods could be bought cheaply. Not needing any clothes, Winter handed over her whole six-month supply.

The scale of the error she had made became clear when she went to buy a mug, a couple of plates, a knife and fork and a one-ring electric heater to make breakfast and supper in her room, the hotel serving only one meal a day in the dining room at that time.* A single plate cost $25. A journalist told her, 'You gave away 10,000 dollars' worth of roubles in a day.'†

She had another lesson in the Metropol economy when an expensively dressed young woman with a large sapphire on her manicured hand knocked at her door and asked for a job as her courier. 'I live in the hotel with a fur buyer,' she added. Winter could not see why this young

* Ella Winter, *I Saw the Russian People*, p. 19.
† Ibid., p. 19.

woman's love life had any bearing on her ability to act as an errand girl. Only later did she realise that the visitor expected her, an American woman, to understand that she, the mistress of a fur buyer, should not spend the summer chopping wood in the forest and ruining her nails and so needed an excuse to avoid compulsory war work. She did not get the job.

Winter never got over her shock at what she found in the Metropol. She was not ready for a 'little island of foreigners and reluctant Soviet citizens, where only talk and rumour, complaints and finagling, pettiness and gossip and disaffection could flourish'. It reminded her of a modern-day Circe's isle, the enchanted realm of a sorceress who, in Homer's *Odyssey*, turned Ulysses' heroic soldiers into a herd of pigs. In her view the male correspondents, with their generous rations and choice of young women, were no better than swine.*

When Nadya and Winter finally met in the dining room of the Metropol, they affected, as good communists, not to have seen each other before. Nadya's secret was safe.

If Winter's appearance in Moscow was a surprise, it was as nothing compared to the shock Nadya experienced when, flipping through the pages of *Time* magazine, she saw her old American communist friend Whittaker Chambers listed as a senior editor. 'Who is this Chambers?' she asked the *Time* bureau chief Craig Thompson with studied nonchalance. Thompson told her that he was a former communist who in 1938 had come to offer his services to *Time* and had become a star writer. His pen was so fluent that he could take the most abstruse

* Ibid., p. 30.

topic – the publication of James Joyce's dense experimental novel, *Finnegans Wake* – and get it on the cover of a middlebrow magazine. Nadya knew that Chambers had left the Communist Party, but it was a shock to hear that he had swung so far right that he was working for a conservative publication. Recalling their time together in New York, she yearned to tell Chambers that she and Alex had rejected Stalinism and to find out how he had come to the same conclusion.* She persuaded Thompson to write to Chambers, adding a line at the end of his letter, 'Nadya also sends her greetings.' When Chambers read it, he had no idea who Nadya was – he had known her as Maria – and worried it could be a provocation. It was only when Thompson returned to New York and gave Chambers descriptions of Alex and Nadya that he was convinced they were his old controllers, 'Ulrich' and 'Maria'. Nadya acknowledges she had 'frank conversations' with Thompson, which is borne out by what Chambers later told the FBI, that his Soviet masters had become 'bitterly anti-Soviet and lived in constant fear of being shot or sent to Siberia'.† Even with Nadya's identity confirmed, he did not dare to respond to her, his caution perhaps stemming from Alex's blunt words to him as he and Nadya were leaving New York: 'Remember, Bob, there are only two ways that you can really leave us: you can be shot by them, or you can be shot by us.'‡

* Nadezhda Ulanovskaya and Maya Ulanovskaya, *Istoria Odnoi Semyi*, 3rd edition, (Inanpress, 2013), p. 51.
† Allen Weinstein, 'Nadya: A Spy Story (*Encounter*, June 1977), p. 77.
‡ Whittaker Chambers, *Witness* (Andre Deutsch, London, 1953), p. 234.

In the first weeks of 1945 the *Daily Express* correspondent Alaric Jacob noticed that chairs, rugs and crockery were disappearing from the Metropol. This could mean only one thing: a major conference was scheduled and in wartime it could only be a meeting of the Big Three – Stalin, Roosevelt and Churchill – and it would be held on Soviet territory, and it had to be somewhere warm, Roosevelt's health being too delicate to tolerate the cold. The location turned out to be Yalta, in the Crimea, at the former Tsar's Livadia Palace, which had been comprehensively looted by the Germans.

With the conference taking place in total secrecy and in the absence of the press, it was easy for all sides to claim it was a success: miraculously, it seemed, the Allies were still united as war was drawing to a close. This was the upbeat message given to a joint session of Congress on 1 March 1945 by Roosevelt, a spectral figure who was to die the following month. Stalin had cooperated on many pressing issues and he was no longer insisting on a fixed sum of reparations from Germany, said the president. Stalin had refused to give up the lands in East Prussia, Hungary and Czechoslovakia that the Red Army had conquered, but on Poland, he appeared to be more flexible: he had agreed that the Soviet-installed provisional government should be broadened through open elections to be contested by other parties.

To critics of Roosevelt and Churchill, this looked like wishful thinking: what guarantee was there that Stalin would risk a free election in Poland when he had his Soviet placemen in office already? Stalin believed that Poland must be a Moscow-aligned buffer state against Germany, and he had never hidden this ambition.

In New York, Chambers saw through the blind optimism of the Western leaders: the Yalta agreements were
not 'a start on the road to a world of peace'* as Roosevelt
claimed, but a green light for Stalin to establish an Eastern
European empire. Chambers wrote a piece and laid it on
the desk of *Time*'s managing editor, asking him to read it
but suggesting it might not fit the magazine's ethos. It was
'unlike anything else he had done for *Time* – and unlike
anything the magazine had ever published.'† A deputation
of the staff came to the editor to ask him to bin the piece as
'bitter, irresponsible journalism' that could harm peace
and reflected only the author's bias as an ex-communist.
Despite this, it was published on 5 March under the title,
'The Ghosts on the Roof', and with a disclaimer saying it
was a 'political fairy tale'.

It was an extraordinary piece of journalism. The ghosts
of the last Tsar, the Tsarina Alexandra and their four
daughters and one son, all with Bolshevik bullet holes in
their foreheads, are gathered on the roof of the Livadia
Palace to eavesdrop on the conference. Nicholas has left
his usual haunt – the casino at Monaco – to pursue his fascination with Stalin. 'What statesmanship! What power!'
the emperor gushes. 'We have known nothing like it since
my ancestor Peter the Great broke a window into Europe
by overrunning the Baltic States in the 18th century. Stalin
has made Russia great again!'

Nicholas peers through a hole in the roof to admire

* https://www.presidency.ucsb.edu/documents/address-congress-
the-yalta-conference
† Sam Tanenhaus, *An Un-American Life: The Case of Whittaker Chambers* (Old Street Publishing, London, 2007), p. 190.

Stalin, 'so small, so sure', who had brought the world's greatest statesmen to an old imperial palace to celebrate his becoming the ruler of half of Europe. The emperor explains that Stalin's greatness is to have adapted revolutionary tactics, discarding proletarian uprisings in favour of 'social revolutions' such as are being fomented in Romania, Bulgaria, Yugoslavia, Hungary and Poland. The last word goes to Cleo, the Muse of History, who has joined the imperial family on the roof. 'I never expect human folly to learn much from history.'*

Chambers' heartfelt whimsy was ahead of its time. Readers complained in droves and the magazine tried to dissociate itself from the author's implication that post-war US-Soviet cooperation was doomed.† But within weeks messages were pinging back and forth between London and Washington on the ways Stalin was breaking his promises on Poland by arresting Polish politicians returned from exile. In a couple of years the Chambers view was mainstream.

The article was not signed, as was customary for *Time*, but reading it in Thompson's room in the Metropol, Nadya was in no doubt that the fairy tale could only have been written by Chambers. She smiled to herself as she thought affectionately of the brilliant but chaotic American comrade who, she now realised, had followed the same path as her.

---

* 'The Ghosts on the Roof', *Time*, 5 March 1945.
† Tanenhaus, *An Un-American Life*, p. 191.

# 24

## *The Metropol's invisible wall*

In 1926 an unremarkable, prematurely balding man was allocated room 453 in the Metropol. It was not a suite, but it had its own toilet and a balcony with a view of the Bolshoi Theatre. Small tables had been set up throughout the hotel, and the new arrival could be seen playing chess in the corridor outside his room. His chess partners soon discovered that Vassily Ulrich did not like to talk about his work, but he spoke readily and with great passion about his beetle and butterfly collection. He spent winter evenings sorting the insects he had caught over the summer and mounting them on pins in glass cases.

His wife, Anna Kassel, was the opposite to him in character. She was sociable, loved to chat and would reveal with pride that she had once worked for the great leader himself, Vladimir Ilyich Lenin, an association that made her minor Bolshevik nobility. But even at her most unguarded moments, the garrulous Anna never let slip the nature of her husband's work.

In the early evening as the journalists converged on the room of whichever of their colleagues was hosting drinks, some of their number might pass Ulrich playing chess and not give him a second thought. All the journalists had arrived in Moscow with one burning question – What had really happened during Stalin's purges? – and none of them had the slightest inkling that the man bent over the chess board had been at the heart of the Great Terror unleashed by Stalin in the 1930s.

For twenty-two years, from 1926 to 1948, Ulrich served as one of the USSR's most senior judges with the title of Chairman of the Military Collegium of the Supreme Court, a role he carried out with such zeal that colleagues called him 'Executioner No. 1'.* During the years of the Great Terror from 1936–38 he signed no fewer than 31,456 death sentences, including those of Isaac Babel, the acclaimed writer who described so vividly the lives of the Jewish gangsters of Odessa, two Red Army marshals – Tukhachevsky and Egorov – and four members of the Communist Party politburo.† The Metropol's Old Bolshevik residents – Stalin's comrades in the Revolution –were living under the same roof as a man who at any moment could summon them to a ten-minute hearing and sentence them to death.

Ulrich had no legal training, which suited Stalin perfectly as he followed whatever orders he was given without question. Ulrich had personally assured Stalin that he was working 'under the direct guidance of the highest directive organs'.‡ This meant that, irrespective of the evidence, Stalin and the Politburo edited and approved the indictments and verdicts in the 'show trials' of senior Bolsheviks in the

* Vadim J. Birstein, *SMERSH: Stalin's Secret Weapon* (Biteback, 2011), p. 65.
† Ekaterina Egorova, *Metropol – Stolitsa Moskvy* (Sever, Moscow, undated) p. 251.
‡ Birstein, *SMERSH*, p. 64.

1930s. (The show trials were unlike routine political cases in that they featured a prosecutor and a defence counsel, and the abject confessions of the accused were reported in detail in the press, to promote the image of Stalin as the all-powerful leader.) For routine hearings, usually held in secret, Ulrich was trusted by Stalin to hand down a death sentence to almost all the accused. Once convicted, they were taken down to the basement of the Military Collegium building on 23 Nikolskaya Street, where they were shot in the back of the head, their corpses removed by night in ammunition boxes and cremated at the Donskoi Cemetery.

The Metropol was a mere ten minutes' walk away from all Ulrich's places of work: the Lubyanka where the detainees were held; his office in the Military Collegium; and the House of the Unions, a historic building where he conducted the show trials. At those show trials all eyes were on Vyshinsky, the histrionic prosecutor who vilified the accused as 'stinking carrion' and 'mad dogs' while Ulrich remained in the background taking notes. Despite his high position, Ulrich's face was never well known. As the purges gathered momentum, the wives of the disappeared would queue up at the door of the Military Collegium to ask for news of their relatives, to be told either nothing at all or that their loved ones – who were already dead – had been sentenced to 'ten years without right of correspondence'. The more courageous women would accost Ulrich on the street as he left his office or as he entered the Metropol. He would fob them off – 'I could give you money, but I cannot help you.'* As the daily number of executions reached

---

* Egorova, *Metropol*, p. 252.

dizzying heights in the late 1930s, Ulrich was provided with bodyguards to stop people bothering him.

In 1926, the same year that Ulrich moved into the Metropol, Nikolai Bukharin, a rising star in the Communist Party, settled into a three-room corner suite with its own hallway. A tragic love affair began. Directly above Bukharin's suite lived the Larin family whose teenage daughter Anna developed a crush on Bukharin and wrote girlish love poems to him. On her way down to Bukharin's suite to post a poem under his door, her courage failed. In the corridor she caught sight of Stalin, a regular visitor to the Metropol, where half of the government was billeted, and ran up to him and begged him to deliver her poem in person, which he did. In 1934, at the age of twenty, she became Bukharin's third wife, only to see him arrested three years later, charged with conspiring to overthrow the Soviet state, and executed as an enemy of the people. Anna spent twenty years imprisoned as a 'family member of a traitor to the motherland', and every night she repeated to herself Bukharin's last testament repudiating the confessions he had been forced to make. He had asked her to memorise the text, unwritten, until she could present it as evidence for his rehabilitation.

Bukharin's death sentence was one of the thousands Ulrich signed but it had special significance for his family. He moved them into the Metropol suite once occupied by Bukharin. Profiting from the goods and property of the 'repressed' was a perk of working for the secret police. By the start of the war Ulrich had eaten so well that he was bursting out of his uniform and had become, in the words of a political prisoner, 'a uniformed toad with watery eyes'.* Violating the strict secrecy surrounding his work, Ulrich allowed his wife to interfere in court decisions and gave his mistress a pass to come to his office.† The life expectancy of a secret policeman under Stalin was short but Ulrich, who had sent thousands of innocents to their deaths or to waste their lives in forced labour camps, somehow survived all these purges. After the war the invisible man of Stalin's Great Terror left the Metropol when he was rewarded with his own apartment. He died peacefully at home in the comfort of his own bed.

In contrast to other residents of the Metropol, Nadya and Alex would have known who this unremarkable man was. It was he who had overseen the massacre of the 30,000 White soldiers and officers who had surrendered in Crimea at the end of the civil war, the bloodbath that had convinced Alex never to join the Communist Party. It was Ulrich who signed the death warrant of Jan Berzin, the director of military intelligence who had promoted Alex's spying career. Exceptionally, Ulrich went down to the basement and personally shot Berzin in the back of the head. Both Ulrich and Berzin were of Latvian origin so, by shooting his compatriot, 'Executioner No. 1' proved that his loyalty to Stalin was unwavering.

That Ulrich's presence remained a secret shows how effectively an invisible wall separated the journalists from the Metropol's permanent residents. Very occasionally, however, could an event on the other side of the invisible

---

* Anton Antonov-Ovseyenko, *The Time of Stalin: Portrait of a Tyranny* (Harper & Row, New York, 1983), p. 83.
† Birstein, p. 65.

wall not be hidden. One day in December 1944, journalists were drawn from their rooms by the sweet smell of incense wafting down the corridor and the dissonant sounds of religious chanting and a baby crying. A baptism was in progress, that of the new-born daughter of Alexander Vertinsky, a popular singer in the days of the Tsar, who had returned from exile to show solidarity with the USSR in wartime. His wife Lidia feared taking baby Anastasia out in the cold to a church, so a priest and a deacon with a sonorous voice were invited to their suite. Anastasia cried throughout the ceremony.

When Lidia looked out into the corridor she was astounded at what she saw: guests of all nationalities had emerged from their rooms and were joined by the hotel's maids, waiters and security men, all straining their ears to hear a baptism service 'in the most tightly guarded hotel in the godless Soviet capital'. Having made her presence felt during the christening, Anastasia went on to become a famous Soviet actress, among other roles starring as the bewitched Margarita in the 1994 adaptation of Bulgakov's satire of Soviet life, *The Master and Margarita*.*

The American journalist Eddy Gilmore, who lived in Moscow for eleven years while waiting for permission to take his Russian wife Tamara to live in the United States, witnessed a rare serious breach of the invisible wall. After the end of the war, Gilmore, Tamara and a Canadian diplomatic couple were in the hotel lift. As it was about to begin its trembling ascent, someone banged on the metal grating with a stick and demanded to be let in. The liftman opened the door and in strode a Soviet army general

* Egorova p. 266.

in full dress uniform, the gold star of hero of the Soviet Union gleaming on his chest. Gilmore recognised General Andrei Eremenko, one of the heroes of the defence of Stalingrad, who had been wounded seven times in the battle but continued to exercise command from his hospital bed. Buoyed up by the cocktails he had drunk at a US embassy party, Gilmore introduced himself to the general – who clearly had had a few drinks somewhere else – and the latter recalled that they had met on a press trip to Stalingrad in 1943. When the lift stopped at the second floor, the general was chatting animatedly in Russian to Tamara and the Canadians. He ordered the liftman to wait. 'Close the door and keep it shut until I tell you to open it.'

The lift bell kept ringing as other guests summoned it, and the liftman looked anxious, but the general carried on speaking to his new friends. A concierge appeared, out of breath after climbing the stairs, and begged the general through the grating to vacate the lift, which he reluctantly did. The conversation continued on the landing, a large empty space occupied by a couple of chairs and the woman floor manager sitting at her desk. Gilmore could see her watching the unusual spectacle on her floor and then picking up the phone. He tried to steer the general into one of the dark corridors, but the old soldier would not take the hint. A man in a blue serge suit appeared, one of the many who could be seen lolling around the hotel lobby day and night, and sat silently in a chair. Gilmore broke into the conversation to invite the general to join him and his friends for dinner, and the general readily accepted. At this, the man in the blue suit stood up, approached the general, looked him in the eye and said two words,

'Comrade General'. That was all it took for the hero of Stalingrad to crumple. 'I'm sorry it's impossible for me to have dinner with you,' he told Gilmore.*

Looking back on this incident Gilmore concluded it was no bad thing that a convivial dinner and an innocent exchange of war stories never took place. If it had, the secret police would have found a way to drag the general away in the middle of the meal, which would have been even more humiliating for the man who had shown such simple delight in chatting to an American journalist, his Russian wife and a Canadian couple.

This incident could never have happened during the war. It required a journalist who had been in Moscow long enough to recognise a general he had met several years previously, and one who spoke enough Russian to engage the general in conversation. The lift was back in service, and when alcohol loosened tongues in this confined space, the friendly interest in foreigners that comes so naturally to Russians could not be suppressed.

* Eddy Gilmore, *Me and My Russian Wife* (New York, 1968), p. 174.

# 25

## *May 1945: Winston Smith in Moscow*

Russia's war ended on 9 May 1945, and the news of the crushing of the 'fascist viper' was broadcast to the Soviet people in the early hours of the next day, prompting a wild outpouring of joy on the streets of Moscow that lasted until the following night. In Red Square, thousands of workers released from their twelve-hour shifts formed circles and sang folk songs, while factory girls, their arms linked, swept down the streets. Crowds of students milled around Red Square searching for someone in authority to respond to their exuberance. There was no point in standing by the blank walls of the Kremlin – Stalin would never appear, and no civilian or military leader would risk his career, or even his life, to bask in an ovation from the masses. A strange figure wearing a black cassock edging his way past Lenin's tomb caught their attention. This was Hewlett Johnson, the 71-year-old 'red' Dean of Canterbury, a senior Anglican churchman known for his radical pro-Stalin views, who had come to Moscow to celebrate the victory. He found himself surrounded by boisterous students who, on learning who he was, grabbed hold of him and tossed him into the air. He cried out in terror as he rose above the crowd, his bald pate fringed with long snowy white hair catching the sun and his cassock blowing back to reveal his leather gaiters. Up he went again, but realising they meant him no harm, his features relaxed.

After the students had finished celebrating with the red dean, and with no sign of Stalin appearing to share their joy, they spied the Stars and Stripes fluttering from the US embassy next to the National Hotel and gathered in front of it, dancing and singing. With the ambassador away, deputy head of mission George Kennan sent someone to find a Soviet flag and hang it beside the Stars and Stripes, producing roars of approval from the crowd below. They wanted more. Kennan had been watching the festivities from the balcony of his top-floor apartment and went down to a lower floor, climbed out of a window and stood on the pedestal of one of the great columns adorning the front of the building. With a US army sergeant beside him he shouted in Russian, 'Congratulations on victory day. All honour to the Soviet allies!'* The crowd hoisted one of their number on their shoulders, and he climbed up to join Kennan on his precarious ledge. Embracing the unsuspecting sergeant in a bear hug, the climber dragged him down into the mass of students below, and surfing on a sea of welcoming arms he disappeared into the distance, not to be seen again for many hours.

Such spontaneity had not been seen in Moscow during all the long years of Stalin's dictatorship. The fact that the American embassy was the focus of the young people's acclamation was galling for the secret police. They would use all the tools at their disposal to make sure that this shameful lapse was erased from history.

* George F. Kennan, Memoirs 1925–1950 (Hutchinson, London, 1968), p. 243

Kennan returned to his apartment, where two guests were waiting for him. Ralph Parker had telephoned Kennan early that morning and invited himself and Valentina to watch the celebrations from the balcony. A cerebral diplomat, Kennan was unsettled by his spontaneous involvement with thousands of exuberant young people. Parker asked him, 'Wasn't that wonderful?' He confided to Parker he felt sad for the students – they had suffered so much, yet years of hard slog awaited them to rebuild the devastated western lands of the Soviet Union.* Parker did not forget this conversation. He would rework it four years later when he was under pressure from the NKVD to produce an anti-Western propaganda book portraying British and American diplomats in Moscow as spies bent on the destruction of the Soviet Union. And though Parker and Kennan had been on good terms since they had met in Prague two years previously – Kennan had helped Parker and Milena escape the Gestapo on their midnight flit from Prague – Parker was required to paint the American as the most dastardly of the lot.

In his book, *Moscow Correspondent*, which presents a positive picture of the USSR for British readers, Parker faithfully describes how the students gathered in front of the embassy to demonstrate their support for the alliance and then Kennan responded by delivering an impromptu speech in Russian on American-Soviet cooperation.† This was not damning enough to fit the demands of the Cold

---

* George F. Kennan, *Memoirs 1925–1950* (Hutchinson, London, 1968), p. 243.
† Ralph Parker, *Moscow Correspondent* (Frederick Muller Ltd, London, 1949), p. 12.

War, and he was required to produce a hatchet job entitled *Conspiracy Against Peace: Notes of an English Journalist.* It opens with a version of the Victory Day events rewritten just as Winston Smith, at his desk in the Ministry of Truth, would have done in Orwell's *Nineteen Eighty-Four.*

In Parker's later account, the students were not camped outside the embassy for fourteen hours, but 'pushing past it'. Kennan did not address them, but hid, skulking in sullen silence behind a closed window like an enemy agent. And Kennan was not sympathising with the students but, with a 'petulant, irritated look' on his face, he was already planning the next war against Russia. The words he put into Kennan's mouth about the students were these: 'They think the war is over, but it's only just beginning.' Parker writes that the portrait of the recently deceased Roosevelt in Kennan's apartment had been replaced by that of the warmongering Truman. In fact, the apartment had no presidential portraits on its wall, though both Roosevelt and Truman were on display in the embassy itself in May 1945.* Parker does not mention that he was Kennan's guest: that would not fit the Soviet script about the diplomat who later became famous for setting out the US policy of 'containment' which set limits on Soviet expansionism during the Cold War.

*Conspiracy Against Peace* was translated in many languages and distributed all over Europe and the developing world, becoming a key document of Soviet propaganda in the 1950s, its authenticity confirmed by its author having worked for *The Times.* Generously, Kennan describes the

---

* Ralph Parker, *Conspiracy Against Peace: Notes of an English Journalist* (Literaturnaya Gazeta Publishers, Moscow, 1949), pp. 6–7.

book as 'published over Parker's signature' – he could not believe that the serious and well-informed journalist he knew could have written it.

The great Russia expert Isaiah Berlin was baffled that Parker, who had discussed the USSR so 'sensibly and critically' with him, could publish a book 'denouncing the British embassy, man by man'.* (Due to English libel law, the book was not published in Britain.) A Canadian diplomat had a simple answer to the Parker conundrum: 'Mr Parker is completely under the influence of the Russian woman with whom he lives and it is rumoured that the nature of his writing in recent years is directly attributable to some form of blackmail which his mistress, or her MVD [the title at that time of the secret police] employers, are holding against him.'† The Reuters correspondent John Miller suggested what form the blackmail was taking: in 1949 the Soviet authorities were withholding an exit permit to allow Parker to visit his mother in England. Only when he agreed to produce full-throated propaganda did the exit permit materialise.‡

Kennan cites Parker's rewriting of history as a proof of the Communist Party's need to make reality conform to the image it had cultivated for itself. 'In tens of thousands of instances, over the course of the years, real events had to be denied, false ones invented, or true facts distorted

---

* Isaiah Berlin, *Enlightening: Letters 1946–60* (Chatto & Windus, 2009), letter of February 1951.
† John Watkins, *Moscow Despatches: Inside Cold War Russia* (James Lorimer Ltd, 1987), letter 574 dated 10 December 1948.
‡ John Miller, *All Them Cornfields and Ballet in the Evening* (Hodgson Press, 2010), p. 125.

beyond recognition, in order to produce a version that was compatible with the party's neurotic vision of the environment in which it lived and of its own reaction to that environment.'*

Much of Parker's book is written in the wooden language of *Pravda*, and there are errors so glaring that they could be seen as hints from Parker that he was writing under duress or possibly that key parts of his narrative were 'hardened up' by Soviet editors. One example: the title of one of the most famous songs of the 1930s, 'It don't mean a thing (if it ain't got that swing)' appears as 'It don't mean nothin'' [sic], which looks like what a Soviet editor would write who claimed to know the American vernacular but had no sense of rhythm. As for Parker himself, he wrote to his friend, the artist Julian Trevelyan: 'It's old stuff and I am not proud of it.' Having thrown in his lot with the Soviets, uneasy about spending the rest of his life in Moscow but unwilling to return to Britain, he was going through a personal crisis. 'I am fat and flabby and still highly superficial and unreliable,' he wrote in another letter to Trevelyan.†

Parker may have felt uncomfortable about the book, but it would set the tone of his work in the 1950s. During the Korean War, he served his masters by spreading the lie that the Americans were using biological weapons – a hardy perennial in the Russian propaganda garden which bloomed again as recently as March 2022 during Putin's

---

* George Kennan, *Memoirs 1925–1950*, Kindle edition, loc 4977.
† Trinity College Cambridge archive, Trevelyan papers TREJ 44/12 and 44/13.

invasion of Ukraine.* He dutifully covered the post-war show trials of 'enemies of the state' in Eastern Europe, which the newly installed communist governments conducted to prove their Stalinist credentials.

* 'Mr Ralph Parker', *obituary in The Times [sic]*, 27 May 1964.

# 26

## *1947–48: The knock on the door*

By 1947 the reporters who had fought for the coveted position of Moscow correspondent during the war had left Russia. The Metropol was no longer the home of the foreign press, but a down-at-heel hotel with a famous name. Parker, now married to Valentina, was one of the few who remained, and had been allocated a spacious flat in the historic centre of Moscow. Nadya had returned to teaching English, this time at the Moscow Institute of International Relations, but the Press Department had not forgotten her. With a Moscow conference of the Big Four victors of the war – the United States, USSR, Britain and China – scheduled for March 1947, the Press Department approached her to interpret for the press pack. Nadya accepted the assignment because she hoped to see Blunden again. Since he had left Russia four years previously, she had often recalled their friendship in the Metropol and the secrets she had shared with him and was keen to know whether he had finished his book. She had heard that he had settled in Paris and it would be much easier for him to get to Moscow from there than from Australia. But he failed to appear.

Cyrus Sulzberger told her she was a fool to imagine that Blunden would come. 'Why would he want to return to Moscow? He's been to Germany and met Russians in the displaced persons camps. He learnt a lot more about the Soviet Union in Germany than he did when he was in Moscow. In these camps, people speak freely, unlike here. He got all the material he needed, and he's written his book. Why would he come back?'*

With these blunt words Nadya learned that Blunden's book was out. Entitled *A Room on the Route*, it had been published in the United States two months previously and turned out to be an exposé in thriller format of the dark underside of Stalin's Russia. Much of the action takes place in the home of two women, a tiny room in a communal flat with a window through which an assassin tries to shoot Stalin on his route from the Kremlin to his dacha.

Blunden wrote it in the winter of 1945/46 from notes written in a 'minute indecipherable hand' in the tiny notebook which never left his person, day or night, while he was in Moscow. After leaving Russia, 'this little book accompanied me in thousands of miles of traveling and passed unnoticed by scores of intelligence officers and security officials who were supposed to check all documents brought into or taken out of such countries as Russia.'† Blunden romanticises himself as a literary figure, telling the reader he had written the book in the Algonquin Hotel, where Dorothy Parker and other New York literary luminaries regularly met for lunch, and in Montparnasse, the Parisian haunt of Sartre, de Beauvoir, Hemingway, Scott Fitzgerald and Henry Miller.

* Nadezhda Ulanovskaya and Maya Ulanovskaya, *Istoria Odnoi Semyi* (Inanpress, 2003) p. 86.
† Publisher's blurb of the back page of the first edition of *A Room on the Route*, (Lippincott 1947).

The first review of the book, in the *New York Times* in March 1947, was damning.* The reviewer dismisses the book as little more than 'a series of ill-formulated mumblings' in which the hero is a man called Ferguson, 'with whom most readers will be compelled to identify Mr Blunden himself'. He mocked the war correspondent for relating his work to 'places associated with free artistic creation' such as the Algonquin Hotel.

The American novelist John Dos Passos, who had visited Russia in 1928, leaped to Blunden's defence, saying he recognised the characters in the novel from his own experience. He compared it to Arthur Koestler's *Darkness at Noon*, a classic portrayal of Stalin's Great Terror. *A Room on the Route*, he wrote to the *New York Times*, 'furnishes the only picture we have from the pen of an English-speaking writer of the basic realities of life under Russian despotism. It has the truth you only get from great literature.' But while Koestler had only exposed 'the tortured spirit of the isolated communist idealist', Blunden had painted 'the agony of the great Russian people'.† Alexander Kerensky, the exiled head of the Russian provisional government overthrown by the Bolsheviks in 1917, weighed in to describe the book as 'the only authentic novel about Russia written by a foreigner'.‡

While its merits as a novel were disputed, Blunden's book became a focus of controversy at a time when the wartime alliance with the Soviet Union, during which

---

* 'Dissidents in Moscow', *New York Times*, 9 March 1947.
† 'From the Editor's Mailbag', *New York Times*, 6 April 1947.
‡ Patrick Buckridge, 'A Kind of Exile: Godfrey Blunden – An Australian in Paris', *Journal of Australian Studies*, 2002.

Stalin's bloody history of murder and repression was downplayed, was being replaced by the superpower struggle of the Cold War. The book could not fail to attract the attention of the Soviet secret police.

In 1947 Nadya was teaching English at the Institute of International Relations, an exclusive school where the sons of the Kremlin elite were coached to become diplomats and spies – so exclusive, in fact, that it was the first Soviet institute of higher education to refuse admission to Jewish students. Outside the institute, the drivers of Kremlin-supplied cars sat around all day waiting for the pampered students to come out of class. The staff were expected to dress appropriately, and Nadya felt good in the clothes she had bought to pass as a bourgeois lady: her smart green suit imported from Stockholm and the fur coat she had bought sixteen years before in New York. The American sales clerk had encouraged her to make this once in a lifetime purchase with the words, 'Madam, this is beaver fur. It will last forever.'* The coat would not have turned heads on Fifth Avenue, but in Moscow she cut a film star-like figure.

Having worked in the institute for only a few months, Nadya was summoned by the head of department, who told her sheepishly that her services would not be required beyond the end of the academic year. Nadya's command of English was better than any of the other teachers and the senior classes depended on her, but the head of department gave her no good reason for the decision. 'What difference does it make to you why you're being dismissed?' she said. She told Nadya not to mention her dismissal to anyone.

* Ulanovskaya and Ulanovskaya, *Istoria*, p. 148.

As she left the head of department's office, Nadya puzzled over the reason for her dismissal. Could it be they no longer wanted to employ any Jews? More likely, it stemmed from her work with foreign journalists during the war. Her husband was having problems too – he was being questioned about his pre-war work in military intelligence. And their telephone had been cut off – someone more influential had been given their line.

A few months later, in the early evening of a Saturday in February 1948, there was a knock on the door. In the 1930s, during Stalin's Great Purge, the secret police were notorious for bursting into people's homes in the middle of the night, with neighbours anxiously listening out for boots in the stairwell when they saw the black cars draw up outside. In those days, Muscovites muttered, but never said aloud, 'Only thieves, prostitutes, and the NKVD work mostly at night.'* Now the secret police were more discreet. Nadya opened the door to two men in civilian clothes. 'We need you to come with us to the Foreign Ministry to answer some questions about a correspondent you worked for.' Nadya responded, 'My daughter is ill – I can come on Monday.'

The men insisted. 'It has to be now. We'll drive you there and bring you straight back. You'll only be gone for half an hour.' She went with them, not even thinking to remove from her handbag the medicines she had bought for Irina earlier in the day. Only the uneasy look on her husband's face as she said 'See you later' unsettled her. As she got in the car, she knew for sure this was a secret police

* Anne Applebaum, *Gulag: A History of the Soviet Camps* (Allen Lane, 2003), p. 133.

vehicle, but it did not concern her. She thought, 'How scary it would be to be in this car if you were actually under arrest.' She even remained calm as the car took her directly to the Lubyanka, as she knew that everything to do with foreign journalists was under the control of the secret police. On arrival she was told to sit and wait. As the minutes ticked by, she grew angry. How dare they treat her so rudely? Her family would be starting to get worried. She should be at home making supper for the children. What kind of country was this where they could invite you in for a chat and then ignore you? Eventually, she was summoned into an office and a man stood up from behind his desk and greeted her with a smile. 'We're going to arrest you.'

She smiled back. 'That's interesting. May I ask what for?'

'You know full well why you're being arrested. We will talk later, but remember, everything depends on how you behave.'*

She thought, 'So this is how it happens.' But she felt nothing. When a bullet hits you, at first you feel no pain.

She was kept in the same office overnight Saturday to Sunday then all day Sunday and overnight until Monday morning. The same command, 'Confess your crimes!', was barked at her by a relay of interrogators. Each time she replied: 'I don't know what crimes I'm supposed to confess to. Charge me, and I'll try to prove my innocence.' She was so wound up she did not feel the need to sleep.

On the second day, frustrated at her refusal to volunteer any information, one investigator began to prompt

* Ulanovksaya and Ulanovksaya p. 91.

her. 'What were you really doing for the foreign correspondents? You weren't just translating the newspapers,
were you?' She answered with generalities. The interrogator made clear he was asking her about Blunden's book.
'What about the help you gave the correspondent with his
anti-Soviet novel?'* She refused to admit anything.

Early the next morning she was escorted from the
interrogation centre to a cell with a parquet floor, a bunk,
a chest and a little table. All her life she had dreamed of a
room of her own and here it was. Overcome by tiredness
and hunger, she sat on the bunk and collapsed against the
wall. She longed for a cup of coffee, but there would be no
more coffee. Arrest meant her life was at an end. But given
the life she had chosen, it was a miracle she had reached
the age of forty-four. There were so many times when her
life could have been cut short – when she was part of Alex's
band of teenage revolutionaries fighting the Whites or the
Ukrainian nationalists, and in Shanghai when the Russian lowlifes were out to get her. She would never forget
standing in front of the French firing squad. Maybe she
deserved to die now. But what about her family? Her
daughter Maya would be branded for the rest of her life as
the child of a traitor to the motherland. Alex was already
being harassed and her arrest meant that it was only a
matter of time before he too was taken. She started to
reproach herself for inflicting so much suffering on her
family. What had she been thinking? How could she as a
mother have expressed out loud her dissatisfaction with
the Soviet system?

The silence was broken by a loud clattering from the

* Ibid., p. 91.

food hatch in the cell door, but she ignored it. The guard entered: 'It is forbidden to lean against the wall.'

'So what can I do?'

'You can walk.'

She started to pace back and forth. She lost track of time and did not notice the signal for bedtime when, even though the lights were kept on, prisoners had to lie down. The guard, who had been watching her through the spy hole, hissed through the food trap, 'Get undressed and lie down.' No sooner had she lain down than the door opened, and the guard said, 'Get dressed, the investigator is waiting for you.' The guard led her down gloomy corridors lined on both sides with an endless succession of battleship-grey doors. The only sound was their footsteps and the clicking of the guard's tongue to alert other guards that a prisoner was on the move.

The guard took her into the investigator's office and left her sitting on a stool in the corner. Young and good-looking, the investigator was engrossed in his papers and did not even look up. His name was Motavkin, a name she would never forget.* An hour passed and still he had not said a word to her. She thought, if he's not ready to see me, why did they summon me? It was on the second night when she had to wait even longer that she realised this was done to deprive her of a whole night's sleep.

This time the investigator shoved a piece of paper at Nadya with the words: 'Make a list of all your relatives and

* Motavkin is described by former prisoner Gennady Kuprianov as a 'specialist in knocking out teeth and breaking ribs'. See Memorial website https://nkvd.memo.ru/index.php/Обсуждение: Мотавкин,_Михаил_Александрович

friends.' The list she handed to him turned out to be rather short, as she was careful to limit the numbers, knowing that everyone she named would be interrogated. The interrogator tossed it back to her, snarling, 'Is that all? You can't be serious.'

'My relatives passed away in the typhus epidemic. I made most of my friends in the civil war, and they're all dead now. I wasn't at the institute long enough to make friends with my colleagues. And I haven't got to know my neighbours.'

The investigator interrupted her, and began to reel off names of friends and acquaintances whom she could not deny knowing. With each name, her heart sank further. He revealed that he not only had names but dates and places she had met them. With each person named, he asked her, 'What did you discuss with them?'

Despite her lack of sleep, as a former underground operative she knew she had to give the same answer to each question: 'We talked of literature, theatre and the weather.'* Her obstinacy provoked a stream of curses from the interrogator and Nadya even felt a little sorry for him.

The interrogation ended just before dawn and she was taken back to her cell. She was exhausted, having not slept for three nights. She undressed and went out like a light. Half an hour later she was jolted awake by the wake-up bell. She got dressed and was hoping to sit and doze, but the guard made her stand up. That night the same thing happened as the night before – she was woken up just after having undressed and lain down,

* Ulanovskaya and Ulanovskaya p. 93.

and was brought to the investigator's office, the only difference being that this time she had to wait not one hour
but three hours with the scratching of his pen the only
sound.

Without ceremony he barked at her: 'Those correspondents you worked for, you spied for them, didn't you?
Admit it: you gave them state secrets. You're an anti-Soviet
person and you told them what you thought.'

He brought his fist up to her face, and she feared her
front teeth would end up on the floor. As he circled around
her he kicked her.

'Tell us everything. And if you don't, it'll be worse for
you. We know it all already and we'll expose you.'

At these words, the memory of everything she had said
to the foreign correspondents against the regime, and even
her unspoken thoughts about Stalin, came flooding back
to her. Her body felt like a bag of aching bones from never
being allowed to lie down, but she still held firm and
refused to admit anything to the interrogator.*

'The Soviet regime is sacred to me. I have risked my
life for it many times, and I would do so again.'

'I understand you were once for the Soviet regime, but
which one? Surely not the current one?'

'For the present regime, I would also give my life,'
Nadya replied, betraying her conscience for the first time
with this lie.

The night-time interrogations and days without sleep
continued for thirteen days and nights. Later Nadya would
learn that this treatment was known as the 'conveyor belt',
designed to extract a confession from even the most stubborn

* Ibid., p. 93.

of detainees.* Early one morning, after a night's interrogation when it was still dark, she was not led back to her cell but put in a 'box', a tiny cell used as a temporary holding place, and later taken to a larger cell with two young women in it.

Their first question to the newcomer was, 'What are you in for?'

'Espionage. And you?'

'Also espionage. We've been here for three months. There were three of us, but yesterday they came and took our friend away. We hope it wasn't to Lefortovo.'

Nadya told her new cellmates she was delighted to join them but apologised for having lost her ability to smile. 'I don't think my face muscles work any more.'

Her cellmates were Lola, a ballet dancer, and a young woman called Galya who had been arrested for contact with foreigners. They invited her to join them for breakfast. Laid out on the table were sausage, butter and cheese. 'Where has this come from?' Nadya asked.

'That's put a smile on your face,' said Lola, explaining this was the first food parcel she had received. As they ate, they compared notes on the investigators' techniques and found they all used the same. By the end of the meal, they were not just smiling but laughing.

Galya's sister had married an American embassy

---

* Alexander Buchin, who was arrested and taken to the Lubyanka in 1951, describes the 'conveyor belt' thus: 'They would summon me for interrogation at 10.30pm. No sooner had I lain down than the warders, or to use the prison term the "screws", roused me and took me for interrogation . . . I was returned to my cell around 6am, which was time to get up and we were not allowed to sleep in the daytime.' See Memorial website: https://nkvd.memo.ru/index. php/Обсуждение:Мотавкин,_Михаил_Александрович

employee and had given birth to his child but the Soviet government would not give her permission to go to America with her husband. She had taken refuge in the American embassy, fearing arrest if she set foot outside.

The US embassy was powerless to help her. Unable to get their hands on Galya's sister, the secret police had taken Galya instead. Galya was an attractive and fun-loving girl. The interrogator was obsessed with her sex life and asked her, 'How many lovers have you had?' She named sixteen. Nadya exclaimed, 'Galya, why did you name them all?'

'All?' Galya said in surprise. The three of them fell about laughing. For each of the sixteen she had to recount to the interrogator exactly what he had talked about.

Galya believed it was impossible to hide anything from the interrogator. 'They will torture you until you spill the beans,' she said. It was much better to tell all right from the start. If you didn't, you would be sent to Lefortovo. Galya insisted she did not want to get any of her lovers into trouble and though she had given up their names, she never mentioned their political opinions. One day the interrogator told her to go away and recall everything one of her lovers, a popular Jewish jazz musician, had told her. The next day she said the musician praised American jazz and liked the cut of American jackets. 'That's not good enough. Are you telling me he's satisfied with the Soviet system?'

Galya was indignant. 'What's he got to be dissatisfied about? A little Jew, living in Moscow in a fancy hotel with high-class lovers and pots of money. Of course he's happy, very happy.'*

One day when Galya was summoned for interrogation

---

* Ulanovskaya and Ulanovskaya p. 95.

in the daytime, Lola suggested to Nadya, 'Now we're alone, would you like to hear my story?' Aged thirty-six she was not exactly beautiful, but Nadya saw she had sex appeal. At the age of seventeen she was training to be a ballerina, and despite her spoilt biography – her father had been a wealthy merchant – she was enjoying life. She had plenty of admirers, including highly placed men. When she turned eighteen she was summoned by the NKVD and invited to become an informer. She flatly refused, knowing from childhood that once you agreed to be a police informer you would never escape their clutches. They put more pressure on her. 'What right have you to refuse? Your parents are in exile in Tashkent. And you'll be joining them.' She still held out, even when they threatened to expel her from ballet school. They called her in for a third time, and tried a different tack. 'Sometimes we arrest the wrong person and if you agree to work with us, you can stop us making mistakes. And you won't be short of anything.' Even presented with the prospect of a glittering career and the opportunity to save people, she still refused to cooperate. Without saying anything, the interrogator filled out a form, put it on the table for her to sign and left the room. The hours passed and she felt a desperate need to go to the toilet. It got to the point where she could not hold on any longer. When the door opened, she cried, 'For God's sake let me out!' The answer came, 'Sign and we'll let you out.' She scrawled her signature and ran out of the door.

She was ordered to attend a weekly rendezvous in an anonymous flat with a man whose name she never knew. Her first task was to get close to the avant-garde theatre director Vsevolod Meyerhold, and find out who he talked to and what he said. She thought she could get away with reporting just a few trivial remarks about how much he loved the Soviet system. She congratulated herself that she was not doing him any harm. To start with, her handler treated her as men always did, flirting playfully, and he even promised to make her parents' lives easier. But on the third meeting, the man's tone changed and he cursed and shouted at her, 'What game do you think you're playing? He loves the Soviet regime? Really? You want me to believe that?' The handler revealed he knew exactly what Meyerhold had said to someone else on an occasion when Lola was also present. She was shocked to learn that she was never working alone: another informer was reporting on her. She could never again get away with feeding her handler trivia. With suicide never far from her thoughts, she set about providing the intelligence they wanted.*

When war broke out Lola was evacuated far from Moscow to Central Asia, and she put her encounters with the NKVD behind her as though it had all been a bad dream. But her quiet life was not to last and in 1942 they tracked her down. To soften her up, they portrayed her role as war work. 'The country is in danger. You are a patriotic girl. Moscow is full of spies. You can help us expose them.' She was brought back to Moscow and ordered to circulate among the capital's elite, informing on foreign diplomats and senior Soviet officials, dining out every night at the Hotel National.

Over dinner one night a loose-tongued Soviet general told her about the campaign of terror unleashed by the NKVD in the liberated territories, how they were shooting and hanging girls who had consorted with Germans.

* Ibid., p. 96.

Lola duly reported to the NKVD everything he had told her. When Nadya expressed horror at her denunciation of the general, which led to his epaulettes being ripped off, Lola was indignant: 'I was always being asked to inform on members of the old nobility and wealthy merchants like my papa. And here was a general, a party member.' In her eyes, the general was part of the system, no different from an NKVD officer.

Nadya recalled that before her arrest there had been a spate of articles in the press detailing the nefarious activities of diplomats who were expelled for spying, or as the Kremlin put it, 'activities incompatible with their status'. Nadya was fascinated to hear from Lola the inside story of the provocations that led to their expulsion. Lola and three young women were assigned to work with foreigners and were given precise instructions on whom to befriend and when to sleep with them. A particularly complex trap was set for a French diplomat whom the Russians were keen to expel. The NKVD assigned him a mistress, and when she got pregnant they seized their chance to incriminate him. Abortions were illegal at the time, but the Frenchman was assured by his mistress that she had found a reliable doctor. The NKVD set the stage for his next visit – the mistress lying in bed, a man in a white coat in attendance, and a bucket containing a bloody embryo under the bed. It took five days for the Frenchman to appear, and when he did she told him the procedure had only just been done. The Frenchman was leaning over to kiss her when a policeman entered, made a show of arresting the 'doctor' and then turned to address the Frenchman, who brought out his diplomatic pass. He was promptly expelled as an accessory to a serious crime under Russian law.

As was the fate of all women informers, Lola's handlers eventually turned on her. During her interrogation in the Lubyanka the main charge against her was revealing a state secret – she had warned thirty of her friends not to speak frankly in her hearing, especially if there were witnesses. Lola was sentenced to a term of eight years in an open prison in the Arctic town of Vorkuta. She was assigned to a dance troupe entertaining the forced labourers working in the mines. In 1951, three years after sharing a cell with Nadya, she died of hepatitis.

As for Galya, one day she returned to the cell and told Nadya that the whole interrogation had been about her father. She had already admitted that he had an anti-Soviet attitude, but they wanted names and dates to prove he was engaged in anti-Soviet activity. Nadya was shocked she was prepared to incriminate her father. 'How could I not testify against him? They have to believe I'm not hiding anything from them.' One day Galya found out from a note scratched on the toilet wall that her sister had been arrested and was also in the Lubyanka. She had been holed up in the American embassy for months but had nipped out to do some shopping and was promptly caught. Galya's sister received a twenty-five-year sentence and their father was found guilty of anti-Soviet activity and sent to prison on the basis of Galya's testimony. Galya's belief that telling the interrogators what they want to hear would save her proved correct. She was released soon after her sister's arrest to resume consorting with foreigners and reporting back to the NKVD.

Nadya spent two and a half months with Galya and Lola, during which she refused to provide the evidence that the interrogator was demanding. He threatened to transfer her to Lefortovo prison. 'Once you're there, you'll start singing.' One day after an interrogation session she was put into a 'box' and then taken to a police van which was divided into small cages, one for each prisoner. There was so little air she could hardly breathe. On arrival at Lefortovo she was relieved to find she was not going to be held in solitary. Her cellmate, a woman called Natasha, was in constant pain from inflammation of the ovaries. Nadya was taking the place of a young woman called Maika, whom Nadya had known as a girl from her time working in the Metropol. She was the daughter of Cholerton's translator.*

It was not long after Nadya's arrival before there was a loud tapping on the wall. 'That will be Maika's young man tapping,' explained Natasha. 'The poor fellow is in such a state. He doesn't realise she's not here any more.' She told Nadya that Maika used to spend hours communicating through the wall with the Italian in the next-door cell and that their tapping had developed into a real romance. But she had paid for it: she had ended up in the punishment cell. When they brought her back, she could not stop trembling.

Whenever food was brought, they would hear tapping, which Natasha explained was the Italian wishing them 'bon appetit'. And in the evening he would tap goodnight. Natasha kept urging Nadya to respond. 'Have pity on him.' Nadya said she did not know the prison alphabet, and was too exhausted to learn it. The tapping persisted and she eventually gave in and tapped just once. The Italian responded immediately with a loud pounding on the wall. She took heart from the sound of tapping all around, which mingled with the night-time cries of prisoners going

* Ibid., p. 98.

insane. 'I'm the wife of Marshal Vasilyevsky,' pleaded one woman. In Lefortovo the noise was incessant, and every movement was audible, unlike in the Lubyanka with its parquet floors and carpets which muffled even the sound of footsteps. The loudest sound in the Lubyanka was the clicking of the warders' tongues and the incessant cooing of pigeons which prisoners recalled with repugnance. Lying under a blanket at night, Nadya could tap on the wall unobserved through the spy hole.

As she became more proficient, she learned about the man behind the wall. He had been born in the Italian colony in Odessa and his grandfather was the owner of a well-known bookshop. Maika's 'young man' had been arrested in 1944 in Romania, where he was working in the Italian embassy in Bucharest. He knew nothing of what had happened in the world since his arrest but he had heard the fireworks and artillery salutes and understood that the war was over. Nadya told him that all over eastern Europe communist regimes had seized power. In prison he had been given communist literature to read and the former fascist had revised his view: communism was the future of humanity. Nadya could not help herself and responded to this with a quote from Heine. '*Sie alle beide stinken.*' (They both stink.)

Despite the harsh conditions in Lefortovo, sharing a cell with Natasha and night-time conversations through the wall made life tolerable. She even began to get her strength back. Despite being in so much pain that she was barely able to walk, Natasha was still summoned by her interrogator. On her return to the cell, drained of all her strength, she warned Nadya that if they threatened her she could not hold out and she would tell them everything

Nadya had confided to her. But Nadya continued to speak frankly with her because she was such a good friend. She was so kind and always insisted that Nadya share her food.

Nadya could not understand why she had not received any money from Alex to buy food from the prison shop. All her cellmates received money from relatives. She feared Alex had been arrested or even that he and her children were dead. In time, she understood that access to the prison shop was a reward for good behaviour. In fact, Alex had been sending her 200 roubles a month, but the interrogator ruled that she should be refused any privileges and not even allowed to know that money was being sent to her.

One day her tapping led to her being taken to the punishment cell. She was not surprised to find herself in a bare unheated room, but was shocked to be told to take off her underwear and stockings, leaving her in a thin dress. She curled up on a tiny triangular bench in the corner, blowing on her hands to warm them. The cold made it impossible for her to sleep but when exhaustion overcame her and she fell sideways, the frost on the wall jolted her awake again. She knew she had to endure three days and nights of this torment, but she was in no state even to count off the days. Her thoughts turned to suicide as they had so often since her arrest, however long ago that was. She'd heard how some prisoners tried to kill themselves by cracking their skulls against the walls of their cells, but to do that you needed physical strength, which she no longer had. But there was a way that death could take her. In childhood she had had tuberculosis, and the doctors had told her that if she caught pneumonia, it would kill her. This thought gave her a moment's comfort. Waiting to die, she refused food and water. She did not touch the tiny portions of black bread that were thrown at her. As darkness fell a guard entered and unhooked a shelf fastened to the wall for her to lie on, but without a blanket it was impossible to sleep.*

When she was let out of the punishment cell, she was too weak to walk, and the guards had to drag her to a solitary cell. Once inside, she collapsed onto her bunk. Instead of the cold wooden boards, she felt something warm and soft. It was her fur coat. They hadn't confiscated it after all. She pulled it around her, luxuriating in its comforting embrace. The coat had become like a living being to her, her only companion in her solitary cell. On return to her cell after interrogations, she would always rush to hug it. When they confiscated it to put pressure on her to make a confession, she would whine like a whipped dog.

Her respite was brief. That evening she was summoned to an all-night interrogation. As usual the session began in silence, with her sitting on a stool in the corner of the investigator's office. The silence was broken by a terrible sound, a man's strangled roar through clenched teeth. The roars would stop and then start up again.

The investigator let her listen for a while and then said, 'So how do you like the music?'

She remained silent. 'We do it to women as well, you know.'

'And what are you hoping to get by doing that? The truth?'

'I did warn you that everybody talks in the end.'

Her fear left her. 'Well, go ahead then. Do your worst,' she said.

* Ibid., p. 101.

The interrogator referred to his notes and said: 'You've been tapping on the wall every night. We know who you've been talking to and what you were saying. We know everything.'

For a terrible moment she thought the Italian had betrayed her but then she realised it was the invalid Natasha who had been forced to denounce her. How stupid of her not to realise she had been living with a stool pigeon.

The nightly interrogations with their demands for new names had started up again: she was back on the conveyor belt.

'Now let's talk about your husband. We know he lived in the Metropol with you, and you introduced him to Blunden. What did he reveal to him?'

'I worked for Blunden,' she replied, 'and in civilised society it is customary to introduce one's husband to one's employer when they meet.'

'But you didn't just introduce Blunden to your husband, did you? You introduced him to others. Who were they? And you even took him to their homes. Admit it!'

She refused to confess, and the interrogator launched into a tirade. 'I've been working with you for six months now and you've given me nothing, you evil bitch. You're ruining my career and I've become a laughing stock.'

The nightly interrogations began to take their toll. When she heard them coming to fetch her she began to tremble all over and could barely get herself dressed. She lost her appetite and tipped all her food into the slop pail. She gave up pacing around her cell and just sat curled up on her bunk in a semi-stupor, no longer able to read and just staring into space.

With great clarity, she saw her younger daughter

Irina falling off her bicycle. Irina stared at her mother as she brushed the dust off her blue skirt. But her head was shorn. Why had they cut off the braids that she had plaited each morning? Who was looking after Irina now? Had someone bought the kidney medication she needed? Nadya reproached herself for failing to take her daughter's medicines out of her bag when they came to arrest her.*

One day the cell door opened and a tall man appeared, dressed in a flowing robe and with a gold-embroidered cap on his shaven head. A Tatar! They've let a Tatar into my cell by mistake, she thought. She was terrified that she would be made to take the blame for someone else's mistake. She would be punished – they would send her back to the cooler. She stared at him in fright and he, not noticing her, sat down on the slop pail. At that moment he turned his head towards her, and with an embarrassed smile, let down the flaps of his robe. She looked away, and when she looked back, he had vanished.

The hallucinations continued in the investigator's office. The walls were bare apart from a portrait of the secret police chief Beria above the investigator's head. How could this man with his pince-nez and face of an intellectual be such a monster? For years he had been dragging innocent people from their beds and sending them to die in forced labour camps.

The wall began to bend before her eyes, stretching away from her and in the process disfiguring Beria's portrait, turning him into the monster he really was. Beria had been spotted driving around Moscow in his limousine

* Ulanovskaya and Ulanovskaya, p. 101.

identifying young girls to be brought to him late at night. To escape the ghoulish image, she looked down at her feet. Now a hole was opening up in the floor between her and the investigator's desk. 'This used to be such a solid institution,' she blurted out. 'Look – there's a huge hole in the floor. Can't you get it fixed?'

She began to lose her grip on reality. She no longer saw the interrogator as an enemy but as an acquaintance who needed her help. When he asked her a question about one of her contacts, she replied casually, 'Oh, that's not worth talking about. I won't tell you that.' She kept talking and talking but her words made no sense.

'So this is what's it's come to. You've gone crazy,' he sneered. After that he lost interest in Nadya's case and sent her back to the Lubyanka. He had found another case which was more likely to advance his career.

Still in a state of extreme confusion, she was brought back to the Lubyanka late that night. She was led along a dimly lit corridor. The guard opened a door no different from all the others. From the oppressive gloom of the prison corridor she stepped, under the gleaming light of crystal chandeliers, into the opulent masked ball of Tchaikovsky's opera, *The Queen of Spades*. Before her glided grand ladies with regal bearing. 'Oh, how elegant you all are,' she exclaimed.*

These 'elegant ladies', her nine new cellmates, welcomed the newcomer – it was not the first time they had provided refuge for a woman driven out of her mind by weeks of sleep deprivation and all-night interrogation sessions. They asked her name and how long she had been in prison. Encouraged

* Ibid., p. 102.

by their attention, she could not stop talking. 'Hush now, Nadya,' said one woman gently. 'It's night-time and we need to be quiet but if you like, you and I can talk softly together, all night if you want. I have been here for four years, and I'm allowed to sleep in the daytime.'

As Nadya recovered her equilibrium, the gorgeously coloured ball gowns she had espied from the doorway resolved themselves into the washed-out dresses of her fellow prisoners, and the bright make-up of the guests at the masked ball faded to the grey-blue skin tone of women who had not seen the sun for many months. They were now real people, but still exceptional. They were caring and generous, even to the extent of sharing out their extra food supplies. Although it was forbidden to lie down during the day, the other women took turns to screen her with their bodies so that she was able to sleep wrapped in her fur coat for nineteen hours at a stretch. In two weeks, she had recovered the balance of her mind.

In 1951, three years after her arrest and having been shuttled back and forth between the Lubyanka and Lefortovo prison, she had a final session with the interrogator and was allowed to see the evidence against her. During her three years in pre-trial detention she had seen prisoners return to the cell distraught after discovering who among their friends and family had betrayed them and what they had denounced them for. She opened the cardboard file with her name on it and flicked through the thick wad of closely typed pages until she came to the testimony of her friends. She had once complained to her colleagues at the Metropol that her daughter had come home from Pioneer camp with headlice. On another occasion she had had to do the courier's work as well as her own because of a flu epidemic. Her friend Jackie was asked what secrets Nadya had revealed about her time as a spy abroad. Jackie told them how Nadya had gone shopping to buy a hat in Berlin. She had chosen a pink one and was so delighted with it she put it on straightaway. As she was leaving the shop, a saleswoman approached her. 'You can't go out in that – it's a shower cap.'*

The evidence of anti-Soviet activity extracted from her friends was so trivial that it made her smile. 'Is that all you've got on me? What crime am I supposed to have committed?'

'You'll see. Your failure to cooperate will cost you.'

On hearing this, she thought how wrong he was: if she had admitted everything, the charge against her would have been much more serious. Throughout three years of interrogation she had admitted only one thing: that in 1937 she had doubted that there were so many traitors and enemies of the people in the country. But no matter how much the interrogator had threatened her she had never admitted to sharing these thoughts with anyone, not even her husband. In the words of the indictment, she had 'slandered the security organs in her thoughts'.

The interrogator had once let slip, 'We do not prosecute people for their thoughts, only for conversations.' So on what charge could they convict her? Nadya knew that no suspect was ever acquitted. She convinced herself that for her thought crime she would only get three years.

A week later, she was taken from her cell and led along unfamiliar corridors. A door opened and she found herself in the office of the prisoner governor. She noticed a doctor

* Ibid., p. 108.

standing by. She had barely sat down when she heard her name called out and she was ordered to stand. The voice continued, 'In the name of the Union of Soviet Socialist Republics, you are sentenced to fifteen years in a corrective labour camp'. The doctor moved towards her, but she just smiled at him. If she had heard five years instead of the three she was expecting she would have been disappointed. But fifteen years she could not take in.

From the governor's office she was taken to a special wing of the Lubyanka for convicts due to be transported to labour camps. She had been convicted under Article 58 of the Russian Criminal Code covering a broad range of crimes of 'anti-Soviet activity', including in her case revealing state secrets to Blunden.

All the fight had been knocked out of her and she did not even react to the punishments inflicted on her there. Several days later, when she was walking along the railway tracks towards the prison train, she could not keep up with the other convicts, even though she was carrying only a small bundle. She heard the voice of the convoy commander, 'Slow down – the old woman is falling behind.' Nadya looked around to see who the old woman was. It was her.*

* Ibid., p. 110.

# 27

## *1951: The Hen and the Eagle*

By 1951 the Soviet forced labour camps were dispersed over a vast area, from the Arctic Circle in the frozen north to the burning deserts of Central Asia in the south, and throughout Siberia and beyond, as far as the Pacific coast. It took weeks for prisoners to be transported by rail to their final destination, with numerous stops en route. Since the days of the Tsars, long before the Bolshevik Revolution, political prisoners had been exiled to places so remote there was no need for barbed wire to stop them escaping. In the 1930s the forced labour camps became an integral part of Stalin's rapid industrialisation drive, and political prisoners were sent to work in mines in places where only reindeer herders had lived before.

The first stop on Nadya's journey to the camps was a transit prison in the town of Vologda. Still wearing her fur coat and smart green suit – the last vestiges of her previous life – she waited for a warder to unlock the cell door. The door opened and a sea of faces looked up at her. The women were so tightly packed in there was not an inch of free floor space. The bunks, made of rough wooden planks, were occupied. Nadya, so weak she could barely stand, laid her luxurious coat on the only patch of bare floor, next to the enormous slop bucket.

As night fell, a kind woman took pity on Nadya and persuaded one of her friends to make room for her on her bunk. Although Nadya was so emaciated she did not take up much space, it was still too cramped for her to turn over at night. At least no one felt cold.

The only good thing about the transit prison was that after three years she was finally allowed to communicate with her family. She sent a postcard asking, 'Who's alive and where are you all?' She was overjoyed to receive a telegram from her daughter Maya asking if she could visit. Nadya responded, 'Come as soon as you can.'*

Every morning Nadya waited nervously to hear the names of prisoners who were to be moved on that day. She was terrified of hearing her name: her daughter would come to visit her, and she would be gone. Her new friends in the cell shared her distress.

While waiting for the visit, she received a letter from Maya which skilfully outwitted the censor to convey the news that Alex had been arrested: 'Papa was at liberty until last year.' This confirmed what Nadya had inferred from questions about Alex put to her by the interrogator in the Lubyanka. As she would later discover, Alex had written to Stalin, recalling the time when they were young revolutionaries in Siberian exile drinking cocoa together, to plead for Nadya's release. Alex received no response to his letter, but was arrested soon after sending it.

Nadya had not seen her daughter since the morning of her arrest three years before. Fifteen-year-old Maya had been reading a book on astronomy in the library and

* Nadezhda Ulanovskaya and Maya Ulanovskaya, *Istoria Odnoi Semyi* (Inanpress, 2003), p. 111.

had come home in the evening to find the flat unusually silent. It seemed no one was at home, and then she noticed her father slumped in a chair. 'Where is Mama?' she asked.

'I'm afraid mama's been arrested,' he said in a barely audible voice.

Now eighteen and having graduated from high school, Maya had applied to the top universities but been rejected as the child of enemies of the state. The only institute willing to accept her was the Food Technology Institute, which took anyone, even Jews, who were subject to quotas throughout the higher education system. With both parents in prison, Maya was a social outcast, shunned by friends whose families were afraid to be seen consorting with the traitors to the motherland. Her only friends were from other families similarly cast out of society by Stalin.

When Maya came to visit her mother in the transit prison, they were only allowed fifteen minutes together. Nadya managed to hide from Maya how thin she had become by wearing her green suit, which covered her skeletal body more effectively than the black dress she usually wore, in which two of her could fit. Mother and daughter swapped coats. Maya gave Nadya a sleeveless cotton jacket. Nadya slid off the beaver fur coat which had given her so much comfort during her three years of interrogation, but which was now too heavy for her to carry, and Maya put it on. A year later, on close examination of the coat, Maya discovered forbidden objects hidden by her mother in the lining. There was a tooth from a comb with a hole in it which would be used as needle, a piece of wire and a safety pin.

When recalling this brief meeting more than twenty

years later, Nadya was still unable to put into words the emotions she felt on seeing her daughter again. Maya did not want to add to Nadya's suffering by mentioning her own troubles.

Maya reached the transit prison just in time. Within twenty-four hours Nadya was put on a train to Vorkuta, an Arctic coal-mining city founded in the 1930s where thousands of prisoners worked in slave labour camps. The first stop was another transit prison. At the age of forty-six Nadya stood out – due to the harsh conditions no one over fifty was sent to the Arctic – and a prisoner gave up her place on a bunk so she could lie down, but the bedbugs stopped her sleeping. For the harsh conditions, the prisoners were issued with filthy old coats, from which the cotton padding had mostly disappeared. Putting on this disgusting garment, Nadya recalled how she felt when dressing for dinner in a first-class cabin on the SS *Bremen* on the way to New York. It did not feel right to be wearing such an elegant gown – it was as if she were playing a part. But it did not feel right to be wearing this ragged coat either.

After a few days in the transit prison, Nadya was so weak that she struggled to complete the three-kilometre march under armed guard to her final destination, a labour camp known as Predshakhtnaya. After weeks on the road, only her curiosity about 'the Zone' – as the complex of slave labour camps was known to its inmates – kept her going. They were made to wait in the freezing cold in front of the camp gates while the guards took their time processing the new arrivals. When the gates finally swung open Nadya found herself surrounded by inmates all shouting at once, mostly in Ukrainian. 'Anyone from Drohobych?'

'Anyone from Stanislav?'* The newly arrived Ukrainians were joyously received by their fellow countrymen, who were desperate for news from home. All these Ukrainians – new arrivals and those who had been in the camp for years – had been deported as part of Stalin's campaign to root out the spirit of Ukrainian nationalism and hostility to the Soviet Union that had re-emerged during the war.

On entering one of the huts, Nadya was surprised to find an empty bunk, and laid her bundle down on it. The old lags stared down at her from the upper bunks. 'It's so dirty here,' Nadya exclaimed. 'This must be a really bad camp.'

'I've been in lots of camps and this is a really good one,' said one of her new cellmates. She asked Nadya how long her sentence was.

'Fifteen years,' said Nadya, 'a crazy amount.'

'What's crazy about that? I've survived here for twelve years.'

Nadya was too tired to talk and lay down on her bunk and dozed off. 'Is anyone here from Moscow?' A melodious voice interrupted her slumber. When Nadya responded, a striking figure, tall, erect and seemingly clad in a grey robe approached. On closer inspection, the woman was wearing a washed-out camp dress with her hair tied up in a rag. This was Lyalya, an actress from the Moscow Arts Theatre, and within a short time the two women had bonded. Lyalya set out her rules for survival in camp. 'The most important thing is not to end up doing general work. For this you need to be signed off sick. Looking at the state of you, you should be in the infirmary. Just make sure you don't get better.'

* Today known as Ivano-Frankivsk.

Lyalya put her plan into action, and persuaded the doctor to accept Nadya as a patient in the infirmary, in the bed next to hers. The infirmary was much cleaner than the barracks, and the rations were better. Lyalya had free run of the kitchen and would always add something tasty and nutritious to Nadya's bowl of gruel. One day Nadya was astonished to overhear her friend conversing fluently with a foul-mouthed old villain in the expletive-filled argot of the criminal underworld. The conversation in the kitchen turned to Nadya. 'I know who that woman is. I saw her in that fur coat. She's one of those rich Jews,' said the criminal. Lyalya responded in the tone of a gangster, 'She's my bitch.' The old criminal was taken in by this performance, and Lyalya the gangster woman became a hot topic among the criminals in the camp. 'Why have we never heard of her before?' they asked each other. Lyalya was prouder of her convincing impersonation of a criminal than of any role she had played in the Moscow Arts Theatre.*

With better diet and rest, Nadya's health improved and she was allowed to get up and walk around. At first she walked like an old woman, but after two weeks the doctor reprimanded her. 'What are you doing walking so fast? You've got to act like a sick person if you want to stay in the infirmary. Otherwise they'll set you to work.'

Nadya decided she could not keep up the pretence of being ill. She told the doctor: 'If I have to pretend to be ill to survive, I'd rather be healthy.' The doctor promptly discharged her. Her first job was peeling potatoes in the kitchen, but she was not fast enough and was reassigned to

* Ulanovskaya and Ulanovskaya p. 115.

fuel the boiler room: women worked in pairs to transport loads of coal on stretchers. At first she was so weak she kept dropping her end of the stretcher, but after a few days her body adapted to the work.

One day a Jewish woman named Roza who was in charge of the sanitation brigade offered her a place in her team. She would have a low bunk with its own night table and the work would be light, just sweeping the snow away from the latrines. She would not be required to go down into the pit and dig out the faeces.

Nadya objected: 'People will say that the Jews always look out for each other,' but Roza persuaded her to accept her offer. For two days Nadya swept the snow around the latrines. She could hear her co-workers talking about her. 'Of course Roza will never send her down into the pit.' Nadya decided it was better to shovel faeces than to hear nasty things said about her while she was sweeping the snow. When Roza saw her down in the pit, she exploded. 'Who told you to go there? I'm the boss and I tell people where to work.' Nadya refused to back down, and said she would not accept preferential treatment.

Working in the pit and digging up the solid waste with a shovel, Nadya was assisted by a muscular Ukrainian farm girl who wielded a crowbar to loosen the shit when it was still frozen. 'You're not strong enough,' the Ukrainian kept saying, as she grabbed Nadya's shovel and filled up a few buckets to help Nadya meet the target of fifty buckets a shift.

Sometimes the truck that took away the waste had to be loaded at night. One evening Nadya was standing at the top of a ladder being handed buckets of shit to tip into the truck. All around her the heavens were lit up by the shimmering red, green and gold colours of the Northern Lights, which bathed the barracks and perimeter fence of the Zone in an unearthly glow. Perched up high as she mechanically received bucket after bucket, she was mesmerised by the beauty of the dancing lights and a fierce rage welled up inside her. 'You think you've destroyed me,' she imagined herself yelling in Stalin's face. 'Well, you're wrong. Look at me now. I thank God that he brought me here.' It was more than thirty years since Nadya had abandoned her religious beliefs. But, under the pulsating Northern Lights, she experienced something spiritual.*

Later Nadya discovered why Roza had offered her so many privileges. She was an informer who had been ordered to report on Nadya. Nadya was already on the camp authorities' blacklist. Lyalya had warned her that as an educated Muscovite she would inevitably be put under pressure to become an informer. Sure enough, six weeks after arrival at the Predshakhtnaya camp she was called in by the security officer, who greeted her politely.

'Do sit down. I see you are from Moscow. Your sentence is a long one, but you're a Soviet person. We can sort things out so that you get easier work.'

'How can you say I'm a Soviet person when I was convicted of criticising the security organs to foreign journalists?'

This unsettled him. 'Sometimes mistakes are made.'

'Not in my case.'

'So you are saying you are an enemy?'

'I thought everyone in this camp was an enemy.'

The security officer threatened her. 'Your behaviour

* Ulanovskaya and Ulanovskaya p. 129.

will decide the quality of your life in camp and what happens to you at the end of your term.'

'If I live to the end of my term, I'll be sixty and I am completely indifferent to what happens to me then.' Nadya had won the argument and walked away feeling strangely liberated. For the rest of her term she was never again summoned and asked to be an informer.

The security officer's revenge was to send Nadya away from the relatively mild regime of Predshakhtnaya to a labour camp known as the Second Brick Factory, where the work was harder. It is a Russian tradition before going on a journey to sit on your suitcases and reflect for a moment, and as Nadya sat on her bundle of meagre belongings, her friends gathered round her to say goodbye. One of them pointed out that Nadya had failed to heed warnings that her refusal to cooperate with the security officer would end badly for her. 'For me it's worth suffering if I can keep my self-respect,' she retorted.

At the Second Brick Factory camp, Nadya wanted to work in a sanitation brigade, but instead found herself harnessed to a cart with seven other women hauling coal to keep the military garrison warm twenty-four hours a day. Her next job was in the brick factory itself, where the women had to carry the new bricks up a steep ramp. This was dangerous work, and it was not long before Nadya tripped and fell off the ramp and broke her leg. She lay in pain until the end of the shift. Then, supported by two co-workers, she hobbled to the camp's infirmary, a mile away. There she remained for three months. As soon as she could walk, she was allowed to work in the infirmary. The Vorkuta camp authorities decided to empty all the camps of the prisoners who were no longer productive workers. One

October morning a thousand prisoners, mostly women –
the old, the prematurely aged, the sick, the disabled – waited
in front of the camp gates. Years later, Nadya recalled
their departure as a scene in a film. The gates opened and
the prisoners stepped from the Arctic gloom into the blinding light of searchlights, brighter than a hundred suns.
The prisoners shuffled between two lines of soldiers armed
with rifles, officers wearing tall karakul hats, and prison
guards with dogs straining at the leash. Loudspeakers
broadcast warnings to the prisoners that they would be
shot on sight for stepping out of line or picking anything up
from the ground. Nadya could not believe her eyes. 'All
this just for us?' She looked around and saw that she was
one of the fittest.*

A short distance away was the branch line of the convict-
built railway. They were packed into cattle trucks, with no
room to move, and given salted herring to eat, but there
was little water to drink. Nadya understood for the first
time how you could die or go crazy from thirst. They had
left the treeless Arctic where winter had already set in and
after two days in the windowless cattle trucks, the doors
were opened and the exhausted prisoners emerged blink-
ing into warm sunshine and were greeted by a treat for the
eyes, a forest of green trees. There were carts waiting to
transport them to the camp, but even those who could
barely walk opted to make their way on foot. The opportunity to wander through the sweet-smelling pine trees was
too good to miss. On arrival, they fell upon scraps of food
abandoned by the previous occupants. If there were leftovers, they were not going to be short of food.

* Ibid., p. 123.

The Potma camp was a waystation on the route between Moscow and the labour camps in the Urals, Siberia and the Far East. It was here that news filtered through to Nadya of the calamity that had befallen her daughter Maya. For months she had suspected that something bad had happened at home: her mother had stopped writing to her, only sending parcels. On her arrival in Potma she received a letter after a long silence. Enclosed was a note from Maya, written from a transit camp in Novosibirsk, couched in language which would pass the censor while leaving no doubt as to her fate. 'You know I've always had good health and the climate in Siberia is very good.' This note confirmed one of Nadya's darkest fears, that Maya had been arrested. The horrors of camp life – in Potma the political prisoners were sharing barracks with murderers and other hardened criminals – took on a new significance as Nadya imagined her daughter experiencing the same.

She accosted every new arrival at the camp – 'Have you seen my daughter?' – until one day a young woman arrived from Potma's Camp No. 10, where two of Maya's co-defendants, Tamara Rabinovich and Nina Ufliand, had entrusted her with a message. Nadya's first question was, 'How long is her sentence?' The young woman could hardly bring herself to answer: 'A long one.'

'More than ten?' In these times, ten years was a short sentence.

'Much more,' the woman whispered. 'Twenty-five.'

Nadya could not take this in. When reality hit her, she shrieked: 'They've given my child twenty-five years. They've gone completely mad. It can't carry on like this – giving children twenty-five years.' The young woman tried to calm her down, but Nadya cried out. 'Death is too good for them.'

Nadya was denounced for her outburst but, as luck would have it, her punishment was to be sent to Camp No. 10, where Tamara and Nina, her daughter's co-defendants, were being held. The two young women shared their memories of Maya: meeting her for the first time at the Food Technology Institute, how she introduced herself and even what she was wearing. It cut Nadya to the quick to hear that Maya had spent New Year's Eve alone when she had written to her mother saying what a happy time she had had. Nadya hung on the young women's every word when they described the trial of the sixteen defendants. All of them had admitted their guilt and pleaded for leniency except for Maya. Some of what Maya said to the judges is recorded by another of her co-defendants, Alla Reif: 'I hate you. I have never believed that my parents were enemies of the people. Even if they had done something, they did it honestly.' In court she had vowed never to keep quiet about the injustice suffered by her and her family, unless they 'put a muzzle' on her. Reif recalls all the defendants holding their breath as they heard these brave words. 'We were terrified for Maya. I kept imagining how much pain and insult she had had to overcome in order to think and feel that way.'*

Hearing how Maya had spoken to the court, Nadya was filled with pride. Her life had not been in vain. She herself had never dared to speak out against the regime during her interrogation. With shame she recalled how

* Alla Tumanov, *Where We Buried the Sun* (NeWest Publishers, Edmonton, 1999), p. 121.

she had declared herself ready to lay down her life for the Soviet regime. As she would tell Cyrus Sulzberger many years later, 'I was so proud of Maya. I felt like a hen who had produced an eagle.'*

The full story of the arrest, interrogation and sentencing of Maya and the other defendants was beyond Nadya's worst imagining. Maya had joined a discussion group made up of high school and university students aged sixteen to nineteen who called themselves the Union of Struggle for the Revolution. They debated how to roll back Stalin's dictatorship and return to the true socialist principles of the Bolshevik Revolution. In the group's manifesto, Stalin was accused of holding fraudulent elections, suppressing freedom, following an imperialist foreign policy, and instituting 'state capitalism' which had pauperised the peasantry. One of the group's number was an informer, and in early 1951, the sixteen teenagers were arrested and accused of being members of a 'Jewish anti-Soviet youth terrorist organisation'. The following year all were found guilty of terrorism – the evidence for this being that one of the boys possessed an old gun for which he had no ammunition. The three boys considered to be the ringleaders were sentenced to death and executed; ten of the others accused, including Maya, were sentenced to twenty-five years; and three – including Tamara and Nina – to ten years of forced labour. Over two decades Stalin had executed hundreds of thousands on fabricated charges of anti-Soviet activity, ensuring that by 1951 no adult would dare to voice an opinion against the dictator. Only a few naïve schoolchildren had had the courage to dream of a different future.

* 'The Hen who Produced an Eagle', *New York Times*, 17 July 1977.

In March 1953 Nadya was on the water supply team. They worked in pairs. One woman drew up a bucket of water from the well and handed it up to the other standing on a cart who poured the water into a barrel. During a break Nadya nipped into the barracks to grab a piece of bread. The radio was playing as usual to the empty room but Nadya noticed the announcer's voice had taken on an unusually solemn tone. Her ears pricked up. It was an official announcement that Comrade Stalin was ill. This was the news that Nadya had been yearning to hear. 'At last! They wouldn't be reporting his illness if there was even the slightest chance he would recover.' But who could she share this wonderful news with? She returned to the well with a skip in her step and, with no one else to tell, shared the news with her partner, an illiterate peasant woman who gave her a blank look. Now it was no effort to lift up the buckets – she felt she could move mountains. A young woman who Nadya knew was an informer ran up to her. 'Have you heard? Comrade Stalin is ill.'

'Really?' Nadya feigned indifference. 'Everyone gets ill from time to time. We have excellent doctors. They will cure him.' The informer looked disappointed.

In the evening Nadya waited by the gates for her friends who had been working outside the camp to return. She wanted to be the first to surprise them with the news, but when the gates opened and she saw the glint in the eyes of one of her friends, she understood they knew already.*

*

* Ulanovskaya and Ulanovskaya, *Istoria*, p. 131.

The death of Stalin was announced on 6 March 1953, five days after he collapsed at his dacha with a cerebral haemorrhage. Summoned to the refectory to hear the official announcement, Nadya and her fellow prisoners stared at the floor, not sure what to expect. With the camp bosses fearful of an uprising, the prison regime became stricter. New prisoners sentenced to twenty-five years for non-existent crimes continued to flood into the camps, the victims of the last spasm of Stalin's vindictive paranoia. In July, Beria, Stalin's secret police chief, was denounced as a spy and executed, which heralded the liberalisation of his empire of forced labour camps.

In Maya's camp the prisoners were ordered to remove the numbers from their jackets and were allowed to wear their own clothes. The barracks were no longer locked at night, and prisoners no longer had to suffer the indignity of using the communal latrine bucket. Previously prisoners were allowed only to send and receive two letters a year. Now they could send and receive as many letters as they wanted, and even correspond between camps. Nadya made up a parcel of luxuries for Maya, clothes and a book of poetry. As she folded each item, warm mittens, a nightshirt – whoever heard of a nightshirt in camp? – and a blue cardigan knitted from wool unravelled from an old sweater, she imagined how Maya would react to each item. Her efforts were rewarded by a letter from Maya: 'Imagine me lying on my bunk in a beautiful nightshirt and reading the poetry – this is the life.'

These changes were not mere window dressing. In February 1956, Khrushchev delivered a 'secret speech' denouncing the excesses of Stalinism, and the emptying out of the camps accelerated. Maya was brought back to Moscow and put in a cell in the Lubyanka with her co-defendant Tamara. The two girls had no idea what fate awaited them, but the joy of being together again after five years and a parcel of roast chicken and other treats kept their spirits up. One day a guard opened the cell door and said: 'You're wanted. Get your things together.' They quickly gobbled down the last spoonfuls from a tin of condensed milk – too good to go to waste – and followed the guard to the prison governor's office. Maya went in first and was handed two letters from her father, which unusually had not been opened. 'Do you have family in Moscow?'

'Yes, I have a sister.'

'Well, you are free to go.' He handed her a certificate of release and asked her to sign it. Without thinking she scribbled her name, muttering, 'The way you work makes no sense. You put people in prison for no reason and then you release them with no warning.' The governor objected: 'Given what you were up to, you should have known you'd be arrested.' Before she left the governor's office another piece of paper was put before her. She had to sign that she understood she would receive a three-year sentence if she ever revealed any details of the labour camp regime. Then it was Tamara's turn. Within a short time, the two girls were standing behind one of the Lubyanka's huge wooden doors. A guard opened it and they stepped out into Dzerzhinsky Street. For a moment they stood rooted to the spot in the April sunshine, but then linked arms and set off at a fast pace to get away from the building where tens of thousands had been incarcerated, tortured and killed. Round the corner, the crowds milling around the Detsky Mir toy store paid no attention to two young women incongruously dressed in padded cotton jackets and carrying bundles.

The next day, Maya's sister Irina kitted her out in a smart coat borrowed from a friend.

When Maya was released, her mother was still being held in Camp 10. By refusing to admit any guilt, Nadya had made herself ineligible for fast-track rehabilitation. With the camp destined for closure, the prosecutors had to work out a way to justify her release. They struck out her conviction for treason, retaining only the charge of 'disclosure of an official secret'. They reduced her sentence to eight years, a term she had just completed, and she was thus eligible for release.

Maya took the train from Moscow to Potma to visit her mother. With no train scheduled for the branch line to the camp, Maya walked the final stretch of the journey through the forest, collecting spring flowers that grew beside the railway track. Approaching the camp she saw through the dirty window of the guardhouse a familiar face framed in a cloud of white hair. Maya saw the face recoil in horror. The first thing her mother said to her was, 'You shouldn't have worn that coat. You should have come in your padded jacket. That's how I've been picturing you.'

For Maya, her mother had become a stranger to her. But after three days this sense of alienation faded, and the remaining inmates of the camp derived pleasure from seeing mother and daughter together. One of them even sewed Maya a dress. Maya left after three days, and within a few weeks her mother joined her in Moscow to restart their lives.*

* Ulanovskaya and Ulanovskaya, *Istoria*, p. 200.

# 28

## *1977: From the Arctic to the Côte d'Azur*

One of the consequences of Stalin's repression of the Russian intelligentsia was that educated people sentenced to forced labour in the Gulag regularly came across friends, acquaintances and co-workers from their past. When Nadya was moved as a punishment to Potma's Camp No. 10 she was overjoyed to be reunited with her old friend Rakhil Afanasyevna, who had been arrested in 1947 after the publication of Blunden's book, *A Room on the Route.* The 'route' in the title could be recognised by any Muscovite as the road that Stalin took between the Kremlin and his dacha – it was regularly closed to other traffic to allow the dictator's motorcade to speed through unimpeded. The NKVD regularly updated their file of residents whose windows overlooked the route. Given that Rakhil came to the Metropol from time to time to have a bath in Nadya's room and was well-known to the NKVD as the widow of a victim of Stalin's purges, it did not take long for her to be identified as the resident of Blunden's 'room' who coincidentally was called Rachel, the anglicised version of her name Rakhil.

Out of earshot of the other prisoners, Rakhil told Nadya that the interrogator in charge of her case had demanded she confess to having entertained a foreigner in her home. A defenceless widow of an enemy of the people, she had in the past been pressured by the NKVD to work as an informer, but she had stood up to them. Now under arrest, she still refused to cooperate until one day the interrogator placed in front of her the testimony of Lidia Romanovna, the childhood friend whom she had invited to share her room after the execution of Lidia's husband. Lidia had revealed everything about Blunden's visit.

Nadya was shocked. 'What did they do to her to make Lidia betray you?'

Rakhil explained that not long before their arrest, Lidia's life had changed for the better. She had married an elderly lawyer and moved out of the cramped room they shared. For the first time in years, Lidia had something to lose: if she refused to cooperate, her husband would suffer the consequences. She had become easy prey for the NKVD. Having lived with Lidia for so long through so many privations, Rakhil was devastated by her betrayal. Another victim of Blunden, thought Nadya.

During the weeks they spent together in the Potma camp, their conversation often reverted to Blunden. They tried to imagine how he must be feeling, knowing that his actions had caused so much suffering.* Back then, he had appeared to be a kind and sympathetic man.

In 1959, the sister of one of Nadya's American communist friends came to Moscow. Sometime before her visit, she had met Blunden in Paris, where he had been living since the end of the war. He invited her to dinner and asked for all the details about Nadya's case. All she could tell him was that Nadya had been imprisoned as a result of

---

* Nadezhda Ulanovskaya and Maya Ulanovskaya, *Istoria Odnoi Semyi* (Inanpress, 2003), p. 79.

information she had provided for his book, and her family had suffered the same fate. Blunden stayed in contact with this woman for some time, but never used her to send a message to Nadya. Nadya decided he thought he would put her in danger were he to contact her.

Almost twenty years later, in the summer of 1977, Nadya and Maya found themselves in the south of France, in the hills above Nice, near the medieval walled town of Vence with its glorious view of the Mediterranean. They had come to visit Godfrey Blunden, who had retired there after a successful career as a journalist and author. For years Maya had heard her mother recalling her time working with Blunden in the Metropol, so when Nadya was invited to London to record a TV interview with William F. Buckley, the American conservative commentator, on her career as a spy,* Maya decided they should fit in a visit to Vence on their way back to their new home in Israel. If Maya expected that a reunion after thirty-four years would resolve all the unanswered questions about her mother's working relationship with Blunden, she was to be disappointed.

On arrival at the Blunden villa, they were greeted warmly by Blunden's wife Maria, who had heard about Nadya and her efforts to bring the true story of Stalin's Russia to the world while working as an interpreter in the Metropol. While Maria served refreshments, Blunden sat in silence, unwilling to say anything to his guests, and leaving all the talking to his wife.† When the subject of the

---

* 'Firing Line with William F. Buckley Jr.: The Soviet Intelligence Apparatus', https://www.youtube.com/watch?v=cH6JXMuOSy4
† Interview with Katherine Blunden, October 2022.

book and Nadya's time in the Gulag came up, Blunden would only say he did not remember anything.

The only written report of this meeting is a five-line note from Maya. Her mother had an explanation for Blunden's silence: he was so 'traumatised' by the fact that Nadya had suffered on his account that 'he could not speak about it, or even recall any prison sentences'. Maya added that she herself could not understand such 'sensitivity' but her mother did.*

It is hard to accept Nadya's explanation that Blunden was too traumatised to speak about his role in sending her to the Gulag. A more likely explanation is that Nadya wanted to think the best of a friend to whom she had entrusted her secrets and, at the age of seventy-four, she had no interest in forcing him to accept the blame. Nadya's grandson, Alexander Yakobson, says that his grandmother spoke about Blunden 'very charitably' in later life: he remembers her as someone who was never vengeful despite her strong moral sense. When her daughter Irina died in hospital in 1961 as a result of gross medical negligence – some nurses were prosecuted for administering a deadly overdose of medication – she never wanted to know what happened at their trial.†

Neither of Blunden's children – Ronald who had a career in publishing and Katherine who worked in finance – was present at the meeting in Vence, but both insist that their father's silence had nothing to do with any trauma or sense of guilt over his role in Nadya's fate.

'I remember my mother telling me my father was not that interested in talking to Nadya when she came to visit,'

* Ulanovskaya and Ulanovskaya, *Istoria*, p. 80.
† Interview with Alexander Yakobson, 24 July 2022.

Ronald Blunden told the author. 'He did not take part in the conversation in the way he was expected to, so my mother did all the talking at the meeting. Never at any point did he confide to me that he felt in any way responsible for what happened. He never mentioned any feeling of guilt or any regret about Nadya. In his view, she was trying to get a message across to the West and she was taking a tremendous risk in doing so. I don't see him being silent because of some deep-felt emotion that he could not express. But his silence could have been an expression of indifference – that is something I could imagine.'

Katherine Blunden's recollection of her father is that he was more than indifferent – he was furious at being held responsible for Nadya's imprisonment. She has a theory why it suited the Kremlin to have Nadya behind bars in 1948. Moscow knew that the American communist Whittaker Chambers, who had been recruited by Nadya's husband to spy for Soviet military intelligence in the 1930s and had later become a militant anti-Stalinist, was about to reveal the extent of the penetration of Washington by the spy ring run by the Ulanovskys and their successors. 'The Soviets knew these revelations were going to come out and the last thing they wanted was someone in Moscow who could be asked by the correspondents to reveal all.' Chambers did indeed reveal his explosive testimony in August 1948, but by that time there were few American journalists in Moscow, and anyway it would have been hard to track Nadya down. Nadya was never asked about Whittaker Chambers during her three years of interrogation, nor does Katherine Blunden's theory explain why the secret police went to such efforts to extract a confession from Rakhil Afanaseyevna for welcoming Blunden into her home.

The family's view, according to Katherine Blunden, is that Nadya was 'steeped in Soviet spy culture' and knew what she was doing. 'She gave a lot of information to journalists. Did she think they would sit on it? She was not a naïve peasant girl. She had been a spy in China and the US, sufficient [sic] experience to know what journalists do for a living. Such people know that if you unburden yourself to a journalist the information is going to come out.'

The last word should go to Nadya's grandson, Alexander. 'There is a huge difference between a journalist under normal civilized conditions quoting someone who spoke carelessly and thus hurting people – which may be regarded as legitimate [sic] part of professional journalism, even if sometimes a bit tough and heartless – and exposing someone who lives under a murderous dictatorship to a grave danger. Maybe Blunden did not fully understand the Soviet system. Many Western people thought they understood it but in reality they didn't. This was an extreme case, and the normal rules of journalism did not apply to someone you talked to in Stalin's Moscow.'*

Ronald Blunden would like to see his father remembered as a journalist who was ahead of his time in presenting the reality of Stalinism, while the Western Allies were still enamoured of the exploits of the Red Army. While Blunden was writing the book in Paris, where communists were a potent force in society, he felt very much alone. He found a soulmate in Maria, who was working as a fixer for English-speaking correspondents, and she became his wife. Maria had two good reasons to see Stalin

* Ibid

as the enemy: she was born in Poland and had been a Trotskyite in the inter-war years.*

It may be true that Blunden was ahead of his time, but that does not excuse his failure to disguise his sources. The life stories of the characters 'Rakhil' and 'Ivan' in his book match to a large extent those of Nadya and Alex in real life. The book does not state explicitly that the couple were working abroad for Soviet military intelligence, but it is evident to the reader they were involved in cloak-and-dagger work, and the parallel was close enough for Nadya to be convicted in 1951 of revealing state secrets.

The Blundens and the Ulanovskys will never see eye to eye, but there is one further mystery. Any reader of *A Room on the Route* who knows the fate of Nadya will wonder what was going through the author's mind when he wrote a chilling scene that appears in the final pages of the book. A train has stopped at a station in Ryazan, and a little girl sees what looks like a group of dwarves on the opposite platform. The girl's mother looks out of the window and sees that they are in fact prisoners squatting on their haunches, guarded by two soldiers ready to shoot if any try to stand up. She tells her daughter to look away. 'They are political prisoners. They are being taken – who knows where? To Kazakhstan perhaps.' When the train moves she cannot help noticing that one of the prisoners squatting uncomfortably on the platform on their way to the Gulag is Rakhil, the heroine of the book. It is Rakhil whose life is closely modelled on Nadya's.†

---

* Interview with Katherine Blunden, October 2022.
† Godfrey Blunden, *A Room on the Route* (Lippincott, 1947), p. 317.

# 29

## *Post-War*

### The Ulanovsky Family

In 1956, after eight years of separation, the Ulanovsky family was reunited in Moscow. Three were released from different outposts of the Gulag, Nadya from Potma in Mordovia, Alex from Karaganda in Kazakhstan and Maya from eastern Siberia, while Irina, now a beautiful young woman, returned from Ukraine where she had been living with her grandmother. They found their flat empty of all their possessions. When the NKVD had come to arrest Alex they had ripped the flat apart, removed documents and pocketed all the cash that Alex had set aside for Maya to live on should he be arrested. A year later, after Alex was sentenced to ten years of forced labour and confiscation of his property, the NKVD returned to the flat to seize all the family's possessions and sold them off at a discount to their colleagues – a perk of the secret policemen's job. What they didn't want they burnt. The only thing left behind was the piano, which Maya, alone in the flat and still a schoolgirl, sold to support herself.

While the family rebuilt their lives they stayed with

friends. 'In every home we were greeted as martyrs, as heroes,' Maya recalls.*

In 1958 their lives improved. The Soviet regime awarded Alex a 'personal pension' – more generous than a standard pension – in recognition of his years of service to the state. In the same year, a judicial review of Nadya's case acquitted her of the last remaining charge against her, revealing state secrets. She too was given a personal pension, enabling the family to live in reasonable comfort.

Other ex-prisoners who received these benefits put their years in the Gulag behind them and became regime propagandists, writing about the exploits of old friends while omitting to mention that they had been executed in the basement of the Lubyanka.† Gifts from the regime had no influence on Nadya. She settled into the role of dissident intellectual, translating banned works into Russian to be circulated hand-to-hand in samizdat ('self-publishing') among the Moscow intelligentsia. The texts were typed up secretly in up to five carbon copies, the last being a barely legible smudge. Nadya and her family lived in a twilight world, honoured by the state but active in the dissident movement that was to challenge the Kremlin until the collapse of communism. When summoned by the KGB and warned to stop her samizdat activity, Nadya responded, 'You cannot hurt me any longer.'‡

In 1960 she translated into Russian Arthur Koestler's *Darkness at Noon*, a book the journalists at the Metropol had

---

* Nadezhda Ulanovskaya and Maya Ulanovskaya, *Istoria Odnoi Semyi*, (Inanpress, 2003),), p. 201.
† Ulanovskaya and Ulanovskaya, *Istoria*, p. 201.
‡ Allen Weinstein, 'Nadya – A Spy Story', *Encounter*, June 1977, p. 78.

told her was the key to understanding Stalin's purges, and she helped to circulate samizdat editions of banned Russian works such as Solzhenitsyn's *Cancer Ward*, the manuscript of which she hid at her home. For years the 'Chronicle of Current Events', the only unofficial source of news in the USSR, was typed up in secret at Nadya's flat by Lyudmila Alexeyeva, who recalled: 'My nerves were frayed to the limit especially late at night when it seemed as if the clicking of the typewriter could be heard by all our neighbours.'* Nadya slept peacefully while her friend pounded the typewriter keys with enough force to produce five legible copies.

Robert Conquest's exhaustive research into Stalin's purges, *The Great Terror*, was circulated in samizdat translation at the end of the 1960s. After reading it, Alex told his wife, 'The story is told and it will survive. Now I can die in peace.'† Alex died in 1970 at the age of seventy-six.

While Nadya had rejected Judaism and the enclosed life of the shtetl as a teenager, she was always aware of being Jewish and bristled when she heard anti-Semitic comments and saw Jewish stereotypes in the official press. But for Maya, her engagement with all aspects of the Jewish experience in Russia – in terms of culture and history – was deeper, even to the extent of her learning Yiddish, a language which was not spoken at home.

Between 1969 and 1973 large numbers of Jews were allowed to emigrate from the Soviet Union to Israel, presenting the Ulanovskys and the wider Jewish community in the USSR with a dilemma. Permission to emigrate

* Ulanovskaya and Ulanovskaya, *Istoria*, p. 212.
† Weinstein, 'Nadya – A Spy Story', p. 78.

from the USSR, a privilege denied to the Soviet population in general, was making assimilation into Soviet society even harder. As a schoolboy, Maya's son Alexander found that 'Isn't it time you went to Israel?' was added to the list of anti-Semitic barbs. At the same time, no one expected the opportunity to emigrate to last for ever – it was now or never. And so Maya, her husband Anatoly and 14-year-old Alexander left for Jerusalem in 1973, arriving just weeks before the Arab-Israeli war. Nadya followed two years later.

Nadya took with her two mementos from her past. The first was the beaver coat that had comforted both her and Maya in the Lubyanka. In Jerusalem they used it as a blanket on cold winter evenings.

Alexander became a professor of ancient history at the Hebrew University of Jerusalem. He treasures another family memento from the thirties, the Cantonese shawl that the super-spy Richard Sorge had bought his grandmother so she could pass as a 'bourgeois lady' in colonial-era Shanghai. 'If Russia was a normal state, the Cantonese shawl would be held in Moscow in a museum of military intelligence,' he remarked recently. 'But I will never allow the Russian state to have it.'

## Cholerton

After being refused a visa to return to Moscow in 1943, Cholerton never wrote another word about Russia. The journalist who had witnessed the show trials of the 1930s and whose opinion had been sought by every diplomat and correspondent in Moscow failed to write the defining book of the era. His daughter Katerina Porter believes he was paralysed by the fear that, should he write anything, Natalia, his translator and the love of his life who had been sentenced to ten years in the Gulag, would suffer further persecution. 'My father used to say that he had stayed much longer in Moscow than any other journalist, so he was always expecting that he'd be expelled one day and it was just a matter of time. I think he never stopped worrying about what could happen to Natalia.'*

His many years of reporting on the Soviet Union were not wasted, however. He was generous with his time in speaking to researchers, including Robert Conquest when he was researching *The Great Terror*. Edward Crankshaw, a prolific writer on Soviet affairs, wrote of Cholerton, 'He gave me the run of his extraordinary mind, in which profound political, aesthetic and moral judgments emerged disguised as an endless series of anecdotes, usually comic, often cheerfully scurrilous. He knew more about the Soviet Union – and about most other matters – than I shall ever know.'

## Ralph Parker

The 1950s was a difficult decade for Ralph Parker: nobody he came into contact with professionally or socially in Moscow thought well of him or trusted him. The British embassy treated him with suspicion. When a British intelligence officer drew up a list of British correspondents living in Moscow – all of them married to Russian women – he wrote

* Interview with Katerina Porter, August 2022.

off Parker as 'a slimy character dominated by his extremely forceful Russian wife'. Despite Parker's impeccably pro-Kremlin coverage, the *Daily Worker* came to doubt his commitment to the communist cause (he had never joined the party) and at the end of 1955 dispensed with his services. In a 1958 conversation secretly recorded by MI5 in London, Harry Pollitt, the British Communist Party boss, said he had heard that the Russians wanted to 'get rid of' Parker. In the recording, a party official expresses mild surprise, but adds that Parker has 'nothing to do with us'.*

As Parker's journalistic career faded he sought a different role for himself, as a cultural mediator in the Cold War between East and West. Inevitably, his first efforts were greeted with suspicion. On a press trip to Leningrad to meet sailors from a visiting Royal Navy ship, Parker offered to help them get tickets for the ballet. Under the heading 'Communist activity during Fleet visit', the naval attaché reported that Parker was 'actively ingratiating himself with junior officers' and 'insinuating himself into their confidence'.†

But as the 'Khrushchev thaw' gathered pace and Stalinist repression was relaxed, Parker had more success in his new role. When the Shakespeare Memorial Theatre was invited to Moscow in 1959, Parker threw a party for the actors, including Michael Redgrave, at his flat in the city's historic centre. The 1962 publication of Solzhenitsyn's *One Day in the Life of Ivan Denisovich* – the first account of a Stalin-era forced labour camp to pass the censor – was Parker's opportunity to prove himself as a literary translator.

* TNA KV6 190b, 30 May 1958.
† TNA KV6 120/10136, 29 November 1955.

He dashed off an English translation which was published by Penguin, to the anger of Solzhenitsyn, who complained his work had been 'mauled into English by the pot-boiling parasite R. Parker'.* Encouraged by Valentina he secured parts in two Soviet movies, in which he plays a 'good' Englishman rebelling against his country's Cold War hostility to the USSR. In one he is an RAF pilot who was shot down over Nazi-occupied Russia and falls in love with an alluring Soviet kindergarten teacher who hides him from the Germans. Unable to forget his one true love, he returns years later to the Soviet Union to find her. The second is set in a Soviet international children's summer camp where a Japanese girl from Hiroshima tragically dies from radiation poisoning. Parker plays an English doctor who sees it as his 'debt of honour' to come to Russia and denounce the barbarous cruelty of the British and American forces, who were allied with the USSR during the war but are now enemies.†

In his last years Parker finally found a position which suited him perfectly, as the Moscow representative of the New York impresario, Sol Hurok, helping to arrange the visits of Soviet artists to the United States. When he died in 1964 his funeral was attended by two British diplomats. Opinions were divided as to why they came. Was it to pay their respects to a British citizen who, despite MI5's suspicions that he was a communist agent masquerading as a journalist, had become a prominent member of the British community in Moscow? Or were they hoping to identify

---

* John Miller, *All Them Cornfields and Ballet in the Evening* (Hodgson Press, 2010), p. 126.
† https://www.kino-teatr.ru/kino/acter/m/sov/29143/works/

representatives of the Soviet security organs who might have come to pay their respects?

If Valentina had been a colonel in the secret police, as the wartime press corps liked to believe, there was no sign that the 'competent organs' were taking care of her after Parker's death. She was thrown out of the central Moscow apartment they had shared and moved into an anonymous new block on the outskirts of the city. One year after Parker's death, she was grief-stricken, short of money and with no prospect of earning any. 'All I wish is that he will call me to him soon,' she wrote in a letter to Julian Trevelyan and his wife Mary Fedden. She likened her bereavement to her first parachute jump: 'You pull the ring and then you are separated from everything, there is no time, no real shapes around you, only clouds underneath. But that experience lasts just for a moment. Now this is what I feel all the time . . . I feel just a nuisance, like a worn-out horseshoe.'*

One summer Saturday afternoon John Miller, the Reuters correspondent who had helped Parker with English prison slang for his translation of Solzhenitsyn, set out to find Valentina in her new home. A Hogarthian scene greeted him: on the grass and paths between the blocks of flats there were men lying dead drunk. 'It was a terrible place for her to spend the last years of her life, but she accepted what had happened to her with a shrug of the shoulders.'

A similarly dismal picture is painted by Parker's nephew

* Valentina Parker to Mary Fedden and Julian Trevelyan, Julian Trevelyan archive TREJ 44.27, Trinity College Cambridge, February 1965

and godson, Neil Parker, who went with his wife Anne to Moscow in February 1981. Armed with Valentina's address written in Russian on a scrap of paper, they took the metro to the end of the line and then a trolley bus, finding themselves in a maze of buildings. In the bitter cold, lifeless bodies lay in the underpasses under the ring road. They took the stairs to the third floor. A boy answered the door. It was obviously the wrong flat. His mother was about to slam the door on them when Anne whipped a tube of Smarties from her pocket and the mother put on her coat and showed them the way to the correct address. A young man in a silk dressing gown answered the door and, at the sound of the visitors, a voice from inside shouted out in English, 'Who is it?' Valentina had lost her sight. When Neil spoke, she said, 'It's Ralph again. I hear his voice.' She ran her hands over Neil's face. 'Yes, it's Ralph.' There was no food in the flat to offer her guests. She was plainly not being granted the privileges afforded to a colonel in the Soviet secret police. Her circumstances were more like the just deserts of a Soviet citizen who had dared to marry a foreigner. 'She had come down in the world dramatically,' Neil recalls.*

A third visitor from abroad provided an insight into Valentina's character that would have surely surprised all her detractors in the British community. She never lost touch with the Czech family of Parker's first wife. Milena's son-in-law was an architect who came to visit Valentina while on business in Moscow in 1973. When he told Valentina that his daughter Zsuzsanna was getting married, Valentina, in one of those impulsive acts of Russian

* Interview with Neil and Anne Parker, September 2022.

generosity that so impresses foreigners, slid off her wedding ring and said to him, 'Give this to Zsuzsa. Then she
will not have to buy a ring, it's hard to get high-quality
gold these days.'

At his home in a pretty village in Cheshire and still
sprightly at the age of eighty, Neil Parker recalls his uncle
Ralph as an international man of mystery who would des-
cend on the family from time to time, wreathed in an aura
of wealth and sophistication. When in London he was
reputed to stay in a suite at the Savoy and he told everyone
his car was a Chevrolet. Neil's wife Anne joins in, 'I don't
believe he was a communist – he bent with the wind.' Neil
recalls the memorable occasion when Uncle Ralph came
to Cambridge and took him out of his boarding school for
the day. Parker had come to pick up his MA degree and
invited Neil to the ceremony. Afterwards, he took Neil to a
ballet school in a Cambridge loft where young dancers
performed in the hope that Parker would select one or two
to train with the Bolshoi Ballet in Moscow. This is how
Parker would want to be remembered, as a man of the
world bringing together people from hostile countries
through the medium of culture.*

## Alexander Werth

Alexander Werth, the Russian-born journalist who worked
at various times for Reuters, *The Sunday Times*, the BBC
and the Manchester *Guardian*, was more deeply affected by
his wartime experience than any other correspondent

* Ibid

because of his strong emotional connection to the land of his birth. He had grown up in a German-speaking milieu in St Petersburg until his family fled to Britain to escape the Bolsheviks, giving him a cultural heritage that was Russian, German and British. As he witnessed the Nazis' racially motivated war against Russia, he refused to speak German, the language of his father. In the words of his son Nicolas, he 'amplified the Russian part of his heritage and culture'.

During the war Werth never quite got to grips with the treadmill of daily journalism, tending to refer too frequently to the plays he had seen on the Moscow stage, and his cheerleading for Stalin raised questions at the BBC about his 'objectivity'. Sometimes he appeared too ready to accept the Soviet propaganda lines fed to journalists. In one of his weekly radio talks he described Stalin's 1936 constitution, which was adopted just as the bloodbath of the Great Terror got under way, as Russia's Magna Carta, and looked forward – naïvely as it turned out – to its implementation after the war.* The BBC's doubts about his pro-Russian sympathies were reflected in its refusal to run his eyewitness report from the Majdanek Nazi extermination camp, which had just been liberated by the Red Army. A BBC executive told him: 'Not credible. A Soviet propaganda operation, just for show. You were misled.'† In this the BBC was wrong.

Not a natural broadcaster, his weekly radio talks were

---

* James Rodgers, *Assignment Moscow: Reporting on Russia from Lenin to Putin* (I. B. Tauris, 2020), p. 113.
† Nicolas Werth, foreword to Alexander Werth, *Russia at War 1941–45* (Skyhorse Publishing, 2017), p.xvi.

sent to London as scripts to be read out by a professional announcer.* Werth intended to stay on in Moscow after the war, but he left in 1948 when tightened restrictions on foreign journalists made working in Moscow impossible even for a journalist well-disposed to the Soviet regime.

He returned to Moscow on regular visits during the Khrushchev 'thaw' in the early 1960s, by which time some of the blank pages in the history of the Soviet war effort – Stalin's cataclysmic errors, the extent of the Moscow 'panic' of October 1941, the genocide of the Jews – had been filled in by the publication of some generals' wartime memoirs, Yevtushenko's poem Babi Yar about the massacre of 33,000 Jews in Kiev, and Simonov's novel, *The Living and the Dead*.

During this period he worked on the book he had been intending to write for twenty years, now with the benefit of new material and a historian's perspective. In his 1,000-page *Russia at War 1941–45* he found his true metier: 'the dual perspective of historian and witness gives both a depth and an intensely human character to *Russia at War*', Nicolas Werth wrote in a foreword for a later edition of the book.

His timing was perfect. It was published in the Soviet Union in 1964, just a few weeks before the fall of Khrushchev. Over the next three years he worked on a new book, *Russia in Peace*, which would chart the flourishing of Soviet culture and civil society after the terrible sacrifices of the war years. The book was never finished. In August 1968 Soviet troops invaded Czechoslovakia to crush the Prague Spring. As a believer in 'socialism with a human face',

* Rodgers, *Assignment Moscow*, p. 107.

Werth was devastated. In March the following year he took his own life.*

## Charlotte Haldane

When Charlotte Haldane was writing *Russian Newsreel* about her time in Moscow, the Communist Party of Great Britain worried that in turning her back on communism she would toss a grenade at the party at a time when its fortunes were on the rise. But Charlotte was not going to give Hitler any free propaganda, and she suppressed, with a great effort of will, her real feelings about Stalin. The book was full of praise for the Russian people and dedicated to 'the Red Army and the heroic defenders of Moscow'. A careful reader might notice that what she left out was more significant than what she included. She writes, 'I have purposely refrained throughout the book from discussing the social, political and economic system which prevails in the Union of Soviet Socialist Republics.'† This was heresy for a Communist intellectual, given that in Marxism, political economy trumps everything. When party members came upon her book in libraries, they defaced it.

It was not until 1949, long after the war was over, that she revealed her true feelings in her autobiography, *Truth Will Out*. Comparing her writing in 1941 and eight years later, one can detect moments in *Russian Newsreel* when she skates around what she is really thinking. In 1941 she

---

* Werth, *Russia at War 1941–45*, p. xiii
† Charlotte Haldane, *Russian Newsreel* (Penguin, 1943), p. 184.

praised the Red Army for transforming unkempt peasant youths with feet wrapped in rags into 'smartly shaven soldiers, with close-cropped heads, wearing good coats, breeches and overcoats and fine high leather or felt boots'.* In 1949, she contrasts the 'pinched, pale faces and rags of the workers' with the 'smart uniforms of the Red Army men' who are now part of the new elite, along with the well-nourished political bosses and the NKVD officers, the 'real rulers of the country' with their 'powerful, insolent faces'.†

She realised she had been 'an intolerable bore' since joining the party in 1937. 'I had lied, cheated, acted under false pretences, obeyed and carried out orders from on high – this is called democratic centralism – denied all my inner ethical tenets and spiritual codes for the good of the cause, convincing myself that the end, the glorious and most worthy end, justified the means. I had not even had pleasure from it.'‡

As her husband J. B. S. Haldane had predicted, she lost contact with all her party comrades except for those who were sent to snoop on her. This was particularly harsh for her because when her marriage had failed to provide the sexual fulfilment, companionship and parity with her husband she yearned for,§ she had found lovers within the party, including William Rust, who later instigated a

* Ibid., p. 80.
† Charlotte Haldane, *Truth Will Out* (Weidenfeld & Nicolson, 1949), p. 239.
‡ Ibid., p. 238.
§ Judith Adamson, *Charlotte Haldane: Woman Writer in a Man's World* (Macmillan, 1998), p. 178.

campaign of vilification against her. She was branded a traitor and the guilty party in the break-up of the marriage. Party gossip threw up several reasons for her change of heart – she had failed to find any man in Moscow who wanted to be her lover; it was revenge for Stalin's refusing her an interview. At the same time, the activities of her husband were magnified to eclipse her own role in the party's history.

Charlotte lost her job at the *Daily Sketch* and found herself unemployable in the newspaper industry – communist sympathisers were influential in Fleet Street at the time. She conceded that, in her earlier life, she would have been the first to blackball a lapsed comrade who wanted a job on a national newspaper. She and JBS separated in 1942, and divorced in 1945.

As a divorced woman – she was now 'Miss Haldane' under the conventions of the time – she needed to raise her earnings, and the BBC archives record her demands for a pay rise for her radio talks, her main source of income.

In 1948 Charlotte clashed in public with JBS over the bitter East-West scientific controversy of the 1940s. Stalin had promoted a little-known geneticist, Dmitry Lysenko, who argued that he could improve wheat yields by treating the seeds before germination, and that the improvements would change the wheat seeds' genes and be passed on. According to the scientific consensus this was nonsense, but the Kremlin repressed scientists at home who disagreed and insisted that all good communists aboard endorse this mumbo jumbo. For a long time JBS sat on the fence and refused to condemn Lysenko, arguing that British science was hardly perfect with its reliance on funding from big companies. In an article in the *News Chronicle* addressed to 'British communists who are scientists', Charlotte laid down a challenge to her husband. Was it possible, she asked, to reconcile scientific knowledge based on experiment and observation with 'loyalty to a political creed which denounces this same knowledge, these principles, and this practice as criminal and fascist'?* The pressure on JBS – and not just from his ex-wife – became intolerable and he broke with the Communist Party in 1950. He later moved to India and took up Indian citizenship, a move prompted in part by his embrace of Hinduism.

Charlotte's later years were taken up with a series of biographies of women of talent and political influence. She died in 1969. She would have been appalled that her obituaries tended to mention her marriage in the first sentence, whereas had she been a man, the wife would have been relegated to the final sentence, if she appeared at all.†

## Alice Moats

Before the war Alice-Leone Moats had written nothing more substantial than a tongue-in-cheek book of etiquette, *No Nice Girl Swears*. During her time in Moscow, she discovered talents in herself that, on her return to the United States, led to her becoming a syndicated columnist and commentator. Despite her expensive education and connections to the Roosevelt White House, she was as comfortable talking to a Russian chambermaid as to

* 'Mine is a Moral Objection', *News Chronicle*, 22 December 1948.
† Adamson, *Charlotte Haldane*, p. 198.

an ambassador, and she fitted in with the laddish – even loutish – culture of the male journalists, who all called her 'Moatsie'.

On one memorable occasion she was arrested for breaking the midnight curfew. In the police station she was given a chair at the end of a line of curfew breakers, women with bundles and kerchiefs on their heads. They fingered her yellow summer dress, and asked if it was real silk and why she wasn't wearing any stockings – hadn't she got any? She told them she didn't wear stockings in summer because it was too hot, an original idea which intrigued the Russian women. Then an old woman wanted to know what she wore under her dress, and she gamely lifted it to show them what a panty girdle was. While the other correspondents moaned that they were banned from meeting real Russians, later that night Alice was accompanied to her home through the blackout by a 'charming' policeman who confided in her that the air-raid patrol was far too zealous in detaining people who broke the curfew.

In her memoir, she hints strongly at a secret love affair in Moscow with a twenty-four-year-old Soviet fighter ace named Sergei, a test pilot for the latest aircraft who was deployed wherever the battles were fiercest, from Murmansk to Kharkov. On meeting Alice he did not hide that for him it was love at first sight and they had assignations in an empty apartment. He was fascinated by the United States and promised that after the war he would come to New York. Alice's evacuation to Kuibyshev happened so suddenly that she did not have the chance to say goodbye to him. She never found out if he had survived the war. Even if he had been allowed to go to America, he would never have found her: as a precaution Alice and Sergei did not tell each other their surnames. In later years Alice would claim to have been engaged eight times, but she never married.

## Tanya Matthews

After a year living in Egypt, in July 1945 Tanya Matthews sailed for France with her infant son Christopher to be reunited with Ronald in Paris. Having arrived in Cairo with a single bag, she boarded the ship with thirteen pieces of luggage as well as a 'mental load of mannerisms' acquired to help her fit into bourgeois society – insincerity, double talk, good table manners and a superior air. Life in post-war Paris was cheap, and the family lived in style with a maid and a nanny, while Ronald became doyen of the Anglo-American Press Association, a group of men who traded political gossip at the long bar of the Hotel Crillon.

When the newly married Princess Elizabeth came to Paris in 1948, Tanya and Ronald were invited to a reception at the British Embassy. Tanya hired a Balmain dress of heavy pink silk with an enormous skirt covered with layer of white muslin. As she stood in front of the mirror she did not recognise the figure before her as the girl from the dusty oil town in southern Russia who had spent the summer digging potatoes on a collective farm. At the reception the ambassador's wife accompanied the princess, stopping from time to time to introduce her to the guests. Though Tanya gazed imploringly at Lady Harvey she was not introduced and did not have the opportunity to perform the curtsey she had been practising.

Despite her claim to have mastered the art of talking

without saying anything, Tanya was not afraid of making herself unpopular when the conversation around her dinner table turned to praise of Stalin. When a Labour Party official said, 'You won't deny that illiteracy has been eliminated in Russia?' she retorted: 'Yes, but would you like to live under a system which allowed you to read only one kind of book – the kind that the Kremlin chooses for you?' When the official praised the giant industries built by the communists, she shot back, 'They were built by slaves and run by slaves.'*

When Ronald sent her to London to learn about his homeland, she found the city cold, grey and unwelcoming. For solace she turned to a priest at a Catholic church in Mayfair and they talked for hours about Russia and her guilt at having abandoned her daughter. Getting herself out of Russia had required one miracle, and rescuing Anna would require a second, she told him, but the priest was convinced it would happen if she prayed. After two weeks in London, she fell ill and a Harley Street doctor told her she had a malignant growth, and needed an urgent operation. She retired to bed for three days, but feeling better on the fourth day, she went to see the priest, who saw the hand of God in her misfortune. He told her to send a doctor's certificate with her diagnosis to her ex-husband in Moscow and ask him to seek permission for her mother and Anna to come to visit her in Paris on urgent medical grounds.

That done, she went for a second opinion to a doctor who told her she was perfectly healthy, had no malignant growth and did not need an operation; the first diagnosis

* Tanya Matthews, *Russian Wife Goes West* (Gollancz, 1955), p. 78.

was the result of misinterpreting damage caused by a clumsily performed Soviet operation to remove an abscess under her womb. A second miracle did happen, and a year to the day after her arrival in France, on Bastille Day 1946, her mother and Anna landed at Orly airport. With Babushka looking after him, three-year-old Christopher was soon fluent in Russian, his fifth language, after speaking Greek and Arabic in Egypt, French with his Parisian nanny and English with his father.

Tanya had started to write her life story. After ninety pages her enthusiasm was flagging but Arthur Koestler encouraged her, saying, 'You've got something there. Go on, finish the book.' *Russian Child and Russian Wife* – Tanya hated the title – described in all its shocking detail the life of an ordinary Russian girl. Readers accused her of writing an anti-Soviet book. Newspapers requested features about ordinary life in Russia – but nothing 'political or biased'. Tanya provided what they wanted but, with her family safely out of Moscow, she was aching to write the truth about Stalin's regime, not just light features about vodka and mushrooms.

Ronald encouraged her in her ambition to be a serious journalist. He was convinced there was a good story to be had from interviewing Red Army deserters and escapees from the Soviet zone in Germany, and Tanya was the person to do it. Given the absence of serious reporting from Moscow, Ronald believed that these refugees could be the source of exclusive copy on the rising tide of discontent with Stalin's rule. He fixed it for Tanya to get a British press card, and from 1951–54 she travelled regularly to refugee camps in western Germany, providing hard-hitting copy for the *Observer*, the *Daily Telegraph* and *Time* magazine.

Her work turned out to be vital for the family finances after the *Daily Herald* closed its Paris bureau and Ronald found himself out of a job. Tanya and Ronald had swapped roles: the secretary-translator had become the correspondent. There was one problem she never managed to solve: she was treated with suspicion by a CIA operative in Germany whose mission was to unite the disparate strands of Soviet defectors into a credible opposition force to Stalin. Wherever he went, he found the blonde Russian-born reporter was there before him. With the looks of a Hollywood Mata Hari, Tanya could never convince the Americans that she was not a Soviet spy. Her dream since childhood in Grozny had been to go to the United States, but when she applied for a visa, it was refused.*

In the mid-1950s Ronald was recruited by the BBC to cover the collapse of the French empire in North Africa and the family moved to Tunisia and settled in a blue-and-white Moorish house in the charming seaside village of Sidi Bou Said. When Ronald died in 1967, Tanya took over his job. Her voice, carefully enunciated English with a slight Russian twang, was known throughout Africa: she dared to report what others would be expelled for saying – that Tunisia was a police state.

When I knew Tanya she was seventy, strikingly good-looking and elegantly dressed. She was as competitive in journalism as she was in sports – she had been a table tennis champion in her youth and now played a mean round of golf. She was untouchable because she had built up an unmatched network of contacts in Tunisia who would protect her. Government ministers, ambassadors and

* Matthews, *Russian Wife Goes West*, p. 239.

glamorous people from the film world would gather for dinner in her courtyard on warm evenings. Around 9 p.m. Tanya, an early riser, would slip quietly off to bed, the guests knowing they could stay chatting as long as they wanted. Generous by nature, she was always giving away copies of her book, *Russian Child and Russian Wife*. As I said goodbye to her on leaving Tunis to return to work in Russia, she went to her bookcase to find a copy to give me. It was her last.

In 1993 Tanya returned to Moscow after a fifty-year absence. As part of a BBC radio documentary, she visited the small room, now occupied by one old lady, where she, her daughter, her mother, her ex-husband and a nanny had all managed to find a place to sleep. She interviewed shoppers queuing up to buy Nina Ricci cosmetics outside one of Moscow's new branded stores and finally she went to visit her ex-husband Nick, the cameraman who had won an award for documenting the defense of Moscow in 1941, now living with his second wife and daughter in a new block on the outskirts of the city. Though they chatted amicably, it emerged that Nick had paid a heavy price for enabling their daughter Anna and Tanya's mother to visit Tanya in the West. When they failed to return to Moscow, Nick was expelled from the Communist party. This ruined his career: he was banned from working on prestigious documentaries in Moscow and had to scrabble around for work in the provinces. This revelation seems to have made Tanya regret her decision to return to Moscow. 'One should never go back to see the ghosts of the past.'*

---

* Tanya's return to Moscow was the subject of a BBC Radio 4 documentary, 'Going Back', broadcast on 27 December 1993.

## The Metropol Hotel

While I have been writing this book, the Metropol Hotel has been undergoing a major refurbishment. The hotel has never been frozen in time; in the 1980s, after decades of neglect, its ageing fabric was restored to its original glory. The rooms were all upgraded with ensuite bathrooms, but the look and feel of the hotel was little changed since its opening in 1905. During the Covid pandemic, however, modernisation has speeded up and become more radical. More than half of the rooms have been upgraded, with all signs of the hotel's early twentieth-century roots replaced with a décor that critics describe as 'international hotel beige'. The famously wide corridors have been narrowed and ceilings lowered. A group of journalists taken on a press tour were said to be 'up in arms' at the loss of some of the authentic character of the hotel, the scene of so many momentous events in Russia's twentieth-century history.

Rumours are now circulating among Moscow conservationists that the next stage of modernisation will reconfigure the dining room. No plans have been published, but fears are growing that the famous marble fountain is to be removed, and two of the gilded uplighters are to disappear to allow modern lighting to be installed. The fountain is an iconic feature: it is at the heart of memories of generations of visitors, both Russian and foreign. Muscovites now in their sixties recall dancing around the fountain as a high point of their youth; Russian pilgrims cupped their hands to catch water from the fountain and bathe their faces, believing it to come from a holy spring, and not the municipal supply; in the wilder times since the collapse of the Soviet Union in the 1990s the Russian new rich have fancied the gentle flow of the fountain to be a sparkling stream of champagne endlessly filling a marble goblet. It would be a terrible shame if the fountain that inspired memories over so many decades were to disappear for ever.

# Afterword

In November 1944, after four months in Moscow, Edgar Snow had a nightmare which had such an effect on him that he had to write it down. A little animal, perhaps a bat, is hiding in the fur of a dog and rushes out to attack a small child, sinking its teeth into the back of the child's neck and sucking its blood, before retreating to the warmth of the dog fur. Analysing this dream, Snow concluded that it represented his life in the Metropol during wartime: 'The vampire represents the correspondents, and the child represents the war dead at the front on which they feed and then crawl back to warmth and security.'* Snow was not the only correspondent who felt guilty that while other men were fighting and dying, the correspondents' only battle was with the censor. He was particularly alive to the absurdities of the life of the Moscow correspondents who, unable to cover the war as they wished, occupied themselves writing books on Russia. He shared some jaundiced thoughts with the Reuters bureau chief, Harold King, over lunch in one of the balcony rooms that overlooked the Metropol dining room:

* Papers of Edgar Snow, Book 45 1944, p.132.

'Look at us, I said to King. Never before have so few owed so much to so many. In this room are two dozen men whose names are made famous by being linked with the deeds of the Red Army. Never before have 25 men all covering the same story, with exactly the same sources of information, been asked each and every one of them, to write a book about it. Never before have 25 newspapermen confined to a hotel been asked to write a book about their experiences.'*

When Churchill visited Moscow in October 1944 he invited correspondents to meet him in Clark Kerr's study at the British embassy, a room overlooking the formal garden which the ambassador had turned into a vegetable patch. As an 'old journalist', Churchill told them he knew the difficulties and disappointments of their profession and complimented them on the 'care and tact' they had shown, by which he meant not complicating the already difficult relationship with Stalin. 'Well done,' he said. 'Considering the paucity of material, it's been a case of making bricks without straw.'†

But these were empty words. His early enthusiasm for a contingent of war correspondents in Moscow whose front-line reports would bring to life the Anglo-Soviet alliance had waned after the United States joined the war. With Britain no longer alone, and confident that the Allies would win, he decided that only one thing mattered: that the Russians continued to kill German soldiers in their hundreds of thousands.

* Ibid., Book 40, p. 111.
† Ibid., Book 45, p. 113.

As the war drew to a close the British embassy re-assessed the role of correspondents in Moscow. With Stalin and the Western Allies now in disagreement over the future of Europe, the Kremlin's manipulation of the British media changed from a wartime necessity that had to be tolerated into a peace-time problem that needed to be resolved. The embassy started a regular bulletin detailing the censorship of British correspondents' copy. Once the war was over and most of the press corps had left Moscow, the embassy assumed the newly liberated correspondents would reveal the censorship and restrictions they had operated under. In fact, the whole press pack and their employers kept their dirty secret quiet. Edgar Snow felt he should come clean – in a book perhaps to be called *Confessions of a Correspondent* – but such a publication would have cast doubt on the veracity of his phenomenally successful *People on our Side*, which had a print run of half a million copies in the United States.

The one exception to the journalistic code of omerta was Paul Winterton, who worked for the *News Chronicle* and the BBC overseas service: he offered his editor a tell-all article, but the newspaper refused to run it. All Fleet Street turned it down. At the end of May 1945, *World Press News*, a trade journal read only by journalists, interviewed Winterton and published a thin piece under the headline 'Foreign Correspondents in Moscow Reduced to Yes-Men'.*

The editor of the *News Chronicle* received an angry letter from a shocked reader, Ms L. A. Murdoch Bliss, an 'ordinary woman in the street' who by chance had read

* *World Press News*, 24 May 1945.

Winterton's revelation in *World Press News* that he had been broadcasting and writing 'stuff and nonsense'.

'I shall not pay any attention to reports from Moscow in future,' she wrote. 'I never dreamt for one minute that Mr Winterton was being told what to say and not being allowed to follow his own judgment. It never occurred to me that the *News Chronicle* would tolerate this state of affairs for one moment, especially on important affairs.' She understood that Russia was easily offended but she could not accept 'grovelling' before the Kremlin.

'Surely Mr Winterton must have been aware of the harmful repercussions? He can be quite assured that he has misled millions of people in this country and abroad.'*

With the newspapers refusing to reveal the truth, the British Embassy went into action, compiling a four-page report on the journalists' working conditions that was circulated among the Cabinet at the end June 1945. Clark Kerr, the British ambassador, wrote that the purpose of Soviet censorship was not just to preserve military secrets but to rewrite articles that did not fit the Kremlin line. Journalists were expected to parrot *Pravda* and *Izvestia*, and the censors did their best to make it look like the views of these official organs were the opinions of the writer.

While sympathetic to the difficulties experienced by journalists, the document went out of its way to reveal the 'temptations' offered to correspondents who toed the Kremlin line. The financial rewards for journalists working in Moscow were huge: they paid no income tax to the Soviet government, could live on their expenses, save their

* Letter to Gerald Barry, editor, *News Chronicle*, 1 June 1945. Trinity College Cambridge Library, Layton Papers 86/200.

salaries and rake in royalties from book sales. 'In these circumstances the frontier between professional integrity and material expediency is apt to be uncertain,' the ambassador noted.

The report ended with a warning: the Kremlin's ability to manipulate resident correspondents in Moscow was likely to be 'a constant source of friction' in future between the Soviet Union and the Western democracies. It urged the government to make British newspaper owners and editors aware of the harm they would be doing to Anglo-Soviet relations if they chose to keep a correspondent in Moscow.*

That Stalin won the propaganda war and was able to suppress all negative coverage of the Soviet Union – in part thanks to the complicity of the press – is not in doubt. The correspondents known as the 'Kremlin stooges' got together in London in November and December 1945 to celebrate their success in bolstering Stalin's image. Victory parties brought together Ralph Parker and Valentina (who was allowed a visa to visit Britain despite fears she would be a threat to national security); Alaric Jacob, the *Daily Express* correspondent who was an avowed Marxist despite having the tastes of a wealthy bourgeois; John Gibbons, the *Daily Worker* correspondent; and John Aldridge, the *New York Times* staffer who would go on to be awarded the Lenin Peace prize. No expense was spared: the party hosted by Parker was held in the Pinafore Room at the Savoy, the hotel's most famous private dining room.†

---

* TNA FO 371 47918/76.
† Diary of Alaric Jacob, 16 November 1945 and 3 December 1945.

Winterton, the only correspondent who had tried to tell the truth about the whole enterprise, was not invited.

Journalists often exaggerate the effect of their writing on public opinion, but it is clear that the British public, fed for years on a sanitised image of Stalin, was ill-prepared for the confrontation that set in after the war. They had been led to believe that Britain and Russia would work together to usher in a period of peace and prosperity in Europe, allowing Britain to focus on creating a more equal society at home. In fact what lay ahead was rearmament and the huge expense of creating a nuclear deterrent.

Vernon Bartlett, the MP who had sailed out to Russia in the early days of the war and challenged Stalin in public to accept the principle of a free press, wrote in 1960 that democracy had allowed itself to be dangerously weakened by illusions about 'Uncle Joe' during the war years.

'Subsequent shocks to public opinion would have been less deep, and therefore less dangerous, if we had flouted the policy of the moment by telling the whole truth, and not merely that part of it which was in the immediate interests of the allies,' Bartlett writes in his autobiography, *And Now, Tomorrow*. 'Years elapsed before people in Great Britain could accept the fact that the communist leaders were found to be hardly less dangerous than the Nazis had been.'

He concludes: 'If I have learned anything in some forty years of journalism, it is that it does not pay to wrap up the truth in fine phrases.'*

*

* Vernon Bartlett, *And Now Tomorrow* (Chatto, 1960), p. 81.

The world has changed since 1941, but there are similarities between the ages of Stalin and Putin. When Stalin imposed censorship on foreign correspondents' output in 1940 after he launched his Winter War on Finland, the *New York Times* correspondent G. E. R. Gedye was taken aside by an official and told not to refer to the new press regime as 'wartime censorship'. Why not? asked Gedye. Because the USSR is not at war, came the reply. It was an operation to liberate the 'revolutionary masses' of Finland from the grip of the 'White Guards' in power in Helsinki.*

Change the country from Finland to Ukraine and substitute 'White Guards' for 'drug-addled Nazis' and you can see why Putin called his war a 'special operation'. It is often forgotten that the Second World War in Europe began with Hitler and Stalin's joint campaign in 1939 to wipe Poland off the map of Europe. Stalin's reasons for obliterating Poland are echoed in Putin's intention in 2022 to destroy Ukraine as an independent state. Putin's annexation of four Ukrainian provinces later that year recalls Stalin's land grab in 1940, when he extended the frontiers of the Soviet state by adding the western Ukrainian territories which had previously been part of Poland.

Russia is a country with no defensible borders to the west. A president who promises to extend the country's defensive perimeter – even when no aggressor is in sight – will be seen as following in the footsteps of Russia's most celebrated leaders. Peter the Great conquered the Baltic States to give Russia a 'window onto Europe' in the north. Catherine the Great extended the Russian empire to the

* Draft article on Soviet censorship, G. E. R. Gedye papers, Imperial War Museum. GERG27, item 1343.

south, taking Crimea and the northern shore of the Black Sea. Russia lost some of these possessions with the Bolshevik Revolution in 1917. Stalin regained them in wartime, but his conquests were reversed when the Soviet Union collapsed and Boris Yeltsin let go the periphery of the Tsarist empire, leaving only the Russian heartland under the Kremlin's sovereign control. It is not surprising that Putin, once he had established himself as an immovable leader, set out to recover the most valuable of the territories 'lost' in the 1990s and the one closest to the hearts of the Russians: Ukraine.

This book has focused on the extraordinary lengths that Stalin took to control the media narrative in Second World War. It is not fanciful to suggest that Putin has been following Stalin's playbook and he has had some success in using twentieth-century methods to control twenty-first-century media at home. In the Russian heartland, away from the more sophisticated big cities, he appears to have convinced people that his ill-conceived and unnecessary war is an existential struggle for the survival of Russia. The ground was well-prepared. The first step in Putin's path to autocracy was to reassert control over the media. This process was so near completion by the time Putin launched his invasion of Ukraine that it took just a few days to close down the few remaining independent media outlets. It is hard to imagine Putin being able to go to war against Ukraine without the full control of the media that enabled him to engender in Russian society a new militarism based on nostalgia for the glory of the 1945 victory and an officially nurtured sense of victimhood.

So important for the Kremlin is the connection to 1945 that the Moscow-backed separatists in eastern Ukraine hang alleged spies and collaborators with signs around their necks marked SMERSH (Death to Spies), the name of Stalin's wartime counter-espionage service. Russia's Channel One TV has been so keen to identify Putin with the heroic 1940s that it has claimed that the president's father died defending Leningrad from the Nazis. Putin was born in 1952.

In 1944, during Churchill's visit to Moscow, Stalin made an excursion through history that he knew would please his allies. Russia and Britain together had seen off Napoleon, he told Churchill in a toast, but a century later it had required a little help from the Americans for the Allies to win the First World War. In the war that was drawing to a close as Stalin spoke, the Americans were 'an absolutely indispensable partner', providing not only soldiers but also the Lend-Lease supplies of arms and raw materials that helped the Red Army to victory.*

Putin would do well to reflect on the fact that the Lend-Lease of today – the airlift of American weapons to fight the aggressor – is going not to Russia but to Ukraine. These supplies have prevented Russia from eradicating Ukraine as an independent state, a task that Putin rashly thought could be done in three days.

As these words are written, there is stalemate on the battlefield. The survival of Ukraine depends in large part on the continued flow of American weaponry. Just as Stalin spared no effort to manipulate the media and keep the Western onside during the Second World War, victory for Putin now depends on him doing the opposite: undermining American support for Ukraine so that Washington tires

* Papers of Edgar Snow, Book 45, p. 109.

of being Ukraine's armourer at a time when the United States should be focusing on China not Europe. America bowing out of the fight would leave President Zelensky outgunned by Russia, and forced to accept humiliating peace terms. Just as Stalin insisted on total control of wartime propaganda, we can be sure that Putin will use every weapon available in his arsenal, from the broadcast propaganda of his TV stations to the darker arts of social media manipulation and the hacking of emails, to turn American opinion against the Ukrainians. That is his path to turn what looks like defeat into victory.

January 2023

# Bibliography

Adamson, Judith, *Charlotte Haldane: Woman Writer in a Man's World* (Macmillan, 1998)

Anders, Władysław, *An Army in Exile* (Macmillan, London, 1949)

Antonov-Ovseyenko, Anton, *The Time of Stalin: Portrait of a Tyranny* (Harper & Row, New York, 1983)

Applebaum, Anne, *Gulag: A History of the Soviet Camps* (Allen Lane, 2003)

Atkin, Malcolm, *Section D for Destruction: Forerunner of SOE* (Pen & Sword, 2017)

Bartlett, Vernon, *And Now, Tomorrow* (Chatto & Windus, 1960)

Berlin, Isaiah, *Enlightening: Letters 1946–60* (Chatto & Windus, 2009)

Birstein, Vadim J., *SMERSH* (Biteback, London, 2011)

Blunden, Godfrey, *A Room on the Route* (Lippincott, 1947)

Bourke-White, Margaret, *Shooting the Russian War* (Simon & Schuster, 1943)

Braithwaite, Rodric, *Moscow 1941: A City and its People at War* (Profile, 2006)

Bruce Lockhart, Robert, *Memoirs of a British Agent* (Putnam, London, 1932)

Carroll, Wallace, *We're in This with Russia* (Houghton Mifflin, 1944)

Carter, Eric, *Force Benedict* (Hodder, 2014)

Chambers, Whittaker, *Witness* (Andre Deutsch, 1953)

Cienciala, Anna M. et al., *Katyn: A Crime Without Punishment* (Yale University Press, 2007)

Cripps, Stafford and Gorodetsky, Gabriel, *Stafford Cripps in Moscow 1940–1942: Diaries and Papers* (Valentine Mitchell, 2007).

Day, Peter, *Trotsky's Favourite Spy* (Biteback, 2017)

Driberg, Tom, *Ruling Passions* (Cape, London, 1977)

Egorova, Ekaterina, *Metropol – Stolitsa Moskvy* (Sever, Moscow, undated)

Gilmore, Eddy, *Me and My Russian Wife* (Greenwood Press, New York, 1968)

Griffith, Hubert, *R.A.F. in Russia* (Hammond, Hammond Ltd., London, 1942)

Grossman, Vasily, *Stalingrad* (Vintage Classic, London, 2020)

Gruliow, Leo, 'The Soviet Press: "Propagandist, Agitator, Organizer"', Journal of International Affairs, Vol. 10, No. 2, The Press in World Affairs (1956)

Haldane, Charlotte, *Russian Newsreel* (Penguin, 1943)

Haldane, Charlotte, *Truth Will Out* (Weidenfeld, 1949)

Harriman Averell, and Elie Abel, *Special Envoy to Churchill and Stalin, 1941–1946* (Random House Inc., 1975)

Inber, Vera, *Leningrad Diary* (St Martin's Press, London, 1971)

Israelyan, Victor, *On the Battlefields of the Cold War: A Soviet Ambassador's Confession* (Pennsylvania State University Press, 2003)

Jordan, Philip, *Russian Glory* (Cresset Press, London, 1942)

Kennan, George F., *Memoirs 1925–1950*, (Kindle edition)

Kirk, Irina, *Profi les in Russian Resistance* (Quadrangle, New York, 1975)

Bibliography

Leningrad Faces New Winter of Siege, *Daily Telegraph* (Sydney), 17 September 1942

Maisky, Ivan, *Complete Diaries*, vol. 3 (Yale University Press, 2017)

Matthews, Owen, *Richard Sorge: An Impeccable Spy* (Bloomsbury, 2019)

Matthews, Ronald, *Red Sky at Night* (Hollis & Carter, London, 1951)

Matthews, Tanya, *Russian Child and Russian Wife: An Autobiography* (Gollancz, London, 1949)

Matthews, Tanya, *Russian Wife Goes West* (Gollancz, 1955)

McDonald, Iverach, *The History of The Times 1929–1984* (Times Books, 1984)

Miller, John, *All Them Cornfields and Ballet in the Evening* (Hodgson Press, 2010)

Moats, Alice-Leone, *Blind Date with Mars* (Doubleday, New York, 1943)

Morley, Iris, *Nothing But Propaganda* (Peter Davies, London, 1946)

No Pessimism in Russian Retreats, *Daily Telegraph* (Sydney), 10 July 1942

Overy, Richard, *Russia's War* (Penguin, 2010)

Parker, A. R., Gresham Cooke, R., Green, Felix (eds), *A Declaration of Tory Principles. Essays by Undergraduates of Oxford and Cambridge* (Heffer & Sons, Cambridge, 1929)

Parker, Ralph, *Conspiracy Against Peace: Notes of an English Journalist* (Literaturnaya Gazeta Publishers, Moscow, 1949)

Parker, Ralph, *Moscow Correspondent* (Frederick Muller Ltd, London, 1949)

Parker, Valentina to Mary Fedden and Julian Trevelyan, Julian Trevelyan archive TREJ 44.27, Trinity College Cambridge (1965)

Plokhy, Serhii, *The Gates of Europe: A History of Ukraine* (Penguin, 2015)

Purvis, Stewart and Hulbert, Jeff, *Guy Burgess: The Spy Who Knew Everyone'* (Biteback, London 2016)

Ransome, Arthur, *Six Weeks in Russia in 1919* (Allen & Unwin, 1919)

Rodgers, James, *Assignment Moscow: Reporting on Russia from Lenin to Putin* (I. B. Tauris, 2020)

Ruge, Eugen, *Le Metropol* (Chambon, Paris, 2021)

Salisbury, Harrison, *Disturber of the Peace* (Unwin, 1989)

Sanford, George, *Katyn and the Soviet Massacre of 1940: Truth, Justice and Memory* (Routledge, 2005)

Sheridan, Clare, *Mayfair to Moscow* (Boni & Liveright, New York, 1921)

Slezkine, Yuri, *The House of Government* (Princeton University Press, 2017)

Snow, Edgar, *Journey to the Beginning* (Random House, 1958)

Sudoplatov, Pavel, *Raznye dni tainoi voiny i diplomatii* (Olma Press, Moscow, 2001)

Sulzberger, Cyrus, *A Long Row of Candles* (Macdonald, 1969)

Sykes, Christopher, *Nancy: the Life of Lady Astor* (Collins, 1972)

Tanenhaus, Sam, *An Un-American Life: The Case of Whittaker Chambers* (Old Street Publishing, London, 2007)

Topolski, Feliks, *Fourteen Letters* (Faber, 1988)

Trevelyan, Julian, *Indigo Days*, (Macgibbon & Kee, London, 1957)

Tumanov, Alla, *Where We Buried the Sun* (NeWest Publishers, Edmonton, 1999)

## Bibliography

Ulanovskaya, Nadezhda and Ulanovskaya, Maya, *Istoria Odnoi Semyi*, 3rd edition, Inanpress, 2013)

Watkins, John, *Moscow Despatches: Inside Cold War Russia* (James Lorimer Ltd, 1987)

Werth, Alexander, *Moscow '41* (Hamish Hamilton, 1942)

Werth, Alexander, *Russia at War 1941–45* (Barrie and Rockliff, London, 1964)

Winter, Ella, *I Saw the Russian People* (Boston, 1946)

Zetkin, Clara, Lenin on the Women's Question, *My Memorandum Book* (2004)

# Picture Credits

1a     Margaret Bourke-White/The LIFE Picture Collection/ Shutterstock

1b     Photographer unknown/National Portrait Gallery, London

2 (all)     Margaret Bourke-White/The LIFE Picture Collection/ Shutterstock

3 (all)     Courtesy Alexander Yakobson

4a     National Archives, Kew

4b     Courtesy Christopher Matthews

4c     Courtesy Australian War Memorial

5a & b     Courtesy Zsuzsanna Szunyogh

5c     Trinity College Cambridge Archive, Trevelyan Collection

6a     Courtesy Alexander Yakobson

6b     © Imperial War Museum (E19024)

7a     Courtesy Sian Snow

7b     World Telegram photo by Fred Palumbo/Library of Congress Prints & Photographs Division, Washington D.C.

7c     Courtesy Katerina Porter

8a     © Imperial War Museum (HU 106382)

8b     Alan Philps, author's collection

8c     Courtesy Alexander Yakobson

# Acknowledgements

This book would never have been written if my friend Natasha Groznaya had not remembered a chance remark by me that I wanted to find out more about the Metropol Hotel in wartime. 'This will help,' said Natasha as she handed me a newly published history of the hotel by Ekaterina Egorova, a teacher who in the 1990s had supplemented her meagre wages by moonlighting as a receptionist in the Metropol. The fruits of her research appear throughout the book.

Natasha gave me the impetus to write the book, but it has required the support of many others for the wartime story of the Metropol to see the light of day. I would like to thank my agent, Annabel Merullo, for believing in the project, Iain MacGregor for taking it on, and Yvonne Jacob, Cathie Arrington and Raiyah Butt at Headline for seeing it through to publication.

I am grateful for the cooperation of Professor Alexander Yakobson who generously provided memories and photographs of his mother Maya Ulanovskaya and grandmother Nadya Ulanovskaya and allowed me to quote from their memoir, *Istoria odnoi semyi*. Though an English version has been published under the title *The Family Story*, I have preferred to translate from the original Russian. I am grateful to Chris Matthews who shared memories of his parents, and provided images of his mother Tanya but sadly died before the book came out. I am indebted to Anna Hajkova who introduced me to Helena Kopecká, daughter of Milena Hofbauerová. As she lay dying, Helena arranged for me to meet her son, Daniel Kopecky, and her niece Zsuzsanna Szunyogh. My thanks go to Daniel and

Zsuzsanna for sharing their family's story and providing me with photos and letters. I am grateful to Sian Snow for permission to use the diaries of her father, and to Jasper Jacob, for the use of the diaries of Alaric Jacob. If there is anyone who I have failed to trace, I would be glad to hear from them. Interviewees who have been generous with their time include Katherine and Ronald Blunden, Neil and Anne Parker, and Katerina Porter.

I have had the benefit of the resources and the helpful staff of the London Library, the British Library, the National Archives in Kew and the News UK Ltd archive, but I still needed the services of experienced researchers. Catherine Mullier's incomparable sleuthing in archives in London and Cambridge revealed aspects of Ralph Parker's character and career. Oleg Boldyrev followed up leads in Russia, Irina Shumovich unearthed photographs of Jewish life in Ukraine and Clara McMichael researched archives in New York. Julian Graffy educated me about the role of foreigners in Soviet propaganda films. An article by Richard Cockett, 'In wartime every objective reporter should be shot', provided me with many fruitful leads.

Among those who have helped, inspired, or otherwise improved the work are Fay Anderson, Richard Parrack, Michael Binyon, Patrick Buckridge, Giles Elgood, Helen Fitzwilliam, Sir Roderick Lyne, Barry Moody, Judith Matloff, Catherine Philps, Simon Renton, James Rodgers and Rachel Smith. But the book would have been a half-formed thing without my wife Sarah, my harshest critic and sworn enemy of journalese.

# Index

Afanasyevna, Rakhil 233–6, 388–9, 392
air raids 124, 282
aircraft production 228
Albania 140–2
Alexeyeva, Lyudmila 397
All-Union Society for Relations with
  Foreign Countries 52–3, 186
American aid 27
American Communist Party 198, 201
American embassy 15
Amery, Julian 140, 141, 293
Anders, General 255–64, 274
  appointed commander of army of
    Polish deportees 257–8
  captured by the Russians 257
  evacuation plan 261–4
  meets Moats 255–6
  meets Moats in Tehran 264
  recruits 258–60
  task 258–60
Anders' Army 255–64
  evacuation to Iran 261–4
  officers 261–2
  recruits 258–61
Anderson, Fay 218
Anglo-Soviet alliance 109
anti-Semitism 67, 167, 230, 397–8
Archangel 34, 37, 45–6, 137, 147
Armstrong, Harold 248–9
Astor, Nancy 54

Babel, Isaac, death sentence 331
Baillon, General Joe 318
Baku 313–15
Balfour, Jock 311, 321

Barrington-Ward, Robert 297
Bartlett, Vernon 34–5, 37–8, 40, 108, 424
  censorship 106–7
  Smolensk front visit 90, 99
  Smolensk front visit report 101–2
  Stalin interview 107–9
Batiushkova, Katerina 277–8
BBC 40, 101, 103, 107, 191, 219, 284
BBC Middle East service 318
Beaverbrook, Lord 95, 107, 108
Bechyne 139
Beilis, Mendel, trial 67
Belgrade 140
Beria, Lavrenty 274, 385
Berle, Adolf 214–15
Berlin 159, 162–3, 165–6
Berlin, Isaiah 342
Berling, Zygmunt 274–5
Bershad 11, 68
Berzin, Yan 197, 213, 334
Bierut, Boleslaw 275
Big Vera (prostitute) 177
blackmail 342
Blunden, Godfrey 218, 365
  A Room on the Route 345–8, 351, 388–9,
    393–4
  answers readers' questions 232
  failure to disguise his sources 393–4
  German prisoner of war interview 231
  interviews Alex and Nadya 226–7
  Kharkov reports 229–31
  leaves Russia 236
  Ortenberg interview 223
  reunion with Nadya 390–1
  seeks information on Nadya 389–90

439

Blunden, Godfrey – *cont'd.*
  Stalingrad visit 228–9
  suffering caused by 388–94
  visits a Russian home 232–6, 388–9
  works round restrictions 222–5
Blunden, Katherine 392–3
Blunden, Ronald 391–2
Blunt, Anthony 291–2
Bolshevik Revolution 9–12, 49, 69,
    209, 426
Bourke-White, Margaret
  arrival in Soviet Union 82–3
  Dorogobuzh visit 97–8
  dress 84
  Smolensk front visit 82, 84, 88–9, 91,
    93, 95, 96–7, 97–8
  Vyazma bombing raid 91–2
  Yelnya photograph 96–7
*Bremen* (liner) 197
British Communist Party 157–8, 291
Bruce Lockhart, Robert 48, 48–9, 49
Buchin, Alexander 355
Buckley, William F. 390
Bukharin, Nikolai 211, 333
Burdenko, Nikolai 272, 274
Burgess, Guy 56, 292, 299
Buzuluk 255–6

Cairo 317–22, 412
Caldwell, Erskine 82–3, 91
Carr, E. H. 297–8, 301
Carroll, Sidney 19–20, 24
Carroll, Wally 35, 37–8, 45–6, 126–7
Carter, Eric 40–1
Case, Martin 23
Cassidy, Henry 116–17, 132, 155, 242,
    273, 282
Částková, Slávka 139
casualties, numbers hidden 100
Catherine the Great 425
censorship 17, 32, 64, 96–7, 106–7, 134,
    152, 223–4, 232, 421, 425
Central Telegraph Office 62
Chaliapin, Feodor 47–8
Chambers, Esther 199
Chambers, Whittaker 198–200, 204–5,
    214–15, 323, 325–6, 327–9, 392
  The Ghosts on the Roof' 328–9
Champenois Jean 267

Cheka 52, 163, 164–5
Chelyabinsk 217
*Chicago Daily News* 63, 121
China 165, 166
Cholerton, A. T. 112–13, 177, 261
  apartment 281–2
  beard 281
  evacuation to Kuibyshev 133
  experience 276
  holiday in Britain 276–7
  Kharkov reports 230
  marriage 277–8
  Moats interviews 282–3
  Moats takes Sanctuary with 117
  Natalia writes to 285–6
  post-war 398–9
  secretary–translator arrested 276, 277,
    284–5
  Smolensk front visit 84–5, 86, 92, 94
  temper 283–4
  visa refused 276–81, 286–7
  in winter 283
'Chronicle of Current Events' 397
Churchill, Winston 2, 18, 34, 40, 57,
    83, 110, 221, 285, 306, 327–8,
    420, 427
Clark Kerr, Sir Archibald 277, 278–9,
    281, 286, 298, 305–6, 308–9,
    422–3
Cold War 301, 340–3, 348
collectivisation 54, 203, 217
*Collier's* magazine 14–16, 116, 117, 258
Comintern 291
Communist International 163
Communist Party, fall of 56
Conquest, Robert 397, 399
*Conspiracy Against Peace: Notes of an English
    Journalist* (Parker) 341–2
conveyor belt interrogation 354–5
Crankshaw, Edward 399
Cripps, Stafford 101–2, 108, 109–11,
    124–6, 129, 295–6, 306
Czechoslovakia 28, 138–9, 406

D-Day landings 318
*Daily Express* 21–2, 24, 192, 327
*Daily Herald* 194
*Daily Sketch* 19–20, 34, 103, 110, 409
*Daily Telegraph* 84–5, 281

# Index

*Daily Worker* 100, 301, 399–400
Deakin, Ralph 146, 296–7
Dekanozov, Vladimir 311–12
Denmark 206–7
diplomat expulsions 359
Dorogobuzh 97–8
Dos Passos, John 347
Driberg, Tim 299
Driberg, Tom 56
Dzerzhinsky, Iron Felix 227

Eden, Anthony 279–80
Egorova, Ekaterina 53
Egypt 317–22
Eremenko, General Andrei 335–7
Estonia 160–1, 162–3
Exham, Colonel 255–6
eyewitness reports, importance of 18

factories, return to production 227–8
famine 155, 164
fascist beasts 193, 193–5
Fedden, Mary 292, 402
Fido (coat) 84
Finland 425
First World War 69
floozies 177
food shortages 135–6
Food Technology Institute 373, 382
Foot, Michael 231
foreign language institute students 177–9
Foreign Office 109–11, 195, 280–1, 298, 315, 321–2
foreigners, Russians and 1
Fourth Directorate 165–6, 206, 207

Galya (Lubyanka prisoner) 355–6, 360
gangster pact, 1939 36
Gedye, G. E. R. 18, 425
General Mud 86–7
German Communist Party 164–5
German invasion 13–15, 18
Germany, 1921 159–64
Gestapo 230–1
Gibbons, John 106–7
gilded cage 155
Gilmore, Eddy 147, 148, 267, 268, 304, 335–7
Gilmore, Tamara 335–7

girls of the Metropol 48
  reputation as prostitutes 176–9
Goebbels, Joseph 265, 266, 270
Great Britain, thirst for information 104–5
Great Patriotic War 4
Great Purge, the 55, 58, 207–15, 226–7, 267, 330–4
Griffith, Hubert 38–9
Grossman, Vasily 225–6, 228, 229–30
Grozny 246–51, 316
GRU 165–6

Haldane, Charlotte 7
  arrival in Archangel 45–6
  background 21–3
  crisis of faith 156–8
  divorce 409
  'Domestic Life in the USSR' lectures 33
  Dorogobuzh visit 97–8
  dress 83–4
  epiphany in Kuibyshev 134–6, 137
  evacuation to Kuibyshev 125–7, 127–31, 132–3, 134–6
  faith in Stalin 42
  flight to Moscow 46
  and George Hill 130–1
  German advance on Moscow 123–7
  ghoulishness 94
  heightened emotions 32
  intentions 110
  jealousy of 93–4
  job interview 19–20, 23–4
  journey back to Moscow 99–100
  later years 410
  leaves Russia 136–7
  lecture to Topolski 44
  loss of faith in the Communist Party 134–6, 137, 156–8
  lunch with Cripps 109–10
  marriage 157
  outlawed by BCP 158
  and Pilot Officer Wollaston 40–1
  post-war 407–10
  pro-Sovietism 93–4
  *Russian Newsreel* 137, 156–7, 407
  secretary–translator 181
  sense of unease 98

# Index

Haldane, Charlotte – *cont'd.*
  Smolensk front visit 81–2, 83–4, 88, 90,
    91, 92, 93–4, 97–8, 99–100
  Smolensk front visit report 103
  Spanish Civil War experience 83, 88
  on Stalin's Russia 157–8
  *Truth Will Out* 407–8
  voyage to Russia 33–46
  Vyazma bombing raid 91, 92
Haldane, J. B. S. 22, 23, 24, 157–8, 408,
    409–10
Hamburg uprising 164–5
Harriman, Averell 95, 107, 112, 305
Harriman, Kathy 271, 273
Hebrew University of Jerusalem 398
Hill, George 130–1, 294–5
Hitler, Adolf 2, 15, 36, 148, 204, 255
Hodson, Flight Lieutenant 39–40
Hogg, Quintin 290
Holt, Paul 233, 238, 240–1, 242–3
homosexuality 56
Hong Kong 175
Hungary 139
hunger prostitution 177

Ibárruri, Dolores 88
impotence, sense of 181
Inber, Vera 219–20
industrialisation 128, 197–8
information, sources of 180–1
informers 357–60
intelligence services, British press
    relationships with 32
interpreters, privileged position 60
invisible wall, the 330–7
Iran 316–17
Israel 397–8
Istanbul 30, 141–2
Istra 152–6
  banquet 154–5
  New Jerusalem monastery 153
  suffering 153–4
  survivor interviews 153–4
Italian campaign, 1944 262

Jackson, Michael 56
Jacob, Alaric 192, 327
Japan 165
Jews, Nazi massacre of 229–31

Joe (Airedale terrier) 125, 127
Johnson, Hewlett 338–9
Jordan, Philip 84, 133–4

Kamenev, Lev 208
Kassel, Anna 330, 334
Katyn massacre 265–7, 270–4
Kennan, George 339–41, 342
Kerensky, Alexander 347
Kerr, Walter 147, 179
Kharkov 100, 229
Kherson 75–6
Khrushchev, Nikita, secret speech 385
Khrushchev thaw, the 400, 406
Kiev 42
King, Harold 267–8, 419
Klyachin, Alexander 57
Knickerbocker, H. R. 17
Koestler, Arthur 414
Kollontai, Alexandra 51
Korean War 343
*Kremlin Chimes* (play) 176
Kremlin stooges 192–3, 193, 195–6
Kuibyshev 156, 256
  accommodation 132–4
  Charlotte Haldane's epiphany in
    134–6, 137
  evacuation to 121, 122–3, 125–7,
    127–37, 138, 147–8, 150
  food shortages 135–6
  Grand Hotel 132–3, 136, 148
  Intourist hotel 132
  refugees 134–6
kulaks 208
Kuprianov, Gennady 352n
Kurgan, Rafail 170–5
Kursk, Battle of 270

labour camps 371, 374–84
  food 376
  prisoners released 385–7
  sanitation brigade 377–8
  survival rules 375–6
  water supply team 384
Lawrence, William H. 301
Lefortovo prison 370
Lend-Lease supplies 427
Lenin, Vladimir Ilyich 49, 52, 69,
    303, 330

Leningrad 400, 427
Leningrad, siege of 219–20, 224
Lepeshinskaya (prima ballerina) 304
Lerner, Naum 211–13
LeSueur, Larry 147, 195–6
Lily (secretary–translator) 181
Lithuania, Sovietisation 312
living conditions, ordinary Russians
    232–6
*Llanstephan Castle* (ship) 33–46
    absence of promised Soviet escort
        43–4
    arrival in Archangel 45–6
    cargo 36
    convoy 37
    lectures 33, 38–40
    lifeboat drill 34–5
    passengers 34, 36–7
    passes North Cape 43
    press pack 34–5
Lola (Lubyanka prisoner) 355, 357–60
London 19–24, 26, 413
    King Street, Covent Garden 158
London Blitz 156
*London Evening Standard* 218, 231
London Poles 265–7
Lord Haw-Haw 103
Lozovsky, Solomon 24–5, 26–8, 81–2,
    283–4
Lyalya (labour camp prisoner) 375–6
Lysenko, Dmitry 409
Lyudmila (prostitute) 177

McDonald, Iverach 296
McLaughlin, Eric 63–5, 152, 156
Maisky, Ivan 105, 111
Majdanek Nazi extermination camp 405
Mao Tse-tung 179
Margolis, Jack 58, 61, 112, 323
Mary (American communist) 122–3
Mason-MacFarlane, General 263
Matthews, Christopher 412, 414
Matthews, Ronald 6, 268
    bag full of soap 237
    birth of son 303
    covers D-Day landings 318
    death of 415
    death of father 311–12
    as fascist beast 194–5

leaves Russia 310–15
post-war 141, 413, 415
proposes to Tanya 237–8
reunited with Tanya 412
Revolution Day celebrations toast,
    1943 307
secretary–translator 188–91
on Tanya's exit permit 322
wedding 238–41
wedding reception 241–3
Matthews, Tanya (nee Svetlova) 6, 7,
    194–5
    background 245–54
    BBC Middle East service broadcast
        318–19
    birth of son 303
    change in status on marriage 243–5
    childhood 247
    cloud of suspicion 247–8
    comparison with Nadia 244–5
    divorce from Nick 252
    in Egypt 317–22
    eighteenth birthday 248–9
    and evacuation of Moscow 253
    exit permit 315, 321–2
    as fascist beast 193–4, 195
    first shopping trip 317
    first impression of abroad 316
    in Iran 316–17
    as journalist 141–5
    leaves Moscow 313
    leaves Russia 310–15
    marriage to Nick 250–1
    Matthews proposes to 237–8
    passport irregularity 314–15
    path to freedom 243, 253–4
    permission to leave Russia 312
    Polish crisis press conference 267–8
    post-war 412–16
    receives British passport 317
    refuses to return to Russia 321–2
    rendition of *Life is Just a Bowl of
        Cherries* 251
    return to Moscow 416
    reunited with Ronald 412
    Revolution Day celebrations, 1943
        302–4, 306–7, 308
    *Russian Child and Russian Wife* 414
    secret police encounters 249–53

# Index

Matthews, Tanya (nee Svetlova) – *cont'd.*
  secretary–translator recruitment
    183–91
  security check 320–1
  social life 244
  wedding 238–41
  wedding reception 241–3
media environment 4
media management 219–22, 421–4, 426
  hospitality 87–91
  operation launched 81
  Smolensk front visit 80–104
  success 104
Memorial 182
Metropol economy, the 324–5
Metropol Hotel 3, 32
  anarchic spirit 62
  authors experience of 5–7
  Bolshevik Revolution 49–50
  Boyarsky Zal function room 55
  *cabinets privés* 48–9
  conditions, 1920s 50–3
  current owner 57
  dining room closure 58–9
  dissolute atmosphere 48
  and German invasion 13–15
  the Great Purge 55
  heating 60
  history 47–56
  invisible wall 330–7
  journalist occupation 56–62
  lobby 61
  long-term residents 58
  meals 58–9
  at opening 47–8
  permanent residents 330–7
  post-Stalin 55–6
  reception desk 61
  refurbishment 417–18
  renamed Second House of Soviets 50
  restaurant 49
  role 57
  secretaries' dining room 244–5
  United Press office 59–60
  waiters 59
  working day 61–2
Meyerhold, Vsevolod 357–8
MI5 27–8, 142–3, 144–6, 291
MI6 293, 295

Military Collegium of the Supreme Court
  331, 332
Miller, John 342, 402
Ministry of Information, British 24, 32,
  34, 141
Moats, Alice-Leone 182
  arrest 411
  arrival at Metropole 112
  avoids evacuation 113–18
  Cholerton interview 282–3
  connections 112
  decision to become a journalist 15–16
  evacuation to Kuibyshev 131–3
  and German invasion 13–15, 18
  glamourous figure 131
  journey to Moscow 16–17
  leaves Russia 262–4
  meets Anders 255–6
  meets Anders in Tehran 264
  named *Collier's* Moscow correspondent
    117–18
  Polish deportee interviews 258–60
  post-war 410–12
  problem of 111–18
  Steinhardt's slurs against 263
  takes Sanctuary with Cholerton 117
Molotov, Vyacheslav 14, 108, 125,
  279–80, 302–8
Moorehead, Alan 218
Morley, Iris, *Nothing But Propaganda* 192–3
Moscow 47
  abandoned feel 152
  air raids 124, 257, 303
  American evacuation 113–18
  Bolshoi Theatre 25
  camouflage 25–6
  Churchill visits 427
  the Cocktail Hall 241–2
  defence of 128, 148–9
  evacuation 121–3, 123–7, 253
  German advance on 119–27
  and German invasion 13–14, 18
  Hotel National 358–9
  the Lubyanka 26, 119–20, 211–12,
    252–3, 257, 332, 350, 364–70
  Maly Levshinsky Pereulok 281–2
  National hotel 124
  Pascoe mission 291
  preparations to mine 120

Red Square 25, 338
St Catherine's Hall 107–9
Spaso House 117
Tanya's return to 416
TSUM 224
Victory Day celebrations 338–41
Moscow House of Actors 183–4
Moscow Institute of International
Relations 345, 348
Motavkin (investigator) 352–3
mud 86–7
Murdoch Bliss, Ms L A 421–2
Murmansk 156

Narkomindel 62
Natasha (Lefortovo prisoner) 360, 361–2,
365
Naumov-Glatman, Naum 208–9
Naumov-Glatman, Sara 209
Nazi-Soviet non-aggression pact 14,
17–18, 83, 214
New Jerusalem monastery, Istra 153
New York 197–205
*New York Post* 323
*New York Times* 17, 29, 84, 138, 149, 156,
230, 301, 347
*News Chronicle* 84, 219, 421–2
Nick (TS's ex -husband) 250–1, 252–3,
312–13, 416
Nikolayev 73–5
NKVD 129, 130, 132, 137, 149–51, 177,
178–9, 183, 194, 196, 211–13,
230–1, 262, 270–4, 277, 280,
293–6, 388–9
non-fraternisation 137
North Cape 42
Northern Lights 378

Obyedkov, Ivan 295–6
Odessa 9–12, 68–73, 77–8, 164
Operation Typhoon 119
Operation Uranus 228
Ortenberg, David 223
Oumansky, Konstantin 136–7

Paléologue, Maurice 38–9
Palgunov, Nikolai 27–8, 80–1, 85, 106,
153–6, 219–22, 269
Palkovská, Ludmila 143, 144

Palmer, Commander 185–6, 242
panic mongers, liquidation order 226
Parker, Anne 403, 404
Parker, Jan Ralph Heyrovsky 143, 146
Parker, Milena 28–9, 30, 31, 403–4
birth of son 143
in Czechoslovakia 138–9
death of 143–4, 145
flees Prague 139
marries Ralph 141
Parker, Neil 403, 404
Parker, Ralph 7, 345
anti-western propaganda 340
appointed Moscow correspondent 293
as ardent young Conservative 289–90
attempt to fill Cholerton's shoes 286–7
background 288–93
birth of son 143
blackmail 342
briefing notes 297–8
*Conspiracy Against Peace* 289
*Conspiracy Against Peace: Notes of an English
Journalist* 341–2
contradictions 300–1
in Czechoslovakia 138–9
death of 401
death of Milena 143–4, 145
death of son 146–7
evacuation to Kuibyshev 138, 147–8,
150
fight with King 267–8
flees Prague 139
heightened emotions 32
in Hungary 139–40
intelligence work 140–2, 293
invented childhood 289
as Kremlin stooge 193, 195–6
last years 401
marries Milena 141
MI5 interrogation 144–5
MI5 investigation 28–31, 142–3,
144–6
Moscow assignment 31–2
*Moscow Correspondent* 340
movie career 401
*One Day in the Life of Ivan Denisovich*
translation 400–1
Polish crisis press conference 267–8
Polish diaspora report 275

Parker, Ralph – *cont'd.*
  political rebirth 290–3
  position at *The Times* 296–8
  post-war 399–404
  relations with the American embassy
    300–1
  relations with the British embassy
    298–301
  relationship with the NKVD 293–6
  relationship with Valentina Scott
    150–1
  replaces Sulzberger 149–51
  return to Britain 142
  rewriting of history 340–3
  scholarship to Cambridge 288–9, 290
  secretary–translator 187–8
  sense of impotence 181
  show trial coverage 344
  sources of information 181
  Stalin Q&A 269–70
  suicide attempts 147
  time in Yugoslavia 28, 29–30, 293
  *The Times* appointment 146
  *The Times* drops 301
  undercover work 30
  Victory Day celebrations 317–18,
    423–4
  voyage to Russia 147
  VS assigned to 150–1
Pascoe, Joe 291
patriotism 100
Paulus, General Friedrich von 228, 229
Pearl Harbor, attack on 152
People's Commissariat for Foreign
  Affairs 62
Pera Palace Hotel, Istanbul 30
performing seals 2
Pervomaisk 77
Peter the Great 425
Petliura, Symon 71
Petrograd 161
Philby, Kim 292, 294
Philps, Alan 5–7
Pick, Captain 173, 175
Poland 36–7, 44, 255, 262, 269–70,
  274–5, 327, 329
  government-in-exile 275
  Katyn massacre 265–7, 270–4
Polish Communist Party 275

Polish crisis press conference 267–8
Polish deportees
  Anders' Army 255–64
  condition 258–60
  evacuation 261–4
Polish diaspora 275
Pollitt, Harry 400
Polyakov, Alexander 105
Port Arthur 168
Porter, Katerina 399
Potma's Camp No. 10 labour camp
  381–4, 387, 388–9
Prague 138–9
Prague Spring 406
*Pravda* 189, 223, 265–6
Predshakhtnaya labour camp 374–9
prison labourers 137
Profintern 164
propaganda 101–3, 105
propaganda posters 240
prostitutes 176–9
Putin, Vladimir
  invasion of Ukraine 4–5, 343–4, 425,
    426–7, 427–8
  media control 4–5, 426

questions, stock answers 53

Rabinovich, Tamara 381–3, 386
radios 191
Ransome, Arthur 51
Raphael of Bershad, Rabbi 11
ration vouchers 183
rations and rationing 3, 183, 219–20,
  224–5
Red Army 37, 42
  crisis of morale 225–6
Red International Labour Unions 164
*Red Star* 189–90, 223
Red Terror 227
Redgrave, Michael 400
refugees 134–6
Reif, Alla 382
Revolution Day celebrations,
  1943 302–8
Reynolds, Quentin 132, 133, 283
Roberts, Sir Frank 298, 300
Robeson, Paul 22
Romanovna, Lidia 233–4, 235, 389

## Index

Roosevelt, Franklin D. 327–8
Rostov University 251–2
Rostropovich, Mstislav 56
Royal Air Force mission 34, 36
Royal Navy 37
Roza (labour camp informer) 377–8
Ruhr, the 162
Russell, John 13–14, 15, 115–16
Russian Civil War 68–76, 79
Russian empire 47
Russian home, Blunden visits 232–6
Russian names 7
Rust, William 158, 408–9

Sakharov, Andrei 182–3
Salisbury, Harrison 59, 271, 273
samizdat 396–7
*Saturday Evening Post* 180
Scapa Flow 36
Schulenberg, Count von 113
Scott, Henry 150
Scott, Valentina
    assigned to Parker 150–1
    as Kremlin stooge 193
    post-war 404
    relationship with RP 150–1
    reputation as Anglophobe 311
Second Brick Factory labour camp
        379–80
second front, the 221, 318
secretary–translators 181–3
    duties 190–1
    influence 180
    recruitment 183–91
    reliance on 179–81
    role 180
Section D 140–2, 294–5
Senior, Margaret 232
sex-trade subculture 176–9
Shanghai 165–75
Shaw, George Bernard 53–4
Shaw, Marjorie 238, 239, 305
Shcherbakov, Alexander 220–1, 287
Sheridan, Clare 50–1
Shostakovich, Dmitry 304–5
show trials 207–11, 212, 283, 331–2, 344
Siberia 159–60, 371
Skopje 140–2
Smolensk front visit 80–104

Bourke-White joins party 82
    censorship 96–7
    Charlotte Haldane joins party 81–2
    Dorogobuzh 97–8
    dugout 87–8
    farewell banquet 98–9
    first stop 85–6
    frustration 93–4, 94–5
    German spotter planes 86
    hospitality 87–91, 98–9
    journey back to Moscow 99–101
    journey to 85
    meals 98–9
    mud 86–7
    party 83–5
    propaganda 101–3
    reports 101–3
    sleeping arrangements 90
    subterfuge 94
    success 103–4
    trial-by-vodka 88–90
    visit announced 80–1
    Vyazma 85–6
    Vyazma bombing raid 91–2
    Yelnya 80, 94–7, 101
Snow, Edgar
    Kharkov reports 230–1
    Matthews wedding 238–9, 240–1
    meets ordinary Russian 1–2
    on Metropol Hotel 3
    on Palgunov 222
    *Red Star Over China* 179
    and reliance on secretary–translators
        179–81
    sources of information 180–1
    staff 181
    thoughts about experiences 419–21
soap 237
Sofiano, Tatyana 181–3
Sokolovsky, Vasily 102
Solzhenitsyn, Aleksander, 400–1
Sorge, Richard 166, 169–70, 175, 398
Southport 143–4
Soviet press 26
Soviet Union, comparison with Britain
        38–9
Soviet War News 105
Soviet women, emigration ban 311
Spanish Civil War 22, 83, 88, 291

# Index

'The Special Commission for
 Determination and Investigation
 of the Shooting of Polish
 Prisoners/nlof War by German-
 Fascist Invaders in Katyn
 Forest' 270
Special Operations Executive 145
SS 229–31
Stalin, Josef
  Anders' Army plan 261
  antisemitism 230
  anti-Ukrainian policy 374–5
  appearance 107
  Bartlett interview 107–9
  censorship 17
  Charlotte Haldane on policies 157–8
  death 55, 384–5
  drinking 308
  emigration ban 311
  foreign policy 297–8
  German advance on Moscow 122
  the Great Purge 55, 207–15, 226–7,
    267, 330–4
  industrialisation policy 128, 197–8
  interviews 109
  journalist policy 57
  Katyn massacre 274
  Khrushchev denounces excesses 385
  not one step back order 226, 228
  Order No. 227 226
  Parker Q&A 269–70
  Poland policy 36–7, 255, 266–7,
    269–70, 274, 327, 329
  propaganda war victory 423
  reporter policy 2, 4
  Revolution Day speech, 1943 302
  role in Hitler's rise to power 204
  sanitised image 424
  sense of self-interest 228
  Shaw/Astor meeting 54
  show trials 207–11
  Siberian exile 159–60
  status 3–4
  suspicious nature 27
  Three Power Conference 104
  toasts the free press 108
  Yalta conference 327–9
Stalingrad 225–6
Stalingrad, battle of 228–9, 267

Standley, William 185
starvation 135–6
Steele, Archibald 63, 65, 121, 122, 131
Steffens, Lincoln 323
Steinhardt, Laurence 15–16, 17, 112,
  113–15, 117–18, 132, 262–4
subterfuge 94
Sudoplatov, Pavel 294
suffering 153–4
Sulzberger, Arthur Hays 149
Sulzberger, Cyrus 139–40, 141, 142,
  222, 383
  evacuation to Kuibyshev 132, 138
  marriage 149
  Smolensk front visit 84, 89–90, 92, 93,
    94–5
  Smolensk front visit report 102–3
  trial-by-vodka 89–90
Sunday Express 22
Sverdlov, Yakov 159–60
Svetlova, Anna 414, 416
Svetlova, Nick 183
Svetlova, Tanya. see Matthews, Tanya
  (nee Svetlova)
Sydney Daily Telegraph 218

T-34 medium tank 87
Tallinn 161
tank production 228
TASS 18, 221
Tehran 263, 264, 316–17
temperatures 60
Thatcher, Margaret 292
Third International 291
Thompson, Craig 325–6
Three Power Conference 96, 104
Time magazine 325–6, 328–9
The Times 29, 31, 146, 230, 275, 293,
  296–8, 301, 341
Tirpitz (German battleship) 37, 42
Tolstoy, Alexei 272
Topolski, Felix 33, 34, 35, 37, 41–2,
  44–5, 262
torture 356
Trans-Siberian railway 167–8
Trevelyan, Julian 145, 290–3,
  343, 402
Trotsky, Leon 220, 227
Turukhansk 160

# Index

Ufliand, Nina 381–3
Ukraine
  collectivisation famine 54
  liberation of Kharkov 229–31
  Nazi genocide 229–31
  Putin's invasion of 4–5, 343–4, 425,
    426–7, 427–8
  Russian Civil War 68–76
  White prisoners of war massacred 79
Ukrainian deportees 374–5
Ulanovskaya, Alex 7, 24–5, 26–7, 70, 72,
  77–9, 351, 362
  American assignment 197–205
  arrest 372
  arrested in Denmark 206–7
  Blunden interviews 226–7
  death of 397
  denounced 212–13
  escape from Shanghai 174–5
  escape from Siberia 160
  family reunited 395
  Hamburg uprising 164–5
  journey to Shanghai 166–7
  Kurgan affair 170–5
  mission to Germany, 1921 159–64
  New York spy network 198
  personal pension 396
  post-war 395–7
  Shanghai mission 165–75
  and the show trials 207–11
  Siberian exile 159–60
  spying career 159–75
  wariness of Stalin 207–8
  wounded 216
Ulanovskaya, Irina 217, 391, 395
Ulanovskaya, Lyosha 217
Ulanovskaya, Maya 210–11, 217,
  351, 372–4
  arrest and imprisonment 381–3
  emigrates to Israel 398
  engagement with Judaism 397
  family reunited 395
  meets Blunden in Vence 390–1
  release 385–7
  reunited with mother 387
Ulanovskaya, Nadya 7, 63–79
  acquitted 396
  and Alex 72–5
  Alex's return 77–9

American assignment 197–205
American role 200
arranges Blunden's visit to a Russian
  home 232–6
arrest 349–50
arrival in Shanghai 169
assigned to McLaughlin 63–5
birth 66
birth of daughter 200
Blunden interviews 226–7
and Blunden's Stalingrad visit 228
breaks leg 379
childhood 66–7
comparison with Tanya 244–5
conviction 370
daughter visits in transit camp 372–4
daughters arrest and imprisonment
  381–3
death of family 164
disillusion with the Communist Party
  210–11, 211–13, 218
dismissed from Moscow Institute of
  International Relations 348–9
as dissident intellectual 396–7
emigrates to Israel 397–8
enrols in Foreign Languages Institute
  205–6
epiphany 152–6
escape from Shanghai 174–5
evacuation to Kuibyshev 122–3, 133
evidence against 368–9
family background 245
family reunited 395
first meets Alex 70
fur coat 348, 364, 368, 371, 373, 398
German advance on Moscow 119–23
good deed in a naughty world 178–9
goodbye to Blunden 236
grandfather's influence 66–7
hallucinations 365–7
Hamburg uprising 164–5
health improves 376
identities 66
influence 180
interrogation 350–6, 360–1, 364–9
Istra trip 152–6
journey to labour camp 371–4
journey to Shanghai 167–9
Kurgan affair 171–5

Ulanovskaya, Nadya – *cont'd.*
  labour camp sentence 370
  learns of Stalin's death 384–5
  looses grip on reality 367
  on Matthews 194–5
  mental strength 32
  mission to Germany, 1921 159–64
  move to Odessa 68–9
  Northern Lights experience 378
  Odessa beating 9–12, 72
  past life 65–79
  post-war 395–8
  post-war assignment 345–6
  at Potma's Camp No. 10 labour camp
    381–4, 387, 388–9
  at Predshakhtnaya labour camp 374–9
  in punishment cell 363–4
  reconnects with Chambers 325–6
  refused privileges 362
  relationship with Victor 76–8
  relatives in America 202–3
  release 387
  reunion with Blunden 390–1
  reunited with daughter 387
  Russian Civil War 68–76
  on sanitation brigade 377–8
  at Second Brick Factory labour camp
    379–80
  sense of justice 12, 67
  shame 154
  Shanghai mission 165–75
  Shanghai wardrobe 169–70
  and the show trials 207–11
  spying career 159–75
  and Tanya Svetlova 195
  thoughts of suicide 363–4
  told Alex dead 76
  transfer to Lefortovo 361–4
  translator appointment 24–8
  visit to Uzhovka 216–17
  and VS 150–1
  Winter's appearance in Moscow 323–5
Ulrich, Vassily 330–4
Union of Polish Patriots 275
Union of Struggle for the Revolution 383
United Press agency 35
United Press office 59–60
United States of America 197–205,
    214–15

useful idiots 52–3
Uzhovka 216–17

Veger, Evgeny 55
Veger, Solange 55
Vence 390–1
Vertinsky, Alexander 335
Vertinsky, Anastasia 335
Vertinsky, Lidia 335
Victor 76–8
Victory Day 338–41, 423–4
*Ville d'Anvers* (ship) 137
visa-appeal 193
visas 254
  supply of 111
  weaponized 276–81, 287–8
Vishnevskaya, Galina 56
Vladivostok 115–16, 165
Vodovozova, Maika 360, 361
Vodovozova, Natalia 278
  arrest 277, 278–9, 280, 284–5
  charges against 285
  letter to Chollerton 285–6
  sentence 285
VOKS 52–3, 186
Vologda 371–4
Vorkuta 360, 374
Vyazma 85–6
  bombing raid 91–2
Vyshinsky (deputy foreign minister)
    267, 268, 307–8

Wall Street Crash, 1929 201
Webb, Sidney and Beatrice, *Soviet
    Communism: A New Civilisation* 226–7
Webb, Sydney and Beatrice 54–5
Werth, Alexander 287
  coat called Fido 84
  death of 407
  family background 101, 404–5
  journey back to Moscow 100–1
  Katyn massacre report 272
  Kharkov reports 231
  naïvety 273
  post-war 407
  Revolution Day celebrations, 1943 304–5
  *Russia at War 1941–45* 231, 406
  Smolensk front visit 84, 90–1, 95, 100–1
  Smolensk front visit report 102

# Index

West Chester, Pennsylvania 202–3
Willi (creepy German communist) 167
Winter, Ella 323–5
Winter War 425
Winterton, Paul 219–20, 421–2, 423–4
Wollaston, Pilot Officer Dicky 40–1
working conditions 192, 422–3

Yakobson, Alexander 391, 393, 398
Yalta conference 327–9

Yelnya 80, 94–7, 101
Yeltsin, Boris 274, 426
Young Revolutionary International 69
Yugoslavia 28, 293

Zagorsk 275
Zelensky, Voldymyr 428
Zeppel (German wireless operator) 173, 174
Zhukov, General Georgy 228
Zinoviev, Grigory 208